THE POLITICS OF CRIME PREVENTION

NEW PERSPECTIVES IN CRIME, DEVIANCE, AND LAW SERIES

General Editor: John Hagan

The Politics of Crime Prevention

Race, Public Opinion, and the Meaning of Community Safety

Kevin H. Wozniak

NEW YORK UNIVERSITY PRESS

New York

NEW YORK UNIVERSITY PRESS
New York
www.nyupress.org

Library of Congress Cataloging-in-Publication Data
Names: Wozniak, Kevin H., author.
Title: The politics of crime prevention : race, public opinion, and
the meaning of community safety / Kevin H. Wozniak.
Description: New York, NY : New York University Press, 2023. |
Series: New perspectives in crime, deviance, and law |
Includes bibliographical references and index.
Identifiers: LCCN 2022036522 | ISBN 9781479815722 (hardback) |
ISBN 9781479815753 (paperback) | ISBN 9781479815777 (ebook) |
ISBN 9781479815784 (ebook other)
Subjects: LCSH: Crime prevention—United States. | Crime and race—United States. |
Police—United States—Finance. | Police—United States—Public opinion.
Classification: LCC HV7432 .W69 2023 | DDC 363.2/30973—dc23/eng/20220822
LC record available at https://lccn.loc.gov/2022036522

This book is printed on acid-free paper, and its binding materials are chosen for strength
and durability. We strive to use environmentally responsible suppliers and materials to the
greatest extent possible in publishing our books.

Manufactured in the United States of America

10 9 8 7 6 5 4 3 2 1

Also available as an ebook

*To my parents, for supporting my education
and raising me to have an inquisitive mind*

*To Aaron, for your unconditional support
during good times and bad*

*To Representative Bobby Scott and his dedicated staff,
David Dailey, Rashage Green, and Carrie Hughes,
for showing me how the legislative sausage is made firsthand*

Law enforcement is just one aspect of public safety. . . . [The other aspects of public safety] are affordable housing, good schools, availability of healthcare, being able to deal with homelessness in our communities, and . . . mental health.
—Cedric Alexander, former president of the National
  Organization of Black Law Enforcement Executives

The greatest way to honor the loss of life on all sides, loss of life due to gun violence, would be to invest in our communities.
—New York City Councilwoman Kristin Richardson Jordan

CONTENTS

Introduction

Race, Redistribution, and the Politics of Crime Control

"Defund the police." This slogan emerged among activists and echoed across the media and the halls of government in the summer of 2020 following the murder of George Floyd, a Black man, at the hands of Derek Chauvin, a White Minneapolis police officer. The police were called because a store clerk suspected that Floyd paid with a counterfeit twenty-dollar bill. While arresting Mr. Floyd, three officers pinned him to the ground, and Officer Chauvin knelt on Mr. Floyd's neck for over eight minutes, inflicting a fatal injury.[1] A bystander filmed the arrest and posted the recording on social media, and the video went viral. Protests against the police killing of Mr. Floyd first erupted in Minneapolis and later spread to cities and towns across the United States over the course of the summer. Some analysts judged this wave of mass public protests to be the largest protest movement in American history.[2]

Mr. Floyd's tragic murder repeated an old cycle in American history: police violence against civilians of color sparks public backlash.[3] Several police killings of Americans of color received extensive media coverage and sparked large protests in the years between 2014 and 2020, notably the deaths of Michael Brown in Ferguson, Missouri, and Freddie Gray in Baltimore, Maryland.[4] The Black Lives Matter (BLM) movement rose to prominence during this period. Founded by a trio of community organizers, BLM grew into a loosely organized but widespread multiracial coalition that called not just for an end to police violence, but also for much broader efforts to ameliorate the social and economic manifestations of systemic racism in the United States.[5]

Much of the discussion around defunding the police was fundamentally a debate about budget priorities. Proponents of defunding argued that government and the business community invested less and less money and resources into working-class and impoverished communities over the course of the twentieth century, especially majority-Black communities. Divestment caused criminogenic social conditions to fester, but rather than rebuilding and revitalizing communities, elites chose the criminal justice system to be the "first responder" for all the nation's social problems that are related to poverty, deindustrialization, and unemployment.[6] To reverse this trend, the Electoral Justice Project of the Movement for Black Lives proposed the BREATHE Act. If enacted, this legislation would divest federal resources from incarceration and policing; invest in nonpunitive, noncarceral approaches to community safety; and allocate new money to build healthy, sustainable, and equitable communities.[7]

Though the slogan "defund the police" was new, the civil rights debate about budget priorities stretches back decades.[8] President Lyndon Johnson convened the National Advisory Commission on Civil Disorders to study the causes of dozens of riots that swept through cities across the nation in the late 1960s. In their final report, the members of the commission concluded that acts of police violence against Black civilians caused Black Americans' long-standing frustrations and grievances over segregation and poverty to ignite. The commission famously wrote, "Our Nation is moving toward two societies, one black, one white—separate and unequal. . . . Segregation and poverty have created in the racial ghetto a destructive environment totally unknown to most white Americans. What white Americans have never fully understood—but what the Negro can never forget—is that white society is deeply implicated in the ghetto. White institutions created it, white institutions maintain it, and white society condones it."[9] To prevent future unrest, the commission advised that the government launch desegregation and enrichment (meaning investment) initiatives "aimed at improving dramatically the quality of ghetto life."

The commission echoed a position advanced by Martin Luther King, Jr., and other key leaders of the civil rights movement.[10] In 1964, Bayard Rustin, a contemporary of MLK and fellow leader in the civil rights movement, wrote,

> What is the value of winning access to public accommodations for those who lack money to use them? The minute the movement faced this question, it was compelled to expand its vision beyond race relations to economic relations, including the role of education in modern society. And

what also became clear is that all these interrelated problems, by their very nature, are not soluble by private, voluntary efforts, but require government actions—or politics. . . . At issue, after all, is not civil rights, strictly speaking, but social and economic conditions. Last summer's riots were not race riots; they were outbursts of class aggression in a society where class and color definitions are converging disastrously.[11]

Rustin soon after co-authored *A "Freedom Budget" for All Americans*. The Freedom Budget comprised an ambitious antipoverty agenda centered on federally guaranteed full employment and a universal basic income. Rustin wrote, "public responsibility, especially at the Federal level, must move immediately and at an accelerating rate toward increased investment in our human resources in the form of health services, education, and training."[12] Contemporary advocates of defunding the police are carrying Rustin's vision into the twenty-first century.

Despite the repeated pleas of civil rights advocates, a robust program of government-funded community investment has never really taken root and flourished in the United States—at least, not to a degree that meets the magnitude of poverty and unemployment in the nation.[13] The Johnson administration rejected the Freedom Budget, partly because President Johnson preferred his Great Society programs that combined means-tested welfare assistance programs and market-friendly interventions designed to achieve "equality of opportunity" in society, such as affirmative action.[14] In other words, the government largely chose the path of individual-level aid to help people experiencing poverty "pull themselves up by their bootstraps" and become competitive in the labor market rather than investing the resources necessary to eliminate neighborhood poverty and improve community infrastructure. Subsequent presidential administrations committed even further to free market–based policies that promised tax breaks to lure corporations and developers to invest private funds into impoverished communities designated as "enterprise zones." Critics argue that enterprise zones predominantly benefited wealthier people who purchased newly developed properties without substantively benefiting the original less affluent residents of the neighborhoods or reducing overall poverty rates.[15]

The government shied away from direct financial investment in crime control policy as well. In the 1990s, the federal government launched the

Weed and Seed program in cities across the country. The purpose of this program was to "weed out" crime by identifying, arresting, and prosecuting violent and drug offenders while also preventing future crime by "seeding" high-crime neighborhoods with financial investment to support "human services" programs and neighborhood revitalization efforts.[16] Critics argued that many implementation sites poured far more resources into the "weeding" than they did the "seeding," thereby making the program little different from other types of aggressive policing practices that exacerbated tensions between law enforcement and communities of color, such as "stop and frisk" and "broken windows" policing.[17]

The intellectual premise of Weed and Seed was recycled in the twenty-first century in the form of the Justice Reinvestment Initiative (JRI). Under the JRI model, state governments worked to revise their sentencing laws and reduce the number of people incarcerated in the state. Fewer prisoners should lead to fewer prisons, allowing states to shrink the budgets of their correctional systems and "free up" money that could be reinvested into alternatives to incarceration. As of 2020, over half the states participated in JRI, but analysts disagree about the extent to which JRI achieved its incarceration reduction goals.[18] Critics more consistently agree on one point: the JRI significantly diverged from its original vision, which was "to redirect some portion of the $54 billion America now spends on prisons to rebuilding the human resources and physical infrastructure—the schools, healthcare facilities, parks, and public spaces—of neighborhoods devastated by high levels of incarceration."[19] Note how similar this vision was to the Freedom Budget for All Americans and the BREATHE Act. With few exceptions, most states that participated in the JRI chose to reinvest money either back into other branches of the criminal justice system, like police or probation, or into "criminal justice system-adjacent" organizations like drug treatment programs, rehabilitation programs, and halfway houses.[20] These investments are an improvement over simply "warehousing" people in prisons, but they still prop up the criminal justice system or fund services that are largely limited to helping former offenders successfully reenter the community as law-abiding citizens instead of preventing crime in the first place.[21]

These choices are a far cry from the kinds of broad-based antipoverty, crime prevention, and community improvement investments that generations of activists have demanded. Though a surprising number of both Democratic and Republican policymakers grew to support criminal justice reform in the early twenty-first century, most of the reforms pursued as of 2022 were technical changes to the justice system itself. Sociologist Patrick Sharkey argued that politicians failed to shift away from Nixon- and Reagan-era paradigms of withdrawing government financial support from cities (divestment or abandonment) and shift instead toward supporting a paradigm of investment designed to fight concentrated disadvantage, deindustrialization, and urban decay.[22] This is a profound missed opportunity because the evidence is quite clear that neighborhood divestment and concentrated disadvantage are highly correlated with violence.[23] Violence is a social phenomenon, not just an individual phenomenon.

Various organizations that worked with elected policymakers, notably the Pew Charitable Trusts, pressured early advocates of justice reinvestment to abandon community reinvestment. Policy analysts perceived community reinvestment to be firmly aligned with a liberal political perspective, and they feared that committing to that goal would sabotage efforts to secure bipartisan support from political conservatives for efforts to ramp up justice reinvestment and expand it to new states:

> That was the price that had to be paid for following Pew's strategy, which focused on squeezing the most reform possible out of politicians' existing preferences, rather than organizing to try to fundamentally change them. . . . In practice, Pew's goal of cultivating unlikely bedfellows translated into targeting conservatives, on the assumption that liberals were likely to already be on board. As [Pew director of the JRI project Adam] Gelb put it, "Conservatives hold the cards on this issue, and we work closely with them."[24]

Thus, as with so many policy proposals before it, the JRI was largely shorn of its community investment roots in order to make it palatable to politicians.

In short, several decades' worth of elected policymakers in the United States chose to fund police and punishment to fight crime and social disorder instead of choosing to fund community institutions to fix the root causes of crime. This book is an effort to understand whether the American public would make the same choice as their elected leaders. Drawing upon original data that I collected through focus groups and a national survey of Black and White Americans, I will make the case that politicians misjudge Americans' crime prevention preferences. I will show that civilians recognize that social conditions, like poverty and a dearth of good jobs, cause crime. Likewise, they believe that a robust crime prevention strategy must address these root causes rather than focusing solely on arresting individual offenders. When asked to brainstorm their own crime prevention budgets, most people choose to fund a mix of both criminal justice and community-based institutions. Few civilians made the same choice as politicians have to neglect community investment. Even fewer people indicated that they would vote against a politician who funded community institutions to fight crime and disorder. However, there is some evidence that racial divisions among the public endure. I will argue that a politically viable path exists for policymakers to support and fund community-based crime prevention without provoking public backlash as long as advocates are mindful of the language they use to make their case.

In the remainder of this chapter, I review the existing evidence regarding American public opinion about punishment, crime prevention, and antipoverty programs. I will then describe two bodies of political science theory, framing theory and racial priming theory, that help explain why Americans tend to support antipoverty programs in general but oppose many particulars of the programs. In brief, when Americans' racial stereotypes are activated, their antipathy toward programs that they believe benefit the "undeserving poor" rises. This consistent pattern of racial backlash presents a major political problem for advocates who demand community investment as a means of undoing systemic racism. I examine how racial backlash could manifest in discussions of crime prevention strategies. Later in the book, I present evidence of rhetorical strategies that may be able to bypass backlash and maximize public support for the kinds of community investment programs dreamed of by civil rights advocates from 1960 through 2020.

Public Preferences to Reduce Crime and Poverty

To understand the politics of community investment for the purpose of crime control, we must draw on knowledge about public attitudes toward both criminal justice and financial assistance programs for the poor. Political scientist Peter Enns combined data from dozens of public opinion surveys fielded over several decades to create an estimate of mass "punitive sentiment."[25] This measure captures the American public's overall support for criminal justice policies that punish offenders. Higher levels of punitive sentiment indicate that Americans are more supportive of long, harsh punishments for criminals, while lower levels indicate less support for tough punishment. I present Enns' updated timeseries of punitive sentiment that he graciously agreed to share with me in figure I.1. It shows that public punitiveness declined over the course of the 1950s, began to climb in the mid-1960s, peaked in the late 1990s, and has been declining ever since.

Since overall public support for harsh punishment is lower than it was during the "tough on crime" era of the 1980s and 1990s, many Americans may be open to activists' calls for the nation to make greater use of non-criminal justice responses to crime and deviance. The ebbing of public punitiveness likely opened the door for criminal justice reform.[26] However, criminologists disagree whether public support for harsh punishment and public support for rehabilitation and more "merciful" responses to crime are mutually exclusive or whether Americans can support both punitive and progressive responses to crime

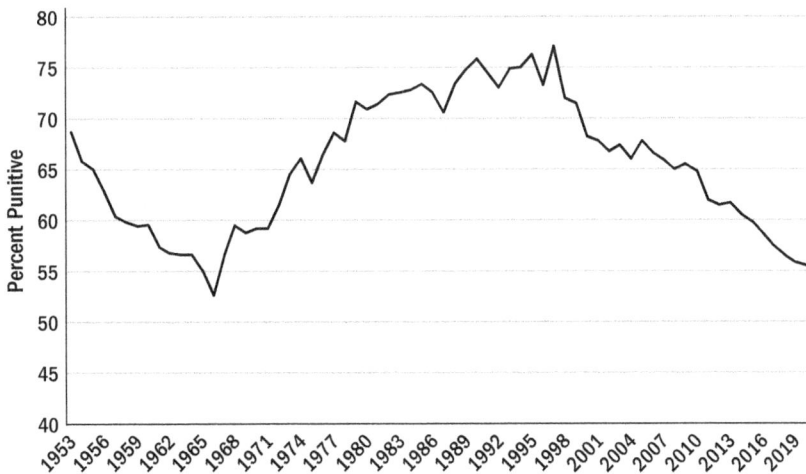

Figure I.1. Peter Enns' Measure of Mass Public Punitiveness: 1953–2019.

simultaneously.[27] For example, a person might support life imprisonment for an offender who commits murder but community-based treatment for a petty drug user. Peter Enns had to use publicly available surveys to construct his measure of public punitiveness, and the overwhelming majority of US public opinion polls ask narrow questions that only measure Americans' support or opposition to punishment.[28] If support for nonpunitive responses to crime is indeed independent of support for tough punishment, then there might be a "shadow" unmeasured trend of progressive sentiment that could be mapped alongside punitive sentiment.

Unless surveys start consistently asking Americans about their support for nonpunitive responses to crime, we will never possess the data necessary to create a proper longitudinal measure of progressive sentiment. I am aware of only one survey that equips us to gauge Americans' progressive sentiment, albeit in a limited manner. The Gallup Organization asked national samples of the US population the following question with just enough sporadic frequency over the 1990s and 2000s that we can assess changes over time: "Which of the following approaches to lowering the crime rate in the United States comes closer to your own view—do you think more money and effort should go to attacking the social and economic problems that lead to crime through better education and job training or more money and effort should go to deterring crime by improving law enforcement with more prisons, police and judges?" This question is similar to the "defund the police" debate in that it asked respondents to state whether they would prefer that the criminal justice system or nonpunitive, civil institutions receive more resources. I present the responses to this question in figure I.2.

The Gallup data provide an interesting counterpoint to Enns' punitive sentiment measure. Both measures show that Americans' support for the criminal justice system was highest in the early 1990s. However, even at the peak of American punitiveness, most Americans still said that they would prefer to give civic institutions more resources than the criminal justice system. The public was nearly split on this question in 1994, but in every other year that Gallup asked this question, a far larger percentage of respondents preferred attacking social problems over giving the criminal justice system more support. As of 2020, 63% of respondents said that "more money and effort should go to addressing social

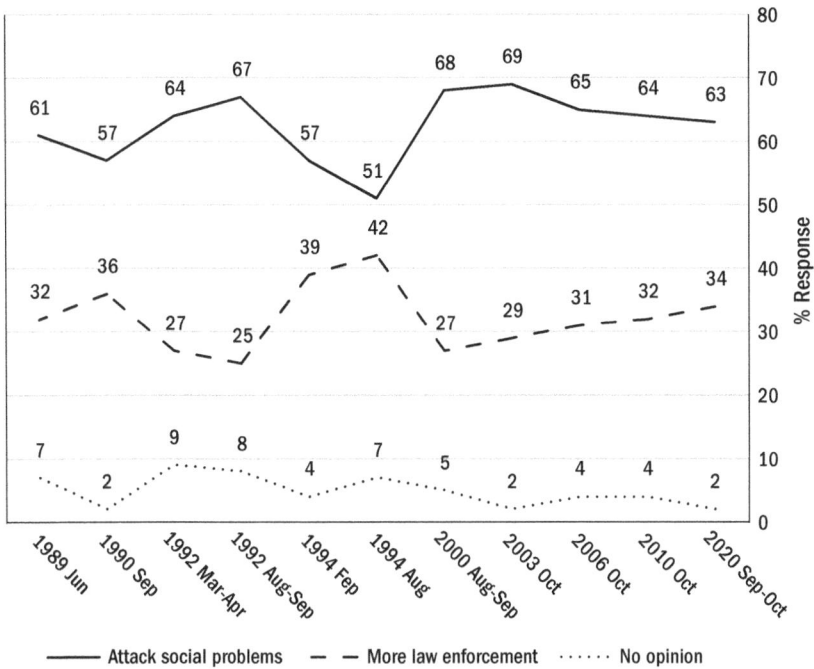

Figure I.2. Gallup Survey. The Public's Crime Prevention Preference.

and economic problems such as drug addiction, homelessness and mental health" versus only 34% saying that "more money and effort should go to strengthening law enforcement" (note how the wording was slightly altered in 2020 compared to the other years that Gallup asked this question). Not only do the Gallup data suggest that most Americans today share activists' desire for greater investment into health-promoting community institutions, but this also may have been the majority public preference for decades.

Public opinion about government spending to aid people experiencing poverty tells a similar story. From 1984 to 2018, the General Social Survey asked respondents this question: "We are faced with many problems in this country, none of which can be solved easily or inexpensively. I'm going to name some of these problems, and for each one I'd like you to tell me whether you think we're spending too much money on it, too little money, or about the right amount. First, are we spending too much, too little, or about the right amount on assistance to the

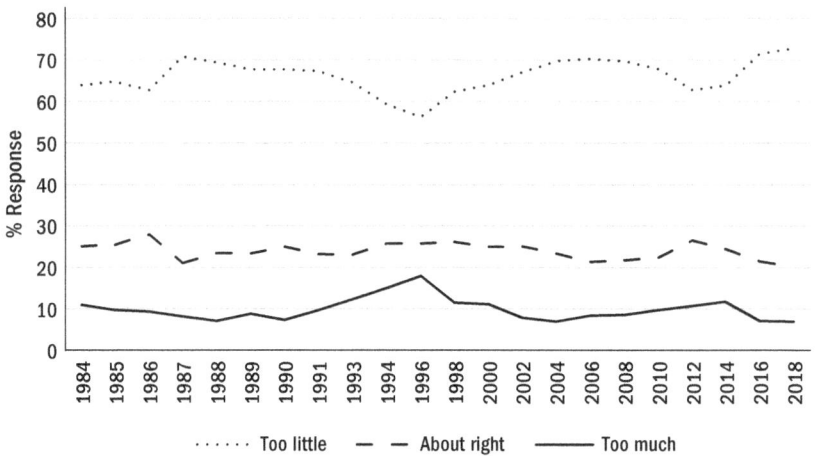

Figure I.3. General Social Survey. Public Attitudes toward Spending on Assistance to the Poor.

poor?" Figure I.3 presents these data. It shows that, from 1984 to 2018, between 56% and 73% of Americans said that the country spends "too little" on assistance to the poor. Much smaller minorities of Americans said that the country spends about the right amount of money or too much money on assistance to the poor.

Scholars have also found that a large majority of Americans expresses support for programs designed to ameliorate income inequality, improve Americans' quality of life, and aid the poor. According to a 2007 survey, 78% of all Americans, 71% of Republicans, and 77% of wealthy Americans expressed support for their tax dollars being used to pay for food stamps and other assistance to the poor. Eighty-one percent of all Americans, 74% of Republicans, and 82% of wealthy Americans supported using their tax dollars to fund early childhood education programs. Eighty percent of all Americans, 72% of Republicans, and 73% of wealthy Americans supported using their tax dollars to fund retraining programs for people whose jobs have been eliminated.[29]

Based upon the various public opinion polls I just reviewed, it appears that politicians were quite wrong to assume that Americans would oppose direct community investment programs to address the social causes of crime.[30] Is that all there is to the story—politicians simply misunderstood their constituents all along? Unfortunately, there are theoretical reasons to expect that the trends presented in figures I.2 and I.3 may mask significant underlying disagreements among Americans that can be triggered under particular circumstances. To assess this possibility, we must first understand the nature of public opinion about policy issues—and the ways that racism can shatter consensus among Americans.

Framing, Racialized Stereotypes, and the Politics of Resentment

Americans are ambivalent about government policies to aid people experiencing poverty. Figure I.3 showed that a large majority of Americans has said that the nation spends "too little" on "assistance to the poor" since at least the early 1980s. In contrast, figure I.4 shows the General Social Survey data on public opinion about government spending on "welfare."[31] This question reveals a very different pattern. For most of the past forty years, a majority of Americans believed that the government spends too much on welfare. It is only since 2018 that a majority of Americans has stated that the government spends about the right amount of money on welfare, and nearly as many people said that it spends too little as the proportion of people who said that it spends

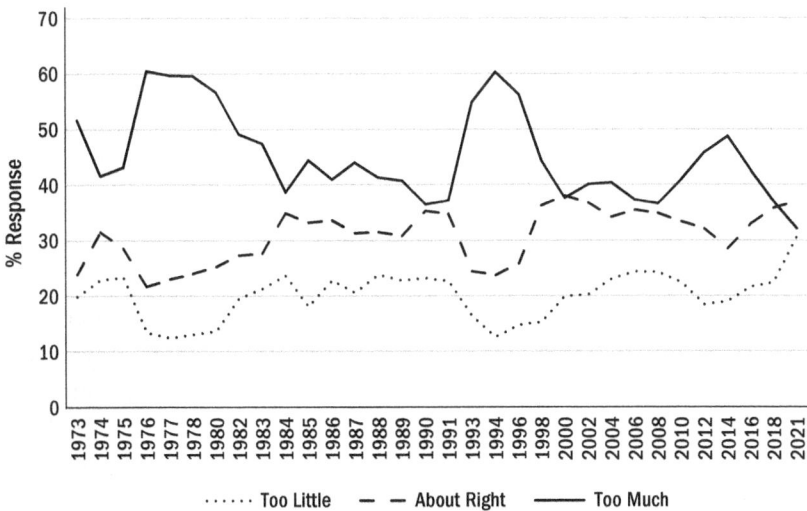

Figure I.4. General Social Survey. Public Attitudes toward Spending on Welfare.

too much. But welfare is financial assistance to the poor. How can a strong majority of Americans say that the government spends too little on assistance to the poor in the same year that a majority also says that the government spends too much on welfare?

The answer is that the word "welfare" evokes different thoughts, images, and emotions for most Americans than the phrase "assistance to the poor," and these different reactions activate different values. Most Americans of all racial and ethnic backgrounds broadly accept the "Protestant work ethic" and believe that it is important for people to exercise personal responsibility and "pull themselves up by their bootstraps" rather than accept a "government handout."[32] Political scientists Benjamin Page and Lawrence Jacobs observe,

> Most Americans are philosophical conservatives but also pragmatic egalitarians. They look to government for help in ensuring that everyone has genuine equal opportunity plus a measure of economic security with which to exercise that opportunity. America's conservative egalitarianism involves blends or compromises among three pairs of inclinations that push in different directions: belief in individual self-reliance but dislike of extreme economic inequality; skepticism about government but pragmatic willingness to turn to government when needed; and hostility to taxes but realistic acceptance of the need for tax revenue.[33]

In other words, a typical American is willing to support government-funded aid to the "deserving poor"—people who use the aid to better themselves and work to change their circumstances—but not the "undeserving poor"—"lazy" people who "choose to live on the public dime" instead of working.[34]

Some psychologists argue that feelings of anger toward lazy people who receive financial benefits are rooted in human evolution.[35] Thousands of years ago, when humans lived in small groups of hunters and gatherers, any person who consumed food without using their own labor to contribute to the group's collective resources increased their individual likelihood of survival without also increasing their groupmates' likelihood of survival. Such people were essentially cheaters, and humans (like many other social animals) evolved to punish cheating behavior in order to maintain a fair distribution of resources within groups.

However, humans' predisposition to dislike laziness and freeloading can become exceptionally dangerous when it interacts with stereotypes. When a society's majority or ruling class stereotype entire minority or disempowered groups of people as being prone to laziness, elites use that stereotype to justify denying the subordinate groups access to aid—or even to justify oppressing and punishing the members of that group.[36] It is the critical difference between imposing consequences upon an individual person who is known to be engaging in freeloading behaviors versus denying benefits to an entire group of people on the assumption that most of the members of that group would abuse the benefits system in the future—prospectively punishing large numbers of people for an action most of them will likely never commit.

Many White politicians and other Americans in positions of power intentionally stereotyped Black Americans as lazy and prone to violence throughout the nation's history in order to justify slavery, then Jim Crow segregation, and, most recently, discriminatory policies that disproportionately block Black people's access to public benefits and financial resources.[37] In fact, racial stereotypes about laziness took on terrible new importance following the end of the civil rights movement in the early 1970s. Over the course of the 1960s, the social construction of the poor underwent a significant change. Sociologist Martin Gilens analyzed stories about poverty that were published in *Time* magazine, *Newsweek*, and *U.S. News and World Report*, and he found that

from [1950] through 1964, poor people were portrayed as predominantly white. But starting in 1965 the complexion of the poor turned decidedly darker. From only 27 percent in 1964, the proportion of African Americans in pictures of the poor increased to 49 percent and 53 percent in 1965 and 1966, and then to 72 percent in 1967. Nor has the portrayal of the poor returned to its previous predominantly white orientation. Although there have been important declines and fluctuations in the extent to which blacks have been overrepresented in pictures of poverty . . . , African Americans have generally dominated news media images of the poor since the late 1960s. From 1967 through 1992, blacks averaged 57 percent of the poor people pictured in these three magazines—about twice the true proportion of blacks among the nation's poor.[38]

Furthermore, White people were more likely to be depicted in stories of the "deserving poor," such as elderly people, while Black people were more likely to be depicted as the "undeserving poor" in stories that juxtaposed poverty, chronic unemployment, drug use, and crime.

Modern politicians amplify and politicize racial stereotypes of laziness in order to attack government-funded aid programs for the poor. The most infamous example of this political tactic was Ronald Reagan's castigation of the "'Chicago welfare queen' with 'eighty names, thirty addresses, [and] twelve Social Security cards [who] is collecting veteran's benefits on four non-existing deceased husbands. She's got Medicaid, getting food stamps, and she is collecting welfare under each of her names. Her tax-free cash income is over $150,000."[39] Reagan never explicitly called the welfare queen a Black woman, but by evoking stereotypes that lazy people want government handouts instead of working an honest job that were long applied to Black Americans, he implicitly racialized this woman. Reagan argued that government assistance causes people to become dependent, lazy, and incapable of taking care of themselves, their families, or their communities. He essentially flipped the script; rather than acknowledging that government divestment over the course of the 1970s sparked urban decay, he claimed—without irony—that government investment was, in fact, the cause of urban decay. With these justifications in hand, Reagan launched a massive rollback of New Deal policies and significantly slashed government assistance to poor people and impoverished communities.[40] Scholars argue that Reagan's emphasis on a small, lean federal government that provides as little fiscal support to people or localities as possible was still the dominant—albeit contested—paradigm through at least the Trump administration.[41]

Political rhetoric like that employed by Reagan resonated with the shifting media depiction of the poor and taught a generation of Americans to associate "welfare" with (stereotypes of) lazy, undeserving Black people. White Americans' antipathy toward lazy Black people is, in turn, the strongest predictor of public opposition to welfare policies.[42] Lazy welfare consumption violates the Protestant work ethic, which triggers feelings of resentment in many Americans.[43]

A number of political scientists have demonstrated that exposing Americans (particularly White Americans) to words or images that evoke thoughts about Black Americans often activates underlying prejudiced attitudes and causes them to express greater support for policies that control Black people (such as punishments for criminals) and less support for policies that aid Black people (like welfare). This body of work is called racial priming theory. Political scientist Tali Mendelberg argued that post–civil rights era social norms pressure White Americans to avoid appearing openly racist.[44] As such, when a policy is explicitly framed as benefiting Black Americans or addressing racial injustice, Mendelberg predicted that White Americans would express more support for that policy in order to signal that they are not racist. In contrast, implicitly racialized frames still trigger racist stereotypes and pejorative cognitive associations, but because they do not explicitly mention race, they give White Americans "cover" to argue that their political beliefs have nothing to do with race or racism.[45] As such, this theory predicts that implicitly racialized cues cause White Americans to backlash against racially progressive policies.

Racial priming theory suggests that the way that activists, journalists, and politicians talk about community investment might impact public support. Due to long-standing patterns of segregation and the legacies of discriminatory policies, most of the types of neighborhoods that advocates argued should receive justice reinvestment funds are urban, majority minority (predominantly majority Black), and characterized by high levels of numerous different social problems, including crime, poverty, unemployment, and poor population health.[46] This means that the communities in question could be described using different implicit and explicit racial cues.

For example, advocates could explicitly emphasize racial justice by arguing that "African American communities" should be targeted for investment. Alternately, advocates could emphasize the need to address social problems as the justification for investment. For example, they could discuss the need to invest in "high-poverty communities" or "high-crime communities"—phrases that do not explicitly mention race. Other equally accurate ways of describing many at-risk communities evoke the kind of implicitly racialized language that historically causes punitive White backlash, such as "inner-city communities" or "communities with many residents on welfare."[47] I hypothesize that frames that trigger White Americans' stereotypes about lazy recipients of public benefits decrease public support for community investment, just as they decrease support for welfare. Precisely which adjectives about at-risk communities might trigger public backlash remains an open question.

Data and Context of the Study

It is my goal in this book to "map the margins" of public support for community investment as crime prevention and assess whether it would be electorally safe for legislators to support the kind of direct community investment that has been a major political demand of activists for at least a half century. To do so, I draw on two sources of data that were both collected in 2016: six focus groups with forty-four Black and White residents of the greater Boston metropolitan area, and a national survey of Black and White Americans. I restricted my data to only non-Hispanic Black and White Americans for two reasons. First, most of the work on racial priming theory, which is the foundation of this project, has been based on the history and politics of Black-White relations in America. I did not want to "shoehorn" Americans of other races or ethnicities into a body of theory that might not properly reflect their group's unique historical and political experiences. Second, White and Black Americans often represent the two "poles" of public opinion on criminal justice and public benefit policies. White Americans are typically the most supportive of punitive punishment and least supportive of welfare, while Black Americans tend to be the least punitive and most supportive of welfare. I am simplifying a body of literature with a great deal of nuance, but that general pattern holds. Ergo, if we understand where Black and White Americans stand on the question of community investment and crime prevention preferences, there is a good chance, we can infer, that other racial and ethnic groups will have preferences that fall in between those of those two groups.

I also split the focus groups across participants' level of formal education, which I employed as a proxy for social class. I made this choice because class, like race, also significantly affects Americans' likelihood of experiencing involuntary contact with law enforcement, the quality of their interaction with the justice system, and the severity of the punishment they receive.[48] Two focus groups contained only Black participants, two contained only White participants, and two contained a mix of both races. Within each pair of racial groups, one group included participants with, at most, a high school degree, and the other group included participants with some college education, a bachelor's degree, or graduate education. I discuss the implications and limitations of the racial composition of my data in the conclusion chapter, and I provide more details about my data collection processes in the research methodology appendix.

While I was conducting this research, the United States was still experiencing what criminologists called "the Great Crime Decline."[49] Rates of both violent and property crime began rising in the 1970s, peaked in the mid-1990s, and continued an overall downward trajectory through the time I collected the data for this study in 2016. However, the first cracks in the crime decline began to arise at that time. The nation's overall violent crime rate increased by 6.3% between 2015 and 2016, and the murder rate rose by 7.8%. However, these increases were driven by crime spikes in a small number of the nation's largest cities; the rate of violence continued declining in most cities. Even in the cities that saw crime spikes, their overall level of violence was still only about half as high as during the 1990s peak. Boston was not one of the cities that experienced an uptick in crime as of 2016.

Most Americans consistently overestimate the true prevalence of crime in the nation, and most erroneously report that crime was rising all throughout the decades of the crime decline.[50] As you shall see in later chapters, some of the participants in my focus groups knew the real facts about the crime decline, but others insisted that crime was still rising no matter what they were told. On the other hand, research indicates that collective American punitive sentiment did change in response to genuine fluctuations in the crime rate, which indicates that there is a degree of "wisdom of the crowd" at play when it comes to American public opinion about crime.[51] As I noted earlier in this chapter, mass American punitiveness was substantially lower in 2016 than it was during the crime peak of the 1990s. It is possible that some Americans who paid very close attention to the news might have learned about the recent, isolated spikes in violent crime in 2016 and grown more fearful and punitive as a result. However, it is unlikely that such individuals were so numerous that they would create an overall punitive spike in my data. These focus groups and survey present a snapshot of White and Black

American public opinion at a period of generally low crime and low punitive sentiment.[52]

That being said, Americans' attitudes about criminal justice are influenced by more than their beliefs about crime alone. People's support for harsh punishment is partially driven by their concerns about the overall state of society, which encompasses culture and the economy; scholars theorize that people will support harsher punishment when they feel that society is "out of control."[53] There were reasons for Americans to feel both optimistic and pessimistic about the state of the nation in 2016. On the positive side, the economy had recovered substantially since the Great Recession of 2008. The national unemployment rate was near a fifty-year low, job growth was steady, and median household income had increased for a few years in a row.[54] In October of 2016, the Boston-Cambridge-Nashua metropolitan area registered the lowest unemployment rate out of fifty-one metro areas.[55] On the negative side, rather than benefiting all Americans equally, the post-2008 recovery exacerbated a trend of rising income inequality that began in the 1980s. Only the wealthiest 5% of Americans enjoyed wage gains over this period. The remaining 95% maintained their financial stability by increasing their personal debt. In fact, adjusted for inflation, average hourly wages in 2018 had about the same purchasing power as average hourly wages in 1978.[56]

Similarly, the percentage of American children who earn more than their parents over the course of their lifetime dropped from about 90% for children born in 1940 to 50% for children born in the 1980s. Massachusetts mirrored most of the national averages in regard to income inequality and wage stagnation. Median home prices in Boston also began to increase after the Great Recession; this rate of increase was higher in Boston than in the rest of Massachusetts and substantially higher than the national average. As of 2018, median rent in the city would consume 51% of median Bostonian household income. Bostonians grew increasingly worried about gentrification and displacement during this period.[57]

The participants in my study might have also felt anxious about the fact that the United States was experiencing an opioid epidemic. Beginning around the year 2000, the rate of deaths related to prescription opioids began to dramatically increase, followed several years later by an increase in deaths attributed to illegal heroin and fentanyl. This drug epidemic played a major role in causing adult Americans' average life expectancy to begin declining—a reversal of population health trends that is virtually unheard of among developed nations in the modern world.[58]

Finally, the focus groups and survey occurred only a few months before Americans began casting votes in the primary and general elections of the 2016 presidential race. The topics of race, policing, and crime featured prominently in the campaign, with Democratic candidate Hillary Clinton and Republican candidate Donald Trump taking opposing positions. Clinton endorsed reforms to both the police and justice system more broadly, and she expressed support for the BLM movement. In contrast, Trump framed support for the police and support for BLM in zero-sum terms, emphatically aligned himself with police, and maligned BLM protesters. Trump also extensively focused on the topic of illegal immigration as a threat to the nation's stability. Scholars argue that he resuscitated the "law and order" theme employed by Republican candidates of decades past, including using a great deal of "dog whistle" rhetoric to appeal to racist and xenophobic sentiments.[59]

In sum, Americans had some reasons to feel optimistic at the time of this study, but other reasons to feel that the American dream was slipping away. As we shall see in the analysis of the focus groups, participants raised some of these contextual issues when they talked about the causes of crime. Despite the contentious nature of the ongoing presidential campaign, focus group participants said surprisingly little about the candidates. If these participants' opinions about crime and punishment were affected by candidates' statements on the campaign trail, that change did not come through during the focus group discussions.

Outline of the Book

I begin by analyzing the focus group discussions. In chapter 1, I examine the various factors that participants believe cause crime. I pay particular attention to the ways that respondents blame individual people or social environments for crime because these beliefs have profoundly influenced the politics of government social spending. People who place more emphasis on social and environmental factors tend to support government intervention to address social problems, whereas people who place more emphasis on personal choice and autonomy tend to oppose welfare and government assistance to the poor, instead preferring to discipline the individual people whom they perceive to be solely responsible for their bad choices. I find that most of the participants in my focus groups argued that both personal and social factors cause crime, but they placed greater emphasis on social factors like poverty and unemployment.

In chapter 2, I analyze the focus group participants' ideas about the best ways for society to prevent and reduce crime. Some common ideas emerged across groups, but I discuss the ways that participants' race and social class shaped their willingness to rely upon government or criminal justice interventions for crime control, as opposed to "turning inward" and helping communities police themselves. Though the high school educated participants placed greater emphasis upon social causes of crime, their first ideas about crime prevention placed greater responsibility upon individuals and communities. I interpret this pattern as evidence of less affluent Americans' distrust of government.

In chapter 3, I assess Americans' crime prevention policy preferences by requiring people to make choices between policy alternatives. I asked both the participants in my focus groups and the respondents to my national survey to construct a hypothetical crime prevention budget. I designed this task to reflect the heart of the "defund the police" debate: should the nation invest additional resources into criminal justice institutions, or should we invest more resources into health-promoting community institutions to prevent crime? Contrary to the assumptions made by many policy analysts and politicians, I demonstrate that White and Black Americans express ample support for community investment.

In chapter 4, I analyze the results of an experiment I embedded in the national survey. I manipulated the language used to describe the communities that would receive justice reinvestment funds, employing both implicitly and explicitly racialized language according to the predictions of racial priming theory. I show that White and Black Americans' crime prevention investment preferences are largely immune to framing effects, which means that advocates have greater leeway to talk about community social problems without provoking public backlash than prior racial priming studies lead us to expect. Unfortunately, I do find evidence that White Americans "backlash" against a proposal to specifically invest in "African American communities."

In chapter 5, I test whether politicians' support for community investment would significantly affect people's likelihood of voting for or against them. Most respondents in my survey said that a politician's choice to invest in criminal justice institutions probably would not affect their likelihood of voting for that person one way or the other, whereas a majority of respondents said that they would be more likely to vote for a politician who supported investment into community institutions. I also test how Republican, Democratic, and independent respondents evaluated a politician's investment choices.

Finally, in the concluding chapter, I discuss the implications of this book for the study of both public opinion about criminal justice and racial priming, as well as the politics of community investment and the "defund the police" debate. I argue that my findings suggest that politicians did, indeed, substantially underestimate voters' willingness to support community-based investment and look beyond the criminal justice system to solve the problem of crime. I consider the lessons of my framing experiment for crafting political messages that would maximize the likelihood of assembling the largest coalition of voters to support a new community investment policy paradigm. I conclude by discussing lingering questions that this book cannot answer and proposing new avenues for future research to better understand the politics of crime prevention in the United States.

1

What Do People Believe Causes Crime?

What causes some people to engage in deviant behavior? Why is crime more common in some places than in others? The answers to these questions matter to policymakers, not just to professors. Public policies are not natural reactions to social problems. Policymakers must believe that it is possible to change the causes of a particular problem through government action.[1] Furthermore, policymakers' understanding of the causes of a problem shape the solutions they enact. If policymakers believe that social conditions cause a particular problem, then the logical response is to enact policies to change the problematic aspects of society. Scholars refer to this understanding of causality as "structural" or "situational" in nature (referring to the structure of social situations and environments). In contrast, if policymakers believe that social problems are caused by people's choices, then the logical response is to change people's behavior or neutralize their ability to affect other individuals. Scholars refer to this understanding of causality as "volitional" or "dispositional" in nature (referring to people's voluntary choices and personality characteristics). If crime is understood to be a freely made bad choice, then punishment to express moral judgment and teach offenders the error of their ways is the most logical response.[2]

In the 1960s, structural understandings of crime dominated, and policymakers focused on rehabilitation and antipoverty initiatives as the solutions to crime. A prime example was President Lyndon Johnson's "war on poverty." However, in the 1970s, policymakers began to lose faith in rehabilitation, and their focus shifted to a volitional understanding of crime during the 1980s and 1990s, which led them to focus on punishing offenders instead of addressing social causes of crime. This ideological shift was quite explicit. For example, in a 1968 speech, Richard Nixon declared, "Our opinion-makers have gone too far in promoting the doctrine that when a law is broken, society—not the criminal—is to blame."[3]

Social scientists and scholars possess the formal training to identify the root causes of social phenomena by using the scientific method. However, there are simply too few scholars trained in causal analysis to make up a majority of voters. As such, the causal beliefs of the lay citizens upon whom legislators depend to win elections play a disproportionate role in shaping the forms and goals of public policies—even if those citizens' causal beliefs do not align with scientific evidence.[4] That reality begs the question: what do average Americans believe to be the causes of crime?

In this chapter, I analyze the discussions of the participants in my focus groups. Each focus group began with a simple prompt: "On the piece of paper in front of you, please list five things that you think of that cause crime." The moderator gave participants a few minutes to write down their thoughts on a provided worksheet, and then she prompted participants to discuss their answers with each other. I assess the degree to which the participants' explanations for the causes of crime matched or diverged from criminologists' major theories of crime. I consider whether the participants favored structural explanations for crime, volitional explanations for crime, or a balanced perspective. Finally, I compare the perspectives of these participants to older research in order to judge whether Americans' understanding of the causes of crime has changed over time.

Lay versus Scholarly Causal Attributions

Strain: Deprivation, Stress, and Desperation

Strain theorists argue that the experience of significant stress can push people into criminal behavior as a coping mechanism. Since Americans are socially conditioned to value economic success, people who experience poverty suffer not just the material harms of poverty itself, but also the emotional frustration of feeling denied the American dream. When the stresses of poverty build up too much, some people will do whatever it takes for relief, even if that behavior is criminal. An archetypal example of classic strain theory would be a person stealing medicine to give to his sick child because he cannot afford to purchase it legally. Later strain theorists argued that financial stress is not the only source of strain. Other sources of stress can be the loss of something valued, such as the breakup of a relationship, or exposure to sources of harm or distress, such as domestic violence. Contemporary strain theorists argue that people are most likely to engage in criminal coping behavior when they feel angry because they perceive the source of their strain to be unjust.[5]

Participants in all six focus groups identified causes of crime that are consistent with the principles of strain theory, making it one of the most salient theories in this study. To give some illustrative examples:

Poverty, lack of education and choices, options and opportunity.
(Lacey, 69, W, CE, FG1)[6]

Better opportunities for everyone as a whole, because like in the inner city, you know, the youth there that resort to selling drugs . . .
(Chrissy, 46, B, HSE, FG2)

I want to say, when you talk about causes of crime . . . Okay, you have to look at the individual first, and look at the pressures on the individual and you have pressures like serial unemployment or underemployment. You have serial homelessness. You have incompetent political and social leadership. You have a de-emphasis of art and music and you have lousy teaching or school, or, okay, those are all the pressures pointing at the individuals who say, "I'm gonna act out, I'm gonna commit the crime." Okay, but all the pressures are there if people decide, if leadership decided, "We're gonna do something about those causes so that the individual won't have those pressures," I think crime would go down.
(Christopher, 68, B, CE, FG3)

You got environment up there? That's a big part of crime, where you live at. Because there's a lot of poverty in some neighborhoods, and that causes a lot of crime, you know. People will get jealous and want what you have, and that starts a lot of . . . [did not finish sentence]
(Susan, 53, B, HSE, FG4)

I was going to say, that's like desperation. I have that one thing with something, the poverty, the unemployment, the need for cash. And then just desperation. But that's an extreme.
(Wallace, 57, W, CE, FG5)

People in desperate situations. Like for their child or you're in an abusive relationship and you feel like you have no choice and you have to steal from other people. . . . A young girl with two kids to feed and they can't afford and the kids are crying because they're hungry, she's going to steal something to feed her kids.

(Camille, 29, W, HSE, FG6)

Participants demonstrated an intuitive understanding of the principles of strain theory. Note how Christopher talked about "pressures" upon individuals, Camille talked about "desperate situations," and Susan argued that strain causes negative emotions like anger or jealousy, which push people into criminal behavior. However, within this relatively broad agreement that strain causes crime, participants' understanding of and relationship to strain varied across race and class.

Strain was a dominant theme among the White, high school educated participants of Focus Group 6. All seven participants talked about poverty, substance abuse, and addiction during the discussion, often in very personal terms. Consider the following exchange:

CAMILLE: Yeah, like incentives for you to get on your feet, to get like a get-well job to be able to go back to school—

JASON: A kick starter.

CAMILLE: —if you got whatever reasons, drugs or you had to get whatever and just didn't follow through, just make those things more available to those people that don't have a lot of education or money.

MODERATOR: I feel like it's not adult education but more like, um—

JUDY: Vocational opportunities! I think.

MODERATOR: Vocational opportunities, okay.

CAMILLE: I mean, I just think it's hard to get jobs and get back on your feet and get back to school and try to go about your life when you kind of got off track, you know? And if you get on track, then maybe there won't be crime, you know?

Throughout the discussion, Camille frequently expressed how difficult it is for people to overcome drug addiction and past contact with the criminal justice system and return to a law-abiding lifestyle, especially if those people are also poor and disadvantaged in the labor market. Though Camille never explicitly stated that she was speaking from personal experience during the discussion, she did report on her exit survey that she served one to five years in prison.

Other participants in Focus Group 6 echoed Camille's sentiment that addiction compounds poverty and pulls people into a downward spiral that is difficult to escape.

> JUDY: Smoking cessation, I mean smoking is very expensive. Cigarettes are how much? I don't know because I—
>
> ALBERT: Ten dollars a pack.
>
> PAMELA: Oh my god.
>
> JUDY: I mean, what I'm saying is if you were a family with a small income and you're a single-parent household, your kids are not even going to have a ball to bounce because all that money is going on cigarettes. Even if you don't drink or gamble or use scratch tickets. Smoking cessation groups, I mean, and even giving them products that will help them to get off.
>
> PAMELA: Yeah.
>
> JUDY: Because those are addictions. Now people think marijuana is a gateway. Cigarettes is the gateway, then marijuana. The initial gateway, the real actual gateway: cigarettes. Marijuana and so forth.

These participants viewed even cigarettes as dangerous because all addictions, even those that are legal, can mean the difference between barely getting by to support one's family versus spending one's money on an addiction instead of paying the bills. Poverty is the key factor here; it is unlikely that a wealthier person's overall family finances would be jeopardized by a smoking habit.

The White, high school educated participants of Focus Group 6 show the deleterious impacts of poverty and addiction on adults' ability to refrain from criminal behavior. In contrast, the Black, high school educated participants of Focus Groups 2 and 4 focused more on youths. Their comments about strain had less to do with personal desperation and more to do with their efforts to prevent youth from being tempted into crime. For example, Jacklyn (32, B, HSE, FG2) said,

It's kind of like that tug of war thing when you've got parents, or whoever is in your life, or yourself, and you're tug of warring with everything that's happening around you that's negative. You know what I'm saying? So, to visually always see it, you're like, you can either look at it like "Huh. Okay, well, that car sitting is selling drugs, so they're making money. They're being able to provide for their family and so forth and so forth," you think of it from that aspect, so you seeing it, you know, I always tell my kids, like, "Okay, just 'cause you see the good part of it, doesn't mean that's it, you know what I'm saying? You get to see the dealers with the nice clothes, luxurious cars, whatever the case may have you. But there's a bad side that you don't get to see, you know what I'm saying?"

Similarly, Matthew (55, B, HSE, FG4) stated,

It always . . . It goes back to home. These kids ain't got nothing to look forward to. A lot of these kids go home, they ain't got no food. . . . Because most of them, they live in one-parent homes, either the mother's trying to work and these kids got a lot of time on their hands to do nothing. You see what I'm saying? So half of them don't go to school. They might leave to go to school, but they never actually make it to school. No, really, because if you drive around the block, if you drive around my neighborhood right now, it's just 10:30, you'll see kids, thirteen, fourteen, fifteen, sixteen years old outside, hanging out. Why? You should be in school. And the first thing comes [inaudible due to cross talk], "I'm trying to eat. I got to get money." You know what I'm saying? I got to get money. You know what I mean? They want to wear these $180 sneakers. They want to wear these $200 f—ing, excuse my language, jeans. They want to wear all this stuff, and they don't understand that that stuff can come later, man. Get an education, because you know . . . [did not finish sentence]

Jacklyn and Matthew both live in Dorchester, a large neighborhood that contains a high concentration of Boston's Black residents as well as some of its most concentrated pockets of poverty. In neighborhoods of concentrated disadvantage, where legal job opportunities are uncommon, many teenagers are tempted into joining the drug trade because they see drug dealers who flaunt material possessions. This gives the impression that the drug trade is a way to achieve financial success when other, legal avenues to make money are out of reach due to poverty, undereducation, and discrimination. Jacklyn and Matthew speak to the struggle that Black parents who live in such neighborhoods face when trying to keep their children from being drawn into criminal networks with a promise of easy money.[7]

Many college educated participants expressed beliefs about the relationship between strain and crime that were similar to those of the high school educated participants. However, they typically spoke about the effects of strain from the perspective of liberal ideology or social service professions (like social work), not personal or vicarious experience. Consider this statement made by Inez (72, W, CE, FG5):

> Well, I think of places that society has abandoned in terms of that . . . , I mean, in California and Detroit and parts of Illinois, it's just there are no jobs. There's no hope. And these are . . . what do the smart people do? They get together, they join gangs. They rob, they steal, they figure out a way to survive. I don't blame them. So why are these places being abandoned? I mean, it doesn't seem like local government, their state governments, or the feds are really doing anything.

Later in the discussion, Inez said,

> And I think one of the big things, being impoverished, poverty, areas of extreme poverty, not just the cities, but rural areas. West Virginia, those kind of places. They don't have options, so whatever, it's got to have them, that's . . . you've got to give them more options.

Inez lives in Quincy, one of Boston's immediate suburbs. For her, impoverished areas are "those kind of places." While she states that she doesn't "blame" disadvantaged youth for joining gangs in order to "figure out a way to survive," she also clearly expresses her social distance from the people and places that are most impacted by systemic strains. Similarly, Marianne (30, W, CE, FG5) said,

> I think systemic oppression and discrimination against individuals who are part of different racial, cultural, socioeconomic backgrounds, and the isolation that I think structures perpetuate in terms of . . . for people. So

I think when you're already marginalized in a society that is expecting the worst of you, it pushes you to feel less required to adhere to . . . And I think limited access to opportunities for social and economic mobility, really . . . And I think rage at injustice, when I think people who've experienced, and can witness that there's a lack of access to them, but other people have excessive amounts of access, why not take what you can, if it's . . . you know, if you're able to get away with it?

Marianne disclosed at the end of the discussion that she is a social worker. Unsurprisingly, then, she expressed one of the most "academic" understandings of strain and systemic oppression of all the participants in this study; her statement most closely aligns with social scientists' causal understanding of the relationship between concentrated disadvantage and crime.

Some criminologists theorize that people who can truly empathize with criminal offenders are more likely to support rehabilitation and second chances instead of harsh punishment.[8] The statements of Inez and Marianne highlight the challenges caused by racial and socioeconomic segregation in the United States. Though these White women with advanced education who have little to no firsthand experience with crime expressed sympathy for people who suffer the criminogenic strains of poverty, their feelings may fall short of the depth necessary for true empathy. I saw some evidence that middle-class White people's social distance from poverty leads to a greater variety of beliefs and disagreements. Consider the following exchange:

NATHAN: Well, my experience with it is that, like in the poor neighborhoods, most people that are interested in helping youths at risk are, uh, is not the government, neither the federal or the local government. It's just local, what do you call them . . . ?

MODERATOR: People in the community?

NATHAN: People in the community. Exactly. So a lot of times there's lack of resources. And young people, they're like succumbed to peer pressure all the times, joining gangs because they're kind of forced to. And there's nothing to prevent that, pretty much.

INEZ: I agree. They get together, some of the people in gangs are also very, very smart. They just . . . that's their way of succeeding.

ALICE: Is it because of lack of respect for others?

INEZ: Because other avenues of succeeding aren't open to them.

Nathan (55, W, CE, FG5) was the only participant in Focus Group 5 who reported an experience of arrest and incarceration (less than one year in jail), so it is likely that he was the only person in this group with a personal experience with criminogenic strains. Whereas Inez agreed with Nathan's statement that lack of resources and peer pressure can cause youth to join gangs, Alice (54, W, CE, FG5) seemed to blame gang membership on youths' lack of respect for other people. Inez pushed back and emphasized the criminogenic influence of blocked opportunities. This disagreement between Nathan and Inez versus Alice represents an ideological conflict between a structural versus volitional attribution for crime, respectively. I will return to ideological conflicts among the White participants of Focus Group 5 throughout this book.

Preventing Youth Deviance: Relationships and Culture

Perhaps the single least controversial thing you could say to a criminologist is, "I worry about unsupervised teenagers getting into trouble." The evidence is unambiguous that teenagers and people in their early twenties (especially males) are significantly more likely to engage in deviant and criminal behavior than older adults, and most of the crimes that occur each year are committed by offenders who fall in this age range.[9] Participants in these focus groups frequently commented on youth offending and interventions to keep youth out of trouble. For example:

> In China, and my roommate was Korean at [college], he told me their school day consists of a twelve [hour] school day where they go to school, they clean the school, and they learn martial arts in school, then they go right home. So it's like, we just ship the kids off in half day school, what's gonna happen? They're gonna . . . Rolling up weed, they're gonna be . . . Then when they're rolling up weed and then they, "Oh let's have someone go to the liquor store, oh I'm drunk, let me go steal the car, oh you know what, let me, forget that job for part time, 'F' a part time job, yo my brother says we can go buy this eight ball and go sell crack over to these people." And it's like saying, they could still say to the mother, the parent

whomever, "Oh I was at the rec center," while the kids were out there smoking weed, drinking liquor, and selling crack.
(Adam, 37, B, CE, FG3)

Some of the younger kids need like a curfew. . . . Uh-huh, yeah, they be out there. That's what they need to try to do, get them kids off the street that time of the night.
(Susan, 53, B, HSE, FG4)

Part of boredom and other things that they don't have anything to do. They might be too young to get a job or maybe there's no jobs in their community, so they're out doing stupid things, breaking into cars, whatever they're doing.
(Janet, 56, W, CE, FG5)

Participants offered several explanations for youth deviance that reflected two major classes of criminological theory, as well as one causal belief that criminologists view with much greater skepticism. First, several participants expressed the belief that youth who establish relationships with deviant peers or adults will be more likely to commit crime themselves:

They're sending all the kids to the Y, where they can fight in the back and meet up on the corner and start their little gangs. Do you know what I'm saying? The Y is not an after school program. It's an all-day program for anyone to come to. . . . These kids are meeting up with adults that are older than them that, oh . . . pushing them all the way towards, "Oh, let's take this park around the corner. And let me introduce you to a little of this and a little of that and a little more of this. And take this gun and go rob the corner store for me, because I think you're prepared for that."
(Dorian, 35, B, HSE, FG4)

Peer affiliation, like getting into gangs, getting in with the wrong . . . [did not finish sentence]
(Wallace, 57, W, CE, FG5)

Like monkey see, monkey do, everyone is doing it and you do it.
(Camille, 29, W, HSE, FG6)

This perspective echoes social learning theory, which contends that people learn criminal behavior through relationships with deviants who both teach them the skills to commit crime and give them positive reinforcement for breaking the law. This positive reinforcement instills deviant proclivities in the new offender.[10]

A common theme across the focus groups was that youth can "pick up" deviant beliefs not just from interpersonal relationships, but also from consumption of morally corrosive media. Here, a difference emerged across the race of participants. Several White participants spoke in somewhat general terms against violence and sex being shown on TV. For example, Judy (70, W, HSE, FG6) said, "Actually the media. I think young people are very influenced by things they see on television. All the movies, R videos and whatever else, it's kind of pushing the envelope kind of thing and one-upmanship and in other words, you know, edgy, who can out, who can be edgier than the next person?" Debbie (64, W, CE, FG1) was even more pointed:

DEBBIE: I have a bigger, broader issue. I think what I'm running into, and I have a lot of twenty-something's I'm dealing with, is they're really not clear what right and wrong is.

MODERATOR: Okay, so how do we reduce or prevent crime with what you just said?

DEBBIE: Well, I think part of the problem are the movies people see today and the TV shows they see today. Just watch Dr. Phil sometimes or one of these other . . .

LACEY: Or morally.

DEBBIE: Yeah.

LACEY: You want more moral education and less violence in the . . . ?

DEBBIE: No, I'm thinking even broader than that. I remember the day when they wouldn't have violence on till after ten, eleven o'clock at night.

MODERATOR: Okay, so you want less violence on TV?

DEBBIE: Well, that would be a start. And have better labels for videos too. Movies and videos. Because I think . . . I was sitting in front watching a TV show the other day, I had no idea there was gonna be nudity in it, and this was at 7:00 p.m., and I had somebody in the room that was very young.

Both Judy and Debbie implied that exposing youth to "adult" content on television would start a kind of slippery slope that would put kids on a path to crime.

Several Black participants expressed a more pointed critique about the dangerous effects of media on youth, which brings me to the third criminological theory reflected in participants' discussions of youth crime. The sociologist Elijah Anderson argues that poverty, lack of opportunities for jobs or upward mobility, the presence of drug dealers and violent offenders, and the absence of reliable police protection in neighborhoods of concentrated disadvantage create a self-reinforcing cycle of violence. Youth in disadvantaged communities feel the need to get in fights to prove their toughness because youth who are perceived to be weak and vulnerable are the most targeted for violent victimization. Within this particular social context, violence and retaliation win respect, and drug dealing brings wealth. Anderson called this behavioral adaptation to a dangerous, toxic social environment the "code of the street."[11]

Several Black participants who live in the neighborhood of Dorchester spoke of the influence of the code of the street on youth in their communities. Consider the following exchange between Bettie (23, B, CE, FG1) and Debbie (64, W, CE, FG1) in Focus Group 1:

> BETTIE: I think some causes of crime . . . like I live in Dorchester, I'm twenty-three years old . . . I think sometimes, like certain kids might drop out, but weapons get in the wrong people's hands and basically, the way they think they're immature, so of course they're gonna use weapons, all that. Kids, the ones that don't have jobs. Like it almost happened to me, I almost got robbed for my phone. So, it's more like the youth, like maybe eighteen to sixteen, that's making wrong decisions to cause crimes. And most of them they would drop out or just not go to school at all, and that's what makes . . . I think it's more like all the youth that's making more violence for Boston, right? That's how I feel.
>
> DEBBIE: Do they feel they have no future?
>
> BETTIE: I think sometimes with the way neighborhoods are, you have kids that claim streets, and then here comes, like, that's a going back and forth thing. And then it escalates to this, someone dies, that's

just, it's sad. And then the people that get mad, like the ones that really cared about that person try to get revenge on the other person, so it turns into more violence. So, I think, not trying to be . . . I am Black! I'm not being racist, but it is like all Black, like all the Black kids that's kind of corrupted a little bit.

While Anderson stressed social environment as the cause of the street code, several Black participants also expressed the belief that the code can be transmitted through media. For example, Mary (33, B, HSE, FG4) said, "I like rap music, but I do feel a lot of . . . Like, a lot of the things we expose our kids to encourage a lifestyle that the people actually talking about it don't even really live, you know. And so these kids want to be like these gangsters and stuff like that." Later in the discussion, Matthew (55, B, HSE, FG4) said to Mary:

> MATTHEW: The only role models that your kids have are either your sports stars or your rap stars. There's a lot of people in our community that are positive that try to talk to these kids, but, see, these kids don't want to hear that because of what social media and the television are then showing.
> MARY: That's what I'm saying! That's where they get their value.

Similar sentiments about the criminogenic influences of television, social media, and rap music were also expressed by Chrissy (46, B, HSE, FG2) and Adam (37, B, CE, FG3).

This is where participants' beliefs diverged from research evidence. Most criminologists who have tested the relationship between consumption of violent TV, video games, or music and actual criminal or violent behavior find little evidence that consuming media causes the behavior.[12] As for rap music, specifically, criminologist Charis Kubrin argues that this genre of music does not create the code of the street but rather reflects aspects of life in neighborhoods of concentrated disadvantage. In other words, "gangsta rap" is an artistic outlet for people who are surrounded by violence to make sense of their social world and to assert their autonomy and human dignity in the face of a white hegemonic culture that would reduce them to criminal stereotypes. Gangsta rap is a product of the code of the street, not its cause.[13]

Several Black participants recognized the limited influence of rap music even as they were critical of it. Consider the words of Dorian (35, B, HSE, FG4) and Susan (53, B, HSE, FG4):

DORIAN: But again though, I hate when people find the blame for something, not just saying, you know . . . I hate when people find the blame. At the end of the day, my kids listen to rap music too.

SUSAN: Mine too.

DORIAN: And this is the thing. Like a couple of days ago, they're sitting down, I walk in the living room, like what the? What are you all listening to in here? But at the end of the day, I said, you know what, I can't stop them from listening to this crap, because when they're out of the house, they're listening to it. Like I told them, "you know this ain't reality, right? These guys make money to say these things." So again, it goes back into . . . It's following what you teach your child. At the beginning. They have to be getting it. You know what I'm saying?

It Takes a Village: Parenting and Communities

Several bodies of criminological theory address the relationship between parents' behavior and children's likelihood of engaging in crime later in life. Social learning theory dictates that youth will learn deviance from criminal parents. According to social control theory, youth who feel close to law-abiding parents will avoid criminal behavior so as not to disappoint and jeopardize their relationship with their loved ones. The general theory of crime argues that poor parenting causes youth to develop inadequate self-control, and this impulsiveness forever after predisposes them to crime. Much empirical research has confirmed that variation in parenting styles is related to criminal behavior.[14]

Participants in all six focus groups asserted that bad parenting causes crime, and most took it as such a commonsense proposition that they provided little additional explanation. The way that participants' discussion of parenting varied across the focus groups was more interesting. Several of the high school educated participants implicitly or explicitly recognized that poverty impacts parenting. Consider the perspective of Jacklyn (32, B, HSE, FG2):

But like Ginger said, for the kids that have parents and so forth, or aunts and uncles, they aren't stepping up to the plate. Personally, you know what I'm saying? They're not. Then you have the parents that have to kinda drop down my former work. You got the parents that are working two jobs, or one job, you know what I'm saying? So they can't focus on their kid, or they're not, they're choosing not to focus on their children as much. You have all these kids having kids, so they're crazy naive, so you see them and you're like, "Listen, your daughter shouldn't be . . ." Even if you approach it nicely, "Your daughter shouldn't be twerking around the table," and they're very defensive and it's like, "Listen, I'm just trying to help you because I'm a mom too," you know what I'm saying?

Though Jacklyn critiques parenting styles with which she disagrees, her judgment is tempered by her recognition that the need to work multiple jobs decreases the time some people can spend parenting their children. Similarly, Judy (70, W, HSE, FG6) said,

This is something that has to happen from within, but a stable home life, reasonable boundaries for parental involvement and so forth. And there's no, there's very few programs addressing single-parent homes. What I'm saying is, here in Boston, if you're two seniors you get more help from the mayor's office than if you're a single parent with four kids trying your best to keep the kids out of trouble and pay your bills. Saying this from personal experience.

Judy echoes Jacklyn's perspective that many parents struggle under various strains, but she also bemoans the lack of government programs to help single parents overcome those strains.

Sociologist William Julius Wilson argued that the marked increase in the number of single-female-headed households in majority-Black neighborhoods of concentrated disadvantage during the latter half of the twentieth century was both a consequence of widespread joblessness and poverty and a force that exacerbated poverty.[15] There was a difference of opinion on this point among the high school educated Black participants of Focus Group 4. Joseph (54, B, HSE, FG4) said, "Have that education growing up. I don't care if it's one parent or two parents.

As long as you teach your kids right from wrong, they would know the difference. As they grow up, they keep that virtue with them and that spiritual life as they grow." In contrast, Mary (33, B, HSE, FG4) identified a "lack of fathers in homes" as a cause of crime. Matthew (55, B, HSE, FG4) agreed with Mary, saying,

> Hey, listen. It took me to do just what I'm saying I don't want these kids to do, and that was to go to jail to become a man. And that's the worst place to be to learn to be a man. You know what I'm saying? When society's all messed up, when most of us are older, older men are incarcerated. There's not guidance out here for these kids, and a woman cannot teach a man how to be a man. You know what I mean? . . . She cannot do that. She can raise him. She can discipline him. You, my son, and I break your neck, but I can't teach you how to be a man. And we're teaching kids not knowing . . . having this guidance how to be a man, they don't know how to treat a woman. They don't know how to respect no one because it's not being handed down to them.

Whereas many of the high school educated participants expressed empathy for the challenges faced by poor, single parents, the discussions about parenting among the college educated participants once again showed greater social distance and ideological disagreement. Adam (37, B, CE, FG3) expressed one of the most critical judgments against parents in the entire study:

> There's terrible parenting in the homes, you have to say this, [cross talk, Rachelle: "yes there is"] the parenting is, I'm sorry . . . In White, Black homes, whatever, Latino, I'm sorry, because . . . If you, someone who's constantly in the same system and it was even harder for my elders in the past 'cause of civil rights, now that these kids are disrespectful, they're lazy, they act like they're supposed to have everything handed to them . . .

Adam judged bad parents for raising lazy, disrespectful children, and he neither acknowledged nor granted leeway for social constraints upon people's parenting capacity. Rachelle (60+, B, CE, FG3) agreed with him.[16] Their perspective is much starker and more critical than that expressed by most of the high school educated participants. However, Melissa (44, B, CE, FG3) quickly responded to Adam's criticism of bad parents:

> I think, and this is where I would like to come in, it's, if it were that bad, we would be . . . All of us would be a lot worse off. [*laughter*] I mean, you look at the communities, especially, we're focusing on one generic population, regardless of culture. Well, there are kids who do very well, and we don't focus on that. So, what helps them? Strong social . . . you know, their church, their parents.

This the first example of a role that Melissa consistently played in her focus group. She often acted as a "voice of reason" who pushed her fellow highly educated Black participants to focus on the many examples of successful Black families in their communities rather than narrowly, cynically, and judgmentally focusing on poor, struggling Black families. She served as a counterbalance to the tendency of participants in this group to fall into "respectability politics."[17] Respectability politics refers to class-based divisions within communities of color and the efforts of more affluent individuals to morally distance themselves from "deviant" members of their same racial group.

A similar disagreement occurred among the college educated White participants of Focus Group 5:

NATHAN: Most of the time, it comes down to bad parenting.
JANET: Well, that's a loaded answer.
INEZ: Well, you know, a very laissez-faire parenting style can . . .
  I mean . . .
JANET: But there are also wonderful parents whose children . . . make choices to do things that . . .
INEZ: Oh, no . . .
DYLAN: Yes. Yes.
NATHAN: Yeah.
INEZ: No, I know, but . . .
JANET: I'm just saying, I think it's a loaded thing.
INEZ: I think . . . if there's nothing that inhibits your behavior and you basically learn that, I believe.

NATHAN: Yeah.

INEZ: Mostly. Um, you know.

This exchange was marked by its awkwardness. Similar to Adam and Rachelle in Focus Group 3, Nathan (55, W, CE, FG5) and Inez (72, W, CE, FG5) expressed judgment against bad parenting that was not tempered by recognition of social constraints on parents. Janet (56, W, CE, FG5) intervened and expressed discomfort with the implications of Nathan and Inez's answers. You can see Inez stumbling over her words in response. Dylan (25, W, CE, FG5) and Nathan interjected agreement, but it was not quite clear with what they were agreeing. It felt to me like Inez realized she had expressed a stereotype about people experiencing poverty and attempted to save face when called out by Janet.

Viewed all together, these findings indicate that people's understanding of the relationship between parenting and youth crime varies as a function of race and class. Working-class people are more likely to have a structural understanding that many parents are unable to devote as much attention to their children as they would wish to because of the numerous demands on their time to make ends meet. Poorer Black people are more likely to live in neighborhoods with a higher number of single-female-headed households and hold different beliefs about whether that family structure has different effects on children than two-parent households. Wealthier people are more likely to express volitional understandings that interpret bad parenting as a matter of choice or ineptitude, not a function of environmental constraints. However, there is also ideological disagreement among more affluent people on this point that seems to flow from liberal political ideology or a feeling of "linked fate" attachment to fellow people of color.[18]

Another common theme across the focus groups was concern with collective efforts to raise children. This concept is captured in the old aphorism, "it takes a village to raise a child," which was explicitly referenced by participants in Focus Group 3:

SHELDON: You need the community, that's what you really need. It's not just your kids and your family, okay? It's yours and yours and yours, it's everybody's . . . Like back in the old days, back before.

RACHELLE: A village, a village.

SHELDON: Takes a village.

Criminologists address this concept in their theories of informal social control and collective efficacy, which analyze the ability of people in a community to work together to supervise youth, prevent crime, and solve collective problems.[19] However, Sheldon alluded to a dominant concern of participants across the focus groups when he said, "like back in the old days, back before." These participants overwhelmingly believed that the quality of social bonds between neighbors has eroded over the course of their lives. The college educated White participants in Focus Group 5 had the following exchange:

WALLACE: I would say even before the police, more community involvement, people policing their own neighborhoods, but short of vigilantism. I mean, get to know your neighbors . . . Yeah. Kind of look out for each other. The . . . again, Bruce, are you . . . the way it was . . .

BRUCE: I agree.

WALLACE: Back in the day, neighborhoods kind of looked out for . . . if you knew something was weird going on . . .

INEZ: But look at what's happening to neighborhoods today. They're totally changing. They're not being organized the way they used to.

WALLACE: Well, people aren't close, you don't know your neighbors.

INEZ: That's it.

WALLACE: If you live in a building or you live in a street, you don't even know who's living next door to you.

INEZ: And they don't . . . It's much more insular.

WALLACE: So you hide in your house and things go on and you don't want to get involved. So I guess people getting involved in their neighborhood.

Though participants frequently expressed this belief that community bonds between neighbors have decayed over time, few participants explained why they believed this has happened. The high school educated Black participants in Focus Group 4 were the exception:

MATTHEW: Well, like she said, the curfew. I say community involvement. You know what I mean? In the neighborhood you live in, these kids are going to do this. Society got people so afraid to even say anything to anybody. You know what I'm saying? If you see a kid doing something wrong, people are scared to say something because you don't know if these kids are going to pull out a gun or whatever. You don't know if they're going to come back and blow up your house. So more on community involvement. You know what I mean? The neighborhoods need to be better structured.

SUSAN: Mmm-hmm. Like a neighborhood crime watch also.

MATTHEW: Yeah, just more involved with the neighborhood, with the young kids. You know what I mean?

SUSAN: Neighbor helping neighbor. Mm-hmm.

MATTHEW: Because that . . . You know, a lot of people say just throw these kids away, but you can't throw them away.

Matthew (55, B, HSE, FG4) attributed the decline in neighbors' willingness to supervise other people's children to the rise in youth violence. He reiterated this observation at another point in the conversation, and Joseph (54, B, HSE, FG4) agreed with him that fights among youths decades ago would involve "no guns, no knives." Chastising a teenager who is not your own child is a very risky proposition if that teenager is likely to be armed and retaliate against you with violence. Though this dynamic is likely restricted to impoverished neighborhoods with high concentrations of violence, it reveals how violence creates a self-reinforcing cycle by undermining the very collective efficacy that might be able to prevent violence in the first place. The village cannot raise its children when the children are armed and feel the need to resolve conflicts themselves because they do not trust the police to safely protect them.[20]

Social Control and Deterrence: Stopping Bad People and Bad Choices

The theories that I have discussed so far share an underlying assumption that criminal behavior is not innate. Strain theory argues that people must be pushed into crime by situational pressures that provoke feelings of anger or jealousy. Social learning theory argues that people are pulled into crime through peer pressure or the desire to please a role model who engages in crime. Code of the street theory argues that engaging in fights to earn respect and protect oneself against greater victimization is a (mal)adaptation to an unsafe neighborhood environment. At this point, a lay reader is likely thinking, "But aren't some people just bad?" There is a body of criminological theory that considers the roles of personality and values in criminal behavior.[21] Social control theories start from the premise that all people are self-interested. When people believe that they can get away with criminal acts, and they believe that committing crime would benefit them, they are likely to do it. As such, social control theorists generally assume that people are motivated to commit crime and instead ask why most people *do not* break the law.

If a person's morals align with the mainstream values of society, some social control theorists argue that breaking the law would also feel like a betrayal of one's own values; it is rare for such people to feel that the benefits of a criminal action would outweigh the guilt they would feel.[22] Other theorists argue that people with high levels of self-control will not give into the temptations they feel to break the law.[23] Unlike the strain and social learning theorists who argue that criminogenic social circumstances can change throughout a person's life, the older social control theories lean toward the position that once people's values or self-control are set in childhood, their adult personality will forever after make them prone to law-abiding or lawbreaking behavior.[24]

The key word here is "prone" to criminal behavior. A variety of factors can alter people's judgments about whether the benefits of engaging in crime will outweigh the risks and potential costs. The more positive connections people have in life (i.e., "social bonds"), the more they stand to lose if they are caught breaking the law. Person who are convicted of a crime will likely lose their job and will (at a minimum) cause their loved ones to feel disappointment, pain, and anger if they believe it is important to obey the law. At worst, their loved ones may cut them out of their lives. The fear of losing the good things in one's life increases a person's willpower to resist the temptation of crime. That is why most people do not break the law even when there is a very low likelihood that they would be caught by the authorities.[25]

But what about people with few good connections in their lives? What do people with no spouse, no close family or friends, and no job have to lose if they commit crime? When social bonds are absent or inadequate to prevent crime, the state must step in. Deterrence theory formalizes the proposition that punishment influences people's decision whether to commit crime. If people believe that there is a high likelihood of being caught by the authorities for a particular criminal act, and they also believe that the punishment is more severe than they are willing to suffer, then they will not commit that crime.[26]

Several participants expressed beliefs that are consistent with the spirit of social control theory. They attributed criminal behavior to poor choices or a deficit of values:

> I put things like disregard for others and consequences of actions. I put greed. And then I was thinking of violent crime, I was thinking of anger for various reasons. You know, social reasons.
> (Lance, 60, B, CE, FG1)

> I did write the same thing you wrote, just common sense and morals.
> (James, 46, W, HSE, FG2)

> Lotta times nowadays, people will lack empathy and they don't have that moral guidance [cross talk, Adam: "Moral standing"], you know . . .
> (William, 67, B, CE, FG3)

> Some people just like to commit crimes. They enjoy doing it.
> (Bruce, 58, W, CE, FG5)

> On that vein actually, a deficit of ethics, scruples. Lack of scruples, like not knowing right and wrong. Indifference to . . . A lack of values. A lack of values.
> (Judy, 70, W, HSE, FG6)

These participants saw character deficits as a factor that contributes to crime, one that interferes with offenders' ability to think about how their criminal behavior affects other people.

Some participants talked about choice and responsibility in different ways depending upon their personal experience with crime (or lack thereof). Chrissy and Matthew both disclosed during the discussions that they are former offenders. Their own life history shaped their perspectives on the process of desisting from crime:

I happen to run into [a relative who resumed drug use after exiting prison], just on a fluke, and I could see the shame and the guilt all over his face. You know what I'm saying? I've tried to help him as best I can, but, if you're not willing to help yourself, then I can't do anything for you, because you're not going to bring me back down. You know? 'Cause truth be told, there was a good part of my life where I was in and out of jail. And I've done some crimes, and I've done a lot of things that I'm not proud of, but you get to a certain age and a certain stage in your life where, you just, your priorities change, they have to change, you know what I mean? And it wasn't just because I needed them to change, I wanted them to change. You know what I mean? So there was a difference in the need and the want. I wanted to change. I just got tired of that life, that lifestyle, and everything that came with it, so I made a choice to change, and you know, I just keep my circle very small . . .
(Chrissy, 46, B, HSE, FG2)

But they do have these programs in these [correctional] institutions, but guys don't want to take advantage of it because they don't want to come out here and put no effort in, no sweat, nothing into it. They want to come out, and they want to get fast money. They want to come out. . . . And I've seen it done because I've got three boys. You know what I mean? And they've been in and out the system. As soon as they come out, "Man, let me call my dog." And then, "Yo, hit me off with a pack." Man, what are you doing? You're going back to that, man? "You know, I'm trying to get some money, pop." Come on, man, you know. It's recidivism, whatever it is, but it's on the individual that wants to do better. You know what I mean? Because like I said, you don't see no old drug dealers out here. You know what I'm saying? They all in jail.
(Matthew, 55, B, HSE, FG4)

We have already heard from Chrissy and Matthew in earlier sections in this chapter. Throughout their respective focus groups, they both clearly described the criminogenic effects of strain and the code of the street in their neighborhoods. Here, however, they also express the belief that extricating oneself from a criminal lifestyle requires personal choice and a commitment to change.[27] For Chrissy and Matthew, they arrived at this belief the hard way, through personal experience.

The discussion among the college educated Black participants in Focus Group 3 hints at a range of views on personal responsibility and crime among middle-class Black Americans. Sheldon (30, B, CE, FG3) placed blame on "greed . . . because some, like, those who have and those who have nots here, and people who have not . . . Instead of working to get it, they just go out and take it." Among people experiencing poverty, he draws a distinction between those who choose moral versus immoral means of alleviating their financial strains. In other words, within the context of structural constraints, Sheldon draws volitional character distinctions. Similarly, Adam (37, B, CE, FG3) said,

> ADAM: Addiction. For example, some people have family members who have the same opportunity as you and become substance abusers because, first of all, the mental instability, then the addiction . . .
>
> MODERATOR: Okay.
>
> ADAM: Greed, because some people always feel that they're very self-centered. And, you know, excuses.
>
> MODERATOR: Tell me more about excuses.
>
> ADAM: They don't . . . Laziness. They teach . . . A lotta times people say, they use someone, like saying, "Oh, this, that" and they're like, at this point in time a lotta people they want education especially here in Massachusetts, which is the mecca of education, there isn't much of an excuse to say, "Oh I did it because of this or that." I mean, there are certain stances that revolve around why someone could have committed the crime, but at the end of the day, it all just seems like an excuse, or just a probable cause. And it's whether you choose right or wrong.

Adam began his statement by identifying addiction as a cause of crime. Addiction can be thought of in either structural or volitional terms; it can be characterized as a force that reduces people's agency and pressures them into destructive behavior, or it can be characterized as a freely chosen habit. It quickly becomes clear that Adam thinks of addiction in volitional terms. He talks about substance abusers who "have the same opportunity as you," and his explanation pivots to character judgments about greed, self-centeredness, and laziness. By the end of his explanation, he no longer says anything about addiction and instead frames crime solely as a choice between "right or wrong," and he judges those who make "excuses" for their wrong choices.

In contrast Rachelle, (60+, B, CE, FG3) offered an explanation that mirrored Adam's:

RACHELLE: And poor self-esteem. Poor, very poor. You're set up, you come with the understanding if you're a person of color that you're not gonna succeed. Even though you're trying, the expectation is very low. In the school system, starting with education, knowing you're not expected to excel. So then it just starts a cycle of crime. The other thing is deviant behaviors that are not identified on time. I mean we are no more deviant than the White folks.

MODERATOR: So, deviant behaviors like . . . ?

RACHELLE: Well, they have criminal activities and from early in school, they're not given the help so that they can get the help to get out of that behavior.

MODERATOR: So you weren't thinking more about, sort of, mental health problems?

RACHELLE: Oh I have mental health here! [*laughter*] Not identified with the mental health problems, the kids are not given the opportunity to go to counseling and deal with those things. It's like it doesn't exist. So we have that and then we have greed. We have this illusion with society. If you speak to young people like, "Why am I gonna do that anyway?" This illusion . . .

Whereas Adam began his statement by identifying a cause of crime that could be thought of as structural in nature (addiction) and then offered a very volitional explanation, Rachelle began by identifying a volitional cause of crime (poor self-esteem), but she went on to explain it in structural terms. She attributes youth deviance to a racist school system that undermines Black youths' self-esteem because teachers expect them to fail. She also identifies greed as a cause of crime, but unlike Lance (quoted at the beginning of this section) and a few other participants who simply stated greed as a values deficit, Rachelle locates the source of greed in an "illusion with society," not simply bad morality. These conflicting volitional and structural attributions vocalized by Sheldon, Adam, and Rachelle reveal variance in the degree to which middle-class Black Americans simply blame offenders for choosing to engage in crime versus recognize environmental pressures and constraints on people's choices.

The college educated White participants in Focus Group 5 showed a similar split between structural and volitional attributions for offending:

> INEZ: I was also sort of thinking unmet social and psychological needs.
>
> MODERATOR: Can you say more about that?
>
> INEZ: People who should be treated for mental illness or emotional upsets but aren't. People who, um, poverty I think is in all the things that accompany that. Many unmet . . . in terms of Maslow . . . the unmet needs and stuff, it all gets kind of . . .
>
> WALLACE: There's a basic . . . it kind of encompasses a lot, opportunity.
>
> INEZ: Yeah.
>
> WALLACE: And making poor choices.
>
> INEZ: I had that too.
>
> WALLACE: When you have that . . . Sometimes it's just making bad judgments.
>
> MODERATOR: Did you say lack of . . . ?
>
> WALLACE: Opportunity and bad judgment. Poor choices. Yeah.
>
> ALICE: I said stupidity.
>
> WALLACE: There you go.
>
> MODERATOR: Can stupidity fit with bad judgment?
>
> WALLACE: Basically. Same thing. The same thing.
>
> MODERATOR: Is that kind of what you were going for?
>
> ALICE: I . . . I guess. Yeah.

This exchange was interesting because Inez (72, W, CE, FG5) started by talking about poverty and unmet needs—structural attributions for crime. Wallace (57, W, CE, FG5) sounded like he agreed with Inez, but he began steadily pivoting away from structural pressures and toward volitional factors: poor choices and bad judgment (which Inez endorsed too). Alice (54, W, CE, FG5) went a step further, attributing crime simply to "stupidity." When the moderator asked Alice if she equated stupidity with bad judgment, Wallace put words in her mouth, but Alice's final response did not give the impression that she truly agreed with Wallace. It felt to me that she raised stupidity as a true character defect, something even more fundamental than making bad choices.

Participants of both races and with multiple levels of education echoed not just a social control theory perspective on morality, personality, and choice; they also endorsed deterrence theory's focus on punishment as a force necessary to keep motivated criminals in check. Consider the statements of Patricia and Jacklyn:

> I'd say more jail time, don't give the people too many chances. Sometimes they get too many chances and they go out and commit more crimes. (Patricia, 49, B, CE, FG1)

> And then the consequences. I put, I mean, it sounds crazy and it may be if I were sitting around a table full of convicts, they'd be like "What?" [*laughs*] But, the consequences are not hard enough. They don't level out to the crime. And when I say that you have pedophiles who may get probation or a year, eighteen months. Versus someone that violated their probation. They're in there for a year to two years, you know, plus, it's like "what?" It doesn't even, you know what I'm saying? You just, they don't level out, so, I've been around people who have said things like, "Oh, I'm going to do X, Y, and Z. You know, I don't care, what they're gonna give me? Probation?" You know what I'm saying? Or, "What am I gonna have to do? Pay a fine?" You know, stuff like that. It's like, "Whatever. You know, I can do it, and this is the consequence," or, "I don't have a record, so I'll be good." You know, "I can bail myself out." You know, I can't lie, I've made that statement. Listen, with altercations, it's like, "Listen, I don't have a problem, you know, I have forty dollars on me now, so . . ." You know, type of thing. They don't level out, the consequences, they just don't. (Jacklyn, 32, B, HSE, FG2)

The college educated Black participants in Focus Group 3 reacted enthusiastically to the idea that people commit crimes because they do not adequately fear punishment:

WILLIAM: I have fear of retribution of the law enforcement. Harsher . . . Fear of harsher sentences.

MODERATOR: You said fear of harsher sentences, as opposed to harsher sentences themselves?

WILLIAM: Yes, well make sentences the, um . . .

PAIGE: Deterrent.

WILLIAM: Deterrent.

MODERATOR: Okay, so it's harsher sentences . . .

WILLIAM: I think you mentioned it, someone mentioned, about in the Muslim countries or something . . .

ADAM: Right, yeah.

WILLIAM: They cut your hand off for stealing. You know what I mean, so, if you know you're gonna get your hand cut off I don't think you . . . [*laughs*]

CANDICE: Caned! In Singapore, the kid got caned 'cause he [inaudible]. And he got those lashes. He cried! [*laughs*] But he got 'em, so . . .

WILLIAM: Exactly, in [North] Korea the guy got twelve years of hard labor for stealing a poster, right, so you know, if those were obvious and evident I think you would refrain from doing things, as much as . . .

ADAM: Did you hear the saying, "Fear lasts longer than love?" Because that's what's happening in those countries.

I end this section by quoting Alice because she vocalized one of the strongest ideological commitments to the theory of deterrence out of all the participants in this study. When some other participants in her group began pondering the possibility of decriminalizing some minor forms of deviance, Alice said,

ALICE: Yeah. But is it okay for people to just not . . . If they go and do get convicted and do get caught, and they have to . . . there has to be consequences, somehow, or it's going to be worse. If there's no consequence . . .

BRUCE: They pass.

ALICE: . . . then people will just . . . it's going to just explode because people are just going to go, "it doesn't matter." I can go and get convicted of something serious and then get released. I can just go get it again and not even go to jail, you know, it's like I'm not even going. I'm just going to take the school system, just as an example. The teacher is like the police or the person that's supposed to have respect, and if you have a classroom of fifth graders and the kids are allowed to throw pencils and spitballs and call the teacher, uh, f-ing asshole and not be told discipline, and then, hey, he can do that. So now I start . . .

MODERATOR: I can do it. Hmm.

ALICE: Now, the teacher can't control the kids. And the teacher's being punished. And so, what happens to the kids? They don't get "Oh, just be a good boy." It's, "No, I can get away with this," so now it's going to get . . .

BRUCE: [cross talk] And they get put into some program.

ALICE: . . . worse and so . . . and you know what, I understand how programs are supposed to work, but if you don't have a little . . . some discipline and some consequences . . . I mean, I'm not talking about beatings and things like that. I'm just talking like to show . . .

MODERATOR: Respect.

ALICE: . . . there is respect and there is . . . there are rules. And if you don't follow the rules, there has to be consequences.

Alice strongly believes that deviance, be it childish misbehavior or adult criminality, occurs when people doubt that violations of the rules will be followed by punishment. This is about as textbook a definition of deterrence theory as could be written. For Alice, "there has to be consequences."

Crimes of Opportunity and Vulnerable Victims

Routine activities theorists argue that a crime will occur when a motivated offender and a potential victim happen to be in the same place at the same time in the absence of effective deterrents. For example, a person might be robbed if he or she encounters a motivated offender alone on the street at night, but it is unlikely that the potential offender would act if a police officer were present. Routine activities scholars spend a lot of time trying to identify the most effective forms of "target hardening": changes to physical space or human behavior that make it harder for motivated criminals to successfully commit a crime.[28]

Echoing the tenets of routine activities theory, several participants argued that crime happens when people are insufficiently mindful of their belongings:

> I'll just give you the easy example. If you ever read . . . the community newspaper for Back Bay, South End, Beacon Hill. I cannot tell you how often, it has a little police report, people leave their computers and tablets, cell phones totally unattended. Or they're walking down the street and using their iPad or whatever, totally oblivious to everybody around them! In fact, I read some this week where people left their front doors and their apartment doors unlocked when they left. Again, I think it's because they're paying attention to their media and not what's going on. Car doors unlocked, you know, just leaving things on tables.
> (Debbie, 64, W, CE, FG1)

> If I see you sitting there with a five-hundred-dollar cellphone by the door on that train and I don't have that phone . . . snatch!
> (Joseph, 54, B, HSE, FG4)

Debbie was particularly critical of people who paid insufficient attention to protecting their belongings, referring to them as "stupid victims."

Likewise, some participants argued that crimes are more likely to occur where target hardening measures are absent or inadequate:

> There was a thing in Detroit before this whole water thing, there were, I guess, miles of streets that, the street lamps were out and nobody wanted to put the money into fixing them. So because there was all these dark streets, bad things could more . . . that whole opportunity thing that we were talking about before. You know, on a well-lit street, people might not have these things happen and people might be more inclined to walk down the street. And give money to a business.
> (Janet, 56, W, CE, FG5)

> The total lack of proper police enforcement. When I see policemen sitting by the road trying to catch speeders, they're called patrol cars, [but] they're not patrolling like they used to. . . . When I look back as to how the police did their business when I was growing up, and being

younger compared to now, there's a huge difference. When I was growing up, the police actually walked a beat. You get to know that officer in
your area. There was someone on the streets that people were aware, hey,
there's a police officer on the street. There was actually patrolling going
on as opposed to sitting by some intersection with a red light where the
odds of catching someone is so slim. It's a complete waste of time, money,
and manpower.
(Bruce, 58, W, CE, FG5)

Participants in these focus groups did not mention themes consistent
with routine activities theory as frequently as they mentioned themes
consistent with the previous theories I discussed, but it was another
example of lay citizens demonstrating intuitive logic consistent with
formal criminological knowledge.

The Justice System as Cause of Crime: Labeling Theory

A few participants identified the criminal justice system itself as a cause
of crime. They argued that people can fall back into criminal behavior
because they are blocked from new, legitimate opportunities by their
criminal record. Participants typically expressed this perspective though
critique of "CORIs." CORI is an acronym for "criminal offender record
information," which is the complete record of a person's criminal court
appearances in Massachusetts, whether or not those court appearances
ended in conviction. CORI reform was a salient topic in state politics
around the time these focus groups were conducted, and several participants were aware of this fact. Consider the following statements:

[There are] barriers to reentry that follow people back into criminal
behavior.
(Lacey, 69, W, CE, FG1)

You gain a record and after a while you start to live by your record.
(James, 46, W, HSE, FG2)

There's so many people that can't get jobs because of their CORI. You
know what I mean, and then one thing leads to another, leads to another,

so something's gotta be done with, I did my time, let's get, you know
let's . . . [did not finish sentence]
(William, 67, B, CE, FG3)

I know guys that have . . . When that college degree they've got from jail.
And once they go out in society, they wouldn't focus on . . . Because once
they say, "Where did you [get that degree]?" "I got it through the Department of Corrections." So they're just like balling it up and throwing it to
the side.
(Matthew, 55, B, HSE, FG4)

Particularly for folks who possibly already committed a crime. There are
so many . . . the restrictions and the limitations on you societally after
having committed a crime, you know, it goes on your CORI, we basically
continue to punish people for crimes after committing one for the rest of
their lives, so preventing them getting jobs, difficult to vote, difficult if not
able to vote at all . . . if we basically marginalize people after one crime, so
why . . . it gives them no motivation to not commit more crimes, because
you've already put them in this other class as individuals in our society.
(Marianne, 30, W, CE, FG5)

Labeling theorists argue that a criminal record—especially for people
who spent time incarcerated—burdens people with stigma.[29] Whether
out of rational risk avoidance or pure prejudice, many employers choose
not to hire a former felon, many people choose not to purchase a house
if they learn that the neighbor has a criminal record, and so forth. If
former offenders continually fail to reestablish a law-abiding life despite
their best efforts because no one will give them a second chance, they
become more likely to fall back into their old criminal habits. Labeling
theory has some connections to both strain and social control theories; being unable find gainful employment and treated like a social
outcast and second-class citizen is both stressful and prevents people
from establishing new, positive social bonds. Unlike these other theories, labeling theory explicitly "casts blame" for this state of affairs on a
criminal justice system that punishes offenders too harshly and does too
little to help them successfully reintegrate back into society following
incarceration.[30] Like routine activities theory, participants in this study

mentioned themes consistent with labeling theory less frequently than themes consistent with other theories. However, these findings reveal that some Americans believe that there are aspects of the criminal justice system that actually make crime worse.

Summary

To summarize the analysis so far, the participants in these focus groups expressed numerous beliefs about the causes of crime that are remarkably consistent with the formal theories and evidence produced by scholars over many decades. Most criminologists would only seriously question the participants' belief that exposure to television or music with violent content or adult themes causes youth to develop a propensity toward deviance; this was the one "lay" belief about the causes of crime that lacks a body of supporting scientific evidence that criminologists find convincing. How do these beliefs of citizens and criminologists relate to the "volitional criminology" theories that dominated criminal justice policy throughout the 1980s and 1990s? Did a change in citizens' understanding of the causes of crime explain policymakers' shift between the 1960s and the 1980s away from a structural understanding of crime toward a volitional understanding? We must compare the data from these focus groups to older research in order to answer those questions.

Do Structural or Volitional Beliefs Dominate?

As policymakers changed their beliefs about the causes of crime over the course of the 1970s, American crime control policy shifted away from antipoverty initiatives toward an emphasis on tougher punishment.[31] The politics of this era influenced criminologists too. Social learning and (especially) strain theories are more structural in nature than volitional, and these theories were widely influential in the first half of the twentieth century. Just as volitional beliefs about crime grew in popularity among policy makers during the 1970s and 1980s, social control theories concurrently grew in influence among criminologists.[32] Though social control theories do address some structural factors, such as employment opportunities, they have more to say about volitional causes of crime than do social learning and strain theories.

These dynamics are not unique to scholars. Many public opinion studies find that beliefs about the causes of crime influence lay citizens' preferences for crime prevention or punishment too. In general, the more strongly people endorse a volitional or dispositional attribution for crime, the more strongly they favor punishment over rehabilitation or crime prevention; the more strongly they endorse a structural or situational attribution, the more strongly they favor rehabilitation or crime prevention.[33]

However, the participants in these focus groups endorsed many different causes of crime. All six focus groups identified both structural causes, such as poverty and neighborhood context, and volitional causes, such as greed and immorality. It is possible that some individual participants endorsed solely volitional causes of crime. To address this possibility, I reviewed the focus group transcripts and participants' written answers on the worksheets. Only a few participants seemed like they might embrace a purely volitional criminology.

I quoted Lance (60, B, CE, FG1) in the section on social control theory. He identified "disregard for others and the consequences of actions," "greed," and "anger" as causes of crime. During the discussion, he explained that he was thinking of anger "for various reasons; for social reasons." He did not clarify further, but on his worksheet, he wrote, "anger over grievances (real or imagined)." His causes are mostly volitional in nature, but anger could have an element of a structural understanding depending upon the kinds of grievances he had in mind. Timothy (54, B, HSE, FG2) stayed silent during his group's discussion about the causes of crime. On his worksheet, he wrote, "drugs," "bad person," "getting ez money," "alcohol," and "gambling." Like Timothy, Melissa (44, B, CE, FG3) did not vocalize her causes of crime during the discussion, but she wrote on her worksheet "anger, frustration, stress," "retaliation," "boredom," "pride," and "ignorance." Similar to Lance, some of Melissa's thinking could have been structural in nature. Frustration, stress, and retaliation are most often caused by negative social stimuli according to strain theory and code of the street theory. On the other hand, all her answers related to people's emotions and personality, which could fall under the "volitional" category. We cannot know for sure precisely how Melissa would classify her answers because she did not vocalize them. Lastly, Bruce (58, W, CE, FG5) vocalized "the drug trade," "lack of proper police enforcement," and "some people just like to commit crimes" during the discussion. On his worksheet, he also wrote, "stolen items/cars that people resell" and "lack of funding." His only answer that was not clearly volitional in nature was lack of funding. Since he did not mention this during the discussion, we cannot know what he felt was inadequately funded.

I identified two respondents who only vocalized volitional causes of crime during their group discussions, but they had first written at least one structural cause of crime on their worksheet. Baldwin (52, B, HSE, FG2) only vocalized "drugs," "bad people," "gangs," "alcohol," and "gambling," but he also wrote "no money (homeless)." Alice (54, CE, FG5) only vocalized "stupidity," "lack of morals," and "lack of respect for others" during her group's discussion about causes of crime. However, she wrote "drugs" and "poverty." I cannot determine whether Baldwin and Alice chose not to vocalize their structural answers because they felt that other participants had already covered those topics or because they felt more strongly about their volitional answers.

Overall, these findings from the focus groups suggest that there is not a deep well of support for a single-minded embrace of volitional criminology among contemporary Americans. Perhaps, though, the participants in my focus groups have substantially different beliefs about the causes of crime than the rest of the American population. After all, they are a self-selected group of residents of a single metropolitan area. Or perhaps Americans' beliefs about the causes of crime have changed since the 1970s and 1980s. Fortunately, I can compare the statements of the participants in this study against older research to address these possibilities.

Decades of surveys reveal that, in the 1940s and 1950s, Americans predominantly attributed youth crime to poor parenting and lack of adult supervision. In the 1960s, Americans continued to identify poor parenting as the primary cause of "lack of respect for law and order and the increase of crime," but they also began to call for tougher law enforcement and identify unemployment as a cause of crime. By the mid to late 1960s, Americans began to endorse structural causes of crime in larger numbers. According to a 1966 poll, 38% of Americans attributed crime to "upbringing," but 30% attributed crime to "bad environment."

"No education" and "not enough money in home" also began to be endorsed as causes of crime by at least 10% of respondents, whereas these answers were largely absent prior to the 1960s. By 1971, over 50% of respondents identified factors like "lack of parental discipline," "too lenient sentences," and "poverty conditions" as major causes of an increase in crime. Interestingly, Americans have long identified bad media as a contributing factor to crime. Three percent of respondents to a 1946 poll identified "bad movies; too many movies; radio programs; newspapers; bad books" as the main reason teenagers commit crimes. In a 1971 poll, 30% of Americans stated that "violence on TV and [in] the movies" was a major cause of rising crime. Other answers given by the participants in my focus groups that showed up in polls taken many decades ago were lack of properly trained police officers, greed, alcohol and drugs, and moral breakdown in society.[34]

Polls from the 1970s and early 1980s show that Americans predominantly blamed bad parenting for crime in the middle decades of the twentieth century, but the percentage of Americans who endorsed structural causes of crime like poverty also significantly increased during this period. The increased popularity of structural attributions coincided with a rise in the number of Americans who also blamed crime on inadequate punishment.[35]

More recent polls indicate that Americans continue to endorse a variety of both structural and volitional causes of crime that are consistent with several different criminological theories.[36] A study conducted by sociologists Victor Thompson and Lawrence Bobo is a particularly valuable point of reference because the authors conducted a nationally representative survey of White and Black Americans in 2001. They found that White Americans were significantly more likely to favor volitional attributions for crime over structural attributions than were Black Americans. However, these relative differences do not change the fact that large numbers of both White and Black Americans endorsed statements consistent with both types of causal attribution. Thompson and Bobo put respondents into one of three categories: those who endorsed more individualist causes than structural, those who endorsed more structural causes than individualist, and those who endorsed a roughly equal number of causes of each type. They found that 51.7%

of White respondents were individualists, 15.2% were structuralists, and 30.2% were mixed. In contrast, Black respondents were roughly evenly distributed across the three categories.[37]

Sociologist Ted Sasson's book *Crime Talk* provides a second, particularly valuable comparison to my research because he also conducted focus groups about crime with White and Black Bostonians in the early 1990s.[38] Comparing our two studies suggests that there has been both continuity and change in Bostonians' understanding of crime. Sasson categorized his participants' explanations about the causes of crime into five key themes, all of which were also vocalized by the participants in my 2016 focus groups. Sasson's first theme was "faulty system," which captured participants' belief that people commit crime because punishments are inadequate and offenders believe they will be able to get away with their crimes. About half of the focus groups in his study unanimously endorsed faulty system logic, including 57% of the Black participant groups. The faulty system theme corresponds to the beliefs expressed by the participants in my study that I described in the section on social control and deterrence theories. Sasson's second theme was "social breakdown"; it captured participants' beliefs that the bonds within families and between neighbors within communities were worse today than in decades past. Sasson reported that this was the most popular theme among his participants, unanimously endorsed by 60% of his focus groups. It corresponds to my findings discussed in the sections on parenting, code of the street, and collective efficacy.

Sasson's third theme was "blocked opportunities"; it related to participants' beliefs that inequality, poverty, and discrimination pushed some people to commit crime. He characterized this as a substantially less popular theme than faulty system and social breakdown; of all the themes in his study, it was the one that the largest number of participants discredited and disputed. This theme corresponds to the findings I discussed in the section on strain theory. Sasson's fourth theme was "media violence"; it captured participants' beliefs that exposure to violence on TV or in music could corrupt youths' values. Sasson classified media violence as a secondary frame because it was only mentioned by participants in five (out of twenty total) focus groups. This theme almost perfectly mirrors the sentiments expressed by participants in my study that I discussed in the section on parenting and youth deviance. Finally, Sasson's fifth theme was "racist system"; it referred to participants' beliefs that the criminal justice system was an oppressive force that actively discriminated against people of color. Sasson observed that this theme was frequently discussed in focus groups among Black participants, but it was rarely discussed by White participants. This theme corresponds to some of my findings that I discussed in the section on labeling theory.

Combined with the findings from the survey research studies I discussed, the fact that the participants in my 2016 focus groups expressed most of the same beliefs about the nature of crime as did Sasson's participants in the early 1990s shows that Americans' understanding of the causes of crime is relatively consistent over time. It appears to take several decades and significant social changes for Americans to collectively prioritize new causes of crime that were overlooked or dismissed in earlier times. Furthermore, study after study finds that Americans endorse both volitional and structural causes of crime. There is variance in the degree to which different people embrace one set of causal beliefs about crime versus the other, but very few people exclusively endorse only one attribution style.[39]

There does seem to be some evidence of change, as well. Sasson concluded that the blocked opportunities frame was the weakest, most disputed frame among his participants. In contrast, the participants in my study spoke about the criminogenic effects of poverty and unemployment with great frequency; indeed, strain was one of the most prevalent themes in my focus groups. Strain is arguably the most structural of all criminological theories, and endorsement of structural causes of crime is inversely related to punitive preferences for punishment. If Bostonians' acceptance of a strain or blocked opportunities perspective has, indeed, increased over the past thirty years, it would be consistent with the evidence that Americans' overall level of punitiveness has declined over the same time period.[40]

Even though volitional explanations for crime were more popular among lay citizens during the 1980s and 1990s, the best available evidence indicates that Americans have also endorsed structural explanations for crime since at least the 1960s. If that is the case, why did policymakers overwhelmingly prioritize deterrence-based responses to crime for the past fifty years? Why did structural responses to crime receive little support from the federal and state governments? Perhaps the answer is that even though Americans endorse both structural and volitional understandings of the causes of crime, they might only support volitional responses to crime. I assess that possibility in chapter 2.

2

Brainstorming Responses to Crime

Americans believe that a combination of factors, both from the social environment and from within the morals of people themselves, cause crime. However, even when people agree upon the nature of a social problem's causes, that does not mean that they will also agree upon a course of action to fix the problem.[1] Communities can marshal many kinds of responses to crime, and not all of them involve government or the criminal justice system.[2] People's willingness to call upon the police and the criminal justice system more broadly varies significantly across race, gender, and neighborhood context.[3]

In this chapter, I analyze the focus group participants' discussions about the second prompt: "On the second sheet in front of you, please list 5 things that you think can be done to prevent or reduce crime." As with the first part of the discussion about the causes of crime, participants wrote their responses to the prompt, and then the moderator facilitated group discussion. The open-ended nature of this prompt allows us to analyze the kinds of ideas that organically come to mind when people are asked to think about crime control, rather than asking respondents to state their support or opposition for a list of possible crime control policies that are predefined by the pollster or researcher. I instructed the moderator to ask participants what the government, specifically, could do to reduce or prevent crime in communities if participants did not initially discuss government initiatives on their own.

Each focus group's discussion about this prompt evoked a more unique "personality" compared to the earlier discussion of the causes of crime in which many similar ideas echoed across the groups. These idiosyncrasies shed light on broader issues about contemporary criminal justice that are intertwined with race and social class in the United States. As such, I organize this portion of the analysis first according to the education (the stand-in for social class) segmentation of the groups, and second, group by group. I then analyze the thematic commonalities across the groups in relation to prior research.

High School Educated Groups
Focus Group 2: Cynicism and Mixed Attributions

The crime prevention discussion among the Black and White high school educated participants of Focus Group 2 sheds some light on the disconnect between policymakers and working-class Americans.[4] Timothy (54, B, HSE, FG2) spoke first, and his response evoked a sentiment of cynicism. He replied, "I don't think you can reduce crime. Or stop crime, because as we already know there's rules and regulations and what have you, and people continue on doing what they want to do and breaking them as it is, so there's really no remedy or method, that I know of, anyway, that's gonna stop anything." Such a sentiment presents a dead end for a legislator who is searching for policy solutions to crime.

Other participants in this group did identify some things they would like to change in society that they believed would reduce crime. However, they expressed these beliefs in a manner that would likely flummox a policymaker. Consider the following exchange between Chrissy (46, B, HSE, FG2) and Jacklyn (32, B, HSE, FG2):

CHRISSY: I think a lot of choices that we as humans, that people make begins and ends with us. You know? Like your own, how you see yourself, what value do you put on yourself. Look, I tell my son all the time, it begins and ends with how you think. You are what you tell yourself, you know what I mean? So, you know, if you were like . . . better opportunities for everyone, you know what I mean?

MODERATOR: Okay. Better opportunities . . . ?

CHRISSY: As far as education. Like getting an education, like, you got to pay all kinds of money. You know, you get a good education and then you're spending a good portion of your life paying it back. You know? So, better opportunities for everyone as a whole, because in the inner, the youth there that resort to selling drugs and all the, the . . .

JACKLYN: Robbing and stealing.

CHRISSY: Exactly, the robbing and the stealing and all the crime against your own kind, you know what I mean? Like, they're looking at . . . TV plays a big part in it, you know what I mean? The media plays a big part in it. Technology plays a big part in it. So, you know, they're looking at, [mimicking a young person] "Yeah, I want this, and I want that, and I want this. Can't go to school to get it. They're not gonna do this for me to get it, so I'm gonna get it the best way that I can." You know what I mean, so, you know, it all begins and ends with that person as an individual.

Jacklyn agreed with Chrissy and responded in a similar manner:

Kind of going off of what Chrissy was saying, I do believe there should be like resources, like she said, for everybody. Just kinda giving everybody that chance. You know what I'm saying? That hope. That equal chance, that hope. There should be compassion, empathy, all of that, to prevent crime from happening. So like you were saying, yeah, even though it starts with yourself, but as children, there's different stages. 'Cause where I'm at now, I wasn't here mentally ten years ago. I was somewhere completely different. You know what I'm saying? So, a lot of that plays . . . therapy is huge, you know what I'm saying? Having some type of positive mental, is huge, you know, all those are influences to let you know, "Okay, you don't have to take this route." You don't have to do that, because, personally, I feel like there's enough money in this world for everyone to at least have some type of decent type of housing over their head, little put-put cars needed and never be hungry. Personally.

But the fact it's not like that, that's why the crimes aren't prevented. So, you throw in things, to kinda help, you throw in education because you want to teach the child in order to graduate and go into college and so forth, so forth. Yes but, because the brain kind of develops and is going through levels as you age and get older or whatever, you know, if that isn't right, it doesn't matter what a person's throwing at you. You know what I'm saying? So just to be able to have that, like, [knocks on wooden table] you know . . . and everything costs. Money is huge. It's like, Oh! If your insurance isn't cool you can't get therapy, so what? You just told me you feel like going to shoot up the grocery store, but your insurance, maybe you should . . . you know what I'm saying?

It's that deep, and it's like, I think if people was just, if there was more unity with each other because that, I mean I'm old enough to know that back then, my mother could send us with five hundred dollars to go pay a bill at age nine and the whole community makes sure we made it there. You know what I'm saying? The whole commun—I mean everybody made sure we made it there, "Are you okay? Are you hungry? Thirsty? Gotta use the bathroom? Tell your mother you're on your way, tell her . . ." You know what I'm saying? You didn't have to worry so I think all of that, as a whole, plays a part in preventing crime. You know what I'm saying?

My hypothesis that most respondents would endorse both structural and volitional responses to crime because they identified both structural and volitional causes of crime is supported by Chrissy and Jacklyn's responses. On the one hand, both women point to community resources that governments can improve, such as expanding access to quality education, affordable housing, sufficient food, and therapy—"resources for everybody," as Jacklyn put it. However, look carefully at the way Chrissy and Jacklyn expressed themselves. To my ears, both participants "bookended" their calls for society to address the structural causes of crime in between very volitional statements. Chrissy began her statement by talking about personal choice and self-worth, but then she talked about the need for better opportunities and access to education so that youth do not "resort" to selling drugs or robbery—a structural perspective that clearly aligns with strain theory. However, she ended her answer by returning to a volitional statement: "it all begins and ends with that person as an individual." Similarly, even though Jacklyn identified various structural causes of crime, she also placed responsibility upon individuals when she said, "like you were saying, yeah, even though it starts with yourself."[5]

Jacklyn evoked another theme that was endorsed by several participants in this focus group: the belief that communities were better "back in the day." Baldwin (52, B, HSE, FG2), Chrissy, and Jacklyn lamented the use of modern technology and social media both to bully people and to record heinous acts that can be broadcast widely and upset many people. For example, Chrissy said,

Back in the '80s, we had more structure. I can remember, you knew when to be in the house when those lights came on. You knew if your parent or your guardian gave you that look, you knew to straighten up, you know what I mean? We manufactured games—doubles, hop-scotch, jacks, you know what I mean? Hide and go seek. You know it was good, wholesome fun. Nowadays, all you see is . . . and I'm guilty of it myself. You know? And like she was saying, you know, you can't like go on Facebook for an entire day without somebody uploading a fight. Or somebody being killed or like, how? What is going through your mind when you see two people fighting each other, and your first instinct is to videotape it? And upload it for everyone. . . .

Also consider the following exchange between Jacklyn and James (46, W, HSE, FG2):

JACKLYN: I am a '80s baby, so my mother could give us wads of money to pay each bill, and it got paid. You know what I'm saying? I don't even remember hearing the word pedophile when I was growing up. You know what I'm saying? It seems like everybody's one. I feel like there needs to be a test that you, "You need to take this test. And we need to figure out, is it positive or negative?" You know what I'm saying? Like she was saying, in that time it wasn't . . . yeah, there was crime, but it wasn't this intense. My kids are scared to go to the movies. Okay? They text me throughout school, literally, 'cause they're probably, my phone was vibrating to say "mom, we're okay." You know what I'm saying? It's crazy my kids have to . . . , we pray anyway, but they pray in school, when they get into the building and when they exit. They shouldn't feel unsafe in their school. You got teachers doing things to these kids, coaches, you got the bombings, the shootings. I have to go to school and say, "Okay, what's your protocol if somebody runs up in here with a gun? What's gonna happen? I need to know how you're gonna do it, how's the exit? What's gonna happen?"

JAMES: Internationally it's worse. International violence is worse, but, domestically, it's gone down a lot.

JACKLYN: I can't tell.

JAMES: It's a proven fact.

JACKLYN: I cannot tell.

Here Jacklyn expresses vicarious fear for her children that is presumably shaped by news coverage of mass shootings that occurred in US schools in the years immediately preceding the focus groups.[6] This contributes to her feeling that society was safer when she was growing up. James accurately observed that the US crime rate had, in fact, decreased since the 1980s, but this information could not override Jacklyn's impression of societal decline that she formed by watching the news and social media.

Unfortunately, many policymakers find themselves at a loss when confronted by constituents like Timothy, Chrissy, and Jacklyn. For example, in *The Perils of Federalism*, political scientist Lisa Miller quoted a staff member of a state legislator's policy team:

> Even amongst those type of groups, there are the groups that have the "Here's what we want you to do, here's the words [i.e., text for legislation] . . ." and then there are the people that just bitch generally about an issue. "I don't have a solution. I don't even know what the problem is, just cops pulling over black people. . . ." I mean, I guess I could try and come up with a definition of racial profiling and say it's a misdemeanor in the third degree to racially profile . . . And that was something I just came up with here sitting with you. Those groups have never even suggested something as simple as that. They don't ever have a solution. . . . We have groups that come in here and have no idea how the legislative process works, or anything like that. . . .[7]

Much of what Chrissy and Jacklyn said could sound like "just bitching generally about an issue" to the ears of policymakers. On the exit survey, Chrissy and Jacklyn both reported annual household incomes in the range of $10,000 to $39,000, and both women served at least a few months in jail or prison. They were clearly expressing how it feels to be poor in America. For them, crime is inseparable from the broader challenges they and their communities face. However, legislators cannot return society to the "good old days" of people's youth. Legislators much prefer to hear about constituent problems for which there is a relatively simple or preexisting solution. If legislators who favor a volitional understanding of crime were to hear these statements by Chrissy or Jacklyn, I think it would be very easy for them to engage in "selective hearing."[8] They could focus only on these women's statements that the solution to crime "begins and ends with us" or "is something that has to happen from within" and ignore their expressed desire for improvement in schools, housing, and healthcare. And Timothy's belief that crime cannot be stopped gives reform-averse policymakers a very easy "out."

Eventually, the moderator intervened in this part of the discussion and asked, "Aren't there things that the government could do to help reduce or prevent crime in communities with high crime rates?" James said that the government could install better streetlights and surveillance cameras, as well as add more "streetwalkers, cops" to the beat. These options are all forms of target hardening consistent with routine activities theory. Roger (63, B, HSE, FG2) said, "stiffer sentences." Jacklyn agreed with Roger that punishments are not proportional to the severity of the crime, and she reiterated her belief in deterrence that I reported in the previous chapter. Thus, even though most of the participants spoke extensively about the strains of poverty, when directly asked what the government could do to prevent crime, their initial responses largely supported the deterrence-centric criminal justice status quo.

Beyond these few ideas about specific government action, the primary response to the moderator's question among several participants was cynicism like that first expressed by Timothy. Roger said that one thing the government could do is "Fix their justice system." Chrissy chimed in, "There are things that they can do, the government can do. But, truth be told, our government . . . they're some of the biggest criminals there is! You know what I mean? You just have that, who was he? That, um, he was molesting or raping the, uh . . . the judge, the senator, whoever he was! Come on! They're some of the biggest crooks there are. You know?" Throughout the discussion, Baldwin, Roger, and James were very critical of the police. Baldwin (52, B, HSE, FG2) called attention to crimes committed by police against civilians—"'cause they're beating up a lot of people . . . the cops are doing the crime of just pulling you over and searching you for no reason. That's against the law, when they do that"— and argued that police need to take anger management classes "instead of getting pissed off because they've got a uniform on, or going riding in Roxbury." Given that Roxbury is home to a significant number of Black Bostonians, Baldwin is likely referring to racial profiling and police harassment of civilians of color.[9]

Focus Group 4: Community Self-Sufficiency and Ambivalence Toward Government

As I explained in chapter 1, the Black, high school educated participants in Focus Group 4 extensively explained how the code of the street pulls youth into deviance. Unsurprisingly, then, many of their ideas about crime prevention revolved around parenting and community-level informal social control of youth. Joseph (54, B, HSE, FG4) provided the first answer to the crime prevention discussion prompt: "education is priority." The moderator asked if he was referring to formal schooling, but Joseph clarified that he was talking about education in a broader sense:

> JOSEPH: Have that education growing up. I don't care if it's one parent or two parents. As long as you teach your kids right from wrong, they would know the difference. As they grow up, they keep that virtue with them and that spiritual life as they grow.
>
> MODERATOR: Okay. So, you're thinking public education, plus you were also just talking about . . .
>
> JOSEPH: The spiritual part.
>
> MODERATOR: Okay. So you also want sort of moral education, like right from wrong.
>
> JOSEPH: Yeah.

Joseph's response is consistent with the tenets of the general theory of crime—appropriate parenting instills self-control in children, which in turn inoculates them against criminal behavior for the rest of their lives.

Other participants called for community-level exercise of informal social control, not just individual parenting. I quoted Matthew (55, B, HSE, FG4) in the previous chapter when he called for more "community involvement . . . [being] more involved with the neighborhood, with the young kids," but he also recognized that it is difficult for residents to personally monitor or discipline errant youth if they fear that those youths are likely to brandish a gun when confronted. Susan (53, B, HSE, FG4) agreed with Matthew, praised "neighbor helping neighbor," and also endorsed "a neighborhood crime watch." She additionally called for "more activities in the community because we don't have no swimming

pools anymore, nothing like that for the kids, for the younger generation." As I noted in chapter 1, Susan also advocated for a curfew to keep
kids off the street at night. Mary (33, B, HSE, FG4) similarly endorsed
"homeschooling and year-round extracurricular activities."

It is likely that these participants first thought of ways that communities can "police" themselves because they hold conflicted and ambivalent attitudes toward government and the criminal justice system
that are typical of Black residents of highly policed neighborhoods of
concentrated disadvantage in the United States.[10] Consider the participants' thoughts about the government's response to the opioid
epidemic:

MATTHEW: And one thing's for sure. We don't bring guns. We don't
make guns. We don't make drugs. And when I say we, I mean our
communities, our young people. This stuff is put there to keep them
down, you know. And what makes it so bad is because while shit was
located in the city and in the lower income areas, it was okay. Now
this stuff is moving out to the suburbs.

SUSAN: Got out of control now.

MATTHEW: You see what I'm saying? Now it's a big issue with the
opiates. Just like last night, I was watching the TV, and then you see
these guys riding up and down the street out here with these motor-
cycles and these dirt bikes. Out in Walpole they had a big drug raid
out there. You know what I mean? Our cousin, she left from the city
to go out there. I mean as long as it's inside our society, it's fine.

JOSEPH: As long as it's inside this circle here. When you start coming
outside that circle, uh-oh, that's when they start worrying about it.

SUSAN: They didn't expect this. It's out of control now.

JOSEPH: Yeah. Keep it in the circle. But once it comes outside that
circle . . .

SUSAN: It's already out of the circle. It's an epidemic now.

JOSEPH: . . . that's when they go in and start doing something about it.

MATTHEW: Just for instance, when Charlie Baker, first thing he did
once he really got in there and became governor, he started talking
about he was going to open up these rehab centers for these opiates
and stuff like that.

JOSEPH: He did.

MATTHEW: And it's all because a friend of his son . . . [overdosed].

JOSEPH: Died.

MATTHEW: Okay. Now you know what I'm saying, all these rehab and everything outside the city.

JOSEPH: Popping up.

MARY: Oh yeah.

MATTHEW: They get outside the city, but they're not for us. You see what I'm saying?

JOSEPH: No, that's outside the circle.

MATTHEW: They're outside of the city for the people that live out there, but there's a lot of White people that's doing it, White kids.

JOSEPH: Yeah.

MARY: There's a lot of people with, like addiction and mental health issues that aren't getting help in our communities. So there needs to be more . . . I think there's one [inaudible due to cross talk; I infer Mary referenced a new treatment center being built], but there's going to be like one place. And if you have MassHealth,[11] you can't even . . . Yeah, yeah.

LINDA: Boston Medical has it. Boston Medical has it.

MARY: That's not enough.

These participants all believed that the government has long failed to provide their communities with adequate healthcare resources to address problems of addiction and mental illness. Yet as soon as rates of opioid overdoes increased in wealthier, predominantly White suburbs, treatment resources flowed into those communities. Matthew situated his disgust about the inequitable opioid epidemic response within a broader argument that the government "puts" guns and drugs into Black communities to "keep them down."

However, this group's discussion revealed some of the tensions that arise within Black communities as a consequence of living in proximity to crime. Susan did propose one policy solution to prevent crime:

SUSAN: Gun control. They need a harsher sentence for the guns.

MATTHEW: Oh, well honestly . . . I just did, I don't know, I guess three and a half years.

SUSAN: You can't tell my son-in-law that. He's gone, so yeah.

Susan implied that her son-in-law was a victim of gun violence, which motivated her to call for harsher punishments for gun crimes. However, having served several years in prison, Matthew was uncomfortable with the prospect of harshening sentences as a means of preventing crime. A similar debate arose between Mary and the men of the group:

MARY: I was going to say more protection for people who want to give an anonymous tip. Like snitching is really looked down upon. I'll snitch in a minute, especially if you have one of my . . . I don't care. But when I was in my twenties, I wouldn't do that because I didn't know that and I was dating a lot of criminals then. Now I'm a changed woman, but I'm just saying it was just so silly. I went to so many funerals with young men. . . . And I don't know if this is a city issue or on a state level, but I think if you give a . . . testifying against someone in a crime, you shouldn't have to go and sit in front of them and they know who you are. Because even if they go to prison, their family's still . . . you know.

MATTHEW: That's just the law. You know what it's called? It's called you have to face your accuser.

JOSEPH: You have to face your accuser.

MARY: Yeah, I know.

MATTHEW: So you're accusing me of something, right? And if you think about it, right, it's only fair. So say I really didn't do the crime, but you say you've seen somebody that looks like me and him, because me and this brother look similar.

MARY: But I . . .

MATTHEW: So just hear me out for a minute.

MARY: All right, okay.

MATTHEW: You see somebody that looks like me and him. I did the crime, not him, but we look alike. You can't tell the difference.

MARY: Right.

MATTHEW: You point out this man, and you go . . . All we see, me and him, you all just process his paperwork. Your name's crossed out, your address, everything. So where do I get to a point in time and say . . .

DORIAN: Prove it. That's what I would say. Prove it.

MATTHEW: . . . I don't know this person. Prove that. You know what I'm saying? So it's just the . . . If the law is making it fair, I'm into the law, okay? Actually, I'm just breaking it down into a reality.

JOSEPH: It's good for both parties.

MATTHEW: It's good for both parties. It's making it fair for both parties. You know what I'm saying?

MARY: I just . . . I'm a martial arts teacher, and I teach a lot of free women's self-defense classes and work with a lot of women who suffer from domestic violence. And a lot of them won't testify because they got to go on the stand. And I'm not just talking about like boyfriend-girlfriend argument but, you know, people who were raped. They won't go and testify because they don't want to face their accusers. So there needs to be . . . And then like, 90% of assault is committed by the same people who never get locked up. So I'm not just talking about like drug crimes or robbery. I'm talking like a broad spectrum. I think there needs to be better laws to protect people who can . . .

MATTHEW: But it sucks, because the law is a large spectrum. [*laughs*] You know what I'm saying?

MARY: I know, I know. So it's like we need more, you know, doors to help everyone.

LINDA: Okay, because with my daughter . . . I'm going to cut it short. When my daughter got . . . She has seen him with the murderer, and I mean in . . . She had to testify. The cops were really watching my house and everything . . . because my daughter was scared. So she was on the run. And then when they did catch her, they brought her in. They had to move me out that same night. They moved me straight out of Dorchester that same night.

On the one hand, Mary and Linda expressed their willingness to cooperate with law enforcement to facilitate the prosecution and conviction of repeat offenders. This finding matches prior evidence that Black women are more likely than Black men to defy the code of the street's prohibition against "snitching" to the police.[12] In contrast, the men of this group—all of whom served a sentence on probation or in a correctional facility earlier in their lives—reiterated the importance of due process protections for the accused. Even though both men and women of color have suffered from the expansion of the carceral state over the past forty years, men have borne the brunt of the arrests and punishments, making them particularly distrustful of the criminal justice system. Ultimately, Matthew cogently summarized the feeling of many poorer Black Americans—that they are caught between the rock of local crime and the hard place of hostile police: "Either you do or you don't. You're damned if you do. You're damned if you don't. You know what I mean? Because nobody wants to be sitting in the house, and next thing you know, your house is on fire, or you got bullets coming through your house. You know what I'm saying? So you know, it's like turning a blind eye to all this. But then, in the same token, while you're turning your head to it, you're condoning it."

As in Focus Group 2, the moderator eventually asked these participants directly whether they believe that there is anything the government can do to prevent crime. Whereas the participants of Focus Group 2 responded to this prompt by largely echoing status quo criminal justice interventions, these participants responded in a very different manner:

MODERATOR: I want to talk more about what could the government do. Is there stuff that the government can do in communities to help reduce and prevent . . . ?

DORIAN: All the way. All the way. They can put the money there. Stop putting . . .

MODERATOR: What do you want to put money in?

DORIAN: In the community.

MODERATOR: To do what?

DORIAN: Listen. They've taken away . . . Since I was a kid, I don't see an after school program anymore. They're sending all the kids to the Y, where they can fight in the back and meet up on the corner and start their little gangs. Do you know what I'm saying? The Y is not an after school program. It's an all-day program for anyone to come to. . . . These kids are meeting up with adults that are older than them that, oh . . . pushing them all the way towards, "Oh, let's take this park around the corner. And let me introduce you to a little of this and a little of that and a little more of this. And take this gun and go rob the corner store for me, because I think you're prepared for that." You know what I'm saying? Come on, the government know what they doing!

MODERATOR: Where else can they put money?

MATTHEW: They can put it back into the schools.

DORIAN: [Agreeing] They can put it back into the schools.

MATTHEW: You know, you got so many schools that have closed down and then so many schools, like if you test these kids, a lot of them don't even . . . They're not up to standard, up to par, at their grade level. They can put the money into the people of the community. Like [Mary] says, she does martial arts, right?

MARY: Yeah. And it is so hard to get . . .

MATTHEW: Fund her program! Get little girls there.

Dorian (35, B, HSE, FG4) and Matthew called for precisely the kind of direct financial investment by government into community organizations and institutions that was the original vision of justice reinvestment. Dorian implies that he desires investment like this as a corrective to the government's neglect of public schools, which he perceived to be intentional abandonment.

Joseph had the last word in the crime prevention discussion, and he used it to end on a note of faith in government:

JOSEPH: Okay. Like I said with city hall, with everything, it's . . . That's true because, um . . . Well, I'm fifty-four years old. I grew up in the '60s and everything. So it's the mayor, Menino, best mayor we had since Kevin White. Okay. He the one got the whole city back up. I mean he got the city of Boston back together again as a whole. The first thing he did was he got rid of all the projects. He said, "Tear them down. Get rid of them all, and build them all back up." And South Boston got mad now and said, "Hey, why we got our projects still standing up?" "Because," he said, "you all were the last ones to be built."

MODERATOR: So you have to go last.

JOSEPH: So you get to go last. So that's why you going to see all projects are gone now. Menino did all that. Look at downtown Boston. That one man did it. He took the whole city around, believe me. It was hard for him, and he did it through the community. He did it with the community, with the church leaders, with everybody, the store owners. I mean everybody loved that . . . I love that man.

LINDA: Yeah. Remember that massacre, when that baby and all that got killed? He was right out there. He came right out there.

JOSEPH: He was, he was there for the city when that Charlie Stuart thing. He was there for it. He kept this city calm through a lot. So that's why I said if you've got a good city hall, boom, the city will be all right.

Joseph and Linda are referring to deceased former Mayor Thomas Menino who held office for twenty-one years. The "Charlie Stuart thing" was the infamous 1989 case of a man who murdered his wife but blamed her death on a fictitious Black robber. His lie prompted the Boston police force to launch an extremely aggressive crackdown on Boston's Black population that exacerbated racial tensions in the city.[13] Despite the heinousness of the crime and its fallout, Joseph and Linda believed that Menino, a White man, exercised effective leadership by working with residents of the communities who were harmed by the police response.

Focus Group 6—Poverty and Cynicism Toward the Medical Establishment

The discussion among the White, high school educated participants of Focus Group 6 provides an interesting foil against the discussions among the other high school educated participants in Focus Groups 2 and 4. As I explained in chapter 1, they echoed the same themes about the strains of poverty, which led them to endorse many structural ideas for crime prevention. However, while some participants in this group also vocalized feelings of cynicism and distrust, they largely targeted their ire toward the medical establishment, in contrast to the participants in Focus Groups 2 and 4 who expressed distrust toward the police or politicians. This difference sheds light on the ways that systemic racism functions in the United States and creates different experiences across groups of people who otherwise struggle with similar challenges of poverty.

Given how concerned the participants of this focus group were about the criminogenic influence of drug addiction, it is unsurprising that the first response to the crime prevention prompt dealt with drugs. Frederick (20, W, HSE, FG6) said, "I'm going to be really specific. Put a ban on marijuana because I feel like that's the major cause of most crimes." Albert (43, W, HSE, FG6) soon added, "I wrote 'better or more recovery centers.' That can be recovery from an issue in life or like a drug, a drug addict recovery center, like to take the core of the person and build them up from nothing. Because if you break it down to the point where you're committing crime to get your needs met and you've pretty much broken down to the bottom of the barrel." Similarly, Jason (46, W, HSE, FG6) said, "I put counseling and guidance." When the moderator asked him to clarify, he added, "Everything in general. Counseling to address the problem, whatever that person may be going through." When the moderator later asked whether there is anything specific that the government can do to prevent crime, the participants immediately returned to the topic of drugs:

ALBERT: Yeah, I think they should do away with the low-level drug addict committing crimes and then doing umpteen million years in jail. When the problem is not . . . he's an addict. He's not a criminal.
PAMELA: Right, he's not violent.
CAMILLE: Yes.
MODERATOR: Okay, yes. So you think changing drug laws?
JUDY: Decriminalize addiction.
ALBERT: Right.

This exchange conflicted with Frederick's initial call for a complete ban on marijuana, revealing disagreement among these participants over whether the best way to address drug addiction is criminalization and punishment or decriminalization and treatment. But, clearly, they all agreed that addiction is a major social problem in need of remedy.

The participants in this group also spoke readily about the need to address poverty to prevent crime. Jack (71, W, HSE, FG6) was the first person to make this point:

JACK: Eradicate poverty if you can.
MODERATOR: Okay, how do we eradicate poverty?
JACK: Maybe just distribute more of the wealth. [*laughter*] Help them out better financially.
FREDERICK: He wants some free money.
JACK: Create jobs. Income for everyone so they don't have to steal.
ALBERT: That's a nice thought. Just print more money, right?

Albert also added, "More stable housing." Camille (29, W, HSE, FG6) advocated for investment into healthcare:

> CAMILLE: Just put more money into resources for these problems.
> PAMELA: Correct.
> MODERATOR: Like what? What kind of resources can they put money into?
> CAMILLE: They took a lot of funding for treatment programs and all that stuff and now you see it on the news, the man is saying okay, we need more counselors, we need more treatment. But they took a lot of money and funding for treatments and stuff. They took a lot of programs away. They took a lot of beds away, you know?
> PAMELA: Correct. It used to be thirty days.
> CAMILLE: Your insurance might pay for four days in a mental health hospital rather than two weeks and what is that going to do for you? They took a lot of money and resources away from things that's helping people and now it's gotten worse and they're like okay, we need more. So, you know, we can't ignore this problem, it's not going to go away, you know?

As I reported in the previous chapter, Camille also called for incentives to help "people that don't have . . . a lot of education or money . . . get on [their] feet, to get like a get-well job to be able to go back to school. . . . And if you get on track, then maybe there won't be crime, you know?"

However, just like the other high school educated participants in Focus Groups 2 and 4, these participants also vocalized some ideas of a volitional nature alongside their structural sentiments. Even though Camille repeatedly talked about impoverished people's need for resources, she also said, "When children are young just teach them better, like work ethics and how to take care of themselves. Because I think now, children are just so spoiled and taken care of they don't really know how to take care of themselves and they grow up and they feel entitled to things and I think that can cause crime." Jason then said, "Just be more informed of what's going on around you." These statements shift responsibility for avoiding crime onto individuals themselves (or their parents) rather than government or society more broadly. Such sentiments were not frequently expressed by participants in this group, but they were present.

Finally, some aspects of these participants' statements of trust or distrust toward social institutions were mirror images of the cynicism and distrust expressed by the high school educated participants in the other focus groups. First, one crime prevention idea offered by Pamela (60, W, HSE, FG6) was, "police working with the children. Yeah, instead of making it out that the police are mean. They always make it on TV, the police are like this and that. They're not. It should start from when they're young. Try to work with them. The police ain't bad." As we shall see in subsequent chapters, other participants in this focus group later expressed very negative attitudes toward the police, but Pamela's statement suggests that working-class White Americans' feelings toward the police are heterogeneous, in contrast to the more consistently negative feelings expressed by working-class Black Americans.[14]

Second, participants in this group targeted their strongest statements of distrust and antipathy toward the healthcare establishment. For example, after Camille complained about how few days of treatment insurance will pay for, Judy (70, W, HSE, FG6) said, "Regulating health insurance because if you don't have, in other words if there isn't the insurance to kick in or what have you, the funding doesn't come from somewhere to pay for this treatment, and the insurance companies are making mucho bucks off people's addictions." A bit later in the discussion, she said, "I live in Charlestown, and I have said often times that the biggest pusher in the town is the health center clinic. . . . The doctors need oversight because they actually get these people dependent on a variety of different meds." Pamela agreed with Judy on this point.

Summary of Themes across High School Educated Groups

I argue that discussions of the three focus groups of high school educated participants shared two important themes. The first theme was a call to alleviate the criminogenic strains of poverty—for the government to provide "resources for everybody" according to Jacklyn or "just distribute more of the wealth" according to Jack. Most of the participants in these three groups spoke powerfully about the struggles faced by poor and working-class people in America, and they drew a direct line between poverty reduction and crime reduction. The second theme was feelings of distrust toward powerful institutions in society. However, the way these two themes emerged across the groups reveals meaningful differences in the experiences of Black and White Americans—even among those who are similar in social class.

Participants in all three groups expressed a mix of both structural and volitional statements during this portion of the discussions, but I perceived a difference in the relative proportion of each type of statement expressed across the three groups. A majority of crime prevention ideas expressed by the White participants of Focus Group 6 were clearly structural in nature and directly focused on financial resources to alleviate poverty. Only Camille and Jason expressed volitional statements that placed responsibility for crime upon parenting, ethics, and personal responsibility, and these sentiments did not eclipse these same participants' overall greater focus on poverty. In contrast, the Black participants of Focus Groups 2 and 4 expressed comparatively more sentiments calling for people to exercise personal or parental responsibility to navigate life in poverty or called for residents of poor communities to work together to take care of themselves. Most of these participants also expressed a desire for financial resources to alleviate poverty, but they seemed more skeptical that their communities would ever actually receive such help.

The different focus of the Black participants feels to me like the consequence of living in "race-class subjugated communities."[15] Government policies have long caused Black communities to suffer divestment, financial exploitation, and oppression by the criminal justice system. This history of oppression yields a particular group consciousness and distrust of government among Black Americans.[16] I think that is why so many of the Black participants in these focus groups advocated first and foremost that Black Americans and Black communities take care of themselves. Though they want to receive proper aid and services from government (see Joseph's comments about Mayor Menino), they are collectively more skeptical that they or their communities will actually receive quality aid (see Focus Group 4's belief that the government only took drug addiction seriously once it began affecting White people en masse).

In contrast, at this stage of the discussion, the White participants of Focus Group 6 did not express that their communities had been victimized by government. Instead, several participants perceived their communities to be preyed upon by doctors, pharmaceutical companies, and health insurance providers. This different perspective seems to have made these White participants more willing to call upon the government for aid. It is very plausible that this finding is partly a function of the composition of my focus groups. Though these data include the voices of several poorer and working-class White Americans, they all live in one of the nation's larger, wealthier metropolitan areas that offers a wider range of services than smaller towns. Other scholars have found that poor and working-class White Americans who live in rural areas in different regions of the nation express significantly more negative feelings toward government.[17] However, this difference simply places greater emphasis on the collective negative experience of Black Americans with government even when they live in cities where municipal government functions well, relatively speaking. Poverty is caused by government abandonment, but not all poor communities also experience oppression at the hands of the criminal justice system, the enforcement arm of the state.

College Educated Groups

Focus Group 1: Diverse Proposals

The crime prevention discussion among the Black and White college educated participants of Focus Group 1 was the most straightforward of the six groups. The participants largely offered a variety of different ideas without qualifying each other's statements or disagreeing with each other, even though some participants had disagreed during the crime causes discussion. These participants proposed several of the same crime prevention solutions that participants in other groups subsequently raised, foreshadowing common sentiments. As such, this group's crime prevention discussion had the least unique character.

Seven of the eight participants in this group proposed various types of community resources, services, or investments to prevent crime. Brandon (49, B, CE, FG1) endorsed "drug treatment." Several participants discussed schools and education. Bettie (23, B, CE, FG1) said, "I think we should encourage high schools and college students not to drop out and have somebody try to make them stay in the program or try to keep going. But mainly the high school students. . . . They should have a consequence for not, just, like trying to encourage students not to drop out to the streets, basically." Amber (49, W, CE, FG1) commented, "I want better education [that] starts from the elementary schools, all the way up to high school." Lacey (69, W, CE, FG1) then added, "We want more investment in education, social and civil programs to . . . And one of the things I've noticed that seem to help at-risk youth is any program where there's an adult getting them interested in one strong interest: chess, sports, music, whatever." Lance (60, B, CE, FG1) echoed Lacey's call for investment into the education system.

Some participants proposed ideas that bridged communities and issues that are typically the domain of the criminal justice system. Jeffrey (67, W, CE, FG1) proposed:

> JEFFREY: I would say like community, you know, after school activities and all kinds of things. But I included in that a kind of, an idea I haven't really heard before about, um, where kids or youth could gain admission into programs . . . you incent them to barter their guns. They bring in their guns and they get something.
> MODERATOR: Okay, so like gun buy-back kind of . . . ?
> JEFFREY: Yeah! It would be like a repurchase program for guns, but what you get is, you get into a program that has a lot of positive things for you, that you maybe want the guns to try and get anyway, which is territory. So, you know what I'm sayin'?

Debbie (64, W, CE, FG1) advocated for greater use of community-based alternatives to incarceration: "I think there are people that if you didn't put them in jail and had an alternative, like go out and do things in the community or something, you would have less crime. Because I think it reinvents itself. You learn more! You learn stuff when you're in jail that you didn't know [*laughs*]. Am I right?" Similarly, Bettie endorsed efforts to create more job opportunities and reentry programs for former offenders:

> BETTIE: They should list more jobs. They should let people with, sometimes like not the harsh-harsh felons, but like the felons that maybe is okay a little bit, they should let them get a job. Maybe they

won't have too much time to sit and think about doing the wrong
thing. Like, you have to keep—

MODERATOR: So, you're thinking once they're out, make it easier for
those with felony convictions to be able to get a new job?

BETTIE: Yeah. I mean, they have programs like that, like halfway
houses, but I don't think those is working anymore.

Several participants spoke directly to the functioning of the criminal
justice system itself. Some of these comments were punitive in nature.
Patricia (49, B, CE, FG1) offered the single most punitive sentiment in
this group's discussion: "I'd say more jail time, don't give the people too
many chances. Sometimes they get too many chances and they go out
and commit more crimes." When the moderator asked her if she was
thinking about violent or nonviolent offenders, Patricia clarified that she
was speaking about violent offenders, like those who use guns. Lance
also called for more consistent punishment of offenders, but he said he
was primarily concerned about white-collar offenders who commit financial crimes.

Other participants called for criminal justice reform. Lacey endorsed
"reducing inequities" in the punishment of drug crimes; she referenced
the severe sentences that were imposed on crack cocaine users and argued that the war on drugs "destabilizes neighborhoods." She also fa-
vorably recalled hearing the head of parole services in Massachusetts
talk about his efforts to make "the whole parole department more of a
service organization and having centers, simplifying . . . provisions for
staying out . . . staying off drugs, basically." Following Bettie's call for better reentry services to help former inmates get jobs, Lacey added, "Some
of that is CORI reform," demonstrating that some Massachusetts citizens are aware of the stigmatizing effects of a criminal record.[18] Lance
also advocated "reigning in the gun industry, the gun sale laws across
states" and "rethinking drug policies [but] not necessarily meaning the
legalization of drugs."

Finally, as in other focus groups, several participants who advocated for structural improvements in community resources or reforms
to the justice system also made some volitional statements that placed
responsibility for crime prevention upon individuals. Consistent with

her disdain for "stupid victims" that I described in the previous chapter, Debbie was the most consistently volitional. She complained that "people coming into the city, like college students, they got to know how to live in the city. They don't! And they've really got to know safety, they've got to know how to be tolerant of different people that they've never encountered. . . . It's unbelievable. But we get a lot of people in my building from the Midwest, no clue! They'll buzz anybody in the world to come into the building! [*laughter*] I mean, talk about not being safe!" Similarly, even though she endorsed investments in education and progressive parole reform, Lacey also said that one means of preventing crime is "people taking more responsibility for their actions."

Focus Group 3: Community Self-Sufficiency to Resist Racism

In many important ways, the crime prevention discussion among the college educated Black participants of Focus Group 3 mirrored the crime prevention discussion among the high school educated Black Participants of Focus Group 4. Both groups decried systemic racism, and both groups predominantly focused on ways that Black communities could help themselves. However, the differences between these two groups' discussions shed light on the ways that class divides can shape perspectives within the Black community above and beyond "linked fate" beliefs about the collective experience of being Black in America.[19]

The Black participants of Focus Groups 3 and 4 all recognized the ways that systemic racism causes Black communities to suffer harms while White communities receive resources or aid. The college educated participants of Focus Group 3 frequently described how racist stereotypes impose additional constraints on Black people above and beyond White elites' majority control of government institutions. For example, Adam (37, B, CE, FG3) argued that elites used the war on drugs to reinforce racist stereotypes of criminality while drawing attention away from crimes committed by wealthy White people like Bernie Madoff: "I mean, he's just the one person that got caught doing that. What about all the other ones who didn't get caught embezzling billions, and then we focus on petty drug dealers who're just trying to feed their family in a community that's not given the opportunity, and we're focusing on that and we're using it as a stigma and a stereotype to put Black men and men of color in [prison]." Similarly, Sheldon (30, B, CE, FG3) said, "A lot of it's historical here because as we all know the system was set up for us to fail to begin with anyway, so no matter how hard we try we'll still be viewed as that thug, or whatever have you. A lack of opportunities here, because a lot of our communities don't have education and we don't have the programs set up so we can do something about it here." Both participants recognized that stereotypes about Black criminality are key justifications for the legal and material criminalization and marginalization of Black people.[20] The participants in this group actively resisted these stereotypes. As Rachelle (60+, B, CE, FG3) asserted, "I mean, we are no more deviant than the White folks!"

While these participants were quite vocal about the ways that systemic racism harms Black communities, they reported fewer direct, personal exposure to those harms than the high school educated Black participants in other groups. Eight of the ten high school educated Black participants of Focus Groups 2 or 4 reported being under criminal justice supervision earlier in their lives; in this group, only William (67, B, CE, FG3) reported serving a sentence of probation and less than one year in jail earlier in his life. Many of the Black participants across the focus groups discussed ways that they were active in their communities, but the nature of their community engagement varied across class lines. In Focus Group 4, Mary talked about how she taught self-defense classes for women, especially those who were victimized by domestic violence or rape, and Matthew and Dorian talked about their efforts to be "redeemed old heads," former offenders who mentor neighborhood youth and try to steer them away from following the same life trajectory.[21] Their community service directly confronted or responded to crime. In contrast, the participants in Focus Group 3 led job training, financial literacy, and professional skills workshops (William and Sheldon); tutored youth (Christopher); taught church-based classes for former offenders (Melissa); and ran nonprofit organizations (Rachelle). Except for Melissa's work with ex-offenders, these participants' community service was geared more toward improving the collective wellbeing of the entire Black community rather than being narrowly focused on poverty or crime. Consequently, much of the discussion among the Focus Group 3 participants bounced between talking about ways to help other Black people overcome discrimination, laments about cultural failures in the

Black community, and efforts to help the Black community repudiate racist stereotypes.

Both Rachelle and William (67, B, CE, FG3) endorsed mentoring as a form of crime prevention. Rachelle called for "role models in the schools." William said, "positive role models . . . people paying forward, the role models paying forward." When the moderator asked him to elaborate, he explained,

> Sure, in fact I'm doing that tomorrow, I'm going up to interview with [an antipoverty, community-development nonprofit] and train young kids to be waiters and to give them skills that they can use all through college and everything like that, because I've been a waiter for over fifty years, I have my own business, I have, um, I hire, I send out waiters and bartenders for private jobs. So, I'm training these young kids because it's no jobs, you can't get jobs without experience. So, I'm training these young kids so they can have these skills, so they can have something, you know? . . . One of the things I'll be doing, I'll be training them how to go for job interviews, how to dress for a job interview, how to act, how to talk, how to write a résumé, how to fill out a job application.

William's beliefs about the efficacy of mentoring programs veered volitional in nature. Though he seemed to briefly acknowledge the scarcity of job opportunities ("because it's no jobs"), he was focused on training youth to have the skills necessary to be competitive for job openings. He did not call for public policy efforts to increase the availability of jobs in the labor market. Paige (66, B, CE, FG3) expressed a similar sentiment. One of her crime prevention proposals was:

> Access to good education which allows you to broaden your life experiences so that you're exposed to a lot of different things that show you, you can do this or that, instead of just this one or two, there's ten other things out there, because kids don't know. These kids, Black and White, on the . . . they had like corporate people who would help the city to take these kids out of, you know, outings and do stuff and you would talk to them about what you did in your company and how you got there and they would ask some very naive things, they don't know how to get from here to here because nobody ever told them. And the guidance counselors

in many cases are useless, so they didn't know how to get to there, so they made other choices. The other thing on crime prevention is access to a fulfilling career. You know, one that allows you to grow and whatever in something you like, so it doesn't become a boring job. Opportunity to choose a career without discrimination, something you want.

Like William, Paige appeared to believe that the problem is not a paucity of quality jobs, but rather youths' ignorance about the good mentorship programs and job opportunities that do exist. The only structural problem she mentioned here was employment discrimination. Only Candice (49, B, CE, FG3) said that she wrote "more jobs" on her crime prevention worksheet, but after hearing participants like William and Paige talk about mentoring, she said, "more jobs goes probably with job training," leaving it unclear how strong of a distinction she sees between programs to better train people for existing jobs versus programs to create more jobs in communities.

Few participants offered ideas that explicitly targeted structural causes of crime. Even when they did, focus often shifted in a more volitional direction. For example, Adam said, "I'll just say what I [wrote on the worksheet]. Obviously job training, counseling for those that need it, because you start to see certain individuals, okay, that kid needs a certain thing we have to focus on. 'Cause that's what people do, they don't—they're not focused on the individual, just like he said. And then you have extracurricular activities. It's not just the kids are gonna sit there and go after school and play basketball all the time. That's the norm, or they're gonna learn instruments." I quoted the rest of his statement in the previous chapter. He proceeded to discuss how students in China and Korea spend twelve hours at school, leaving them no time to be unsupervised and fall in with deviant peers, and ended by decrying "terrible parenting in the homes" and "disrespectful, lazy kids." His endorsement of better access to job training and counseling to address the criminogenic influences of strains (structural attribution) was balanced by his digression blaming parents and kids with bad character (volitional attribution). William, Rachelle, and Paige also pointed to quality parenting to prevent crime.

Other participants offered additional ideas to help youth develop positive social values. Paige said, "religious training. Because you learn things in church that it gives you choices. Like if you're in a situation with your peers as a teen and they say, 'Hey, let's steal this,' you have some choices because you were trained not to do that. So you have other choices in the situation." Her phrasing places full responsibility on youth to make the choice not to commit crime. Melissa consistently focused on ways to highlight excellence within the Black community. I quoted her in the previous chapter in which she rebutted Adam's critique of terrible parenting and noted that most Black kids "do very well," which she attributed to strong social bonds, church, and parenting. Furthermore, she argued that highlighting Black excellence through social networks and media could help prevent crime:

> Everyone talks about everything else [referring to delinquent youth and bad parents], let's highlight this kid that lives right beside me picked up the garbage. He's only ten, but on his own he took a garbage bag and just cleaned up the trash on the initiative and cleaned up the yard. That was a big deal. That encourages him, and then that sparks that peer pressure. And then that says, okay, parents are now jealous, my kid can do better. So let's, okay, so no we can't have a one up on you, tomorrow you do this. I mean, when it snows we have a group of kids, four kids, that come and plow our yard out. They're sixteen, seventeen, eighteen. And I highlight one of them and what he has done in school, now all of his friends want to be highlighted. So if we keep that up, that would just spur more.

However idealistic her idea was, it assumed that good behavior is simply a matter of choice. She vocalized no consideration of the structural constraints that might impede impoverished parents' ability to spend as much time with their children as they might like, which several of the high school educated participants in other focus groups did recognize as a problem.

Christopher's (68, B, CE, FG3) ideas about crime prevention were the most purely structural in nature of all the participants in this group. He endorsed "clean and safe parks" and "more art and music [and] enlightened schooling" for children. When the moderator asked him to clarify the latter point, he condemned "nativistic images from the early twentieth century as imbued in these IQ tests and stuff like that, you know, that's just putting money in some privileged person's pocket and not doing the kids any good." Christopher was the most ardent critic of white supremacy in this group, and speaking about crime prevention, he added, "But the fifth thing here goes to the power and privilege thing. . . . We've both been saying that for the whole duration of this group. Get rid of, I put eradicate selfish leadership. . . ." Interpreted in the context of his statements throughout the group discussion, Christopher meant that reducing White elites' power to inflict suffering upon Black communities would also cause crime to decline. Though most participants in this group echoed Christopher's critiques of white supremacy, he was the only one who proposed attacking white supremacy itself to fight crime.

Finally, I remind the reader of evidence I quoted in the previous chapter that several of the participants in this group endorsed the theoretical perspective of deterrence and argued that harsh sentences prevent crime. It is notable that they did not completely reject a role for punishment in crime prevention even though most participants in this group clearly understood how disparate criminal justice practices enforce the stereotypical criminalization of people of color. Not all people of color who object to biased criminal justice practices necessarily reject criminal justice as a solution to crime in principle.[22]

Focus Group 5: Contrasting Visions and Sharp Disagreement

Strong disagreements among the White, college educated participants of Focus Group 5 came into full view during the crime prevention portion of their discussion. In fact, out of all the focus groups, only participants in this group moved past calm disagreement; they challenged and rebutted each other's ideas. Much of this conflict arose from ideological differences; these participants expressed some of the most progressive and most conservative sentiments out of all the participants in the study.

Bruce (58, W, CE, FG5) offered the first response to the crime prevention prompt, which I quoted in the previous chapter in the section on routine activities theory. Bruce argued that "proper police enforcement" is an effective crime deterrent, which he defined as "police actually walked a beat . . . as opposed to sitting by some intersection with a red light where the odds of catching someone is so slim." His answer prompted an exchange that gave the first indication that the participants in this group had very different ideas about what constitutes good, effective crime prevention:

> INEZ: You mean like community policing, kind of?
>
> JANET: Yeah.
>
> BRUCE: No, I'm talking police actually doing their job . . .
>
> MODERATOR: Patrolling on the beat.
>
> JANET: Yeah. Yeah. But they call it community . . . that's what they call it.
>
> WALLACE: That's been around for a while, that term.
>
> BRUCE: . . . if that's the term they use now, which I don't consider to be policing.
>
> INEZ: I don't think they do it much.
>
> BRUCE: Oh, they do it. But like someone said, they sit side by side, having a conversation, I think a two-man staff meeting, essentially.
>
> INEZ: Really? They're not walking the streets and getting, you know, profiling?
>
> BRUCE: Walking . . . I haven't seen a police officer walk the street in decades.
>
> INEZ: You know . . . I don't know how to change that.
>
> NATHAN: Well, downtown they have the bicycle patrols and stuff.
>
> WALLACE: Yeah.
>
> BRUCE: In Boston, they do that.
>
> INEZ: Aren't some good things being done in Cambridge?[23] I mean, I think of Cambridge and I think of community policing. No?

Inez and Janet thought that Bruce was advocating for better community policing. Community policing emphasizes relationship building to foster trust and cooperation between civilians and police, rather than hostility and conflict. However, Bruce, who lives in one of Boston's more distant suburbs, clarified that he holds a very dim view of the community policing model, even going so far as to assert that community policing is not officers "actually doing their job." Rather, it sounds like Bruce advocated for police to engage in ubiquitous, highly visible foot patrols throughout the community. This policing tactic is generally considered to be part of the original "standard model" of policing. Decades of research have shown that random police patrols are substantially less effective at reducing crime than newer models of policing, such as "hot spot" polic-ing that focuses patrol and police interventions on known high-crime locales instead of the community as a whole.[24] As such, Bruce's view of policing is conservative in the sense of yearning for a return to an older way of doing things.

Similar to many of the high school educated participants in other focus groups, Janet (56, W, CE, FG5) advocated for an expansion of drug and mental health treatment programs, but Alice (54, W, CE, FG5) ques-tioned their effectiveness:

JANET: And then I put, like, drug treatment and drug courts . . . prevention, not punishment. And the same for mental health. Sometimes they do go hand in hand. But I think too often there's an underlying issue that's not being treated, and so the person is doing petty or worse crimes, and they're just kind of cycling repeatedly through the system without ever getting the treatment that they need for whatever is really going on.

ALICE: The problem is that you have to want to get treatment, so to have . . . I also put drug and alcohol programs, because alcohol is also . . . We didn't say that, but . . .

WALLACE: Yeah.

ALICE: . . . addiction, but there are programs, but you have to want to turn your life around and away from that. So if you don't, it doesn't matter how many programs we have.

JANET: But there's a shortage of beds in those programs, so people who do want it . . .

INEZ: And then long-term is much more successful than . . .

JANET: And there's a thing called "snowbriety," so doing . . . especially in this area, during the colder months, many people will go in to just get a warm bed and so that makes it harder for someone who is maybe in need of the help, but the beds are not here.

Though Alice said that she supports substance abuse programs, she argued that clients must "want to turn [their lives] around," thereby placing primary responsibility for change upon the clients themselves rather than on the quality of the treatment programs. Janet pushed back against Alice's very volitional stance; she made the structural argument that many people are unable to access treatment not because they lack the willpower to change, but rather because the supply of clinic slots does not meet the demand.

Inez (72, W, CE, FG5) critiqued the severity of contemporary punishments: "Every week it seems, I say to myself, why on earth is this person going to jail? Why is that offense being dealt with such criminality? You know, it seems that everything is a crime in this country that requires jail. I mean, I'm just appalled. . . . We've criminalized so much. And some things need to be, but there has to be a much more novel approach to punishment." Wallace (57, W, CE, FG5) agreed with her that the nation today sentences more people to incarceration for minor crimes than previous decades, and Marianne (30, W, CE, FG5) argued that simply punishing more offenses with harsher sentences does not actually prevent crime. However, following Wallace and Marianne's statements of agreement, the following debate occurred:

BRUCE: I'm trying to think of a crime that . . .

INEZ: Oh, I heard of one the other day . . . that whole idea of if you're with somebody who's committing a crime, and you're basically an innocent . . . why put you in jail too?

DYLAN: Mm-hmm [affirmative]. Yeah. Get a known . . .

NATHAN: Yes, they even have a crime called knowingly being in the presence.

INEZ: And that's relatively new, you know.

JANET: In the presence.

DYLAN: Oh, yeah. Okay.

INEZ: Yeah. It's just . . . it's nuts. I mean . . . there's just so much that . . . and I think judges need to be more free, and they used to be. More free to . . .

NATHAN: Yeah.

ALICE: I have a problem with that because if you're with someone, and say I'm with my girlfriend, and she decides she's going to go . . .

BRUCE: Jack up the liquor store.

ALICE: . . . and punch some elderly person in the face, and I'm with her. Instead of . . .

INEZ: Or you're waiting in the car.

ALICE: ... or ... Well, I mean, you gotta have some responsibility for
being with them and laughing and running away.

BRUCE: You let her do it.

INEZ: Yeah. But in jail is from my point of view, jail is not necessarily ...
I mean, gosh. How many people are we going to put in jail?

NATHAN: Yeah. It's a little extreme, yeah.

Bruce and Alice responded with skepticism to Inez's argument that many
actions are disproportionately criminalized and punished. Consistent
with Alice's strong belief in deterrence that I described in the previous
chapter, she argued that even people who are peripherally involved in
a crime must accept "responsibility" for their actions. Bruce and Alice
expressed neither recognition of nor concern about the growth of mass
incarceration. In contrast, Inez reiterated her belief that the United
States relies too heavily on incarceration, and Nathan (55, W, CE, FG5)
agreed with her.

Inez and Bruce similarly disagreed about the criminalization of drug
use. Inez argued that the war on drugs caused many negative consequences in society. In response, Bruce said, "Speaking to this, I actually know someone that was out in Portland, Oregon. And they have
legalized marijuana out there. And what it's done, it's brought in a lot of
people that now want to sell marijuana and make money. So the rents
have gone sky high. So they have a huge problem with the homeless now.
So they have a huge problem with the homeless committing crimes." At
many points in the discussion, Inez recognized that the negative social
consequences of mass incarceration are experienced by offenders and
their communities. For example, she decried the fact that incarceration
"break[s] up families." Bruce perceived the opposite problem. He believed that the absence of punishment for drug use causes an increase
in crime and social disorganization, as well as an increase in rent, that
negatively impacts the law-abiding residents of communities. Bruce
seems to be making a spurious causal argument here; it strains credulity
that an increase in drug sales and the presence of people experiencing
homelessness would cause a neighborhood to become more desirable
and expensive for renters. However, the important part of Bruce's argument is not its accuracy, but rather what it reveals. Here, Bruce expresses

rather textbook "NIMBYism," which is short for "not in my backyard" attitudes. NIMBYism refers to middle- and upper-middle-class property owners expressing support for social services to aid the poor in the abstract, but opposing them if those services would (1) be established in their own communities, (2) negatively impact their own property values, or (3) require a tax increase.[25]

The participants in this focus group even disagreed about the role of education in preventing crime. Alice said, "The whole education system . . . , a lot of the education systems, not all of them, but a lot of especially city . . . it's just pushing the kids through. They're not really teaching them, they're not teaching. And parents have to take responsibility for that, too, as far as teaching respect and what's right and what's wrong." Inez responded to Alice, "May I add something to that? If you go into the suburbs, although now the rich are going into the cities, and the poor are heading out to the suburbs, so there's a shift. But you go into a Newton or a Belmont, those kids are flourishing, you know.[26] So I have a real problem with the way education is funded. I mean, education funding in this country is disgusting." The moderator asked Inez if she thought that more equal funding of schools would reduce crime, and both Inez and Wallace replied that they thought it would.

In this exchange, we see that Alice believes that changing the nature of education to better teach "what's right and what's wrong" is the best way to reduce crime. In contrast, Inez sees underfunding of schools in poorer communities as the problem. Alice explicitly disagreed with Inez on this point:

> ALICE: But there's the way it's being funded. Okay. Lawrence is the next city over from where I live. And they get a lot of federal funding. And they have a brand, you know, not brand new, but a new school, big high school, everything, all federally funded. They have money coming out of everywhere. And those kids are just pushed through and there's no education. They're not . . . the money is going there, but it's not going to teach the kids and discipline the kids and to teach the kids. And so . . .
>
> INEZ: But . . . but that could be for a whole host of reasons, you know. It's not every educational size is going to fit that particular community's students, you know, they might need something much more special and specific.

Alice doubled down on her belief that deficiencies in education are due not to inadequate resources, but rather are due to school culture—specifically a lack of "discipline." Inez responded by essentially saying that Alice should not second-guess how another town's school system chooses to use its funding.

What is going on here? Alice and Bruce live in Methuen, a town thirty miles northwest of Boston. As of the 2010 census, Metheun's population was about 80% White with about a $50,000 median household income. Lawrence, the neighboring town whose schools Alice impugns, had a population that was about 74% Hispanic with a median household income of about $26,000.[27] In addition to high levels of poverty and crime compared to the state average, Lawrence also had a reputation for local corruption, and its public school system was among the poorest performing in the entire state.[28] In 2012, the state took control of the city's school system to implement reforms. As such, Alice's deeply negative impression of the Lawrence schools is partially based on factual, historic events.

However, Alice did not acknowledge that the Lawrence schools' Turnaround Plan under state supervision had achieved impressive improvements on several metrics of student performance by the time of the focus groups in 2016. In fact, the Lawrence public school turnaround is widely regarded as a national model of success—and no analyst attributed that positive change to the imposition of "discipline" on the school system's students.[29] As I discussed in the introductory chapter, a significant component of contemporary racism is White people's belief that public funds are being given to lazy, deviant, undeserving people of color.[30] It is plausible that Alice's belief that the Lawrence school system squandered copious amounts of federal funding, and her refusal to recognize the school system's notable improvement, were at least partially fueled by stereotypes about the town's poorer, majority-person-of-color population.

Not every idea offered during this discussion provoked disagreement. Aside from Alice's concerns about wasteful school funding, several of these participants expressed support for various financial policies to alleviate poverty, unemployment, and crime. For example:

JANET: I would think full employment would help.
MODERATOR: Full employment?

MARIANNE: Livable minimum wage.
WALLACE: There you go. Jobs and minimum wages.
JANET: Minimum wage.
WALLACE: That's good. That's it.
JANET: That's it.
WALLACE: It's a big one.

As I noted in the prior chapter, Janet, like many participants in other focus groups, asserted that bored youth are likely to get into trouble, so she endorsed "after school and summer programs for youth." Wallace advocated for "proper housing of people." Dylan (25, W, CE, FG5) said, "I think having community resources are important and funding for community resources." When the moderator asked him to go into more detail, he explained that he perceives a link between community resources, social bonds, and informal social control:

It could be anything, like strong communities where people actually know each other. And they care about what's going on in their neighborhood. I know, like in the early '90s, when the Crips and the Bloods in LA, at the peak of violence, started a truce and they were saying, we're going to stop killing each other, the LAPD would raid the truce meetings, you know. Instead of saying, hey, city, let's give a bunch of money to supporting these programs, they would actually raid the meetings. But I think, you know, resources where, safe houses, respites, not just mental health, where people are treated like animals being shipped in and out of the thing, but where people can actually go. . . . And I think arts and creative expression programs. If you're a little pissed off at the . . . about things or they have a way to express themselves, you know, and they're supported in doing that.

Echoing Dylan's idea about community arts programs to help individuals process stress in a safe manner, Nathan supported, "school support groups for kids, victims of domestic abuse and violence from their parents, there's all the way going on and usually kids don't talk about." Finally, like many participants in other focus groups, Inez recognized a relationship between poverty and parenting, so she endorsed an expansion of childcare services: "Businesses and their accommodations for parents because businesses, people are working more . . . longer and longer hours. In many corporations and businesses, they have kids they cannot deal with at home. And if they . . . and especially people who are minimum wage workers, if they stay home and take care of their kid, then they're fired. So it seems to me the businesses need to . . . [trailed off sentence]."

Lasty, I will note the contributions of Wallace (57, W, CE, FG5). Wallace's beliefs seemed to fall in between those of the more conservative participants, Bruce and Alice, and the more liberal participants, Inez, Janet, and Marianne. Just as he endorsed both volitional and structural causes of crime in the first part of his group's discussion, Wallace frequently agreed with many of the ideas offered by participants to address structural causes of crime, but the crime prevention ideas he volunteered himself were more volitional in nature. As I noted in the prior chapter, Wallace saw an important role for informal social control ("more community involvement, people policing their own neighborhoods") in the prevention of crime. He also argued that programs to teach offenders empathy for their victims might prompt them to desist from crime:

> This one is kind of going right towards it, the personal aspect of being a victim of crime. And maybe education and awareness of what a victim goes through. If people maybe heard from or knew exactly . . . Say I don't pick any of a myriad of, let's say, domestic violence or just assault . . . things like that. And here it's . . . or see in print, or whatever, well, what exactly . . . how this destroys lives, the victim, everyone around them. Maybe I'm naive and I think that . . . they think about doing something in the future that's going to hurt someone.

Wallace's idea is consistent with restorative justice programs, though he did not make that connection himself. These solutions are less punitive in nature than endorsing tougher policing or harsher punishment, but they still place responsibility for crime prevention upon community members and offenders themselves.

Public Ideas about Crime Prevention across Race and Class

A major theme in early twenty-first century debates about criminal justice reform in the United States was how to rely less on incarceration and

more on community-based forms of rehabilitation and crime prevention. This focus represented a significant departure from the "volitional
criminology" that dominated criminal justice policymaking and
practice during the 1980s and 1990s.[31] However, debates remain over
precisely what form of community-based crime prevention is appropriate or desirable. The work of local community nonprofit organizations
and cooperation between residents in a community can prevent and
reduce crime, but these solutions largely place responsibility for crime
prevention upon the shoulders of civilians themselves.[32] They also have
limited capability to address the deep, systemic harms of segregation,
poverty, and concentrated disadvantage.[33] For this reason, many advocates argue that the most needed form of community crime prevention
is direct investment into neighborhoods in order to alleviate the structural causes of crime. Since it was government divestment that created
concentrated disadvantage in the first place,[34] it should be government's
responsibility to fix it.[35]

This chapter sheds light on Americans' thoughts about crime prevention during this period of change. Does the evidence presented
here suggest that the public would support efforts to expand the role of
community-based crime prevention? I believe that it does, but the patterns of responses that I observed across the focus groups speak to ways
in which policymakers who either prefer the punishment-centric status
quo or prefer to shift responsibility for crime prevention onto civilians
instead of government could manipulate cultural differences among the
public that emerge across the lines of race and social class.

Prior to explicit prompting by the moderator, few of the Black participants in this study clearly called for government action to ameliorate
poverty and prevent crime. Many of the ideas proposed by participants
in Focus Groups 3 and 4 focused on ways that Black communities could
take care of themselves and prevent crime through their own initiatives. For the high school educated participants in Focus Group 3, these
ideas largely revolved around informal social control, mentoring crime-
involved youth, and teaching community members self-defense—all of
which felt like survival strategies for Black people to navigate crime in
their neighborhoods. Few participants in this group proposed ways for
government to prevent crime until prompted by the moderator; only
then did Matthew quite explicitly call for government investment to

alleviate the harms of concentrated disadvantage. The college educated participants of Focus Group 4 proposed ideas that were less focused on navigating around crime and more focused on equipping Black people to improve themselves—both their job skills and their morals. Viewed in light of the fact that their constructive proposals for mentoring were interspersed with several very judgmental statements leveled against Black people whom they judged to comport themselves in a poor manner, the discussion in this focus group had a feeling of "respectability politics."[36] The Black, high school educated participants of Focus Group 2 most extensively spoke of the link between poverty and crime, but they verbally paired recognition of structural problems with very volitional language that places responsibility for avoiding crime upon individuals themselves.[37]

I suspect that these Black participants thought, first and foremost, of things that individuals and their communities can do to prevent crime because they lack confidence that government would actually respond to Black people and provide the kinds of proper law enforcement and anti-poverty resources they desire.[38] In other words, I do not think this is evidence that Black Americans genuinely want nothing from government when it comes to crime prevention; rather, it is evidence that they have historically felt the need to turn inward and care for their own communities because government has abandoned or victimized them. However, a policymaker who heard the discussions among the Black participants in this study could use their dominant focus on self-sufficiency to justify a "hands-off" approach by the government regarding social problems like poverty and crime. Even worse, a truly cynical policymaker could stoke punitive sentiments among higher-class Black Americans in order to create conflict within the Black community.[39]

If the nature of the discussions among the Black participants in this study are generalizable, they may partially explain why policymakers have "selectively heard" only Black Americans' punitive support for empowering the criminal justice system to do what it takes to stop crime, not their desire for government to do more to alleviate segregation and concentrated disadvantage.[40] However, this chapter also contributes to emerging evidence that policymakers did more than discount the full complexity of Black public opinion; they only truly paid attention to the most punitive sentiments among White Americans.[41] The strongest disagreements about proper crime prevention tactics emerged among the college educated White participants of Focus Group 5. There, Bruce and Alice's predominantly volitional, conservative views went head-to-head against Inez, Marianne, and Janet's predominantly structural, liberal views. It must be repeated that statements of support for tough punishment of criminals as an appropriate means of crime prevention were vocalized by at least one or two participants in each focus group—including several Black participants. However, most of these participants also expressed support for initiatives to address the structural causes of crime. Bruce and Alice felt differently. They questioned the wisdom and efficacy of structural solutions to crime, frequently with a tone of incredulity that their fellow participants would pose such ridiculous ideas. They were on a significantly different wavelength than the high school educated White participants of Focus Group 6, most of whom strongly endorsed programs and initiatives to address poverty and drug addiction. Bruce and Alice's contribution to this study suggests that the greatest lingering pool of support for the harsh "volitional criminology" of decades past can be found among middle- and upper-class White Americans.[42]

However, we must remember that this chapter analyzed participants' initial ideas about crime prevention that first came to their minds when queried in an open-ended manner. These findings teach us about the ideas that Americans associate with crime prevention "off the cuff," but they do not necessarily reveal the full scope and "boundaries" of people's crime control preferences. We cannot properly measure people's preferences until we give them the opportunity to choose between several different types of crime prevention proposals. I turn to this question in the next chapter.

3

Public Preferences for a Crime Prevention Budget

The fact that Americans endorse a variety of responses to crime presents a conundrum for policymakers. People may say that they "strongly support" numerous crime prevention policies, but governments only have the resources and capacity to do so much. Crime prevention policymaking at the state level usually occurs within a zero-sum budget. The more money that legislators spend on one crime prevention policy (or any other state expenditure), the less money they can spend on other policies. From a policymaker's perspective, understanding public preferences is more valuable than simply understanding public opinion. In order to assess the former rather than the latter, we need to ask people to make choices between different policy options, not simply state the degree to which they support or oppose numerous different policies without having to make trade-offs.[1]

This brings us back to one of the central questions of this book: how would Americans choose to allocate resources in order to prevent and reduce crime? In this chapter, I analyze the focus group participants' discussions about how to construct a hypothetical crime prevention budget for the state of Massachusetts. I assess the degree to which the participants favored criminal justice versus community-based investment, and I analyze participants' explanations for why they allocated money as they did. Then, I analyze data from my national survey of Black and White Americans who answered a budget allocation question that was very similar to the scenario I presented to the focus group participants. I use these data to consider whether the preferences of the focus group participants are idiosyncratic or reflect widespread American preferences. I also test whether there are significant disagreements among Americans in their crime prevention policy preferences across group characteristics such as race, political partisanship, and urban versus rural residence.

Focus Group Findings

Budget Allocation Preferences

The discussion of participants' crime prevention investment preferences began with the following prompt:

> Now, let's imagine that Massachusetts has some extra money in its criminal justice budget that it can spend on crime prevention. And you're in charge of the budget and get to decide how that extra money will be spent. [Assistant moderator] is handing out a sheet that has some possible ways the extra criminal justice money can be spent. There are also some blank spaces where you can fill in your own ideas—or any of the ideas we've just been talking about. We'd like you to write in what percent of the criminal justice budget you'd want to use for each item. It can only add up to 100%. You can spend it all on one item or spread it out over several items. Please fill it out on your own and we'll talk about it afterwards.

The budget options on the worksheet were:

- Hiring more police officers
- Hiring more probation officers to supervise offenders in the community
- Building new jails and prisons
- Funding clinics to provide improved healthcare and mental healthcare services
- Increasing funding to the public schools
- Creating jobs
- [Blanks—Opportunity for participants to write their own ideas]

I chose these items to reflect the budget choices that lie at the heart of the justice reinvestment paradigm. First, do we prioritize spending on prisons, or do we invest instead in alternatives to incarceration? Second, when choosing among possible alternatives to incarceration, do we prioritize reinvestment back into other criminal justice system institutions, or do we invest in the "human resources and physical infrastructure" of communities?[2] Table 3.1 presents the average percentage of money participants allocated to each budget option broken down across the focus groups and the race and education groupings. Within each group of

TABLE 3.1. Average Percent Budget Allocation for Crime Prevention Options among Focus Group Participants

	% More Police	% More Probation	% Building Prisons	% Funding Healthcare Clinics	% Funding Public Schools	% Funding Job Creation	% Write-In Options
All Participants							
· Average Allocation	12.5%	11.5%	14.7%	29.8%	22.2%	26.3%	17.0%
· Range	2.5–30%	2.5–25%	10–25%	10–45%	5–50%	5–50%	5–75%
· # Zeros	22	22	38	6	5	2	16
White Participants							
· Average Allocation	16.9%	13.4%	21.5%	25.4%	22.6%	21.1%	17.0%
· Range	5–30%	5–25%	18–25%	10–45%	12–50%	18–50%	5–30%
· # Zeros	11	11	21	5	3	1	9
Black Participants							
· Average Allocation	8.0%	9.3%	11.25%	21.3%	21.8%	24%	17.6%
· Range	2.5–15%	2.5–20%	5–20%	1–35%	5–50%	5–50%	5–75%
· # Zeros	11	11	18	1	2	1	7
College Educated Participants							
· Average Allocation	12.8%	11.6%	16.25%	21.6%	21%	24.8%	18.3%
· Range	2.5–30%	2.5–25%	10–25%	10–45%	5–50%	5–50%	10–33.4%
· # Zeros	9	10	20	5	4	2	8
High School Educated Participants							
· Average Allocation	12.6%	12%	14%	24.9%	23.5%	28.5%	16.0%
· Range	5–20%	3–25%	10–18%	10–50%	10–50%	10–50%	5–75%
· # Zeros	13	12	18	1	1	0	8
Focus Group 1							
· Average Allocation	13.8%	9%	15%	23.6%	25%	27.1%	16.9%
· Range	5–30%	5–10%	10–20%	10–45%	15–50%	10–50%	10–30%
· # Zeros	4	3	6	1	1	1	3
Focus Group 2							
· Average Allocation	12%	12.2%	18%	21.9%	23.6%	22.6%	11.7%
· Range	5–18%	3–25%	NA	10–30%	10–37%	10–30%	5–25%
· # Zeros	3	2	6	0	0	0	3

(continued)

TABLE **3.1.** (cont.)

	% More Police	% More Probation	% Building Prisons	% Funding Healthcare Clinics	% Funding Public Schools	% Funding Job Creation	% Write-In Options
Focus Group 3							
· Average Allocation	7.1%	10.5%	10%	22.1%	16.4%	20%	18.9%
· Range	2.5–15%	2.5–20%	NA	10–35%	5–30%	5–25%	10–33.4%
· # Zeros	2	3	7	1	1	1	2
Focus Group 4*							
· Average Allocation	10%	10%	10%	22.5%	28.3%	25%	17.9%
· Range	NA	NA	NA	10–50%	10–50%	10–50%	5–75%
· # Zeros	5	5	5	0	0	0	1
Focus Group 5							
· Average Allocation	19%	16.25%	25%	18%	21.7%	26.9%	22.5%
· Range	10–25%	5–25%	NA	10–30%	15–30%	20–40%	15–30%
· # Zeros	3	4	7	3	2	0	2
Focus Group 6							
· Average Allocation	15%	12.5%	0%	30.8%	18.7%	36.1%	19%
· Range	10–20%	10–15%	NA	15–45%	12–30%	20–50%	10–25%
· # Zeros	5	5	7	1	1	0	4

Note *: One participant in Focus Group 4 struggled with the math involved in writing his budget. The moderator had to provide significant computational assistance. He settled on 10% each for police, probation officers, prisons, clinics, and schools and 50% to jobs. Later in the group, he asked to fill out a second budget form with different allocations. On his second form, he allocated 75% to clinics, 20% to schools, and 5% to jobs. To account for his uncertainty, I include his second allocations in the write-in option estimates. When calculating the average allocation within each group, I incorporated his allocations as the average amount between his two worksheets (e.g., 5% for the first five options, 27.5% for jobs).

participants, I first report the average percentage of money allocated among respondents who chose to allocate money to a particular line item. Second, I report the range of respondents' individual percentage allocation amounts. Third, I report the number of participants who chose to allocate no money to the line item.

I observe a few notable patterns. On average, participants chose to allocate larger portions of their budgets into the community infrastructure options of healthcare clinics, public schools, and job creation than they did into the criminal justice system options of police, probation, or prisons. In fact, these participants devoted the least amount of money to building new prisons, and the highest number of participants chose to devote no money whatsoever to this option. Furthermore, the upper bounds of the allocation ranges reveal that participants capped their allocations to justice system institutions at lower percentages than their allocations to community services. Participants' preference for greater investment into community services instead of justice agencies is mirrored across race and education groups. White participants allocated double the amount of money to hiring more police than Black participants, on average, but the same number of participants of each race chose to give the police no additional money. A few more high school educated participants than college educated participants chose to allocate no money toward police, probation, or prisons, but the range and average allocations into justice institutions are quite similar across levels of education.

Table 3.2 provides additional information about participants' budget priorities. Within each focus group, I categorized respondents into a four-part typology. The first category contains participants who allocated all their funds toward community-based crime prevention programs and institutions without giving any money to criminal justice institutions. The second category contains participants who allocated 70% or more of their funds toward community-based options but a minority of their funds toward one or more criminal justice system options. The third category contains participants who chose a relatively balanced budget, which I define here as respondents who split their money either 50–50% or 40–60% (give or take 5%) between criminal justice and community-based options (40–60% splits could favor either criminal justice or community allocations). Finally, the fourth category contains participants who allocated 70% or more of their funds toward criminal justice options and allocated only a minority of their funds toward community-based options. The sixth column reports the crime prevention options that many participants wrote themselves, which I will discuss shortly.

Table 3.2 reaffirms my major conclusions drawn from examination of table 3.1. Across all the focus groups, we can see that only one single participant (Bruce) allocated a clear majority of his funds into criminal justice institutions (25% each into police, probation, and prisons, and 25% into job creation). No participant exclusively allocated money

TABLE 3.2. Focus Group Participants Categorized by Budget Preferences, Plus Details about Optional Write-In Allocations

	Exclusive Community Investment	Predominant Community Investment	Balanced Community & CJS Investment	Predominant CJS Investment	Optional Write-In Allocations
Focus Group 1	3	3	2	0	· "Public housing standards" (30%) · "More intensive investigating white collar crime" (15%) · "Improvement of technology (e.g., Computerization)" (15%) · "Better training of police officers" (10%) · "Better training for police, more community policing" (15%) · "Reform criminal justice system (more equitable)" (10%) · "After school activities, music, sports" (30%) · "Youth prosecution separate from adults, restorative justice mediation" (10%)
Focus Group 2	1	5	1	0	· "Housing programs" (15%) · "Mental training police" (15%) · "Food organizations" (15%) · "Housing" (10%) · "Better training for officers" (5%) · "Housing" (25%) · "Legalize some drugs" (10%) · "Gun control" (5%) · "Better [street] lighting, like Detroit" (5%)
Focus Group 3	1	7	0	0	· "Non-profit, community-based job training, reentry" (25%) · "Scholarships" (10%) · "PR initiatives highlighting new programs" (10%) · "Creating jump rope clubs in the schools" (33.3%) · "Creating interactive drumming circles in the schools" (33.3%) · "Supporting music performance in parks" (33.4%) · "Affordable housing" (20%) · "Community center" (10%) · "Mentorship programs in the courts (for youth)" (10%) · "Visit (jails) programs" (10%) · "Community awareness" (10%) · "Soft skill classes for adults & children" (20%) · "Classes on future skills, needed finances" (20%) · "Budgeting classes" (20%)

TABLE 3.2. (cont.)

	Exclusive Community Investment	Predominant Community Investment	Balanced Community & CJS Investment	Predominant CJS Investment	Optional Write-In Allocations
Focus Group 4*	5	1	0	0	· "Pay teachers more" (10%) · "Prepare kids for college" (20%) · "Housing, day care" (10%) · "Positive adults & role models" (10%) · "More social learning, networking" (5%) · "Better after school activities" (5%) · "Daycare" (20%) · "Transportation" (20%) · "Grants for extra-curricular [activities]" (15%)
Focus Group 5	3	3	1	1	· "Arts & expression programs to marginalized communities" (25%) · "Drug decriminalization & treatment" (25%) · "Free community college" (25%) · "Funding community-based restorative justice programs to address previous crimes/criminals/offenders with others" (20%) · "Drop-in centers for youth that involves 1-on-1 mentoring" (20%) · "Community resources, like sports" (15%) · "Youth (after school activities)" (20%) · "Create funding for higher education for low income families" (30%)
Focus Group 6	5	1	1	0	· "Outreach [to youth in schools]" (10%) · "More [street surveillance] cameras" (25%) · "Oversight for mental health clinics re: over-prescribing" (18%) · "Vocational programming" (20%) · "Halfway house for combat vet transition" (22%)

Notes: See Note * in table 3.1; CJS: criminal justice system

into criminal justice to the exclusion of all community-based options (hence the absence of that category in the table). Even participants who preferred a balanced approach that roughly evenly divided their funds between criminal justice and community-based options were a minority in this sample. Instead, most participants chose to predominantly or exclusively fund community-based options.

Paige (66, B, CE, FG3) rather adeptly summarized most participants' feelings about community investment when she said, "[Choosing how to allocate money is] hard because things exist now that need to be funded but if they ideally were funded in the past, some of this other stuff would have to go down . . . If people had access to jobs, good education, and good healthcare, then there wouldn't be so much crime and we said, these are problems." Her sentiment that "all of these things are important and should be funded" was echoed by other participants. William (67, B, CE, FG3) specifically explained his allocation for clinics by saying, "I have 20% of funding clinics because a lot of the people are still unaware that people are still dying, large portion of the Black community still dying from Hepatitis C, HIV, AIDS. And so we need more money going to these clinics to save people in the community. 'Cause that's another thing that's being overlooked. People think AIDS epidemic is over." Similarly, Adam prompted the following exchange in Focus Group 3 when he explained his allocation toward clinics:

> ADAM: Thirty-five percent funding clinics to provide improved healthcare, mental healthcare services. Very necessary, especially in Massachusetts.
>
> WILLIAM: All around, all around.
>
> ADAM: Actually there's a whopping statistic that New England or maybe Massachusetts but like New England, that we have the most mental patients per capita than anywhere in the country, more heroin addicts, more per capita than anywhere in the country. And um [cross talk, unidentified female speaker: "It might be the opioids."] Opioid, yeah, well, yeah. Right, and a lot of mental patients also.

However, explanations like William's and Adam's were relatively infrequent. Most participants seemed to assume that the underfunding of public institutions was common knowledge and not in particular need of explanation. Participants across the groups expressed two common themes. The first was clarifying how they would want their money to be used in public schools. For example, Debbie (64, W, CE, FG1) split her budget fifty-fifty between public schools and job creation, but she explained that she would like to blend the two. She proposed government-subsidized programs to bring employers into high schools to provide workshops and professional networking: "You really need to have the employers come in who are actually going to eventually be recruiting, to give the kids workshops, what's required, and actually have on available right there, applications." Lacey (69, W, CE, FG1) said, "And then 20% in increased funding to the public schools, better targeted investment education or sports and other activities among other things. More treatment for learning disabled, disabilities and so forth." On her worksheet, Marianne (30, W, CE, FG5) wrote that her 20% budget allocation toward schools should go "towards socioemotional learning and mindfulness curriculum." As we can see in table 3.2, other participants in Focus Groups 1, 3, 4, and 5 used their write-in spaces to allocate money toward creating or improving various arts and afterschool activities in schools. These allocations reflect participants' belief that structured activities would prevent unsupervised youth from getting into trouble, as discussed in chapters 1 and 2.

The second common theme was participants clarifying or emphasizing that they wanted their allocations toward healthcare clinics to be focused on treatment for drug addiction or mental illness. For example, Lacey from Focus Group 1 said, "I put most of my money in funding clinics who provide . . . well, I didn't mean funding clinics, but improved healthcare and mental healthcare services, and major investment and addiction treatments. So I put that 30%, that was the biggest . . . What about we need more and much better halfway houses for addicts and more people who return to the community, and that's an area that is effective when it's done right, but it's very underfunded." Jack (71, W, HSE, FG6) said, "Fifteen percent on clinics to improve mental health service." On their budget worksheets, Lance (60, B, CE, FG1), Jeffrey (67, W, CE, FG1), and Janet (56, W, CE, FG5) also wrote notes emphasizing that clinic funding should be primarily devoted toward drug treatment services, broadly construed.

In contrast, many of the participants did expressly justify why they allocated little or nothing to police, probation, or prisons. One explanation was far and away the most common: the criminal justice system already has enough money. Consider the following examples:

> I gave less to prisons. 'Cause we got enough prisons. As we can see. You know, you go in, you come out, and you're involved in it, you know, they might get overcrowded, but they get overcrowded because . . . There's just

too much going on, but prisons is not the answer. To build more prisons, it's not the answer.
(Timothy, 54, B, HSE, FG2)

I put 0% for hiring more police. I think we have enough. Zero percent for hiring more probation officers, and 0% for building any new jails. Because we have enough. So I put 30% for improved healthcare and mental health. I put 25% for increase in funding to public schools. 30% for creating new jobs. I put 10% for housing and 5% for better training for our current police officers and probation officers.
(Chrissy, 46, B, HSE, FG2)

We got enough police officers, they've got plenty of cash for them. I wouldn't hire any more probation officers because the ones I see now don't do much of anything anyway and we definitely don't need any more jails, that's for damn sure. I think we need more money in the school system, and we definitely need more jobs, and we definitely need more money into healthcare. That's it. That's cut and dry for me.
(Jason, 46, W, HSE, FG6)

I said 5% for more police officers. I said 0% for more probation to supervise the offenders in the communities, 0% for building new jails and prisons. . . . You have enough. Obviously.
(Adam, 37, B, CE, FG3)

Here, it is important to emphasize that these are people's perceptions. Many corrections administrators would likely gasp in horror at the statement that the criminal justice system has "enough" money. A great many prisons and jails in the United States are overcrowded and understaffed, and many probation and parole officers have downright enormous caseloads. These problems could be significantly reduced with an infusion of cash to hire more criminal justice professionals and reduce the correctional officer-to-inmate or probation-officer-to-supervisee ratio. Remember that the discussion prompt told participants to imagine that Massachusetts had some extra money in its budget, so it may be more appropriate to think of participants' budget preferences here as a statement of priorities for what the state should do to prevent crime above and beyond the status quo. Current correctional budgets may be objectively inadequate to meet proper safety standards, but many of the participants in this study clearly believed that community-based institutions and crime prevention programs were even more underfunded and deserving of financial support than the criminal justice system.

What of the participants who did allocate money into criminal justice institutions? Amber, Lance, Bettie, Melissa, Sheldon, Rachelle, Adam, and Jack allocated money toward police, probation, or prisons, or a combination of the three, but did not explain why or comment further on how that money should be used. With the exception of Amber's 30% to police, all of these participants' allocations were 20% or less into each criminal justice institution. Among this grouping, only Bettie allocated money to prisons (10%). Since these participants did not elaborate on their justice system allocations, we cannot know any more about their motivations. Perhaps they were satisfied with the status quo of the system and simply wished to see it better funded, or perhaps they harbored some criticisms of the justice system that they either felt disinclined to vocalize or felt had already been sufficiently expressed by other participants. All we can know is that these participants expressed some support for police, probation officers, and, to a more limited extent, prisons.

A few participants did have more to say about why they allocated money toward criminal justice institutions, but their explanations did not fundamentally critique those institutions' status quo. Patricia (49, B, CE, FG1) allocated 20% for "better, new jails or prisons" because "they say the jails are really overpopulated, so many to a room." Her answer implies a willingness to build more correctional facilities in order to reduce overcrowding. However, she then said, "Well, I guess when you're in jail you're not supposed to be having a lovely time anyway, so whatever. [*laughter*]" This suggests that Patricia has a level of tolerance for the so-called pains of imprisonment rather than a strong desire for prison reform. Roger (63, W, HSE, FG2) allocated 18% of his budget toward building new jails. When the moderator asked him to elaborate, his answer was a bit rambling and unclear, but it sounded to me like he advocated building separate cell blocks for different categories of offenders. Whether he thought this for reasons of reducing overcrowding or ensuring safety was clear neither from his answer nor context clues in the conversation. Regardless, building more prisons, even to alleviate overcrowding, does nothing to challenge the mass incarceration status quo. Similarly, Alice (54, W, CE, FG5) allocated 20% for hiring more police but specified that she wanted them to focus on gang prevention. Scholars have critiqued gang enforcement tactics as one facet of the "tough on crime" style that dominated policing during the 1990s, contributed to racial disparities in arrests, and increased tensions between police and communities of color.[3]

Many participants clarified that they wanted their allocations toward criminal justice institutions to fund various types of reform, not simply empower the justice system to keep functioning unchanged; this preference is evident in participants' write-in allocations displayed in table 3.2. Albert (43, W, HSE, FG6) said, "I put 10% to retrain the police, 10% for retraining the probation officers and to supervise the offenders. Because there are always going to be offenders out there, and they do need supervision, and they need to be updated constantly." Roger from Focus Group 2 allocated 18% toward probation and requested "more probation officers, more education in the probation system. You know, more educated parole officers." William from Focus Group 3 said, "I changed my first one from hiring more police officers to . . . 5%, to buying video cameras for the police officers. They actually said that there's been a reduction on both sides, the cops' brutality and crime and people committing crimes when they realize they're filming." Candice (49, B, CE, FG3) said, "I had money for jails, but when [another participant] said reentry, that's what I mean. Money into the jail for programs while they're in there. I didn't mean necessarily building."

Several of the participants who exclusively funded community-based institutions and programs clearly expressed why they shunned justice system institutions. Consider the following exchange between the participants of Focus Group 2:

> BALDWIN: See this would've been totally different if we wasn't discussing what we just discussed earlier. We wouldn't have said nothing bad about the police or anything like that. I would've thought it'd be different.
> ROGER: Probably not.
> BALDWIN: I mean, I would have talked the same, you know.
> MODERATOR: But you wouldn't have put it down? If we didn't talk about it?

BALDWIN: I would have given them . . . well, like I said, it's just, what's the way? Are they properly trained police officers, or just young kids that have got a gun? [*chuckling*] And got an attitude for the African American?

MODERATOR: So, if we had done this before we talked, would you have given any money to the police?

BALDWIN: I would have given them some, yes. 'Cause we do need more cops, you know, 'cause crime is [cross talk, inaudible], but *well-trained* cops.

TIMOTHY: We got enough cops. We got enough cops. We got enough cops.

BALDWIN: Well, we do. We do.

This exchange was another clear example of the way that many Black Americans are cross-pressured because they are disproportionately exposed to both crime and hostile or harmful interactions with police officers in their neighborhoods.[4] Baldwin states that "we do need more cops" to address crime in communities. However, hearing other participants recall negative interactions with the police earlier in his group's discussion raised the salience of police bias in Baldwin's mind and led him to withdraw his support for additional funding for police in the absence of reforms and improved training. Timothy's antipathy toward the police was so strong that he would not consider allocating money to the police even for training. Both Baldwin and Timothy are Black men with a high school education, placing them in comparable positions in America's race and class hierarchy.

A discussion in Focus Group 4 made it quite clear that many Black participants were unwilling to allocate money toward criminal justice institutions because they feared and distrusted the system:

MODERATOR: Was there something you looked at and said, "They're not getting anything?"

MATTHEW: Top three. [referring to funding police, probation officers, or prisons]

SUSAN: Yeah, exactly. That's true, top three.

MARY: Me too.

DORIAN: I think that's the worst government funding that they've given us, because . . . they've added new police, right? And if you're within our community . . . Tell me if I'm wrong, right?

SUSAN: You're scared of them.

DORIAN: I'm definitely scared of them.

SUSAN: Yeah, you're scared of them.

DORIAN: If you're walking or driving in the streets, you rarely see a police officer.

SUSAN: You see it on the news every day. They're shooting young people in the back. You see it all over the place.

DORIAN: Now every other three to six months, they're hiring new officers. You don't see them out here, though. You rarely see a police car.

JOSEPH: Where they at?

DORIAN: Tell me. [*laughs*] This is . . . Have you ever called 911?

MATTHEW: No. Hell, no.

On this point, Focus Group 4 was unique. Joseph (54, B, HSE, FG4) particularly struggled with the math of the budget exercise. He filled out two budget worksheets but did not indicate whether he wanted to throw the first one out. On his first worksheet, he allocated 10% of his budget each to police, probation, and prisons—a modest amount, but support nonetheless. On his second worksheet, he did not allocate any money toward criminal justice institutions. In either case, he was the only participant in this group who even considered criminal justice allocations. All other participants in this group exclusively allocated money toward community-based institutions and programs. Their antipathy toward the justice system was clear, and it impacted their policy choices. These participants evoked what criminologists refer to as the "overpolicing-underpolicing paradox." People of color in communities with high rates of crime frequently feel that the police are never there when you need them to stop violence, and yet they seem to be constantly present to question or harass residents who are simply going about their business.[5]

However, some White participants' spending preferences were also influenced by their distrust of law enforcement. Consider this exchange between Albert, Jason, and Camille in Focus Group 6:

ALBERT: I allocated 10% to the police department because they do
  need retraining.

MODERATOR: So how do you want to retrain them?

ALBERT: Well, like the body cameras.

JASON: Yeah, 10% for the body cameras maybe. Maybe I could have
  put that down.

CAMILLE: So we gotta waste money on body cameras because we can't
  trust the cops?

JASON: Yeah, exactly.

CAMILLE: You know what I mean? Like you're a cop, you shouldn't
  trust, your word should be . . .

JASON: Who's policing the police?

CAMILLE: And we're going to waste money on cameras because you're
  not trusted and we're supposed to trust you to save our life? Like that
  makes no sense. That's out of control!

MODERATOR: I take it you did not put any for body cameras.

CAMILLE: No.

This exchange echoed the disagreement between Baldwin and Timothy
in Focus Group 2. Albert is willing to grant some additional funding to
the police, but expressly for the purpose of retraining. That idea seemed
appealing to Jason. However, Camille felt that body cameras would be a
waste of money because the police are untrustworthy. Jason also seemed
to find Camille's perspective compelling, which suggests that the criminal justice preferences of poorer White people may be characterized
by ambivalence. Recall from chapter 2 that Pamela (60, W, HSE, FG6)
expressed support for the police and argued that they were being given a
bad rap by the media in contrast to Albert's suspicion and Camille's hostility. Given the diversity of less affluent White people's feelings toward
the police, this group of the population might be particularly susceptible
to the arguments made by politicians or media pundits to push their
own agendas for criminal justice.

Lastly, we must consider participants' write-in allocations—the
crime prevention options they added to their budgets after listening
to the prior group discussions about causes of crime and possible ways
to address crime. I have already noted that several participants chose

to channel funding toward criminal justice reform programs and extracurricular afterschool activities for youth. In table 3.2, we can also see that several participants wanted greater funding for programs and resources designed to ameliorate the strains of poverty, such as affordable housing and public assistance. For example, Jacklyn (32, B, HSE, FG2) said, "I put another 15% for food. You know you have programs or governmental assistance, whether it's the SNAP benefits or the WIC or whatever. You know food is a huge thing, you know what I'm saying? You have the food pantries, it's just not enough in some cases, and a lot of people go hungry, so for extra I put 15%." Linda (56, B, HSE, FG4) expressed a desire for expanded access to daycare and public transportation:

> LINDA: I put 20% in daycare. And 20% for transportation, even though . . .
>
> MODERATOR: Tell me about transportation. What are you thinking? Are you thinking you want to give the T more money?[6] Or do you want something . . . ?
>
> LINDA: Yeah, give the T more money so these young adults can get out there and buy their bus passes.
>
> MODERATOR: Okay. So you want to be able to give more folks money to use the transportation that we have?
>
> LINDA: Right.

Once again, these participants communicated that they perceived crime to be inextricable from the challenges caused by financial strain and underfunded community resources.

High school educated participants wrote most of the allocations that were designed to improve subsidized housing or public assistance programs. The college educated Black participants of Focus Group 3 also allocated money toward community-based resources, but the programs they proposed echoed the group's dominant theme that Black Americans need to foster personal responsibility and self-sufficiency within their own community (as discussed in chapter 2). Melissa allocated 25% of her budget toward the default "creating jobs" option, but she also allocated an additional 25% into "nonprofit, community-based job training/reentry." She explained,

MELISSA: Twenty-five percent for creating jobs . . . There's an organization that I'm really involved with that provides reentry training,
which I teach for, and we do a literary piece, a job training piece. I
teach them how to interview. I teach them how to do a résumé and
then they get real job training, and we're faith based. So, their success
rate, you know these gentlemen have CORIs and we . . . you know
one of my older students was in his sixties, and he had very low
self-esteem. My role wasn't really to teach them so much as to build
their esteem. [They believe] "I can't do this, I can't do this," but by the
end of it, it's a twelve-week cycle . . . one guy got three jobs. When he
thought he couldn't do anything. So he's on his way.

MODERATOR: Are you putting the rest of your money into that program?

MELISSA: Putting . . . into organizations that are in place that do this,
'cause people like to quit when they see no money, people who are
successful at doing this, who know what they're doing. We give them
the money that they've been fighting to get already, that's always . . .
They're the first to have their money taken away when there's budget
cuts. So, increase their funding. Ten percent for scholarships, for
communities. Scholarships . . .

MODERATOR: For college? Scholarships to where?

MELISSA: Educational scholarships. They could be job training so if
someone wants to be a chef they need the necessary food service
training.

MODERATOR: Okay, so any kind of training.

MELISSA: So any kind . . . HVAC. If you know that you can do electrical
repair, you don't have the money, you'll get the scholarship. And then
10% for PR initiatives because how can people participate in programs
that they don't know are in place? So, it's mandated that you put them
in high-risk communities: billboards, ads, radio spots, websites . . .

MODERATOR: What are high-risk communities?

MELISSA: Um, with high crime. So, we have the data statistics saying
what the crime areas are. What the recidivism rates are, what this
whole in and out's about. Okay, leaflet. No, let's do this. You find an
organization, you have all these nonprofits that are making money off
everybody, that are serving the same populations, that make phone
calls about the same people, okay? Fund them to get ads into them
and say, "Okay, yeah, these things are in place."

William allocated 60% of his budget into financial life skills classes:

> WILLIAM: Five percent in skills or teaching people in the city about purchasing property and real estate laws and rules. . . . So people can buy their own properties, okay? Because the reason why Northeastern [University] is taking over is because no one owns that land, so they don't have any opposition and [community residents] don't know how to do that cause they have no past skills. Twenty percent for teaching soft skills to children and adults because a lot of . . . You can't teach your children if you don't know. I have a friend who's fifty years old, and she can't read or write. I never knew that, and then her son was taking us to her house and he didn't know how to read or write, so I realized it was generational. Twenty percent to classes for future skills needed for financing classes because people don't know how to manage their money. Sheldon works for me, and him and I recently did a thing at [name blinded], a town meeting. . . .
>
> RACHELLE: What was it about?
>
> WILLIAM: It was a town hall meeting [about] what can we do in the Black community . . .
>
> SHELDON: For economics.
>
> WILLIAM: For economics to get more money and more jobs and stuff like that. [cross talk, Sheldon: "And folks came out."] And that's where all this information . . . A year ago I didn't even have any inkling that these are the skills, you know . . . They did a survey on how much money the average Black person in Dorchester or Roxbury have in their bank account, as opposed to someone in Newton,[7] which is $200,000. [*laughter*] It was $700 in Roxbury, the average bank accounts. . . . So Blacks need to know more about financing, to teaching classes on that and that's it, 20% I'm budgeting. Okay?

Like their fellow Black participants in Focus Groups 2 and 4, Melissa and William recognized the Black community's resource deficit.[8] But whereas many of the high school educated participants focused on "giving a man a fish" in order to meet people's immediate needs of food and shelter, Melissa and William focused on "teaching a man to fish" in order to empower Black people to succeed in the labor market and achieve financial autonomy and self-determination.

Lastly, a few participants allocated money toward physical changes to neighborhood infrastructure. Brandon (49, B, CE, FG1) said, "thirty percent for public housing standards. I call that like the 'broken windows' things where you can fix up the buildings in public housing. Maybe the people will care about it more. Because [if] people don't care about their building, then they're not gonna care about crime going on. And that's why if somebody gets shot, nobody says anything, and then the police can't solve crimes because nobody will cooperate with them." Similarly, Jack in Focus Group 6, said:

JACK: I just put down 25% more camera coverage on surveillance.
MODERATOR: Like street surveillance?
PAMELA: They're everywhere.
JACK: Yeah, streets or any place where you think a crime might happen. Because they seem to be very helpful, you know. Put up everything you see on television.

Brandon explicitly referenced the broken windows theory, which posits that crime is more common in run-down, dilapidated neighborhoods because physical disorder signals an absence of informal social control among neighbors.[9] Jack's endorsement of surveillance cameras is consistent with routine activities theory's emphasis on target hardening.[10] Both men recognized that the quality and physical design of neighborhood space affects the things that people do in their communities.

Pondering the Relationship between Allocations and Perceptions of Institutional Effectiveness

When Kathlyn Gaubatz, author of *Crime in the Public Mind*, interviewed members of the public in 1987, she sought to understand why America had arrived at a political consensus in favor of punitive criminal justice policies.[11] She was particularly interested in a puzzle: why did most Americans express support for longer, harsher sentences at the same time that they were not particularly confident that imprisonment actually rehabilitated offenders or deterred crime? Most of the people she interviewed expressed a variety of rationalizations. Some believed that "incarceration would be effective, if only it were more widely used, or the sentences were longer, or the conditions were harsher."[12] Others believed that prisons simply were not making a sufficient effort at rehabilitation. Others supported imprisonment because it kept offenders off the street, even temporarily. And others offered no rationalization; they simply supported imprisonment because, "What else is there to do?"[13]

Public support for harsh punishment has declined significantly since Gaubatz conducted her research in the late 1980s.[14] My focus groups also suggest that Americans are no longer willing to support prisons despite their perceived ineffectiveness. Several participants explained that they chose to give police, probation, or (especially) prisons no money in their budgets precisely because they believed that the criminal justice system is not the most effective means of preventing crime. Consider this perspective from Timothy (54, B, HSE, FG2):

> MODERATOR: Now Timothy, you said that it was really easy. Why was it really easy for you to decide how to split up the money?
>
> TIMOTHY: Because the least effective gets less than somewhere like, for instance, funding for more schools. You know, you give your school more than hiring more police officers.
>
> MODERATOR: So, because the school gives you a better output, a better ending, or . . . ?
>
> TIMOTHY: Well, not so much a better output but just, you know, more money where it's going to be benefit.
>
> MODERATOR: Okay, so more money in the schools is gonna benefit?
>
> TIMOTHY: Right
>
> MODERATOR: Okay. And what did you give less money to?
>
> TIMOTHY: I gave less to prisons.

As I reported earlier in this chapter, Timothy went on to express his belief that "prisons [are] not the answer." Importantly, when the moderator asked if he made his choice because he believed that schools are more effective at preventing crime than prisons, he did not seem convinced that schools actually deliver a "better output," yet he still felt that investing money into schools instead of prisons would be of greater "benefit."

Similarly, Matthew (55, B, HSE, FG4) said the following about his budget:

MATTHEW: It was easy for me because I've been through the court system. I'm pretty sure all of us [in the focus group] been through there at some point in time. I've been through the court system. That court system is full of shit. It's full of shit.

MODERATOR: Okay. So you knew the first three were out. [referring to police, probation, and prisons]

MATTHEW: Yeah, the first three, they get nothing. But the second . . . The rest of them, I said 20% clinics and providing a better healthcare. You've got 20% increasing funds for public schools, 20% in creating jobs, 10% to pay teachers a little more. You know what I'm saying?

However, just as Timothy allocated money toward schools even though he was not entirely confident in schools' ability to deliver better crime prevention outcomes than prisons, Matthew later had the following to say about public schools:

Could I say something? We've been talking about the public school many times. My public school system is supposed to be the best. It's not, be-cause if it was that good, we wouldn't have all these charter schools pop-ping up. You know what I'm saying? You need to have some people that are taking control of the education of these kids. You know what I mean? They open up these charter schools and whatnot because most of the Boston public school system, it sucks. It honestly sucks. These kids go there and if you got like . . . Like I'm a teacher, you're the teacher, we're all the teacher, then we got these bad ass kids in here. We don't know if they got guns in their lockers, in their car, whatever. If they . . . You know, I'm trying to teach you something. You tell me you don't want to do it, I'm going to leave you alone. These charter schools have more family values and more family structure behind them because you have parents like yourself or whatever saying, "Okay, this is where I'm going to put my kid at." You know what I mean? It's going to be better for them, versus getting on the MBTA.[15] It's just sad that that's how it is.

Matthew chose to allocate money into public schools despite his belief that the Boston public school system "sucks." He was not alone in this sentiment. Jacklyn from Focus Group 2 said, "I put increase in funding in public schools, I put 10%. And I know that's kind of low, but I put it because I feel like a lot of stuff they teach you in school is false. That's just my personal opinion. It's not accurate *at all*. . . . I remember being in school, asking the teacher, like, are we gonna ever use this in life? You know what I'm saying? Half the stuff you don't; you just don't."

An important reversal may have happened in American culture. Whereas Gaubatz found that most of her participants in the 1980s were willing to support prisons despite believing they were not terribly effective at preventing crime, a majority of the participants in my 2016 focus groups rejected funding for prisons (and often police and probation) because they deemed them to be ineffective at best or harmful at worst. In contrast, several participants expressed low levels of confidence in the quality of the Boston public schools, and yet they joined most of the other participants in allocating money toward public schools nonetheless. Perhaps today the American public favors investing in community-based institutions even though people feel that such investments might be a bit of a gamble that might not pay off. Americans' willingness to gamble their support on inefficient, untrustworthy prisons may have run out.

Fault Lines and Tremors of Backlash

The focus group data also suggest that Americans' "change of heart" against the criminal justice system in early twenty-first century America may not necessarily be a consensus position. Consider the budget preferences of Alice and Bruce, two of the college educated White participants in Focus Group 5. Bruce was the only participant in the focus groups who predominantly allocated his money toward criminal justice institutions. In fact, he gave the single largest allocation toward prisons. Whereas most participants did not spend a lot of time explaining or justifying their allocations into community institutions, Bruce did not justify his criminal justice allocations. And whereas most participants did explain why they allocated nothing toward criminal justice, Bruce specifically explained why he allocated no money toward public schools:

> MODERATOR: Anything you didn't want to give money to?
> BRUCE: Increasing funding to public schools. It's a cash cow already. Tremendous amounts of money flowing into public schools.

ALICE: I think it's the way they use it, is the way . . .

MODERATOR: Okay. That makes sense. It's your budget. You get to spend it. You divided yours equally, right, Bruce?

BRUCE: Yeah. I did. . . .

MODERATOR: Where'd you put your money?

BRUCE: Hiring more police officers, hiring more probations officer, building new jails and prisons. And creating jobs.

Alice's budget was relatively more balanced between criminal justice and community-based allocations than Bruce's budget, but pay particular attention to her goals for her public school allocation (recall from earlier in this chapter that Alice allocated 20% of her budget toward gang prevention by the police):

ALICE: I also had 10% for probation officers and supervising the offenders in the community, only because if they're already done their time, and they want to come out and get back into the community, they do need training and people to help lead them that way. If you don't have any probation officers watching, like to try and keep them on the right side of the law, then that's why . . . So not like people tailing people, but people helping them to stay out of trouble. I had 20% for clinics; for health care, and mental health care services. Fifteen percent for public schools. But again, that goes to you have to allow the teachers to be able to discipline and teach and . . .

MODERATOR: Right. Rather than just throwing money at the school.

ALICE: Right. And just not hiring more headmasters for exorbitant amount of money and not being able to discipline kids.

MODERATOR: Right.

ALICE: Creating jobs, 20%. And my something else was 15% community resource . . . I put community resources, but arts, sports, things for people. For the community . . .

MODERATOR: Okay, so not just for kids, so everyone can be involved?

ALICE: Yeah. Senior centers . . . everything.

Some of Alice's budget choices are progressive in nature, such as funding community centers and funding probation officers to better connect probationers to resources instead of focusing solely on surveillance. On the other hand, her opinions about schools have a punitive edge. Unlike Bruce, she is not willing to abandon public schools entirely, but her foremost desire is that schools reinstitute "discipline" for youth. Recall from chapter 2 that Bruce and Alice's opinions about public schools were focused on schools in Lawrence, the poorer, majority-Latino town that borders their own, more affluent, nearly 90% White town of Methuen. As such, their opinions about waste and inefficiency in public schools had a racialized undertone.

Beyond the question of school funding, the budget discussion in Focus Group 5 sparked the single most contentious disagreement between participants in the entire study. I report this exchange in its entirety because I think it shines an important light on the ideological fault lines that produce an undercurrent of uncertainty within criminal justice reform efforts.[16]

> INEZ: I was just thinking of something you said, there are lots of levels of crimes and people who commit them. And I think one of the big things, being impoverished, poverty, areas of extreme poverty, not just the cities, but rural areas. West Virginia, those kind of places. They don't have options, so you've got to give them more options. That's why the art programs, they don't even know the stuff is out there for them. They just have no idea. Anyway, I did pretty much what most people did. I gave 25% to demilitarizing the police and allowing enough funding for training. The police have been in the news a lot lately, and one of the things a lot of their leadership have been saying is . . . at the local level, they don't have any money for training. None.
> MODERATOR: So you're giving them some money for training?
> INEZ: Yeah.
> MODERATOR: Okay.
> INEZ: And continuous training for all law enforcement so that they understand how to deal with the mentally ill. How to deal with whoever the committers of crime are . . . and they don't use unreasonable force in those kinds of things. Twenty-five percent to hiring more probation officers, but really training them. And also liaison from prison or jails to the community for nonviolent offenders. And even giving them money, making . . . don't release anyone unless they've got a job and a place to live. And even setting them up, that's where

a lot of the money would go. With some kind of stipend so that they're not going to go back in. [some cross talk between participants omitted] And then 25% creating jobs. Job training and if necessary, well, first of all knowing where the jobs are in terms of our society, then providing job training in those jobs. And even giving them . . . having a pot of money so they . . . if the jobs aren't there in that community, then allowing people to move. Giving them the ability, the means, to get out of their situation. And then 25% for free community college. I know the governor did something, but I just didn't think he went far enough with that.

MODERATOR: Okay. It's your budget. You get to give some more money there. Bruce, did you want to comment?

BRUCE: Oh, yeah. Definitely. If someone stole my car or robbed my house, and they get out of jail and they were going to have a job, an apartment, and a stipend . . . sign me up for that instead! [*laughing*] No way. They should not be getting anything coming out.

INEZ: May I explain myself, Bruce?

BRUCE: Not . . . not . . . not a thing. Sorry.

INEZ: Bruce, may I explain myself?

BRUCE: Sure.

INEZ: This is after they do their time. This is for nonviolent offenders. Nothing that went [inaudible].

BRUCE: They . . . a nonviolent offender, if someone steals my car, they didn't attack me. But you know what? It costs me the loss of my car, my transportation.

INEZ: But you know, Bruce, if that . . . But it's costing society a lot of money in terms of . . .

BRUCE: You want to give them a stipend?

INEZ: . . . just to get back into the community, get their job . . .

BRUCE: Oh, my God! They should have thought of this before they stole my car!

JANET: Oh, boy, there you go.

INEZ: But that kind of reasoning is one of the reasons . . .

BRUCE: Really?

INEZ: . . . I think there are so many people in jail. I think it contributes to it.

NATHAN: Yes, I agree with you.

BRUCE: So you want them to go to jail and get a stipend when they come out of jail? Sign me up.

INEZ: That's not what I'm saying.

ALICE: I think the problem is that . . . there are a lot of people that commit crimes, that get away with it, and then they turn around, they don't think "Great, look at what the city did for me. They're giving me something and they're helping me get better." It's like "Hey, I got away with it. I'm just going to go . . . I like his BMW . . ."

INEZ: No, they're not getting away with it.

NATHAN: No, we don't know. We don't know what goes on in people's minds.

INEZ: They're doing their time. They might spend five years in jail, and then do you really want them to come out with nothing? [some cross talk between participants omitted]

MODERATOR: Everybody gets to choose their own budgets. Okay? Like I said, we're not trying to come up with solutions for all of this. Everyone gets to put money in whatever program they're thinking works. Okay?

NATHAN: But it's true, though, their homelessness for a . . . for somebody released from prison is a cost. To get involved with more crime and go back to prison.

Inez's budget choices were clearly based upon a strain-theory-style belief that poverty is a significant cause of crime—so much so that she advocated that people leaving prison be given direct cash benefits to help them pay for their immediate physical needs (like housing). Giving former offenders stipends sounds like a radical idea, but this policy has been successfully implemented in a few American cities and shown to reduce recidivism.[17]

Bruce and Alice's reactions to Inez's proposal were textbook volitional criminology. Bruce adamantly rejected the idea that a criminal should be rewarded with a stipend. Inez argued that stipend programs would provide greater benefit to society if they helped former offenders avoid being sucked back into crime because they were too poor to legally support themselves. But Bruce replied that criminals "should have thought about" the consequences of their actions before committing a crime. Alice supported Bruce's perspective and argued that a stipend would only teach criminals that they "got away with it." These are volitional attributions that frame crime purely as a free choice based upon anticipated costs or benefits. Though volitional criminology may no longer be the dominant belief among Americans, it is not dead and gone. People like Bruce and Alice who still adhere to a strongly volitional understanding of crime are the kinds of voters who might mobilize against a policymaker who supports criminal justice reform, just as Bruce reacted vehemently against Inez's proposal.

Given the racialized politics of punishment in the United States, it is not surprising that volitional, punitive sentiments emerged in the focus group of more highly educated, comparatively more affluent White participants. However, scholars are increasingly paying attention to the ways in which punitive sentiment among middle- and upper-class Black Americans created class divisions within the Black community and contributed to the rise of mass incarceration.[18] I found evidence of punitive, volitional sentiments among the college educated Black participants of Focus Group 3, as well. Consider the following statement by Adam:

> ADAM: Increasing funding to the public schools is 20%, creating jobs, originally I said 25%, I raised it to 35%, and then the other 0% I said I wanted to have better shelters for the homeless 'cause it seems like there's not enough homeless shelters, and not only just homeless shelters for the homeless but like single mothers who are homeless with kids. Kind of you know the thing is what I noticed is that . . . If you put someone into a program and they're already disenfranchised and then you give them free stuff, that's not teaching them to have the mentality to thrive, to strive. And that's really pretty much what it is.
>
> RACHELLE: That's right!
>
> ADAM: Like these programs that they have in the shelters and then these women wait in the shelters, I know a couple people that happened to, and then they wait and they get put right into a Section 8 home and then they attract the same kind of guy that they weren't supposed to attract . . . [laughter] And house him there, you know what I'm saying? And then all the stereotypes and the statistics start all over again and it's just a setup for a cycle of destruction. That's it.
>
> RACHELLE: That's true.

Adam's budget choices are quite different from Bruce's. Adam only allocated 5% of his budget toward police, and he put the rest of his budget toward community-based institutions. While his allocations might make it seem that he has a solidly progressive ideology, his statement here reveals that he also has a strongly volitional streak to his beliefs.

Adam initially considered writing an allocation for homeless shelters because he perceived that the current supply does not meet the need. However, he changed his mind once he thought about how giving single mothers experiencing homelessness "free stuff" would not "teach them to have the mentality to strive," and would instead only encourage them to "attract the same kind of guy that they weren't supposed to attract." This is the kind of volitional attribution of poverty that generations of (White) politicians, across the administrations of Nixon, Reagan, and Clinton, used to substantially change and restrict welfare programs in the United States.[19] Adam was not alone in this sentiment. Later in the discussion, William said the following:

> WILLIAM: Well, here's a question I have for the group, and it's been bothering me lately, really a great deal and it's . . . I live right in the heart of the opiate, um, they call it "Methadone Mile."[20] And I've called the police so much that they made a hotline that the woman who answered the phone invited me for Thanksgiving dinner. [*laughter*] I'm serious, I am serious, okay. But anyway, what I noticed is there's—because I'm right there and I see it, I'm not just speculating—there's two kinds of different homeless people. You know? It's the people that, mothers that been living paycheck to paycheck and all of the sudden they're homeless or whatever reason, and then there's people who are professional homeless people. And I was asking a friend of mine who was homeless, "How come all the homeless people have brand new sneakers?" He said, because, [cross talk, unidentified female speaker: "Because they get their check!"] no they give 'em to them, they give 'em out. And then at 12:00 in my neighborhood in the afternoon there's no homeless people, so I asked, where . . . They go to lunch. [*laughter*] At 5:00 they disappear. So they have it made. And then they do their . . . Always clean, they have their laundry for forty-five cents. So they have their whole, no responsibilities, so they. . . . [inaudible, cross talk]

ADAM: Enabling, they're enabling them.

WILLIAM: So then you have the ones who they don't have any skills and nowadays with all this new electronic stuff they won't have any skills because these young kids are taking jobs, so they're not even thinking about getting a job because they don't qualify for nothing. And they know they don't qualify. So these people are gonna be homeless, and then how do you separate helping the people who really need homelessness from these people who, you know what I mean? So I don't know, that's the thing, yeah, the shelters and stuff, that's the thing that I'm sort of at a quandary over.

Like Adam, William sees differences between the "deserving" and "undeserving" poor. This perception is likely related to William's allocations toward programs that would empower Black Americans to "pull themselves up by their bootstraps," in contrast to the kinds of direct financial assistance tied to need endorsed by many of the high school educated participants. These findings suggest that the neoliberal cultural emphasis on hard work and individual autonomy has penetrated quite deeply into the upper echelons of the Black community and exacerbated class differences therein.[21] These beliefs are not uniform. Christopher immediately disagreed with William by saying to him, "So you see a difference there, but I'm not so sure that that difference is legitimate." Regardless, the existence of intraracial class divisions in beliefs about whom is deserving of assistance could potentially be exploited to mobilize a diverse coalition of voters to oppose community investment.

National Survey Findings

My focus group data suggest that Americans in the early twenty-first century would prefer to invest more money into community-based institutions and programs than into the criminal justice system to prevent crime. However, the participants in my focus groups were a small, self-selected group who reside in one single metropolitan area. Their policy preferences might be significantly different from those of Americans who reside in different parts of the country. The purpose of qualitative methods like focus groups is to gain deep understanding of people's beliefs and worldviews, not to measure trends across large populations. The latter goal is the purpose of quantitative methods like public opinion surveys. It is time to compare the findings from my focus groups against findings from survey data, which are more representative of wider swaths of the United States population.[22]

I designed a national survey of White and Black Americans to complement the focus group discussion prompts about the core principles of justice reinvestment. I presented the survey respondents with the following scenario: "Now please imagine that you are the governor of a state that has saved money by sentencing more nonviolent offenders to community-based supervision instead of sending them to prison. How would you spend this extra money? Please check all of the options to which you would choose to give money. You do not have to give money to every option unless you want to. Choose only the ones you want to fund." Respondents were then presented the following options:

- Hiring more police officers
- Hiring more probation officers to supervise offenders in the community
- Funding clinics to provide improved healthcare and mental healthcare services for residents of [___ communities]
- Increasing funding to the public schools in [___ communities]
- Funding economic development programs in order to create jobs in [___ communities]
- Give money back to taxpayers in your state through a tax rebate

On a second screen of the survey, respondents were then reshown only the options they indicated that they wanted to fund (with the exact same language), and they were asked, "Now we'd like to know what percent of the extra money you want to spend on these options. The total should add up to 100%." A running tally on the webpage helped respondents allocate a total amount that added up to 100%. Respondents who only selected a single category in the first stage of the question were automatically recorded as allocating 100% of their budget toward that category, thereby skipping the allocation screen.

In contrast to the focus group budget task, the survey respondents' options did not include funding prison construction because this question adhered more closely to the justice reinvestment model, which presupposes that budget savings will come from decarceration.[23] I also added a tax rebate option that was not provided to the focus group participants.[24] Still, the focus group and national survey questions and budget items are similar enough that they both allow us to assess Americans' relative preference for investing in criminal justice system versus community-based institutions. The [___] symbol indicates the presence of a framing experiment treatment, but since I will analyze the experiment in chapter 4, just ignore that symbol for now.

Table 3.3 presents survey respondents' budget allocations. You can compare this information to the focus group findings presented in table 3.1. A few patterns are evident. First, the average percentage of money allocated toward each budget option was substantially higher than the comparable averages among the focus group participants. This is likely because the averages presented in table 3.3 include the "100%" responses from participants who allocated all of their money toward only one budget option. None of the focus group participants chose only one allocation, whereas many of the survey respondents poured all their money into a single pot. The presence of the 100% responses in the calculations raises the mean values. This difference reveals one limitation of the focus group findings; they did not capture the fact that some Americans choose a single-minded focus when offered the opportunity to fund many different policy options.

The second difference between the focus group and survey sample allocations was that the survey respondents allocated similar amounts of money into all six categories, on average. Whereas most of the focus group participants allocated little to no money toward police or probation, the average allocation into hiring more police or probation officers among the survey respondents was relatively comparable to the average allocation into the community institution options of clinics, schools, and job creation programs. The group of Boston-area residents who participated in my focus groups were collectively more opposed to the idea of giving police and probation departments additional money than were Americans at large. Still, the survey findings indicate that the prospect of giving extra funding to police and probation is more polarizing for Americans than the prospect of additional funding for community institutions. Look at the 0% and 100% responses among the full

TABLE 3.3. Average Percent Budget Allocation for Crime Prevention Options among National Survey Participants

	% More Police	% More Probation	% Funding Healthcare Clinics	% Funding Public Schools	% Funding Job Creation	% Tax Rebate
All Participants						
· Average Allocation	40.54%	33.27%	33.21%	36.54%	38.97%	44.64%
· # 100%	95	79	62	62	130	146
· # Zeros	1,173	1,004	965	950	855	1,150
N = 1,812						
White Participants						
· Average Allocation	45.88%	37.15%	35.44%	36.46%	40.97%	53.28%
· # 100%	70	47	29	22	64	91
· # Zeros	510	489	568	598	534	595
N = 914						
Black Participants						
· Average Allocation	31.79%	28.91%	31.59%	36.58%	37.60%	36.28%
· # 100%	25	32	33	40	66	55
· # Zeros	663	515	397	352	321	555
N = 898						
College Educated Participants						
· Average Allocation	38.87%	33.26%	32.13%	37.68%	37.96%	45.58%
· # 100%	56	52	36	43	81	92
· # Zeros	762	623	624	597	550	779
N = 1,176						
High School Educated Participants						
· Average Allocation	43.35%	33.29%	34.80%	34.62%	40.54%	43.47%
· # 100%	39	27	26	19	49	54
· # Zeros	411	381	341	353	305	371
N = 636						
Republicans						
· Average Allocation	49.27%	39.73%	31.00%	35.27%	41.84%	53.09%
· # 100%	55	34	13	9	39	60
· # Zeros	278	306	404	404	353	339
N = 561						

TABLE 3.3. *(cont.)*

	% More Police	% More Probation	% Funding Healthcare Clinics	% Funding Public Schools	% Funding Job Creation	% Tax Rebate
Independents						
· Average Allocation	43.78%	31.57%	34.90%	37.10%	44.06%	56.45%
· # 100%	5	2	3	3	6	10
· # Zeros	51	54	46	46	41	43
N = 74						
Democrats						
· Average Allocation	32.98%	30.32%	33.68%	36.82%	37.85%	39.01%
· # 100%	35	43	46	50	85	76
· # Zeros	844	644	515	500	461	768
N = 1,177						
Metro Area Resident						
· Average Allocation	40.69%	32.57%	33.33%	36.77%	38.98%	43.84%
· # 100%	89	67	57	58	119	122
· # Zeros	1,039	891	851	822	750	1,024
N = 1,600						
Rural Resident						
· Average Allocation	39.64%	37.92%	32.39%	34.61%	38.93%	49.08%
· # 100%	6	12	5	4	11	24
· # Zeros	134	113	114	128	105	126
N = 212						

Note: Average allocation is calculated only from the participants who chose to allocate money toward each particular budget item. It excludes the participants who choose to allocate no money toward the item (the 0% responses). I applied the survey weight to the calculation of the average allocation.

sample of participants. More people chose to give police and probation no money than chose to give clinics, schools, or job creation programs no money, but so too did more people choose to give all their money to either police or probation than allocate 100% of their budgets into clinics, schools, or job programs.

For an easier analysis of the survey respondents' budget allocation preferences across demographic characteristics, I reestimated the average allocations to include both the 0% responses of respondents who skipped a category and the 100% responses of respondents who chose to fund only one category. Including both the 0% responses and the 100% responses in the calculations reduced the average allocation in each category compared to the averages presented in table 3.3, but this calculation condenses the full picture of respondents' preferences into a single measure for each budget category. I present these mean allocations first for the full sample and then divided across participants' race, level of education, political partisanship, and urban versus rural residence in table 3.4.

Table 3.4 shows that, on average, Americans allocated similar amounts of money into both criminal justice and community institution crime prevention options, as well as into a tax rebate for citizens. Some of the differences of priorities across demographic characteristics that we observed among the focus group participants were replicated in

TABLE **3.4.** Average Percent Budget Allocation for Crime Prevention Options among National Survey Participants across Demographic Characteristics

	% More Police	% More Probation	% Funding Healthcare Clinics	% Funding Public Schools	% Funding Job Creation	% Tax Rebate
All Participants	13.7	14.6	15.8	17.5	20.7	16.7
White Participants	18.8[a]	16.8[a]	13.8[a]	12.9[a]	17.2[a]	19.1[a]
Black Participants	8.4[a]	12.3[a]	17.8[a]	22.4[a]	24.3[a]	14.2[a]
College Educated Participants	13.9	15.8	15	18.7[b]	20.2	15.7
High School Educated Participants	13.7	12.9	16.9	15.7[b]	21.4	18.4
Republicans	23.9[c]	17.6[c]	8.9[c]	10.4[c]	16.3[c]	21.7[c]
Independents	12.4[c]	8.4[c]	11.5	13.8	19.3	25.7
Democrats	9[c]	13.7[c]	19.3[c]	21.1[c]	22.8[c]	13.8[c]
Metro Area Residents	13.7	14.4	15.9	18.2[d]	20.8	16.1
Rural Residents	13.9	16.2	14.9	13.2[d]	19.8	20.8

Notes: Average allocation in this table is calculated based upon all participants, including participants who choose to allocate no money toward the item (the 0% responses) and participants who allocated their entire budgets toward a single item (the 100% responses). I applied the survey weight to the calculation of the average allocation.
a = Difference in average allocation between White and Black participants significantly different at $p < 0.05$.
b = Difference in average allocation between high school educated and college educated participants significantly different at $p < 0.05$.
c = Difference in average allocation between Democrats and Republicans or independents and Republicans significantly different at $p < 0.05$.
d = Difference in average allocation between metro area residents and rural residents significantly different at $p < 0.05$.

the survey findings. White participants allocated more money toward police, probation, and a tax rebate than Black participants, on average, and vice versa in regard to clinics, schools, and job creation programs. The average allocation among Black versus White participants was significantly different across all six budget categories, statistically speaking. In contrast, high school educated and college educated respondents allocated similar amounts of money into most categories. These two groups of participants only significantly differed in regard to funding public schools, for which college educated participants allocated more money, on average.

The survey data also allow us to analyze the influence of other demographic characteristics that I did not measure or could not capture in the focus groups, notably political partisanship and urban versus rural residence. The strongest predictor of Americans' vote choices is typically their political party affiliation, which means that legislators pay special attention to the policy preferences of voters who are members of their same party.[25] In addition, Americans who reside in urban versus rural areas are expressing increasingly pronounced political and policy disagreements in the twenty-first century, which is fueling national-level political gridlock.[26] Republican survey respondents allocated significantly more money into police and probation than both independents and Democrats, on average. The average allocations of independents and Republicans into clinics, schools, job creation programs, and a tax rebate did not significantly differ. In contrast, Democrats significantly differed from Republicans in all categories. Democrats allocated significantly more money toward the three community institution options, whereas Republicans allocated significantly more money toward the tax rebate in addition to police and probation, on average. On the other hand, the urban-rural divide that has become so important in American politics may not meaningfully impact Americans' crime prevention policy preferences. Urban survey respondents only significantly differed from rural residents in regard to funding public schools, where the former group allocated more money than the latter group. So far, the survey data indicate that American disagreement about crime prevention policy is much more a function of race and political partisanship than it is a function of education (social class) or urban versus rural residence.

However, the data presented in table 3.4 are somewhat "smoothed" because they present average allocations within different groups of respondents. Not every respondent allocated money into every category, so the conclusion that Americans prefer a balanced crime prevention budget may be a function of the measurement and analysis I have employed so far. To investigate this possibility, I categorized the survey respondents according to their overall investment preferences in the same manner that I categorized the focus group participants in table 3.2. Since I am most interested in assessing Americans' willingness to fund community investment, I grouped investment into a tax rebate alongside investment into police or probation in several categories because both would channel money away from community institutions. I present the results of this analysis in table 3.5.

These findings shine an even clearer light on the different priorities of White and Black Americans. About a third of Black respondents allocated money solely into community clinics, schools, or job creation programs, and an additional third of Black respondents allocated at least 75% of their budget into community institutions. That means that nearly 60% of Black Americans prefer that more money be invested into communities than into criminal justice institutions or simply handed back to individual citizens as a tax rebate. The next largest group of Black

TABLE 3.5. National Survey Respondents Categorized According to Their Budget Preferences across Race

Budget Preference Category	Black Respondents	White Respondents
Only Community	29.33%	21.26%
Mostly Community	29.77%	15.33%
Balanced	18.00%	15.84%
Mostly CJS or Tax	2.10%	6.66%
Only CJS or Tax	8.42%	21.09%
Mostly Tax, then Community	5.06%	3.24%
Mostly Tax, then CJS	0.98%	4.96%
Mostly Tax, Split Rest	0.65%	1.07%
Only Tax	5.69%	10.57%

Note: CJS: criminal justice system

Americans at 18% was those who roughly split their budgets between community institutions and criminal justice institutions or a tax rebate, or both. Only about 10% of Black respondents invested most or all of their budgets into criminal justice institutions or a tax rebate, or both. About 13% of Black respondents prioritized investment into the tax rebate in a variety of ways. About 6% allocated their entire budget into a tax rebate for citizens. About 5% allocated the single largest portion of their budget into a tax rebate but then prioritized community institutions for the remainder of their allocation. Only about 1% of respondents prioritized the tax rebate followed by criminal justice institutions, and even fewer prioritized the tax rebate and then evenly split the rest of their budget between community institutions and criminal justice institutions.

The investment preferences of White Americans were rather starkly different. Only one-fifth of White Americans chose to invest solely in community institutions, and an additional 15% allocated a majority of their funds into clinics, schools, or job creation programs, or a combination of the three. That means that about a third of White respondents prioritized community investments compared to two-thirds of Black respondents. An additional 16% of White respondents balanced their investments between community institutions and criminal justice institutions or a tax rebate, or both. In contrast, close to a third of White respondents prioritized criminal justice investment, and the largest portion of this group (21%) solely funded police, probation, or a tax rebate, or a combination of the three. A larger proportion of White respondents also prioritized the tax rebate compared to Black respondents. Ten and a half percent of White respondents invested all their money into the tax rebate—double the percentage of Black respondents who made that choice. Similarly, more White respondents who allocated the largest portion of their budgets into the tax rebate secondarily prioritized police or probation, or both, (about 5%) than the community institutions (about 3%).

Finally, let us consider the full scope of demographic differences across the American population that map onto political divisions. I ran a multinomial logit regression analysis to test how a variety of demographic and ideological characteristics related to respondents' budget preferences.[27] I present the full results of this analysis in appendix table A.4 for interested readers, but these regression results are very cumbersome to interpret. To simplify interpretation, I derived from this statistical model the predicted probability that a respondent would fall into one of the six budget preference categories.[28] In table 3.6, I present the predicted probabilities for eight different "ideal types" of respondents who vary across four key sources of disagreement in contemporary American politics: race, education, political partisanship, and urban versus rural residence.[29]

Incorporating multiple different dimensions of people's identities somewhat mutes the picture of divergence that emerged when we examined only race. Let's examine the preferences of two types of people who are "most different"—those who represent core bases of the Democratic and Republican parties: college educated Black people who live in urban areas and high school educated White people who live in rural

TABLE **3.6.** Predicted Probability of Budget Preference across Survey Respondent Ideal Types

	Only Community	Mostly Community	Balanced	Mostly CJS or Tax	Only CJS or Tax	Only Tax
			White Respondents			
High School, Republican, Rural	21.8% (13.1–30.5)	18.4% (8.6–28.2)	25.4% (16.0–34.8)	10.0% (3.3–16.6)	17.0% (9.1–25.0)	7.4% (2.9–12.0)
College, Republican, Urban	28.4% (20.7–36.2)	24.7% (17.2–32.2)	16.0% (10.7–21.3)	11.2% (5.5–16.9)	14.8% (8.7–20.9)	4.9% (2.2–7.5)
High School, Democrat, Rural	26.4% (17.6–35.3)	21.8% (12.5–31.0)	25.3% (16.0–34.5)	6.3% (1.6–10.9)	11.9% (6.1–17.7)	8.4% (3.2–13.6)
College, Democrat, Urban	33.7% (26.2–41.2)	28.5% (21.4–35.5)	15.5% (10.7–20.3)	6.9% (3.1–10.6)	10.1% (5.9–14.3)	5.4% (2.8–8.0)
			Black Respondents			
High School, Republican, Rural	22.7% (12.5–33.0)	19.5% (8.4–30.5)	27.7% (16.4–39.1)	5.7% (0.8–10.6)	16.1% (6.6–25.6)	8.3% (2.7–13.8)
College, Republican, Urban	30.0% (21.0–39.0)	26.3% (17.2–35.5)	17.6% (10.5–24.7)	6.5% (2.0–11.0)	14.1% (7.2–21.1)	5.5% (1.9–9.1)
High School, Democrat, Rural	27.0% (17.5–36.4)	22.5% (13.2–31.8)	26.9% (17.1–36.7)	3.5% (0.6–6.4)	11.0% (5.0–16.9)	9.2% (3.8–14.6)
College, Democrat, Urban	34.6% (27.6–41.6)	29.6% (23.0–36.2)	16.6% (11.4–21.9)	3.9% (1.6–6.1)	9.4% (5.6–13.2)	5.9% (2.9–8.9)

Notes: 95% confidence intervals presented in parentheses. Predicted probabilities derived from the multinomial logit model presented in appendix table A.4. Values of the other variables in that model are held constant at their mean values while estimating these predicted probabilities.

areas, respectively. Members of the latter group are predicted to be more likely to fall into the "balanced," "mostly CJS or tax," "only CJS or tax," and "only tax" categories than the former group, and vice versa for the community-based budget categories. However, looking at the confidence intervals, we see that most of these differences are not actually statistically significant across ideal types, and the model predicts that even White, high school educated Republicans who live in rural areas are more likely to fall into the "only community," "mostly community," or "balanced" categories than any of the three more punitive categories. We can also see that people who share race, education level, and urban or rural residence are predicted to be similarly likely to fall into each of the budget categories whether they are Republicans or Democrats.

Summary of Chapter Findings

What is the "big picture" message to take away from the analyses of the focus group and survey data I have presented in this chapter? First, the data presented in tables 3.3 and 3.4 show that the crime prevention spending preferences of White and Black Americans across the country are more varied than the spending preferences of the Boston-area participants in my focus groups. Respondents to the national survey were willing to allocate higher amounts of money toward hiring more police and probation officers than the focus group participants, on average. However, when we shift from examining average allocations into each budget category and instead examine respondents' overall funding preferences in table 3.5, we see that the preferences of the focus group participants were not as divergent from the preferences of other Americans as table 3.3 might have made them seem.

Both groups of White participants were relatively more supportive of criminal justice investment than community investment, but a majority of White participants expressed support for community investment nonetheless. While Bruce was pretty much alone in the focus groups in his strong preference for criminal justice investment over community investment, the survey suggests that about 27% of White Americans share his funding priorities—a notable proportion but far from a majority. Finally, the survey results reveal that when White and Black Americans are given a choice to fund crime prevention initiatives or just return money to citizens in the form of a tax rebate, about 12% of Black Americans and about 20% of White Americans devote a large portion of their budget toward the rebate, if not the entirety of their money. When the full sample of participants is analyzed as a whole, these data suggest that about a quarter of White and Black Americans might resist an effort by politicians to invest directly into the "human resources and physical infrastructure" of communities. However, it seems to me that this is a much smaller portion of people than policymakers assumed when they shied away from community investment, and the focus group data suggest that many Americans strongly believe that policies to reduce poverty and community deprivation would reduce crime.

The data indicate that there is a large audience of Americans who would be receptive to a message in favor of community investment. More important, and perhaps more of a surprise, are the findings presented in table 3.6. Groups of Americans characterized by demographic traits that put them on opposite sides of political fault lines in national politics are predicted to have rather similar likelihoods of expressing the same crime prevention budget preferences. Most respondents were predicted to favor community investment over criminal justice investment or a tax rebate. This is not to say that Americans never disagree. Bruce's vehement rejection of Inez's idea to provide financial assistance to former offenders reentering the community suggests that the minority of Americans who oppose community investment might be particularly vocal about their beliefs. Furthermore, Adam's dispositional attribution of poverty and rejection of allocating more money toward public housing for homeless mothers suggests that class divisions within the Black community might provide an opportunity for opponents of community investment to sow discord among Black Americans. However, the total picture of the findings presented in this chapter does not support many policymakers' assumption that voters would turn against them if they invested in at-risk communities.[30]

The concept of electoral backlash suggests either that people change their political opinions or become mobilized to vote by a particular issue when they might otherwise stay home. In the next chapter, I analyze the results of a framing experiment I embedded in the national survey. I designed this experiment to test the effect of alternative rhetorical framings of justice reinvestment proposals on people's policy preferences. I use this experiment to answer the questions, "Does people's willingness to invest in communities depend upon which communities would receive funding?" and "Does the way politicians talk about community investment alter Americans' policy preferences?"

4

How Framing Affects Public Investment Preferences

How stable is the public's preference for community investment over investment into the criminal justice system? As I discussed in the introductory chapter, debates about the distribution of public funds and benefits have divided Americans across "the color line" since at least the era of Reconstruction. Generations of White politicians weaponized racial stereotypes about laziness in order to disproportionately channel or outright restrict public assistance programs to the benefit of White Americans at the cost of Black Americans and other Americans of color.[1] Do these racial divisions persist in the twenty-first century? Does public support for investment into community institutions and programs depend upon which communities would benefit?

To answer these questions, I analyze the results of an experiment I embedded in my national survey. Recall the text of the key question that I reported in the previous chapter: "Now please imagine that you are the governor of a state that has saved money by sentencing more nonviolent offenders to community-based supervision instead of sending them to prison. How would you spend this extra money? Please check all of the options to which you would choose to give money. You do not have to give money to every option unless you want to. Choose only the ones you want to fund." Respondents were then presented the following options:

- Hiring more police officers
- Hiring more probation officers to supervise offenders in the community
- Funding clinics to provide improved healthcare and mental healthcare services for residents of [___communities]
- Increasing funding to the public schools in [___communities]

- Funding economic development programs in order to create jobs in [___communities]
- Give money back to taxpayers in your state through a tax rebate

My treatment stimulus was different adjectives that described a characteristic of the communities that would receive funding, as indicated by the [___] symbol above. The seven conditions were:

- Control group (only the word "communities" with no modifier)
- High crime communities
- High poverty communities
- Communities with many residents on welfare
- Inner-city communities
- Rural communities
- African American communities

Crime tends to be concentrated in particular places and cooccurring with numerous other social problems, like poverty, unemployment, and poor public health. Due to long-standing patterns of residential segregation in America, these neighborhoods where crime, poverty, and their associated social ills cluster together are also disproportionately majority-Black or majority-Latino communities.[2] Thus, all of the adjectives except for "rural communities" are equally valid descriptions of the kinds of neighborhoods that should receive reinvestment funds according to the original vision of justice reinvestment.[3] However, each treatment condition emphasizes a different aspect of the communities that would receive funds. This differential framing may bring to mind different thoughts, associations, and feelings in the respondents who are exposed to one treatment condition versus another.[4]

In the introductory chapter to this book, I discussed racial priming theory, a body of political science research which shows that exposure to racialized language or images can influence (predominantly White) Americans' policy preferences by activating prejudiced beliefs and attitudes. Importantly, cues can trigger racialized public backlash even if they do not explicitly mention race because generations of politicians learned to talk in "colorblind" language that evoked pejorative stereotypes in a broad manner that gave them plausible deniability about their racist intent.[5] This tactic was most (in)famously explained by Lee Atwater, a longtime advisor to President Richard Nixon:

> You start out in 1954 by saying, "N—r, n—r, n—r." By 1968 you can't say "n—r" —that hurts you, backfires. So you say stuff like, uh, forced busing, states' rights, and all that stuff, and you're getting so abstract. Now, you're talking about cutting taxes, and all these things you're talking about are totally economic things and a byproduct of them is, Blacks get hurt worse than Whites. . . . "We want to cut this," is much more abstract than even the busing thing, uh, and a hell of a lot more abstract than "N—r, n—r."[6]

I designed the treatment cues according to the tenets of racial priming theory. "High crime," "high poverty," "many residents on welfare," and "inner city" are all implicitly racialized cues that evoke Americans' (pejorative) cultural associations with racial minorities (especially Black people) without actually referencing race.[7] "African American" is, obviously, an explicit reference to the racial minority group. Finally, the "rural" condition is designed to be an implicit reference to White people to test whether Americans are simply opposed to particularized benefits directed toward only one group rather than equally available to all.[8] This last condition also evokes contemporary tensions between urban and rural residents regarding taxation and government programs.[9]

I hypothesize that White respondents who were told that "high-crime," "high-poverty," "many residents on welfare," and "inner-city" communities would receive funds would express greater support for funding police, probation, or a tax rebate than White respondents in the control group. In contrast, I hypothesize that White respondents who were explicitly told that "African American" communities would receive funds would express greater support for funding community health clinics, public schools, and community-based job creation programs than White respondents in the control group out of a desire to prove their "anti-racist credentials," as predicted by racial priming theory.[10] Vastly less research has examined how respondents of color respond to racialized cues, and I am aware of no prior study that has included an implicitly White racialized cue like "rural communities," so it is harder to hypothesize the effects of the rural cue or the manner in which cue exposure may affect Black respondents.[11] I leave those as open, empirical questions.

The proper test of framing effects is to determine whether an outcome differs between respondents in a treatment group and respondents in the control group on average. As such, I test whether the mean allocation into each of the six budget categories was lower or higher in the control group compared to each of the six treatment groups that were exposed to different descriptors of the nature of the community that would receive reinvestment funds. When social scientists test whether relationships between the variables in our data are "statistically significant," we are estimating the likelihood that our data would show such a relationship if, in fact, there was no systematic relationship between those social factors in the real world. Roughly speaking, we estimate the likelihood that we are making an error. When we say that a relationship is statistically significant, we are essentially saying that there is less than or equal to a 5% chance that our data would produce such a relationship if it were not an accurate reflection of the broader world.

However, the math behind hypothesis testing is somewhat similar to gambling with dice. Even though 5% is low odds, if you roll the dice enough times, you'll eventually roll a winning outcome. When it comes to an experiment like mine, in which I am comparing outcomes across several different categories, it's like I'm repeatedly rolling the dice. This increases the likelihood that my data will indicate the presence of a significant treatment purely by chance rather than reflecting a robust framing effect. Statisticians address this problem by inflating the standard errors of their estimates when conducting multiple comparisons.[12] Essentially, this makes the hypothesis test more conservative so that if you still find a significant effect, you can be much more confident that the effect is valid. By definition, though, correcting for multiple comparisons increases the likelihood that a researcher may fail to detect a relationship between variables that does, in fact, exist. I chose to split the difference. In this chapter, I report the results of hypothesis tests that employ both "normal" robust standard errors and tests that employ Bonferroni-adjusted standard errors that correct for multiple comparisons. This will maximize our ability to identify significant framing effects with the greatest possible confidence in our accuracy.

Survey Experiment Findings

Do People's Budget Allocations depend upon the
Type of Communities that would Receive Investment?

I present the most basic results of the framing experiment in table 4.1, which displays respondents' average budget allocation into each category (including responses of 0% and 100%) across treatment condition and respondent race. Figure 4.1 presents the same information graphically, which makes it easier to quickly discern the patterns in the data. There is relatively little evidence of direct framing effects. White respondents in the high crime, high poverty, inner-city, and rural conditions did not make budget allocations that significantly differed in magnitude from the allocations made by White respondents in the control group, on average. White respondents who were informed that "communities with many residents on welfare" would receive reinvestment funds actually allocated about 5% less toward hiring more police officers than control group Whites, though this cue did not affect their investments into clinics, schools, or job creation programs. The most consistent framing effect occurred among White respondents in the "African American communities" condition. White respondents who were told that Black community institutions would receive reinvestment funds allocated about 8% more money toward hiring probation officers and 12% more toward giving citizens a tax rebate, but less money toward healthcare clinics (9% less), public schools (7.5% less), and job creation programs (10% less) than White respondents in the control group. Importantly, only the effects of exposure to the African American communities cue on White respondents' allocations toward clinics, job creation programs, and the tax rebate were still statistically significant after correcting for multiple comparisons.

In contrast, the experimental framing only affected Black respondents' allocations toward public schools, not any of the other five budget categories. Compared to Black respondents in the control group, Black respondents who were told that "communities with many residents on welfare" would receive funding allocated about 7% less money toward schools, Black respondents who were told that rural communities would receive funding allocated about 5% less toward schools, and Black respondents who were told that African American communities would

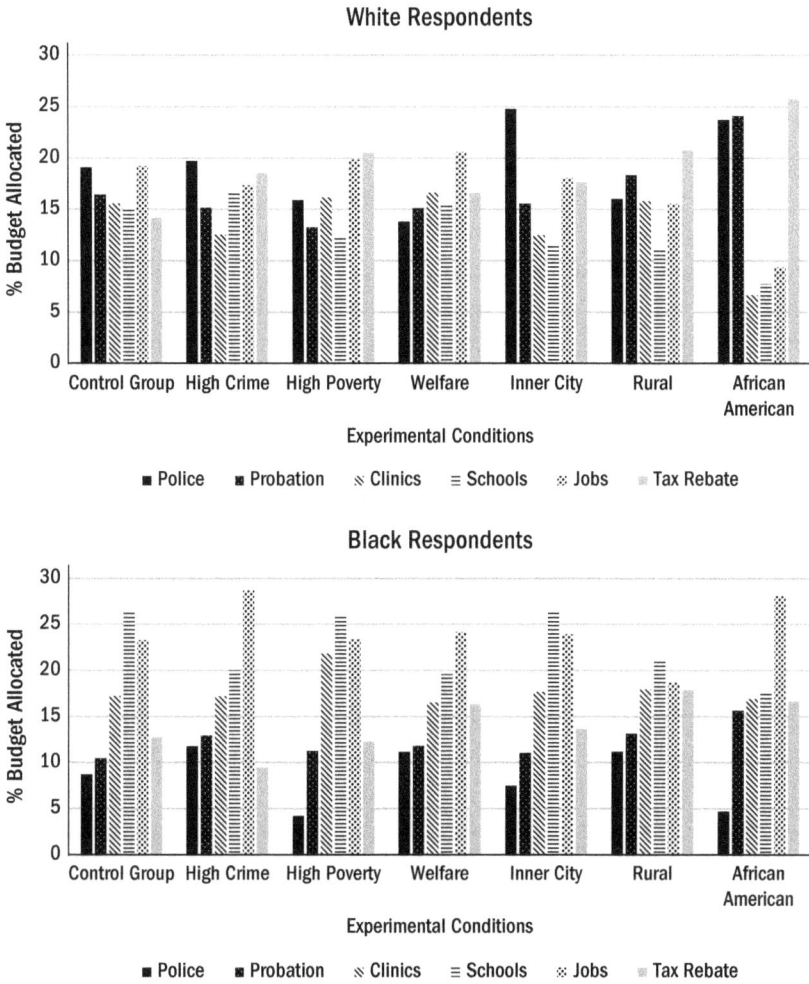

Figure 4.1. Mean Percentage Budget Allocations across Experimental Condition and Race.
Note: Mean allocations include the 0% responses from respondents who chose not to allocate any money toward each category and the 100% responses from respondents who chose to fund only one single category.

receive funding allocated about 9% less toward schools. Recall from chapter 3 that several Black focus group participants were deeply critical of the quality of public schools in their neighborhoods, which may explain the negative effects of the welfare and African American communities cues in the survey data. Likewise, it may be that Black respondents believed that rural schools that disproportionately serve White students are better funded than urban schools that disproportionately serve Black students. However, just as with the White respondents, only the effect of exposure to the African American communities cue was still statistically significant after correcting for multiple comparisons.

So far, between the findings presented in chapter 3 and the findings I just discussed, these data indicate that White and Black Americans would make significantly different choices about how to allocate money between community and criminal justice institutions, but those preferences largely do not change depending on the type of community that would benefit from community investment. The most robust evidence shows that only the prospect of African American communities benefiting from reinvestment caused White respondents to reduce their allocations into community institutions and instead increase their investments into probation and a tax rebate. Among Black respondents, this same treatment condition only caused a decrease in support for public school funding.

However, framing theorists argue that people "filter" frames they hear expressed by politicians and the media through their own personal beliefs and prior experiences.[13] For example, a person who is a staunchly conservative Republican would likely reject an argument that is in favor of increasing taxes because that proposal runs contrary to their own beliefs about limited government. This fact means that frames may appear ineffective if they affect different groups of people in opposite ways; the effects would "cancel each other out" if you do not know to examine subgroups separately. Thus, in addition to racial differences, I also tested whether the effect of frame exposure varied across other theoretically important personal characteristics. I summarize the results of those tests in table 4.2.[14]

Since I presented the full range of respondents' budget allocations across treatment condition and race in table 4.1, in table 4.2, I only fill in the cells of the table for which there were significant differences between a treatment and control group. We see that a broader variety of treatment cues affected different subgroups of the sample. First, there were some differences across education groups.[15] High school educated respondents in the African American communities condition allocated about 8% more money toward hiring probation officers than comparably

TABLE 4.1. Mean Percentage Budget Allocations across Experimental Condition and Race

	Control Group	High Crime	High Poverty	Welfare	Inner City	Rural	African American
				White Respondents			
Police	19.10	19.71	15.87	13.80[a]	24.77	16.00	23.72
Probation	16.40	15.14	13.24	15.09	15.55	18.36	24.09[a]
Clinics	15.54	12.52	16.14	16.60	12.45	15.78	6.66[a,b]
Schools	15.20	16.74	12.21	15.53	11.49	11.27	7.75[a]
Jobs	19.23	17.31	19.84	20.58	18.08	15.55	9.38[a,b]
Tax Rebate	14.16	18.57	20.52	16.60	17.66	20.78	25.76[a,b]
				Black Respondents			
Police	8.71	11.77	4.21	11.12	7.48	11.17	4.69
Probation	10.45	12.92	11.24	11.80	11.03	13.15	15.64
Clinics	17.24	17.19	21.82	16.51	17.68	17.96	16.90
Schools	26.41	20.00	26.05	19.60[a]	26.24	21.01[a]	17.69[a,b]
Jobs	23.29	28.71	23.32	24.15	23.91	18.69	28.09
Tax Rebate	12.73	9.42	12.29	16.33	13.67	17.88	16.67

Notes: a = Within-race difference between control and treatment group significant at $p \leq .05$.
b = Within-race difference between control and treatment group significant at $p \leq .05$ after applying a Bonferroni adjustment for multiple comparisons.

educated respondents in the control group. The frames had a broader impact on respondents who had some college education but no degree. Compared to respondents with some college education in the control group, respondents with this level of education exhibited the following responses to frames: about 8% less money toward probation in the high-poverty condition, about 9% less toward schools in both the welfare and rural conditions, about 9% more toward a tax rebate in the rural condition, and about 13% less toward schools, but a whopping 24% more toward a tax rebate in the African American communities condition. The allocation preferences of college graduates were only changed in regard to their support for a tax rebate; those in the rural condition allocated about 10% more than those in the control group.

More frames affected Democrats than Republicans. Democrats in the welfare condition allocated 8% less money toward public schools but 6% more toward a tax rebate compared to Democrats in the control group. Democrats in the rural communities condition allocated 7.5% less

TABLE 4.2. Mean Percentage Budget Allocations across Experimental Condition and Demographic Characteristics (Significant Framing Effects Only)

	Control Group	High Crime	High Poverty	Welfare	Inner City	Rural	African American
Police	Boomers: 18.9 GenX: 10.4	GenX: 24.6		Boomers: 11.3			
Probation	High School: 10.7 Some College: 16.5 Rep: 14.7 Silent: 6.8 Boomers: 14.0		Some College: 8.4				High School: 18.8 Rep: 26.3 Silent: 29.8[a] Boomers: 23.2
Clinics	Some College: 18.4 Rep: 11.7 Silent: 26.4				Some College: 11.8		Some College: 7.4[a] Rep: 4.5 Silent: 4.3[a]
Schools	Some College: 24.2 Dem: 26.0 Urban: 22.7 Rural: 8.7 Silent 19.8 Millennials&Z: 28.9			Some College: 15.5 Dem: 17.9 Silent: 8.7		Some College: 15.2 Dem: 18.5 Urban: 15.0[a] Rural: 20.4[a] Silent: 5.0	Some College: 10.8[a] Dem: 16.6[a] Urban: 13.6[a] Millennials&Z: 15.0
Jobs	Rep: 19.0 Rural: 28.5				Rural: 10.7		Rep: 6.1[a]
Tax Rebate	Some College: 7.9 College Grad: 9.8 Dem: 9.6 Urban: 12.2 Silent 6.1 Millennials&Z: 8.4			Dem: 15.8		Some College: 17.3 College Grad: 19.7 Dem: 16.9 Urban:19.2 Silent: 23.5	Some College: 32.2[a] Dem: 16.3 Urban: 20.9[a] Millennials&Z: 21.9

Notes: Results presented in this table are within–demographic group differences between control and treatment group that are significant at $p \leq .05$. Cells marked with ([a]) indicate control versus treatment group differences that remain significant at $p \leq .05$ even after applying a Bonferroni adjustment for multiple comparisons.

"High School"=high school graduate; "Some College"=some college courses but no degree; "College Grad"=college or graduate school graduate; "Dem"=Democrat; "Rep"=Republican; "Urban"=resident of an urban metropolitan area; "Rural"=resident of a nonurban area; "Silent"=Silent Generation; "Boomers"=Baby Boomer; "GenX"= Generation X; "Millennials&Z"=Millennial or Generation Z money toward schools but about 7% more money toward a tax rebate. Finally, Democrats in the African American communities condition allocated about 10% less money toward schools but about 7% more money toward a tax rebate. In contrast, only exposure to the African American communities cue significantly altered Republicans' allocations. Republicans exposed to this cue allocated nearly 12% more money toward hiring probation officers, 7% less toward healthcare clinics, and about 13% less toward job creation programs than Republicans in the control group.

There were similarly few differences between respondents who lived in urban metropolitan areas versus those who lived in rural areas. Urban residents in the rural communities condition allocated nearly 8% less money, and those in the African American communities condition allocated 9% less money, toward public schools compared to urban residents in the control group. Rural residents in the rural communities condition allocated nearly 12% more money toward public schools, while those in the inner-city communities condition allocated about 18% less toward job creation programs.

Finally, there were several significant differences between respondents who were members of different generations.[16] Members of the Silent Generation, the oldest respondents in this study, were affected by the largest variety of frames. Silent Generation respondents in the welfare condition allocated 11% less money toward public schools, while those in the rural communities condition allocated about 11% more toward probation and about 17% more toward a tax rebate but nearly 15% less toward public schools. Silent Generation respondents in the African American communities condition allocated 23% more money toward probation but 22% less money toward healthcare clinics. Baby Boomers, the next oldest respondents, were affected by two frames. Boomers in the welfare condition allocated about 7% less money toward police, while those in the African American communities condition allocated about 9% more money toward probation. Gen X respondents were only affected by exposure to a single frame. Those in the high-crime communities condition allocated about 14% more money toward police. Finally, respondents who fell into the youngest generations, the Millennials or Gen Z, were only affected by exposure to the African American communities frame. Those in the treatment group allocated about 14% less money toward public schools and 13.5% more toward a tax rebate.

However, most of these framing effects ceased to be statistically significant once I corrected for multiple comparisons. Here, only two frames met the highest standard of evidence. Again, the African American communities frame showed robust effects that varied in a variety of ways across each of the subgroup dimensions I tested. This frame also caused some of the largest substantive differences, shifting some average allocations by 20% or more. The second frame that met the higher standard of significance was the rural communities cue. Here, participants showed in-group favoritism across the urban-rural divide when it came to the prospect of granting public schools additional funding. Rural residents allocated substantially more money toward schools if they were told that rural communities would benefit, while urban residents allocated less money toward rural schools.

So far, though, this analysis reveals framing effects that are modest at best. The only frame that consistently affected respondents' allocations no matter which subgroups of respondents I examined was the African American communities frame. This was also the only frame whose effects were consistently robust to the statistical correction for multiple comparisons. The second most robust frame seems to be the rural communities frame, which sparked differences across groups of respondents defined by education, political partisanship, location of residence, and generational cohort. The other frames either exerted no effects or affected only one or two specific subgroups of participants. But perhaps examining respondents' allocation choices one by one is too narrow an approach. Perhaps the different frames caused greater changes in respondents' overall funding preference for community institutions versus criminal justice institutions. I turn to that question now.

Do People's Overall Budget Preferences depend upon the Type of Communities that would Receive Investment?

To remind the reader of my method that I first described in the previous chapter, I classified the respondents into one of six groups based upon their overall budget preferences. I distinguished between (1) respondents who only funded community clinics, schools, or job creation programs; (2) respondents who allocated 75% or more of their funds toward community institutions but the remainder toward criminal justice institutions or a tax rebate, or both; (3) respondents who evenly or almost-evenly balanced their allocations across community and criminal justice institutions; (4) respondents who allocated 75% or more of their funds toward criminal justice institutions or a tax rebate, or both, but the remainder toward community institutions; (5) respondents who only funded criminal justice institutions or a tax rebate, or both; and (6) respondents who solely funded the tax rebate. In chapter 3, I analyzed respondents' characteristics that were associated with their likelihood of falling into one preference category versus another. In this section, I test whether framing the nature of community investment changes people's overall investment preferences.

Table 4.3 presents the distribution of respondents' predicted probability of falling into each budget category across the experimental framing conditions and race. Similar to the individual budget allocations presented in table 4.1, we see little evidence of framing effects. Only exposure to the African American communities frame significantly affected White respondents' overall budget choices. White respondents in this treatment group were about 18% less likely to fall in the "mostly community" category, about 21% more likely to fall in the "only criminal justice system or tax" category, and about 11% more likely to fall in the "only tax" category compared to White respondents in the control group.[17] Two frames affected Black respondents' overall budget choices. Black respondents in the high-poverty treatment group were about 4% less likely to fall into the "mostly criminal justice or tax" group than Black respondents in the control group (dropping them to a 0% predicted probability). Black respondents in the rural communities condition were 17% less likely to fall into the "only community" category than Black respondents in the control group. Of all of these differences, only the effect of White respondent exposure to the African American communities cue remained statistically significant after correcting for multiple comparisons.

Consistent with the findings in table 4.2, some demographic characteristics did moderate the effects of cue exposure on overall budget preferences; I present those differences in table 4.4.[18] Exposure to the high-crime communities cue made Silent Generation respondents nearly 30% less likely to fall into the "only community" category, made Gen X respondents about 20% less likely to fall into the "mostly criminal justice system or tax" category, and made Republicans nearly 18%

TABLE **4.3.** Predicted Probability of Budget Preference Categorization across Experimental Condition and Race

	Control Group	High Crime	High Poverty	Welfare	Inner City	Rural	African American
			White Respondents				
Only Community	23.6	22.1	21.0	27.3	20.2	20.1	13.5
Mostly Community	22.6	22.5	27.1	21.7	14.7	16.7	4.3[a,b]
Balanced	16.3	15.0	14.3	17.5	19.8	21.8	13.1
Mostly CJS or Tax	10.2	14.4	9.7	9.6	15.4	12.4	10.0
Only CJS or Tax	20.2	17.0	14.1	15.7	22.8	18.1	41.0[a]
Only Tax	7.2	9.0	13.8	8.3	7.1	11.0	18.1[a]
			Black Respondents				
Only Community	34.0	34.1	36.5	29.8	28.9	17.0[a]	25.6
Mostly Community	31.3	28.9	36.3	28.5	36.6	41.2	40.4
Balanced	19.4	20.5	19.1	16.7	16.7	23.2	15.4
Mostly CJS or Tax	4.2	1.6	0.0[a]	7.0	3.5	2.7	2.1
Only CJS or Tax	7.3	13.1	2.4	10.1	7.2	8.6	10.0
Only Tax	3.7	1.7	5.7	7.8	7.0	7.2	6.5

Notes: a = Within-race difference between control versus treatment group significant at $p \leq .05$.
b = Within-race difference between control versus treatment group significant at $p \leq .05$ after applying a Bonferroni adjustment for multiple comparisons.

less likely to fall into the "mostly community" category but about 11% more likely to fall into the "mostly criminal justice system or tax" category. Exposure to the high-poverty communities cue made Democrats about 5% less likely to fall into the "mostly criminal justice system or tax" category. Exposure to this same cue made Silent Generation respondents about 15% less likely and respondents with some college education but no degree about 12% less likely to fall into the "only criminal justice system or tax" category.

The effect of exposure to the inner-city communities cue only differed across respondents based upon their partisan identification. Democrats exposed to this cue were about 12% less likely to fall into the "only community" category, while Republicans were about 15% less likely to fall into the "mostly community" category but about 13% more likely to fall into the "mostly criminal justice system or tax" category. There were many demographic differences in response to the rural communities cue. Respondents with some college education but no degree were nearly 22% less likely, college graduates were 17.4% less likely, Democrats

TABLE 4.4. Predicted Probability of Budget Preference Categorization across Experimental Condition and Demographic Characteristics (Significant Framing Effects Only)

	Control Group	High Crime	High Poverty	Welfare	Inner City	Rural	African American
Only Community	Some College: 31.7 College Grad: 35.7 Dem: 37.5 Urban: 30.4 Silent: 51.7	Silent: 22.9			Dem: 25.8	Some College: 9.9 College Grad: 18.3 Dem: 19.5 Urban: 16.8 Silent: 5.3ª	Some College: 10.7 Dem: 25.1 Urban: 19.0 Silent: 19.9
Mostly Community	Rep: 25.6 GenX: 37.1	Rep: 8.0 GenX: 17.2			Rep: 10.1		Rep: 2.2ª
Balanced	Silent: 9.6 GenX: 20.2					Silent: 34.6	GenX: 5.8
Mostly CJS or Tax	Dem: 6.7 Rep: 8.8	Rep: 20.1	Dem: 1.5		Rep: 22.2		
Only CJS or Tax	High School: 22.3 Some College: 16.1 Dem: 8.2 Rep: 25.1 Urban: 13.2 Silent: 15.2		Some College: 4.7 Silent: 0.0				High School: 13.0 Dem: 16.3 Rep: 45.4 Urban: 23.6 Silent: 48.6
Only Tax	Some College: 3.0 Urban: 4.7						Some College: 22.9ª Urban: 11.4

Notes: Results presented in this table are within-demographic group differences between control and treatment group that are significant at $p \leq .05$. Cells marked with (a) indicate control versus treatment group differences that remain significant at $p \leq .05$ even after applying a Bonferroni adjustment for multiple comparisons.
"High School" = high school graduate; "Some College" = Some college courses but no degree; "College Grad" = College or graduate school graduate; "Dem" = Democrat; "Rep" = Republican; "Urban" = resident of an urban metropolitan area; "Rural" = resident of a nonurban area; "Silent" = Silent Generation; "Boomers" = Baby Boomer; "GenX" = Generation X; "Millenials&Z" = Millennial or Generation Z

were 18% less likely, urban residents were nearly 14% less likely, and Silent Generation respondents were a whopping 46.4% less likely to fall into the "only communities" category than control group respondents who shared their demographic characteristics. In contrast, exposure to the rural communities cue made Silent Generation respondents 25% more likely to fall into the "balanced budget" category.

Again, the African American communities cue triggered many different effects across respondent demographics. Respondents with some college education but no degree exposed to this cue were 21% less likely,

Democrats were 12% less likely, urban residents were about 11% less likely, and Silent Generation respondents were about 32% less likely to fall into the "only community" category than control group respondents. Republicans were 23.4% less likely to fall into the "mostly community" category. Gen X respondents were about 15% less likely to fall into the "balanced budget" category. Respondents with a high school degree or less formal education were about 9% less likely, Democrats were about 8% more likely, Republicans were about 20% more likely, urban residents were about 10% more likely, and Silent Generation respondents were about 33% more likely to fall into the "only criminal justice system or tax" category. Finally, respondents with some college education but no degree were about 20% more likely and urban residents were nearly 7% more likely to fall into the "only tax" category.

Of all these framing effect differences across respondent demographic characteristics presented in table 4.4, only three remained statistically significant once I corrected for multiple comparisons. Notably, these three were tied to the same two cues that showed the most statistically robust effects in table 4.2: the rural communities and African American communities cues. The contrast between Silent Generation respondents in the rural communities cue versus Silent Generation respondents in the control group in regard to the likelihood of falling into the "only community" category met this higher bar of significance. So, too, did the contrast between Republicans who were exposed to the African American communities cue versus Republicans in the control group in regard to the likelihood of falling into the "mostly community" category. Finally, the difference in the likelihood of falling into the "only tax" category between respondents with some college education but no degree who were exposed to the African American communities cue versus comparably educated respondents in the control group remained significant after correcting for multiple comparisons. We can be most confident that these results predict the way that people would respond to political cues about these topics in the real world.

Summary of Experimental Tests of Framing Effects

What are the "big picture" findings to take away from my framing experiment? First, it appears that White and Black Americans' opinions about how best to invest public funding to prevent crime are not particularly sensitive to variations in the types of communities that could benefit from reinvestment. Most of the different cues affected the responses of only one or two subgroups of respondents and only in regard to one or two budget categories. When a cue did generate significant differences between control group respondents and demographically similar treatment group respondents, the magnitude of this effect was most commonly only about a 5% to 15% change in the amount of money the respondent would put in a particular category or 5% to 15% change in the respondent's likelihood of falling into one overall investment preference category versus another. This finding suggests that politicians have much more latitude to talk about a variety of social problems in communities (such as crime, poverty, and welfare use) without provoking widespread public backlash against community investment than they seem to assume they possess. That's the "glass half full" conclusion.

The second major takeaway from these findings is the "glass half empty" conclusion: the cue that most consistently affected respondents' budget preferences was the African American communities cue. Being told that Black communities would receive reinvestment funds made participants in many subgroups defined by race, education, political partisanship, region of residence, or generational cohort membership less supportive of investing in community institutions and more supportive of investing in criminal justice institutions or a tax rebate, or both. This cue also caused the greatest substantive magnitude changes in the study, by and large. This effect is most clear in table 4.3. White respondents in the control group had a nearly 23% likelihood of allocating most of their money toward community institutions, but Whites in the African American communities condition had only about a 4% likelihood of favoring community investment. This finding does not conform to classic racial priming theory because it was the explicitly racialized cue that provoked backlash against support for Black communities, not the implicitly racialized cues (with only a few exceptions). It does, however, suggest that the "color line" described over a century ago by the sociologist W. E. B. Du Bois continues to divide Americans when it comes to the allocation of public funds and programs. Cueing thoughts about Black people as beneficiaries appears to splinter Americans' investment preferences across numerous demographic cleavages in society.

Third, there is more limited evidence of American resistance to targeted, rather than universal, public benefits that are not specifically (or explicitly) tied to race. The cue that caused the second most frequent changes, and the only cue other than "African American communities" that remained statistically significant after correcting for multiple comparisons, was the rural communities cue. This cue did not so much trigger the racial divide in America as it triggered differences in preferences between groups defined by political partisanship, education, generation, and urban versus rural residence. Most of these subgroups of respondents became less willing to allocate money toward public schools but more supportive of individual tax rebates if they were told that rural communities would benefit—except rural residents themselves who then allocated more money toward public schools.

Fourth, members of the Silent Generation, the oldest respondents in this study, were the most vulnerable to framing effects. Their preferences were significantly affected by a wider range of cues than most other subgroups of respondents, and the changes in their allocations were often substantively much larger in magnitude, shifting 20% or more. I think that this finding indicates two things. First, the Silent Generation holds opinions about public investment that likely hearken back to the Jim Crow era when they were young. Second, these oldest Americans seem to be most vulnerable to politicians' efforts to frame policy debates in a way that sways the public. In contrast, none of the frames significantly affected the likelihood that members of the Millennial or Gen Z generations, the youngest respondents in the survey, would shift from one overall budget preference category to another, though exposure to the African American communities cue did increase these younger respondents' allocations toward the tax rebate but decrease their allocations into public schools. This suggests that disagreements about public funding and community investment among the mass public may be declining over time.[19]

Experiments are best suited for testing whether one factor has a causal relationship with a second factor—in this case, whether different rhetorical phrases provoke policy backlash among people who hear or read them. Experiments provide us less leverage to understand why people hold the beliefs that they do, though. In the last section of this chapter, I return to the discussions of my focus group participants to recount how they believed that public crime prevention funds should be allocated across communities.

Focus Group Findings

Following the discussions of their budget choices (described in chapter 3), the moderator asked the focus group participants which neighborhoods in Boston or towns across Massachusetts they thought should receive reinvestment money to prevent crime. In general, most participants endorsed making evidence-based decisions to target funding in proportion to the magnitude of the local crime problem. Consider the following statements:

MODERATOR: Why did you want to give money to those communities?
JAMES: Those are lower income.
BALDWIN: Lower income, yeah.
CHRISSY: Because there's more crime, poverty, lower income, drug addiction, homelessness.
(Focus Group 2)

MATTHEW: I say look at statistics.
DORIAN: Look at the situation in the town.
JOSEPH: Look at statistics.
MATTHEW: Say if you would have to say ... if you went out to Worcester, go beyond Worcester. Say we go beyond Worcester, Springfield, that way out there. I say look at the crime statistics in that area. The towns with the least amount of crime, those are the towns that get the least amount of money, the least amount of attention.
(Focus Group 4)

MODERATOR: Okay. Where should [the money] go?
JACK: The highest crime rates.
JASON: Dorchester ...
JACK: Roxbury, reading the newspaper.
PAMELA: Roxbury. Mattapan.
JUDY: Charlestown.

FREDERICK: I'll say East Boston. I think it should go there.

JASON: Lynn.

ALBERT: South End.

CAMILLE: Well, Dorchester has the most crime, I think. It's always on the news for shooting and stabbing and robbery and that's Dorchester.

(Focus Group 6)

BRUCE: You would have to start targeting the cities or towns that have the highest crime rates in them.

MODERATOR: I'm not expecting you to know crime rates. I don't know crime rates. But where would you . . .

BRUCE: New Bedford. Springfield. Boston.

INEZ: What about Fall River?

BRUCE: Lawrence. Worcester.

WALLACE: Worcester.

BRUCE: There's a lot of high-crime-rate cities in Massachusetts . . .

WALLACE: The major cities. . . . That's all the big cities.

(Focus Group 5)

Beyond the illustrative quotes above, participants named numerous different Boston neighborhoods, Boston suburbs, or other cities or towns throughout Massachusetts that they thought should receive money. James (46, W, HSE, FG2) and Chrissy (46, B, HSE, FG2) named Roxbury, Dorchester, Hyde Park, Jamaica Plain, and Charlestown—all neighborhoods in Boston. They also named Chelsea and Lynn, towns in the greater Boston metropolitan area. Joseph (54, B, HSE, FG4) named Lynn and Salem, the latter of which is a town about twenty miles north of Boston (famous for its historic witch trials). Linda (56, B, HSE, FG4) named Revere, a suburb of Boston. In addition to the communities named by Bruce (58, W, CE, FG5) and Wallace (57, W, CE, FG5) in the quote above, Nathan (55, W, CE, FG5) also named Roxbury, Dorchester, East Boston, Chelsea, and Revere. Inez (72, W, CE, FG5) named Brockton, a town about twenty-five miles southwest of Boston.

The fact that many of the same neighborhoods, towns, and cities throughout Massachusetts came up repeatedly shows that residents of the Boston metro area share similar "mental maps" of the distribution of crime in the state. Whether these participants' mental maps accurately reflect objective conditions or inaccurately reflect subjective stereotypes about particular neighborhoods and towns is difficult to determine. It is probably a bit of both. On the one hand, criminological research consistently demonstrates that crime is concentrated in a relatively small number of locations that also experience numerous other social problems.[20] Such high-crime locations are disproportionately likely to be located in neighborhoods that are predominantly populated by Americans of color, though research is absolutely clear that this correlation is caused by concentrated disadvantage and segregation, not the characteristics of neighborhood residents themselves.[21] Dorchester, Roxbury, and Mattapan are the three neighborhoods in Boston that typically experience the highest crime rates, especially the highest rates of gun violence.[22] They also contain the highest concentrations of Black residents in the city, as reflected by the fact that at least nine of the Black participants in this study hailed from Dorchester (not every participant named their neighborhood of residence).[23] Other neighborhoods, like East Boston and Charlestown, are predominantly home to blue-collar, working-class families, though some are experiencing gentrification. Similarly, many of the other towns named by participants, such as Chelsea, Lynn, Revere, Salem, Brockton, and New Bedford are also historically working-class towns with levels of crime higher than the state average. Worcester and Springfield are the second and third largest cities in Massachusetts; like many of the state's other post-industrial small cities, they also suffer from relatively high crime rates.[24] These patterns suggest that focus group participants were attuned to real patterns of crime and affluence throughout the state.[25]

On the other hand, numerous studies show that crime and social disorder are racialized in Americans' minds. Americans—especially White Americans—typically believe that neighborhoods with larger populations of people of color, especially Black or Latino residents, experience more crime whether or not that is empirically accurate neighborhood by neighborhood. White Americans also tend to perceive neighborhoods that are populated by people of color as more disorganized and run-down, regardless of objective conditions. In other words, evidence suggests that Whites "see" more crime and disorder than actually exists when they look at neighborhoods where Americans of color live.[26] As such, some portion of the focus group respondents' perceptions of crime across space are likely influenced by racial stereotypes. I suspect this factor was at play in Focus Group 5 when Wallace rather wryly observed that the participants in his group named all of Massachusetts' primary cities as locations of high crime rates, suggesting that some of the college educated White people in that group largely equated cities with crime in a blanket manner.[27] When one hears blanket generalizations, one should be wary of stereotypes. However, even if some of these participants overestimated crime in particular neighborhoods and towns, they demonstrated a baseline level of awareness of real patterns of social problems in the state, and they expressed a desire to target social investment accordingly.

However, other evidence suggests that people might struggle to select particular communities to receive reinvestment funds if the choice were up to them. Participants in Focus Groups 1, 2, 5, and 6 also said that "crime is everywhere." They believed that "problem areas" can be found in most communities. Many participants also believed that the spread of the opioid epidemic caused a widespread increase in crime. Consider this exchange between Wallace and Alice (54, W, CE, FG5):

> WALLACE: In parts of, say, the South Shore and Cape Cod always seem to be . . . everyone's doing fine. But I've heard things about Cape Cod, some of the small towns down there having a lot of drug and crime and problems that, it . . . I'll make a broad statement, crime is everywhere. It's kind of . . . everyone's going to have their problems. So it's hard to pick . . . to send . . .
>
> ALICE: I know people who live in small communities that have heroin rates and things like that.
>
> WALLACE: There you go. Yeah.
>
> ALICE: And they're in, you know, the suburbs and things like that, and OxyContin and things.

Or this similar exchange between Linda (56, B, HSE, FG4), Susan (53, B, HSE, FG4), Matthew (55, B, HSE, FG4), and Joseph (54, B, HSE, FG4):

> LINDA: I'll say New Hampshire.
>
> SUSAN: New Hampshire is beautiful.

LINDA: Yeah, New Hampshire. Now they're starting to do a lot of
crime.

MATTHEW: Oh, no. They're wrecking New Hampshire right now.

JOSEPH: They going crazy up there. They just . . . Two cops just got shot.

SUSAN: I lived there for eighteen years. My son still lives there.

MATTHEW: All this is coming behind these drugs, man.

Perhaps it is not surprising that many of the White participants perceived that the opioid epidemic was creating crime in previously peaceful suburban and rural areas given the fact that the epidemic disproportionately affected White communities in its early stages.[28] It is a bit more surprising that even the high school educated Black participants of Focus Group 4, who recounted the most personal experiences with crime and victimization in their home neighborhoods, also perceived that crime was undermining the social fabric of neighboring New Hampshire, a much more rural and less racially diverse state than Massachusetts.

The belief that crime can be found everywhere lead some of the high school educated participants to say that "all communities" should receive funding. Roger (63, W, HSE, FG2) was the first person to speak in his focus group when the moderator asked which communities should receive money. He replied, "All of them." Jacklyn (32, B, HSE, FG2) agreed with Roger: "I like that one: all of them." In Focus Group 4, Joseph said, "You know, I said the whole city of Boston should get the money. . . ."

How do these findings from the focus groups relate to the survey experiment? Here, we need to think about how the method of the experiment affects response. When a participant is exposed to a cue, that cue activates particular thoughts and associations and brings them to the forefront of the person's mind.[29] If the participant answers survey questions about politics or public policy soon after being exposed to a cue, we infer that the cognitive associations that were primed by seeing the cue shape the participant's answers. So a short experiment like mine (that a participant can complete in one sitting) helps us understand people's immediate, gut reactions to particular cues. If people were to sit and think about an issue for more time, they would likely activate other cognitive associations in their minds, and their answers to the politics or policy questions might then be different.

I suspect that we can see that process at play in the focus groups. When first asked by the moderator where money should be invested to fight crime, the first thought that occurred to most participants was that the most money should go to communities with the biggest crime problem. Some Black participants, like Patricia in Focus Group 1 and Joseph and Mary in Focus Group 4, identified these as "urban" or "inner-city communities" (their choice of language). This feels like common sense. It also dovetails with my experimental findings. The thought of giving high-crime, inner-city communities additional money to prevent crime did not cause any participants to immediately recoil in opposition— even Bruce, the most conservative participant in the focus groups.

However, as participants kept thinking about the question, many of them started to think about the reach of the opioid epidemic, which led them to assert that "crime is everywhere" and, as such, all communities should receive some money. In other words, participants started by thinking about targeted investments based upon need but moved toward thinking more about universal investments because need is everywhere. This feels to me like Americans' predisposition toward universal policies asserting itself.[30] In contrast to the experimental findings, where exposure to the rural communities cue caused urban area respondents to backlash against support for investing in rural public schools, this dynamic actually seemed to increase the willingness of these urban-dwelling participants to allocate money toward rural communities even though they were well aware of the financial need in their own communities.

Among the focus group participants, was there a parallel to the White survey respondents' backlash against the African American communities cue? It is very difficult to assess this question in qualitative research because many Americans—especially White Americans—are deeply uncomfortable talking with strangers about race relations. Americans often cope with this discomfort by speaking in vague, broad terms to avoid facing the problem head-on or insulting people.[31] That being said, I did notice a handful of interactions that felt like participants were uncomfortable with race-targeted investment.

The moderator had enough time in Focus Group 6 to specifically ask the White, high school educated participants what images they thought of when she mentioned different types of communities; she employed the same language as the cues in my survey experiment. Her questions prompted the following responses:

MODERATOR: How about high-crime communities? What do you think? What pops into your mind? What's the first thing you thought of when I said high-crime communities?

ALBERT: Roxbury.

JASON: No jobs.

JUDY: Charlestown.

ALBERT: Dudley Square.

PAMELA: Doesn't matter where you live; things are really bad out there right now.

CAMILLE: Yeah, it's terrible.

PAMELA: It's everywhere. It's not, it's in the suburbs, man, it's everywhere.

MODERATOR: How about White communities?

PAMELA: That's what I'm talking about.

MODERATOR: What pops into your mind when I say White communities?

ALBERT: White communities?

MODERATOR: White communities. I mean something popped into your mind.

PAMELA: It doesn't matter, it's all, it's all mixed.

JUDY: Charlestown at one time was all White and it was a very heavy criminal thing and it had nothing to do with minorities at all. It was a totally Irish American community. I'm saying this as an Irish American. I'm not bragging. In fact, they made a movie called *The Town* that was about Charlestown. The bank robberies.

JACK: Yeah, they used to have the record for bank robberies.

PAMELA: That used to be bad, real bad.

Shortly thereafter, the moderator asked about African American communities:

MODERATOR: How about African American communities? What pops into your head there? What kinds of housing?

PAMELA: Where I live, we're all mixed. It's all mixed.

MODERATOR: Okay, but, what's an African American community, though?

PAMELA: What do you . . . You said it. You said an African American. Where I live people work, mostly they work where I live.

ALBERT: No, but she's talking about an African American community like all-Black communities.

MODERATOR: Because we talked about White communities . . .

PAMELA: But what do you mean? Nowadays everybody's mixed! I lived in Quincy, I lived in the projects in Quincy and everybody is Black, White, Spanish, Asian, I've lived everywhere and everybody's mixed. I've lived in a nice building in Boston, in the West End. If you lived here you'd be home now . . . everybody's mixed. So I don't look at, like, a Black community.

SPEAKER [CROSS TALK, IDENTITY UNCLEAR]: Are you at the [name of apartment community]?

PAMELA: No.

MODERATOR: Right, but we talked about White communities a little while ago. No one had a problem with—

PAMELA: Yeah, but I mean, I keep saying all the time, everybody's mixed.

MODERATOR: Right, okay. So there is no White community and there is no Black community?

JASON: No.

PAMELA: I'm just going to say everybody's mixed.

JUDY: I mean it's getting to be more mixed but there still are Black communities. Like when I'm riding down from Dudley, Warren Street, there's churches on every second corner. Really. I mean—

During the postdiscussion debrief, the moderator and my research assistants who observed the focus group agreed that the discussion about communities agitated Pamela. Because she, herself, had lived in racially heterogeneous public housing communities, she did not even want to discuss racially homogenous communities, and she insisted that crime is a problem everywhere, regardless of the racial demographics of the resident population. Judy echoed her by recalling the history of Irish American gang crime in Boston.

Pamela and Judy's comments strike me as a manifestation of "color-blind racism."[32] The participants in this focus group were collectively the least financially well-off Whites in the study. Several of these participants reported that they currently or previously lived in government-subsidized housing; financial strain and addiction were dominant topics of discussion; five of the six participants had been arrested at one time or another in the past, and three of them served a sentence behind bars. Because of these personal experiences, these White participants resisted the idea that Black communities might experience particularly bad social problems or need particular assistance, in spite of evidence to the contrary. Such thinking could push people to reject race-targeted investment and insist upon universal, race-neutral investments because it "doesn't matter where you live, things are really bad out there right now."

The college educated participants of Focus Group 1 also expressed ambivalence when asked which communities should receive investment. Unfortunately, unbeknownst to the moderator, the tape recorder shut off halfway through this portion of the discussion, rendering the transcript incomplete. I cannot report participants' statements on this question verbatim, but I can summarize their sentiments based upon my field notes. Bettie (23, B, CE, FG1) vacillated over race-targeted investment. She noted that "inner-city schools" are more diverse than schools in other areas, and she also recognized that the "Black communities" and "high-crime communities" in Boston are nearly synonymous. However, at the same time that she acknowledged that inner-city Black communities disproportionately experience crime, she also told the moderator that she did not think that race should be used as a criterion for investment. Even after describing the correlation between Black communities and high-crime communities, she also said that crime "isn't about race; you never know." During the postdiscussion debrief, my research assistants said they felt that Bettie contradicted herself. Even though she was aware of racial disparities in society, she seemed unwilling to abandon American principles of colorblindness when it comes to the distribution of public resources, and this caused her to vacillate in her beliefs about proper crime prevention.

I was surprised to hear some Focus Group 1 participants raise the concept of racial priming on their own (in so many words). Lance (60, B, CE, FG1) and Lacey (69, B, CE, FG1) said that it would be politically problematic to argue for targeted investment into Black communities. Lacey argued that it would be better to use the phrase "underserved communities"; she believed that this terminology would generate more sympathetic reactions among voters and politicians. Lacey also expressed some skepticism toward targeted investing, musing that investing money into high-crime communities "kind of rewards those communities"—a very dispositional assessment of responsibility.

On the other hand, most participants across the focus groups had little trouble judging where money should *not* be invested. They said that the wealthiest communities in and around Boston did not need any additional money for crime prevention. As Joseph put it in Focus Group 4, "Wellesley? No. Too many doctors and dentists and lawyers live out that way." No participant explicitly challenged the principle that affluent communities need no investment, but some did qualify it with the recognition that even wealthy communities can have drug problems and bad parts. The high school educated participants of Focus Groups 2, 4, and 6 most clearly and explicitly rejected funding for wealthy communities, but some of the college educated participants echoed their choices.

I did perceive one difference across education groups that felt meaningful. Only the college educated participants of Focus Groups 3 and 5 expressed concerns about how money would be distributed within communities. In fact, the Black, college educated participants of Focus Group 3 never actually answered the moderator's question about targeting investment across communities. Melissa (44, B, CE, FG3) first responded to the moderator by saying, "But then it goes through the legislation first, and so it's the funnels that we have to work out. Because at the end of the day, who distributes, right?" When the moderator pressed them to choose particular communities, William (67, B, CE, FG3) diverted the conversation with his detailed differentiation of deserving versus undeserving people experiencing homelessness that I recounted in chapter 3. Melissa chimed back in after William argued against giving the "voluntary homeless" financial assistance, and she advocated for money to be invested into nonprofit organizations that "are doing the work." However, she emphasized that we should only choose organizations that have demonstrated "tangible, provable results" and have "a track record . . . on credibility." Rachelle (60+, B, CE, FG3) agreed with Melissa and explained that she worked for many years in nonprofit management, and she recounted how difficult it was to continually appease funders and keep grants rolling in.

The White participants of Focus Group 5 also expressed some concerns about how money would be allocated:

> WALLACE: Talking about just budgetary and where to allot, there's
> that saying, of throwing good money after bad. And so you just
> don't know . . . pouring millions of dollars into an impoverished city
> doesn't necessarily fix the problem.
>
> INEZ: That's right.
>
> WALLACE: If you really got to look at who is where and what they
> need and how much can solve this and it, oh, I can see how it would
> be a huge . . .
>
> MODERATOR: So it may not be just poverty . . . Yeah. But are we all
> sort of agreed that a high-crime area is where we want to spend our
> money?
>
> WALLACE: Hmm.
>
> DYLAN: Well, if the goal is decreasing crime . . .
>
> NATHAN: Well, if you limit the crime, yeah.
>
> MODERATOR: Okay. So we want to throw money into those
> kinds of . . . ?
>
> MARIANNE: Well, I think money should get thrown into those com-
> munities and they should have focus groups with folks and ask them
> what they think would help prevent crime.
>
> DYLAN: Yeah.
>
> NATHAN: Good.
>
> MARIANNE: Because I don't think *we* can know. [*laughing*]

Even though Dylan (25, W, CE, FG5) agreed with Marianne (30, W, CE, FG5) that money should be invested into impoverished communities, he soon expressed some of the same concerns as Melissa and Rachelle in Focus Group 3: "I think it matters too . . . like I think you're probably going to be more effective giving money to community-based organizations that are already doing effective things. Rather than . . . they need money because it was just twenty people that got together and decided they were going to do something. Because you could give even five million dollars to a terribly disorganized, bureaucratic organization, it just evaporates into. . . ." Janet (56, W, CE, FG5) agreed with Dylan. Like Rachelle in Focus Group 3, Janet said that she worked in nonprofit organizations her whole life, and she said, "So I think that comes back to the accountability and making sure that whatever money these places are getting, they are able to show results and put a higher percentage of the dollars towards the people that are being served, rather than towards themselves."

The college educated, White and Black participants of Focus Groups 3 and 5 rather broadly expressed concerns about financial accountability. Though both groups of participants endorsed investment into community institutions (as described in the previous chapter), here we see that they want to ensure that those investments are not squandered. There is nothing inherently wrong with their desire for accountability, but none of the high school educated participants raised this concern. The latter participants only spoke about the magnitude of need in impoverished communities. Thus, it strikes me that only more affluent Americans who possess some degree of wealth express concern that wealth redistribution might be mismanaged. As Wallace said, the college educated participants' largesse seems like it may end at the point at which "good money is thrown after bad."

Conclusion

In chapter 3, I demonstrated that substantial numbers of White and Black Americans express support for the prospect of directly investing resources into community institutions to prevent crime. In this chapter, I tested whether language that evokes America's long-standing racial fault lines might provoke a backlash that would undermine public support for community investment. The findings presented in this chapter show that the potential for backlash exists, but it is more limited in scope than racial priming theory and older studies would suggest. By and large, exposure to cues about crime, poverty, and welfare had little effect on survey respondents' budget choices, and the focus group participants generally agreed that investment should be proportional to the magnitude of crime and poverty in communities. Only exposure to the cues about African American and rural communities caused changes in respondents' budget preferences that met the highest standard of statistical evidence. Unfortunately, these cues did trigger backlash against community investment that is consistent with theories of systemic racism and in-group favoritism. As I said earlier, these findings strike me as "glass half full, glass half empty."

A shift in public opinion only becomes politically meaningful when it is of sufficient magnitude to cause people to vote differently. So even if some Americans are less willing to invest money into African American communities than into communities defined by other features, would they care enough to vote against a politician who supports race-conscious investment policy? More broadly, what kinds of crime prevention and criminal justice reform policies fall outside the public's "zone of acquiescence" in the twenty-first century? I turn to those questions next.

5

The Political Boundaries of Public Support
for Safety Beyond Punishment

The accumulated findings of this book strongly suggest that many politicians substantially underestimate Americans' support for direct community investment.[1] So does that mean that the path toward full and proper implementation of community-based justice reinvestment is smooth and clear for all elected policymakers? Unfortunately, we cannot yet answer that question with a resounding "yes." Survey data which tell us that "X percent of Americans support or oppose policy Y" give us an important starting point when discussing policy reform because they suggest which policy changes might be popular or unpopular among the American public, especially if they are part of a trend of increasing or decreasing public support over time.[2] However, politicians think about public opinion much more broadly than just polls; in fact, many politicians believe that they gain more information about "public opinion" from personal conversations with constituents or news coverage of issues than they do from scientific surveys.[3]

Scholars love nationally representative surveys of the American public, but many politicians are more skeptical of their value. The "electoral connection" explains much of this difference in perspectives. There is only one politician in the United States of America whose constituency is the entire American population: the president. Every other politician is elected by the citizenry of a single state (senators in the US Senate) or a particular electoral district (representatives in the US House and all state-level legislators). To be quite blunt, this fact means that most politicians have little reason to care about the opinions of citizens who live outside their electoral districts because those people cannot provide votes to help them win election. Furthermore, politicians are most responsive to constituents who vote on a regular basis, and they are more likely to ignore constituents whom they perceive as unlikely to turn out to vote.[4]

In single-member, winner-takes-all political systems like the United States, most voters will accept or turn a blind eye to some of their chosen candidate's positions or votes if they believe that the candidate is more favorable than the opponent, overall. This electoral dynamic causes politicians to think about public opinion in a more nuanced manner. They do not necessarily care about taking positions that some (or even many) of their constituents oppose as long as those constituents will vote for them anyway. In other words, politicians are most sensitive to "deal breakers"—the issues that might cause a significant number of their prior supporters to abandon them in the next election or mobilize a significant number of prior nonvoters to show up and vote against them. Politicians pay attention to constituents' "potential preferences"— the policy issues constituents did not know they really cared about until their representative took an action that "crosses the line." Political scientists refer to this as the "zone of acquiescence"—the range of policy positions taken by elected representatives that voters will tolerate before withdrawing their electoral support. Politicians have electoral reasons to care more about avoiding issues or policy choices that fall outside the public's zone of acquiescence than they do to care about the public's preferences on issues that will not ultimately change their vote choices one way or the other.[5]

Criminal justice was a case in point of zone of acquiescence politics for many decades.[6] Politicians learn from electoral wins and losses. They saw that Nixon and Reagan campaigned on "tough on crime" platforms and won the presidency.[7] They saw the damage that was inflicted upon Michael Dukakis' 1988 presidential campaign by the infamous "Willie Horton" TV ad that blamed Dukakis for a violent home invasion committed by an inmate who was temporarily released under a furlough program Dukakis approved as governor of Massachusetts. Dukakis' "soft on crime" reputation only grew worse when, during a televised presidential debate, he stated that he would continue to oppose the death penalty even if his own wife were brutally murdered. The lesson that Democrats in particular learned was that voters would reject a politician who was labeled "soft on crime" no matter how many other desirable qualities they saw in the candidate.[8] Bill Clinton reacted by running on a platform that he claimed was even tougher on crime than that offered by the Republicans.[9] I had the honor of working in the US House of

Representatives on a postdoc fellowship. I will never forget how my former boss, Representative Bobby Scott of Virginia, pithily described politicians' beliefs about the role of criminal justice in elections: "Nobody ever lost an election for being stupid on crime." By this, he meant that far too many politicians believed that "tough on crime" positions fell within voters' zone of acquiescence even if they produced terrible policies with harmful collateral consequences, but "soft on crime" positions—no matter how evidence based—could cost a politician his or her job.

It is not enough to demonstrate that a substantial number of Americans express support for community investment over criminal justice investment. We must also demonstrate either that politicians' choices to support community investment will not mobilize opponents to vote against them or that mobilized opposition is counterbalanced by a coalition of mobilized supporters. If opponents of community investment feel more strongly about the issue than proponents, then politicians would perceive that community investment falls outside the mass public's zone of acquiescence. This appears to be precisely what contemporary politicians believe, especially conservative Republicans.[10] Are they correct?

In this chapter, I use my national survey data to "map the margins" of people's zone of acquiescence for community-based justice reinvestment. First, I revisit the analyses of chapter 3 and test whether voters express significantly different crime prevention policy preferences than nonvoters. Second, I test whether exposure to the community frames I analyzed in chapter 4 affected voters differently than nonvoters. Third, I assess whether survey respondents thought that a politician's choice to support criminal justice or community investment would affect their likelihood of voting for or against that candidate.

Do Voters Have Different Investment Preferences than Nonvoters?

Voting is habitual. One of the strongest predictors of people's likelihood of voting in the next election is whether they voted in the last election.[11] As such, I created a measure to differentiate between survey respondents who self-reported that they voted in the 2012 election and those who said that they did not vote. It is likely that the 2012 voters were substantially more likely to vote in the 2016 election (which occurred six months after they completed this survey). Furthermore, people with more formal education and greater affluence are more likely to vote, which means that distinguishing between voters and non-voters likely captures a substantial portion of the distinction between college educated and high school educated Americans I have discussed throughout this book.[12] Table 5.1 presents the average portion of the survey respondents' hypothetical crime prevention budgets that they allocated into each category. The top rows simply differentiate between voters and nonvoters, while the subsequent rows break down voting behavior across race and political partisanship.

When looking at the full sample, there is little evidence that voters have significantly different crime prevention investment preferences than nonvoters. Only one difference was marginally statistically significant ($p = 0.09$): voters allocated 3% more of their money toward hiring more police officers than nonvoters. However, the full sample masks additional differences across subgroups of the population. White and Black nonvoters' allocations toward hiring more police or probation officers or funding healthcare clinics or job creation programs did not significantly differ, statistically speaking. Black nonvoters allocated significantly more money toward funding public schools than White nonvoters, while White nonvoters allocated significantly more money toward a tax rebate than Black nonvoters.

White voters allocated significantly more money toward hiring additional police and probation officers than Black voters and Black nonvoters, and their average allocation toward police exceeded the comparable allocation even among White nonvoters. Black voters allocated the least money toward police, significantly more money toward funding healthcare clinics than White voters, and significantly more money toward funding public schools and funding job creation programs than both White voters and White nonvoters. In contrast, both White voters and nonvoters allocated significantly more money toward a tax rebate than Black voters. Overall, these findings reaffirm my conclusion from chapter 3 that Black Americans more strongly prefer community-based investment than White Americans, but these interracial differences come into clearer focus when we compare voters to nonvoters. The substantive differences are not overwhelming, though. They range from about a 4% difference to about a 10% difference across the various race-budget category contrasts.

TABLE 5.1. Average Percent Budget Allocation for Crime Prevention Options among Voters versus Nonvoters

	% More Police	% More Probation	% Funding Healthcare Clinics	% Funding Public Schools	% Funding Job Creation	% Tax Rebate
Full Sample						
Nonvoters	11.5†	14.6	16.6	18.4	20.2	18.0
Voters	14.5†	14.7	15.4	17.3	20.9	16.4
White Respondents						
Nonvoters	11.6	16.7	16.1 (WNV<BNV)*	14.7 (WNV<BNV)*	17.9	22.5 (WNV>BNV)*
Voters	20.9 (WV>WNV,BNV,BV)*	16.9 (WV>BNV,BV)*	13.2 (WV<BV)*	12.4 (WV<BNV,BV)*	17.0 (WV<BV*; <BNV†)	18.2 (WV>BV)*
Black Respondents						
Nonvoters	11.4	12.4	17.0	22.1 (BNV>WNV)*	24.4	13.5 (BNV<WNV)*
Voters	7.6 (BV<WNV)*	12.4	17.8 (BV>WV)*	22.6 (BV>WNV,WV)*	25.0 (BV>WNV,WV)*	14.5 (BV<WNV, WV)*
Republicans						
Nonvoters	12.9	15.3 (RNV>INV)*	13.9	15.7	20.3	21.9
Voters	26.8 (RV>RNV,INV,DNV,DV)*	18.2 (RV>INV,DV)*	7.6 (RV<RNV,DNV,DV; >IV)*	9.0 (RV<RNV,DNV,DV)*	15.2 (RV<DV)*	21.6 (RV>DNV, DV)*
Independents						
Nonvoters	10.9	7.5 (INV<RNV, DNV)*	11.1 (INV<DNV)*	16.5	25.4	22.1
Voters	18.8	12.4	3.4 (IV<INV,DNV,DV,RV,RNV)*	10.6 (IV<DNV,DV)*	10.2 (IV<RNV, INV,DV*; <DNV†)	39.1 (IV>DNV,DV)*
Democrats						
Nonvoters	10.9	15.7 (DNV>INV)*	19.0 (DNV>INV)*	20.1	19.1	15.2
Voters	8.6 (DV<RV)*	13.1 (DV>INV; <RV)*	19.3 (DV>INV,IV,RNV,RV)*	21.4 (DV>RNV,RV,IV)*	23.8 (DV>DNV,RV,IV)*	13.5 (DV<RNV,RV,IV)*

Notes: Average allocation in this table includes participants who choose to allocate no money toward the item (the 0% responses) and participants who allocated their entire budgets toward a single item (the 100% responses). I applied the survey weight to the calculation of the average allocation. Voters are respondents who self-reported that they voted in the 2012 election, while nonvoters are those who self-reported that they did not vote in the 2012 election.

WV = White Voter; WNV = White Nonvoter; BV = Black Voter; BNV = Black Nonvoter; RV = Republican Voter; RNV = Republican Nonvoter; IV = Independent Voter; INV = Independent Nonvoter; DV = Democratic Voter; DNV = Democratic Nonvoter   † = $p \leq 0.10$; *$p < 0.05$

A similar pattern emerges when we examine differences across partisanship. There continue to be few statistically significant differences among nonvoters' investment preferences regardless of their partisan identification. Republican nonvoters' investment preferences were not statistically distinguishable from those of independent or Democratic nonvoters with the sole exception of hiring more probation officers. Republican nonvoters allocated significantly more money toward this goal than independent nonvoters. Independent nonvoters also allocated significantly less money toward hiring more probation officers or funding healthcare clinics than Democratic nonvoters.

In contrast, there are some pronounced differences when we examine voters' preferences. Republican voters allocated significantly more money toward police, probation, and a tax rebate and significantly less money toward clinics, schools, and job creation programs than Democratic voters. These same differences were evident between Republican voters and Democratic nonvoters regarding police, clinics, schools, and a tax rebate. Republican voters only significantly differed from independent voters in that they allocated more money toward healthcare clinics, but they allocated significantly more money toward police and probation than independent nonvoters. Democratic voters allocated significantly more money toward clinics, schools, and job creation but less toward a tax rebate than independent voters; these same differences were also significant in contrast to Republican nonvoters for every category except job creation programs. The magnitude of some of these differences is notable. For example, Republican voters allocated 18.2% more money toward hiring police than Democratic voters, while Democratic voters allocated 15.9% more money toward clinics than Republican voters, on average. Independent voters allocated 25.6% more money toward a tax rebate than Democratic voters.

Which of these differences are the most politically meaningful? Since politicians are most responsive to constituents who vote for them, that means that we should pay careful attention to significant differences between voters and nonvoters within each partisan group, as well as significant differences between partisans and the independents who are more likely to be swing voters in an election. These findings suggest that Republican legislators who pay disproportionate attention to active voters will overestimate Republican citizens' support for funding the police and underestimate Republican citizens' support for funding healthcare clinics and public schools. In other words, the investment preferences of self-identified Republican nonvoters are more liberal than those of Republican voters. In contrast, Democratic voters and nonvoters only have significantly different investment preferences for funding job creation programs, for which the former favor slightly greater investment. Interestingly, independent voters emerge as the stingiest of all. Their willingness to invest in the three community institutions was significantly lower than both Democratic voters and nonvoters, and lower even than Republican voters in the case of funding public schools. Independent voters allocated the single largest portion of money toward the tax rebate out of all the partisan groups in this sample. When it comes to allocating funds for crime prevention in society, these findings suggest that independents are more likely to align with Republicans, not Democrats, but they would be most likely to eschew crime prevention spending altogether in favor of returning money to citizens' pockets.

Table 5.2 presents the overall budget allocation preferences of voters and nonvoters according to the investment preference typology I described in chapter 3. The pattern of results is similar to that produced when we examine respondents' budget allocations category by category. In fact, the model estimates that voters' and nonvoters' likelihood of falling into each budget preference category was statistically equivalent when we examine the full sample. White nonvoters were more likely to allocate all their funds toward a tax rebate than Black nonvoters, but there were no other significant interracial differences among nonvoters. This was not the case among White voters. White voters were significantly less likely to allocate all their funds into community institutions than both Black voters and nonvoters, and significantly less likely to allocate most of their funds into community institutions than Black nonvoters. In contrast, White voters were more likely to balance their allocations across both community and criminal justice institutions than Black voters. White voters were also significantly more likely than Black voters and White nonvoters to allocate most of their funds toward criminal justice institutions or a tax rebate, or both, significantly more likely than both Black and White nonvoters to allocate all their funds toward criminal justice institutions or a tax rebate, or both, and significantly more likely than Black voters to allocate all their funds toward a

TABLE 5.2. Predicted Probability of Budget Preference among National Survey Voters versus Nonvoters

	Only Community	Mostly Community	Balanced	Mostly CJS or Tax	Only CJS or Tax	Only Tax
Full Sample						
Nonvoters	26.8	26.3	17.3	4.9	15.1	9.6
Voters	24.7	26.6	17.9	8.2	14.9	7.8
White Respondents						
Nonvoters	22.2	20.3	21.2	7.1	16.0	13.3 (WNV>BNV)*
Voters	21.0 (WV<BNV, BV)*	18.1 (WV<BNV)*	15.7 (WV>BV)*	12.9 (WV>WNV, BV)*	22.5 (WV>BNV*; >WNV†)	9.8 (WV>BV)*
Black Respondents						
Nonvoters	31.5	32.3	13.3	2.8	14.2	6.0 (BNV<WNV)*
Voters	28.6 (BV>WV)*	35.6 (BV>WNV)*	20.3 (BV<WV*; >BNV†)	3.2 (BV<WV)*	6.8 (BV<WNV, BNV)*	5.7 (BV<WNV, WV)*
Republicans						
Nonvoters	29.0	15.8 (RNV<DNV)†	16.9	10.0 (RNV>INV, DNV)*	17.3	10.9
Voters	13.9 (RV<RNV, DNV, DV)*	12.3 (RV<INV, DNV, DV)*	17.1	15.8 (RV>INV, DNV, DV)*	29.7 (RV>RNV, INV, DNV, DV)*	11.1 (RV>DV)*
Independents						
Nonvoters	27.7	33.9 (INV>RNV)†	9.0 (INV<DNV)†	1.1 (INV<RNV)*	11.7	16.7
Voters	5.9 (IV<RNV, INV, DNV, DV)*	17.4	17.2	13.1	19.1	27.3
Democrats						
Nonvoters	25.6	30.0 (DNV>RNV)*	19.0 (DNV>INV)†	3.1 (DNV<RNV)*	14.6	7.7
Voters	30.1 (DV>RV,IV)*	33.3 (DV>RNV, RV)*	18.3 (DV>INV)*	4.6 (DV>INV; <RV)*	7.9 (DV<RV, DNV, RV)*	5.8 (DV<RV)*

Notes: Predicted probabilities are derived from a series of multinomial logit models that first analyzed the relationship between voting behavior and budget preference, and then interacted voting behavior with race and partisanship (in separate models). I applied the survey weight to the calculation of the predicted probabilities. Voters are respondents who self-reported that they voted in the 2012 election, while nonvoters are those who self-reported that they did not vote in the 2012 election.

WV = White Voter; WNV = White Nonvoter; BV = Black Voter; BNV = Black Nonvoter; RV = Republican Voter; RNV = Republican Nonvoter; IV = Independent Voter; INV = Independent Nonvoter; DV = Democratic Voter; DNV = Democratic Nonvoter

†= $p \leq 0.10$; * $p < 0.05$

tax rebate. Notably, Black voters were marginally more likely to balance their budgets than Black nonvoters and significantly less likely to allocate all their money toward criminal justice institutions or a tax rebate, or both, than Black nonvoters. The largest magnitude difference that was evident in these findings was the 15.7% difference in likelihood of allocating all money toward criminal justice institutions or a tax rebate, or both, between White voters and Black voters.

In terms of partisanship, Republican nonvoters were about half as likely to allocate most of their budget toward community institutions as Democratic nonvoters. They were also significantly more likely to allocate most of their budget toward criminal justice institutions or a tax rebate, or both, than both Democratic and independent nonvoters. There were no other significant budget preference differences among nonvoters of different partisan identifications. In contrast, the model predicted that Republican and Democratic voters would have significantly different likelihoods of falling into each preference category except for a balanced budget. Some of these differences are substantively quite large. For example, Democratic voters were estimated to be about 21% more likely to allocate most of their budget toward community institutions and nearly 22% less likely to allocate all their budget toward criminal justice institutions or a tax rebate, or both, than Republican voters.

Focusing on the most politically meaningful contrasts, Republican voters were significantly less likely to allocate all their budget toward community institutions and significantly more likely to allocate all their budget toward criminal justice institutions or a tax rebate, or both, than Republican nonvoters. This finding reaffirms that Republican nonvoters have more liberal investment preferences than Republican voters. In contrast, Democratic voters were only significantly less likely to allocate all their budget toward criminal justice institutions or a tax rebate, or both, than Democratic nonvoters; Democratic voters and nonvoters did not significantly differ in terms of any other preference category. Independent voters and nonvoters only differed regarding their likelihood of allocating all their money toward community institutions; voters were substantially less likely to fall into this preference category than nonvoters. Independent voters only significantly differed from Republican and Democratic voters regarding their likelihood of allocating all their budget toward community institutions; they were predicted to be the least likely group of partisan voters to choose this allocation distribution. However, independent voters' likelihood of falling into each of the other five preference categories was substantively more similar to the likelihood among Republican voters than Democratic voters even if these differences were not statistically significant.

What is the "big picture" conclusion to draw from this analysis? Mass incarceration grew because late twentieth-century policymakers embraced "volitional criminology" and chose arrests and punishment to the profound detriment of community-based crime prevention as America's solution to crime.[13] My findings affirm that policymakers prioritized the preferences of White voters and Republican voters far more so than other groups of people in America when they choose the criminal justice system over community-based crime prevention.[14] Furthermore, even though they are not always statistically distinguishable from partisans, my survey data suggest that independent voters express crime prevention preferences that are closer in substance to those of Republican voters than Democratic voters. This suggests that Republican and independent voters may combine to form the core constituency in America for whom "soft on crime" policies fall outside the zone of acquiescence.

However, it is important to note that "tough on crime" politicians do not just neglect the preferences of Democrats; they also neglect independent and Republican nonvoters whose crime prevention preferences much more closely resemble the preferences of Democrats. Democratic nonvoters do not suffer from a large underrepresentation problem on this issue since their preferences are quite close to their fellow partisans who actively vote. The same cannot be said for nonvoters of other partisan identities. This finding dovetails with prior evidence that there is a much larger pool of "conflicted conservatives"—people who identify as conservative but express many liberal policy preferences—than conflicted liberals in America,[15] as well as evidence that conflicted conservatives hold some views about criminal justice that are more similar to the views of political moderates than consistent conservatives.[16] However, past researchers found that conflicted conservatives tend to vote at high rates, whereas I see evidence of conflicted conservative views among nonvoters in this survey.[17]

In the next stage of my analysis, I tested whether exposure to the community-descriptor frames in the survey experiment affected the budget allocation preferences of voters and nonvoters differently. I found very little evidence of differential reactions.[18] Voters who were informed that African American communities would receive reinvestment funds allocated about 8% less money toward public schools than voters in the control group. There was no such framing effect among nonvoters, and both voters' and nonvoters' allocations toward all other budget categories were unaffected by frame exposure. In terms of respondents' overall budget preferences, voters who were told that rural communities would receive reinvestment funds were about 16% less likely to fall into the "only community" budget category than voters in the control group. Again, no such framing effect was evident among nonvoters, and both voters' and nonvoters' likelihood of falling into all other budget categories was unaffected by frame exposure.

Will a Legislator Who Supports Community Investment Suffer Backlash at the Ballot Box?

So far, the findings of this chapter indicate that Republican voters express a preference for funding criminal justice institutions, while Democratic voters express a preference for funding community institutions to prevent crime. As such, community investment may fall outside Republican voters' zone of acquiescence (but perhaps not the zone of acquiescence of Republican nonvoters), while criminal justice investment may fall outside Democratic voters' zone of acquiescence. However, we cannot yet definitively conclude that this is true. Just because a voter holds an opinion about one policy does not guarantee that the voter feels strongly about that issue, or that it will outweigh all other political issues and become the primary determinant of a citizen's choice to vote for or against a politician. Remember, according to the zone of acquiescence thesis, politicians only fear "sticking their necks out" for policy changes that will cost them reelection. Anything less that voters will tolerate—even if they do not necessarily like their representatives' choice—is politically safe.

I included two questions in my national survey to test whether a politician's crime prevention budget choices would, in fact, significantly affect people's vote choices. After reporting their own crime prevention budget allocations, participants answered the following questions:

1. If a politician in your state voted to spend this extra money on the criminal justice system (like hiring more police officers or probation officers, for example), would this politician's vote make you more or less likely to vote for him or her?
2. If a politician in your state voted to spend this extra money on improving [experimental treatment condition] communities (by funding health care services, public schools, or job creation programs, for example), would this politician's vote make you more or less likely to vote for him or her?

Participants were given the following response options for each question: "Much more likely to vote for this politician," "Slightly more likely to vote for this politician," "It probably wouldn't change my vote one way or the other," "Slightly less likely to vote for this politician," and "Much less likely to vote for this politician." This measure is imperfect since it is hypothetical, and people could change their minds when they are standing in the voting booth. However, I am not aware of any existing exit poll data from a real election that asked voters whether the candidates' criminal justice policy positions determined their vote choices, and most scholars who surveyed Americans' attitudes about criminal justice over the past fifty years likewise neglected to ask respondents whether those attitudes were politically meaningful to them. As such, we possess shockingly little survey data to directly assess which criminal justice policy choices fall outside Americans' zone of acquiescence. This survey is a step in the right direction, even if the measures are limited.

To begin, table 5.3 presents the distribution of the survey respondents' answers to these two questions among the full sample, ignoring the experimental groupings. "It probably wouldn't change my vote one way or the other" was the most prevalent response to each question. Given policymakers' long-standing preference for investing in the criminal justice system instead of community-based crime prevention, it is quite notable that 43% of respondents said that a politician's vote to invest in the justice system would not affect their votes. This is nearly double the number of respondents who said that they would be "slightly more likely" to vote for a politician who funded the justice system. This finding suggests that the political benefit of taking a "tough on crime" position has faded substantially over time, if it was ever even as great as politicians believed.

TABLE **5.3.** Distribution of National Survey Respondents' Answers to Vote Preference Questions

Much Less Likely	Slightly Less Likely	Wouldn't Change Vote	Slightly More Likely	Much More Likely
A Politician's Vote to Invest in the Criminal Justice System				
9.74	12.69	43.07	21.54	12.97
A Politician's Vote to Invest in Communities				
7.6	8.16	29.79	27.05	27.39

Note: Table presents the percentage of respondents who gave each answer among the full sample. This analysis collapsed all the treatment and control groups. The survey weights were not applied to these estimates.

In contrast, only about a third of respondents said that a politician's vote to invest in communities would not affect their votes. Nearly 55% of respondents said that they would be "slightly" or "much more likely" to vote for a politician who funded communities. It may now be more electorally beneficial for policymakers to invest in communities rather than the justice system—a direct repudiation of "tough on crime" politics. To be sure, we must test for differences in people's estimated vote calculus across key personal and ideological characteristics.

For the sake of simplicity, I combined the responses "much less likely" with "slightly less likely" and "much more likely" with "slightly more likely." I then ran two multinomial logit regression analyses to test how respondents' budget preferences, voting behavior, framing experimental group, and personal and ideological characteristics were related to their estimates of the impact of a politician's support for criminal justice versus community investment on their likelihood of voting for that candidate. I present the full results of these regression models in tables A.5 and A.6 in the appendix. In brief, these results suggest that a person's race, overall budget preferences, voting behavior, partisanship, and beliefs about race relations in society and the justice system were significantly related to their likelihood of saying that a politician's policy choices would affect their vote choice. I present the predicted probabilities of respondents' answers to the vote preference questions across key characteristics while holding all other variables in the model constant at their mean values in tables 5.4 and 5.5. Here, we are interested not just in the predicted differences between two categories, such as voters' versus nonvoters' allocation toward schools, but rather various ways that

TABLE 5.4. Predicted Probability of Criminal Justice Investment Vote Preference across Key Respondent Characteristics

	Less Likely to Vote For	Wouldn't Change Vote	More Likely to Vote For
White	11.13 (8.35–13.91)	47.50 (43.42–51.58)	41.37 (37.28–45.45)
Black	28.96 (25.00–32.32)	49.14 (44.91–53.37)	21.90 (18.44–25.36)
Republican	9.69 (6.54–12.84)	41.19 (36.27–46.10)	49.12 (44.00–54.25)
Independent	8.48 (2.17–14.79)	87.35 (79.45–95.25)	4.16 (-0.36–8.69)
Democrat	23.93 (20.63–27.23)	50.39 (46.69–54.10)	25.68 (22.45–28.90)
Nonvoter	15.84 (11.12–20.57)	60.96 (54.57–67.06)	23.19 (17.90–28.48)
Voter	18.98 (15.96–22.00)	47.05 (43.55–50.55)	33.97 (30.67–37.27)
Only Community	35.83 (30.59–41.07)	49.30 (43.76–54.84)	14.87 (11.11–18.64)
Mostly Community	28.71 (23.82–33.61)	51.35 (45.87–56.83)	19.94 (15.77–24.11)
Balanced	10.22 (6.38–14.07)	43.96 (37.71–50.21)	45.82 (39.50–52.14)
Mostly CJS or Tax	2.3 (-0.27–4.94)	32.77 (23.86–41.67)	64.90 (55.71–74.09)
Only CJS or Tax	4.8 (2.12–7.49)	27.04 (21.00–33.08)	68.16 (61.78–74.54)
Only Tax	28.64 (19.14–38.15)	56.44 (46.79–66.09)	14.91 (8.36–21.47)

Notes: Predicted probabilities estimated following multinomial logit regression presented in table A.5 in the appendix. All other variables held constant at their means. Survey weights applied. 95% confidence intervals presented in parentheses.

respondents' answers differed across many categories. Most of the differences between these predicted probabilities were significantly different even after adjusting for multiple comparisons. As such, I also present the 95% confidence intervals of the predicted probabilities to help the reader identify significant versus nonsignificant comparisons.[19]

Table 5.4 presents the predicted probabilities of respondents' judgments about whether a politician's vote to invest money into criminal justice institutions would increase, decrease, or not change their likelihood of voting for that politician. Note how consistently the model predicts that respondents would say that a politician's support for criminal justice investment would not affect their vote choice one way or the other. White and Black respondents, independents and Democrats, voters and nonvoters, and respondents who were classified in the "only community," "mostly community," and "only tax" budget preference categories were all predicted to be most likely to choose this answer. Only Republicans and respondents who were classified in the "balanced," "mostly criminal justice or tax," or "only criminal justice or tax" budget preference categories were predicted to be most likely to say that a politician's support for criminal justice investment would make them more likely to vote for that candidate. However, in the case of Republicans and respondents who balanced their crime prevention budgets, the predicted difference between the likelihoods of choosing "wouldn't change vote" versus "more likely to vote" were modest and not statistically significant.

The multinomial logit models indicated that respondents' predicted likelihood of voting for a candidate who supported criminal justice investment was also influenced by their level of agreement with racist stereotypes that people of color are lazy and their perception of the degree to which the criminal justice system treats people differently depending on their race. I present the effects of these two variables in figure 5.1. These two beliefs had little effect on respondents' likelihood of stating that a politician's criminal justice investment choices would not affect their vote choice one way or the other. In contrast, respondents who most strongly rejected the laziness stereotype and believed that the criminal justice system treats racial minorities worse than White people are predicted to be "less likely" to vote for a politician who supported criminal justice investment rather than "more likely" to vote for the candidate. This pattern is reversed among respondents who more strongly endorsed the laziness stereotype and believed that the criminal justice system treats all people fairly regardless of race. In fact, it was only respondents who scored highest on these two measures who were predicted to reply that this financial choice would make them "more likely" to vote for a candidate than to reply that it "wouldn't change" their vote one way or the other. In other words, these data suggest that "tough on crime" voting can still yield electoral benefit for politicians in twenty-first century America, but only among constituents who most strongly endorse the tenets of colorblind racism.[20]

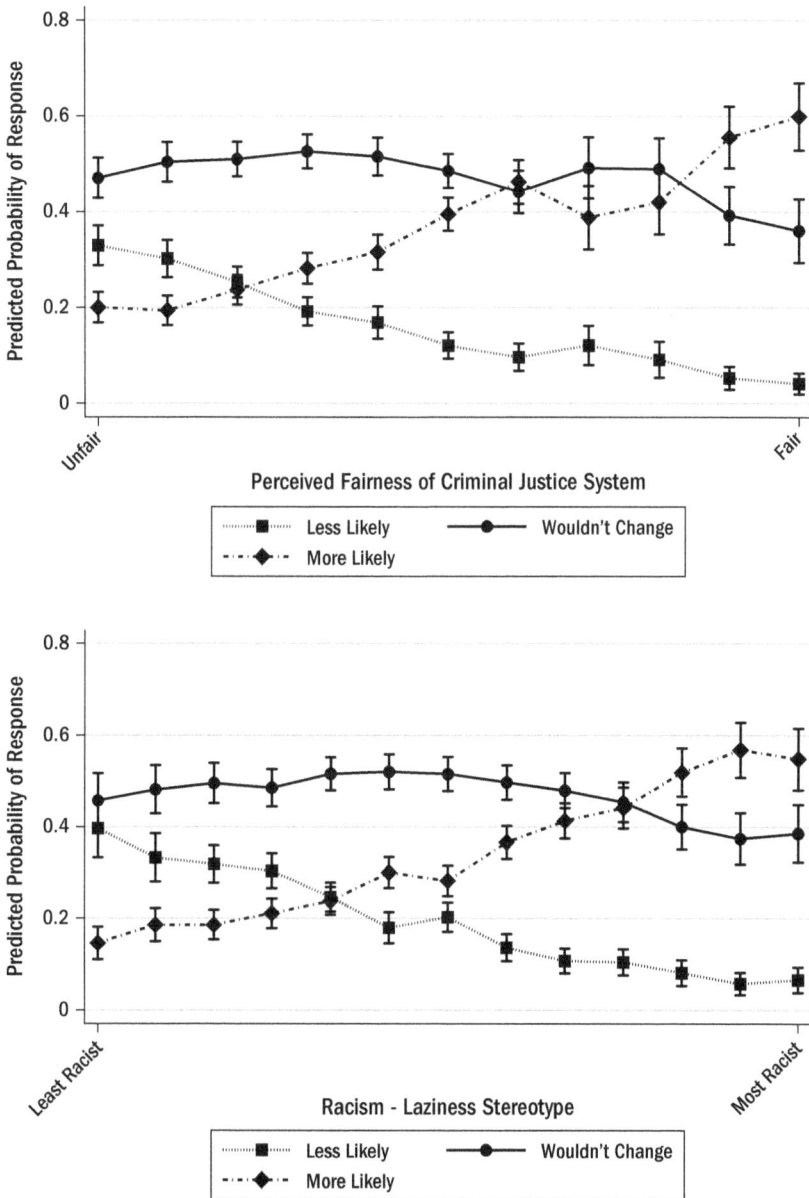

Figure 5.1. Effects of Perceived Criminal Justice System Fairness and Racism-Laziness Stereotype on Criminal Justice Investment Vote Preference.

Next, table 5.5 presents the predicted probabilities of respondents' judgments about whether a politician's vote to invest money into community institutions would affect their likelihood of voting for that politician. These findings paint a very different picture. Here, the model predicted that many groups of respondents would express an increased likelihood to vote for a politician who supported community investment. This was true of White respondents; Black respondents; Democrats; voters; nonvoters; and people who fell into the "only community," "mostly community," and "balanced budget" preference categories. Only Republicans, independents, and respondents whose budget preferences

TABLE 5.5. Predicted Probability of Community Investment Vote Preference across Key Respondent Characteristics

	Less Likely to Vote for	Wouldn't Change Vote	More Likely to Vote for
White	18.94 (15.57–22.30)	36.00 (32.03–39.97)	45.06 (40.79–49.33)
Black	8.17 (5.76–10.58)	23.36 (19.78–26.94)	68.47 (64.48–72.47)
Republican	27.73 (23.03–32.41)	39.64 (34.80–44.48)	32.64 (27.76–37.52)
Independent	14.11 (3.16–25.05)	60.60 (42.96–78.24)	25.29 (9.07–41.52)
Democrat	8.13 (6.11–10.15)	23.18 (20.13–26.22)	68.69 (65.31–72.07)
Nonvoter	9.81 (6.16–13.45)	37.68 (31.18–44.19)	52.51 (45.59–59.43)
Voter	13.94 (11.30–16.59)	28.14 (25.06–31.22)	57.92 (54.44–61.39)
Only Community	5.63 (3.26–7.99)	19.52 (15.09–23.94)	74.86 (70.00–79.72)
Mostly Community	8.79 (5.39–12.19)	18.55 (14.47–22.62)	72.66 (67.75–77.58)
Balanced	9.81 (6.19–13.44)	32.42 (26.39–38.44)	57.77 (51.35–64.19)
Mostly CJS or Tax	29.01 (20.01–38.01)	36.66 (27.19–46.12)	34.33 (24.16–44.50)
Only CJS or Tax	29.87 (23.10–36.64)	50.01 (42.87–57.29)	20.05 (14.46–15.64)
Only Tax	32.40 (23.95–40.85)	40.33 (30.97–49.68)	27.27 (18.49–36.06)

Notes: Predicted probabilities estimated following multinomial logit regression presented in table A.6 in the appendix. All other variables held constant at their means. Survey weights applied. 95% confidence intervals presented in parentheses placed them in the "mostly criminal justice or tax," "only criminal justice or tax," or "only tax" categories were predicted to be more likely to say that a politician's support for community investment wouldn't affect their vote choice (though not all the differences between responses among these groups were statistically significant). No group of respondents was predicted to have the highest likelihood of responding that they would be "less likely" to vote for a politician who supported community investment.[21]

Figure 5.2 presents the effects of respondents' belief about the persistence of racial discrimination in society and belief that the criminal justice system treats all people the same or differently depending on their race. Here, we see that respondents who acknowledged that racial discrimination persists in society and respondents who recognized that the criminal justice system treats people differently depending on their race were predicted to have higher likelihoods of saying that they would be "more likely" to vote for a politician who supported community investment. The probability of choosing "more likely" decreased in a linear fashion as respondents' denial of racial discrimination and belief that the justice system is unbiased increased. The respondents who most strongly denied racial discrimination and insisted that the justice system is unbiased were significantly less likely to say that they would be "more likely" to vote for a politician who supported community investment than to say that they would be "less likely" to vote for such a candidate, or that their vote would not be affected. The predicted probabilities of choosing either of the latter two responses were not statistically different at the highest levels of the racial discrimination and criminal justice system fairness variables.

Finally, I turn special attention to "conflicted conservative" Americans, people who self-identify as conservative and are attracted to conservative political rhetoric and symbols but also express support for a wide range of government policies and benefits. Conflicted conservatives' policy preferences are often quite similar to the policy preferences of self-identified liberals. These Americans make up about a fifth of the electorate, and some evidence indicates that they vote at a higher rate than self-identified moderates or independents, which makes them pivotal swing voters in elections.[22] For the purpose of this study, I defined conflicted conservatives as respondents who labeled their political

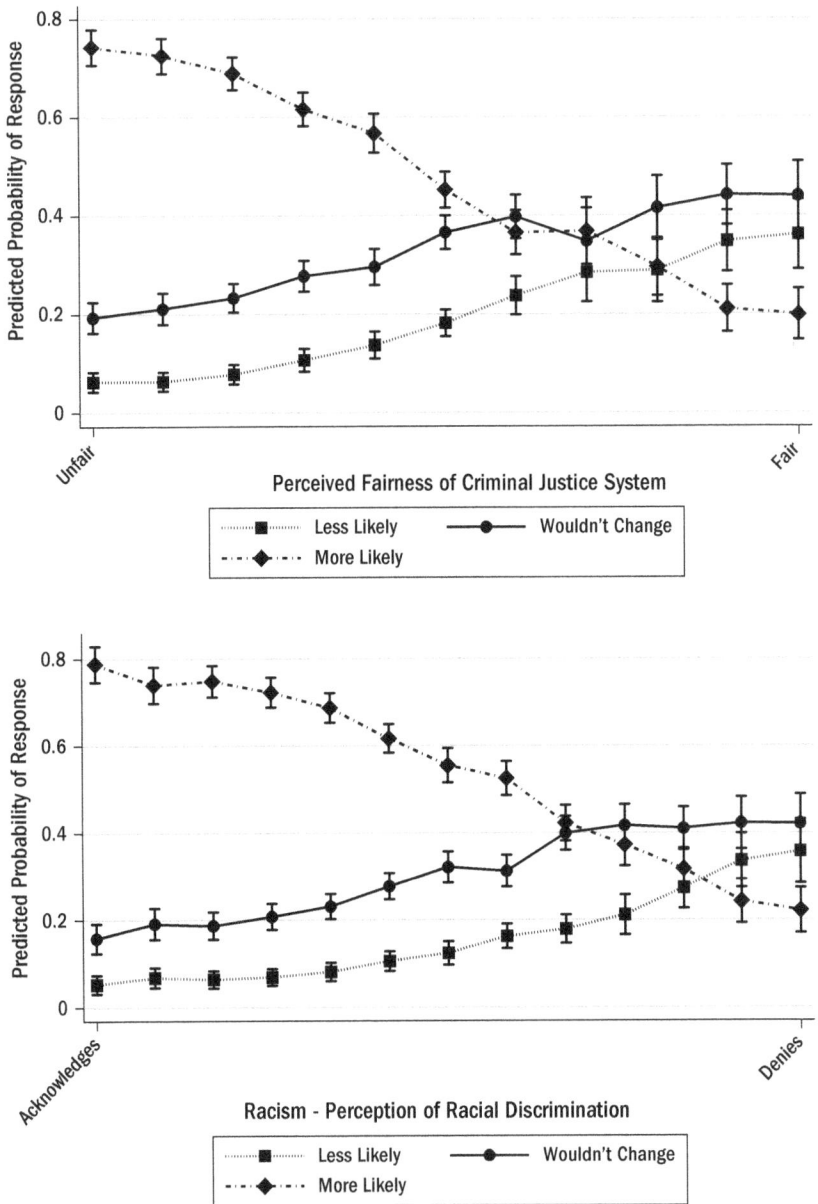

Figure 5.2. Effects of Perceived Criminal Justice System Fairness and Denial of Racial Discrimination in Society on Community Investment Vote Preference.

ideology as "conservative" but whose crime prevention budget preferences placed them in the "only community" or "mostly community" categories. According to this definition, 195 respondents were conflicted conservatives. They made up about 35% of the self-identified conservatives in my survey sample, about 21.6% of the respondents who fell into the "only community" or "mostly community" budget preference categories, and about 9.7% of my sample, overall.

Table 5.6 presents the predicted probabilities of conflicted conservatives' vote preferences. I differentiate between conflicted conservatives who voted in the 2012 election and those who did not. These findings show that most conflicted conservatives were predicted to say that their vote would not be influenced by a politician's choice to invest in criminal justice institutions, but they would be more likely to vote for a politician who supported investment into community institutions. The predicted vote preferences of conflicted conservative voters and nonvoters were not statistically different from each other.

In summary, I see very little evidence in these data that investment into community institutions for the purpose of crime prevention falls outside the public's zone of acquiescence. The statistical analyses predicted that most Black and White Americans would say that a politician's choice to support community investment would make them more likely

TABLE 5.6. Predicted Probability of Criminal Justice and Community Investment Vote Preference among Conflicted Conservatives

	Less Likely to Vote For	Wouldn't Change Vote	More Likely to Vote For
	Politician Who Supported Criminal Justice Investment		
CC Nonvoter	21.15 (13.75–28.94)	65.11 (56.59–73.62)	13.75 (8.69–18.80)
CC Voter	27.87 (20.97–34.77)	52.94 (45.82–60.06)	19.19 (14.38–23.99)
	Politician Who Supported Community Investment		
CC Nonvoter	8.10 (3.69–12.51)	33.83 (24.91–42.74)	58.07 (48.63–67.51)
CC Voter	13.43 (8.38–18.48)	24.64 (18.78–30.51)	61.93 (54.80–69.05)

Notes: Predicted probabilities estimated following multinomial logit regressions presented in tables A.5 and A.6 in the appendix. All other variables held constant at their means. Survey weights applied. 95% confidence intervals presented in parentheses. Conflicted conservative (CC) respondents are those who self-identified as politically conservative but were classified in the "only community" or "mostly community" crime prevention budget preference categories.

to vote for that candidate, not less. Even Republicans and respondents who chose to prioritize criminal justice investment in their own budgets were generally predicted to be most likely to say that a politician's choice to support community investment would not affect their vote one way or the other. Indeed, if we contrast the findings presented in figures 5.1 and 5.2, we see that community investment is predicted to generate more of an electoral payoff among racially liberal Americans (meaning those who reject racist stereotypes and recognize discrimination in both society and the justice system) than the comparable electoral payoff of criminal justice investment among Americans who endorse the tenets of symbolic or colorblind racism. Overall, these findings send a clear signal that many politicians who prioritized funding the criminal justice system over community institutions fundamentally misjudged public opinion and the politics of community-based justice reinvestment.[23]

Conclusion

Toward a Twenty-First Century Politics of Crime Prevention

In this book, I have presented a study of the politics of crime prevention in the United States. Direct investment designed to bolster the "human resources and physical infrastructure" of impoverished communities that suffer from high rates of crime has long been a white whale for liberal activists and politicians—long pursued, rarely achieved, and even more rarely sustained over time.[1] Many politicians who otherwise support criminal justice reform believe that community investment is not a politically viable policy option.[2] In this concluding chapter, I will review my empirical findings and assess whether the evidence supports their pessimistic judgment. I will then lay out the contributions this book makes to scholarship and to contemporary political debates about crime prevention, paying particular attention to questions about political framing and the distribution of public benefits. Finally, I will consider unanswered questions and propose recommendations for future research to continue expanding our understanding of the politics of crime prevention.

Summary of Empirical Findings

In chapter 1, we saw that the focus group participants recognized many different causes of crime—both volitional and structural in nature. By comparing the opinions of the focus group participants to older public opinion studies, I concluded that Americans have long recognized that crime is neither simply a consequence of "bad choices" divorced from social context nor solely a function of environment divorced from personal agency. However, Americans in the early twenty-first century may give greater weight to structural causes of crime than they did in the latter decades of the twentieth century. In chapter 2, we saw that most focus group participants endorsed many different structural solutions intended to address the root causes of crime, but few participants offered such solutions on their own without prompting from the moderator. Instead, many participants—especially Black participants—first offered ideas about how people should take care of themselves and their own communities to prevent crime.[3] I argued that Black Americans in particular may "turn inward" for solutions because they have historically lacked confidence that government will respond to their concerns. This lack of confidence creates a disconnect between what Black Americans want the government to do for their communities versus the self- and community-driven actions that they feel are under their control and worth talking about. The liberal, college educated, White participants spoke most readily about government-led solutions to address the structural causes of crime, but their more conservative peers adamantly disagreed. These findings suggest that race, social class, and community context all shape the way Americans think and talk about crime control.[4] These dynamics have important implications for political representation and accountability.[5]

In chapter 3, I analyzed data from both the focus groups and the national survey in which participants constructed their own hypothetical crime prevention budgets. We saw that the majority of focus group participants allocated most, if not all, of their money toward community institutions like public schools and healthcare clinics instead of investing into criminal justice institutions like police, probation, or prisons. The high school educated participants of both races most consistently and strongly preferred community investment over criminal justice investment. They argued that the criminal justice system already has enough money and that it is not the most efficient or effective means of preventing crime. Some of the college educated participants of both races disagreed with each other and expressed varying degrees of reticence to invest money into institutions that would benefit the "undeserving" poor. Even given these considerations, most of the college educated participants also preferred to invest in community institutions. Among the national survey respondents, about two-thirds of Black Americans and about one-third of White Americans invested predominantly or exclusively in community institutions. In contrast, only about 10% of Black Americans and about one-third of

White Americans invested predominantly or exclusively into criminal justice institutions.

In chapter 4, I tested whether Americans' investment preferences depend upon how the communities that would receive investment are described. We saw that respondents' allocations were largely consistent across all the experimental frame conditions. Only two frames caused changes that withstood the highest level of statistical scrutiny. Urban respondents who were told that "rural communities" would receive investment allocated significantly less money toward public schools than respondents who were simply told that "communities" would receive money, while rural respondents in this condition allocated significantly more money toward schools. The "African American communities" cue exerted the most consistent effect in the experiment. Respondents defined by a range of personal characteristics, but most especially White respondents, allocated significantly less money toward community institutions but more money toward criminal justice institutions or a tax rebate if they were told that "African American communities" would benefit from investment. Most of the focus group participants said that money should be invested in proportion to the local crime problem; locales with higher crime rates should receive more money. However, I also noted how the participants' common sentiment that "crime is everywhere" could potentially undermine their support for targeted investment.

Finally, in chapter 5, I tested whether a politician's support for community investment might fall outside voters' "zone of acquiescence" and provoke public backlash. We saw that self-identified Republican and independent voters were more supportive of criminal justice investment or a tax rebate, while Democratic voters—and Republican and independent nonvoters—were more supportive of community investment. Most respondents said that a politician's choice to invest in criminal justice institutions probably would not affect their likelihood of voting for that person one way or the other, whereas a majority of respondents said that they would be more likely to vote for a politician who supported investment into community institutions. Even the most punitive respondents who favored criminal justice investment in their own budgets were most likely to say that a politician's support for community investment would not actually affect their vote.

Implications for Scholarship

Understanding Public Opinion about Criminal Justice and Crime Prevention

For several decades, the consensus among scholars who studied public opinion about criminal justice was that Americans are "pragmatic."[6] According to this perspective, most Americans believe that both volitional and structural factors cause crime, and they express varying degrees of support for both tough punishments and rehabilitation. Punitive and progressive attitudes are not mutually exclusive. Criminologists Justin Pickett and Thomas Baker argued that the prior evidence supporting the pragmatism hypothesis was a function of survey design choices that increase the likelihood respondents will quickly choose answers rather than think about them carefully. In contrast, their evidence suggests that Americans' punitive and progressive attitudes might be in more tension with each other than scholars had previously concluded.[7]

While I think that Pickett and Baker's work holds important lessons for survey design and the analysis of quantitative data in the study of public opinion about criminal justice, the findings I have presented in this book give me greater confidence in American pragmatism. The qualitative focus group findings I presented in chapters 1 and 2 largely avoid the methodological problems raised by Pickett and Baker and clearly show that people recognize both structural and volitional causes of crime, and they express both punitive and progressive sentiments. American public opinion about criminal justice exists along a spectrum. While the bulk of Americans likely hold pragmatic opinions, a minority of "extreme" Americans may hold exclusively punitive or exclusively progressive policy preferences, a point on which Pickett, Baker, and their critics largely agree.[8] My survey findings in chapter 3 indeed show that some Americans exclusively choose to invest in criminal justice institutions or community institutions for the purpose of preventing crime, but more people chose to invest some of their money into both types of institutions.

If we accept that most Americans hold a mix of punitive and progressive opinions, the more important question then becomes, when does one constellation of opinions become particularly salient and politically meaningful to voters? After all, if people choose a candidate who ran a "tough on crime" campaign because something caused their punitive opinions to be salient at the moment that they step into the voting booth, then these voters will have helped policy move in a more punitive direction regardless of whatever other progressive opinions they also hold. We know that the way we ask survey questions shapes the responses we receive.[9] Scholars need to give survey respondents more opportunity to express both the strength with which they hold particular opinions and indicate their preferred choices when presented with a range of possible policies. Such survey design choices will give scholars greater insight into the electoral implications of public opinion about criminal justice.

Properly measuring people's hierarchy of policy preferences matters far beyond debates among survey researchers. Changes in the overall level of punitive public attitudes caused policymakers to in turn make criminal justice policy more punitive, which is consistent with the theory that politicians respond more to shifts and trends in public opinion than they do to static levels of support or opposition to particular issues.[10] When mass public opinion shifts in a more liberal or conservative manner, this change is usually reflected across all demographic subgroups of the population.[11] Though White and Black Americans consistently differed in their overall levels of punitiveness over the course of the twentieth century, when one racial group grew relatively more punitive, so too did the other group.[12] According to one interpretation of this theory of "dynamic representation," the tough on crime politics of the 1980s and 1990s reflected changes in Black public opinion as much as White public opinion.[13]

Here, I strongly agree with the political scientist Lisa Miller's critiques of this perspective.[14] Miller recognizes that many Black Americans who personally confront the ravages of violence in their neighborhoods express genuinely punitive sentiments. Indeed, many politicians who supported the harshest changes in sentencing law during the "tough on crime" era justified their actions by saying that their Black constituents demanded that they do more to fight gun violence and the drug trade. However, as the findings I have presented in this book reaffirm, few Black Americans express only punitive sentiments. Most Black Americans—especially those who are exposed to crime in their communities—believe that crime is inextricably intertwined with broader social problems that are related to poverty and segregation. As such, their primary demand is that government help them improve their communities; their calls for police to arrest the neighborhood's criminals are important but, in many ways, secondary.

Miller argues that the dynamics of public opinion (interacting with America's fragmented, federalized political system) allow policymakers to engage in what she calls "lowest legislative common denominator politics." She explains, "increasing penalties [is] popular with both lawmakers and the public alike when serious crime is high and spending is largely unnoticed as costs are spread across state populations; meanwhile, improving educational, employment, or other opportunities to ameliorate criminogenic conditions may also be supported by much of the public, but such policies demand increased local spending, which is highly constrained."[15] Since politicians can point to the existence of punitive sentiment among all groups of Americans, they choose policing and punishment as the predominant responses to crime while ignoring Black Americans' pleas for community investment, which would require much greater changes to taxes and the distribution of public spending. Other scholars have called this political choice a profound act of "selective hearing."[16]

The social costs of lowest legislative common denominator politics are inequitably distributed. When policymakers choose to invest only in deterrence-focused criminal justice solutions rather than investments to ameliorate the social conditions that cause crime, the weight of the criminal justice system disproportionately falls upon majority-Black and majority-Latino communities of concentrated disadvantage.[17] Affluent White communities remain virtually untouched by the punitive arm of the state.[18] To use a metaphor, single-minded use of surveillance, arrest, and punishment to fight crime is like chemotherapy to fight cancer. It may reduce the problem, but it inevitably sickens the patient in the process, and it may fail and kill the patient regardless. Mass incarceration has further weakened the social and economic foundations of already-disadvantaged communities.[19] That is why most Black Americans call for community investment to be paired with criminal justice intervention; disadvantaged communities need to be strengthened in order to thrive following the "treatment" of targeted law enforcement. To choose one without the other is to inflict suffering upon minority communities without any balance of restoration, and it privileges the opinions of punitive White Americans over the more nuanced, multifaceted opinions of Americans of color.[20] When dealing with the criminal justice system—the most coercive arm of the state, which is authorized to use violence against civilians—politicians must be very careful when pointing to punitive public sentiments in order to argue that they are "giving people what they asked for." Parallel shifts in punitiveness should not justify a single-minded policy response that will concentrate negative externalities upon minority groups and disadvantaged communities.

Finally, I believe that American criminologists who study public opinion have historically paid far too little attention to crime prevention. When scholars study "progressive" attitudes, they have typically measured them as public support for rehabilitation or second chances for former inmates. If our idea of progressive criminal justice policy is limited to prison rehabilitation programs, drug treatment, or programs to help former inmates reenter the community, then we will be intervening only after a crime has occurred in the first place. The smaller number of studies of public support for true crime prevention typically focused on "child saving" programs designed to prevent juvenile delinquency.[21] This is a step in the right direction, but such interventions do not extend to adult offenders, and the study of delinquency prevention rarely has much to say about community wellbeing in a broader sense. Indeed, two decades ago, the authors of a frequently cited review of the literature only discussed crime prevention within the context of prison-based rehabilitation or early intervention programs targeted toward juveniles.[22] The authors of a more recent literature review devoted only three paragraphs to "attacking the social causes of crime," whereas they wrote six pages on early intervention, rehabilitation as the goal of corrections, and juvenile rehabilitation.[23] In the wake of advocates' calls to fundamentally reimagine public safety as part of the "defund the police" debate, it is time for criminologists to think more expansively about crime prevention when we study the politics of criminal justice.[24]

The Effect of Implicit versus Explicit Racial Cues

According to racial priming theory, racism makes White Americans resist candidates of color and policies designed to ameliorate racial discrimination. However, because post–civil rights movement norms of racial equity put pressure on White Americans to publicly reject racism, the theory predicts that exposure to an explicit (that is, blatant) racial cue will cause White Americans to express greater support for racially progressive policies in an effort to "flash their nonracist bona fides," so to speak. In contrast, exposure to an implicit racial cue will trigger racist backlash against racially progressive policies because implicit racial cues give White Americans "plausible deniability" that racism had anything to do with their decision-making.[25]

For a long time, political scientists rather widely agreed that racial cues can influence White Americans' political preferences, including implicit racial cues like "inner city."[26] However, several scholars have recently failed to replicate racial priming theory's original distinction between implicit and explicit racial cues.[27] Some studies found that exposure to racial cues did little to change people's political or policy opinions, which suggests that the influence of racial cues may be waning as the American public grows more polarized and entrenched in their political positions.[28] Other research suggests that Black politicians, specifically, can gain favor among White voters with moderate or conservative beliefs about race relations if they employ explicitly racialized tropes exhorting Black people to work harder and exercise more personal responsibility, a form of "respectability politics."[29]

My findings are similar to those of other racial priming studies in some ways, but different in others. My experiment failed to produce results that conform to the predictions of the original theory. White respondents who were explicitly told that "African American communities" would receive reinvestment money should have allocated significantly more money into the community-based budget options than White respondents in the control group in an effort to signal their racial egalitarianism. Instead, we saw the opposite pattern; White respondents backlashed and invested significantly less in the community institutions. Racial priming theory predicts that the implicitly racial cues of my experiment should have caused Whites to prefer criminal justice investment over community investment. However, the implicit cues caused few statistically significant differences in opinion between Whites in the treatment groups and Whites in the control group, and none of those differences survived statistical corrections for multiple comparisons. Contrary to another key component of racial priming theory, I also found very little evidence that the effects of cue exposure differed depending upon respondents' preexisting racial attitudes.[30]

Why are my results different from those of prior studies? It is impossible to know for sure, but I think there are two plausible explanations. My results are similar to those of political scientists Jon Hurwitz and Mark Peffley who measured respondents' support for "spending more money on social programs to help people in these neighborhoods get jobs" and "creating more drug rehabilitation programs for people in these neighborhoods." Both questions were embedded under the prompt, "Here are some things that law enforcement might do to deal with the problems of drugs and crime in mostly [Black/White] neighborhoods in the inner city." In this experiment, they found no significant relationship between respondents' endorsement of anti-Black stereotypes and their expressed support for either preventive or rehabilitative programs regardless of whether the neighborhood was described as majority-Black or majority-White.

Hurwitz and Peffley concluded, "In the context of preventive policies . . . stereotypes are much less consequential, presumably because such programs are intended for individuals not yet stigmatized as violent."[31] Their interpretation rings true. When Americans are asked broad, general questions about punishment, their default mental image is of a "worst case" violent offender who has committed many crimes. It is little surprise that many Americans endorse harsh punishments when they are thinking of the "worst of the worst." When people are specifically asked to consider nonviolent and first-time offenders, the punitiveness of their answers declines substantially.[32] Much (though admittedly not all) of the public's racialized fear of crime is tied to stereotypes of Black violence.[33] It stands to reason that racialized punitive attitudes may be less likely to rear their ugly heads when people are considering efforts to prevent crime in the first place.

There is another possibility. Both the research described in this book and the project of Hurwitz and Peffley queried respondents' opinions about neighborhood-level interventions.[34] I am aware of no other racial priming studies on the topics of welfare or criminal justice that employed racial cues about neighborhoods rather than groups of people. This difference might be quite meaningful. Racial priming theory holds that racialized cues activate White Americans' stereotypes about racial minorities—stereotypes that largely revolve around perceptions of work ethic, morality, and deservingness. Many prior racial priming studies oriented their respondents to think about individual welfare recipients or criminal offenders, a cognitive scenario that likely heightens the impulse to judge undeserving, stigmatized persons.[35] But would the average American be equally willing to penalize every other person who lives in the same neighborhood as the individual welfare recipient or offender they have in their mind when responding to a survey with a racial priming experiment? Neighborhood-level programs or institutions can be utilized by many people, innocent and guilty alike.

Viewed in this light, my findings start to make more sense. I designed the implicit racial cues of my experiment to reference particular social problems that are concentrated within disadvantaged neighborhoods. Crime, poverty, and welfare use are all problems that would not exist in a utopia. These three implicit cues gave respondents reasons why those neighborhoods need targeted investment. In contrast, I suspect that the "African American communities" cue triggered White respondents' pejorative stereotype that Black Americans ask for "special treatment," like affirmative action. This provokes resentment among some White people if they believe that race-targeted government programs ignore and overlook White communities that are also struggling with various social problems.[36] I do not have a satisfactory hypothesis as to why the "inner-city communities" and "rural communities" cues also failed to generate robust framing effects. It is plausible that the former cue triggered respondents' associations with crime, poverty, and welfare; after all, it is those associations that have historically made the phrase "inner city" a racialized cue in the first place. Thus, this cue may have also carried an implicit justification for investment. Future research should explore these possibilities, and racial priming scholars should devote greater attention to the prospect that racialized cues may affect public opinion differently when discussed in the context of policies that would affect entire neighborhoods or regions rather than individual beneficiaries of public aid programs.

Implications for Politics

The findings of this research project touch upon a long-standing debate among politicians, pundits, and activists of the American Left. To build a stable political coalition that is powerful enough to fight systemic racism, should the Left focus on race-targeted or universal social policies? Rhetorically, should it emphasize racial justice language or employ race-neutral language to discuss social justice in a manner that emphasizes social class, poverty, and labor justice? These questions have been debated on the Left for decades and continue to the present day.[37]

Distressingly, much empirical evidence indicates that most White Americans respond to racial justice focused arguments about systemic racism with avoidance or hostility.[38] Perhaps more surprising are the findings of law professor Ian Haney López and his colleagues in the Race-Class Narratives Project. They found that focus group participants of all races recoiled when the moderators prompted them to discuss the legacy of slavery and White discrimination against people of other races. White focus group participants typically grew defensive when these topics were raised, arguing that they are not responsible for the actions of White people hundreds of years ago. However, the moderators observed, "people of color in our focus groups tended to resist all express discussions of white-over-nonwhite racism."[39] Instead, many participants of color either defaulted to volitional attributions of responsibility (for example, "I think that passivity has a lot to do with why we may not get ahead")[40] or argued that the problem wasn't even worth discussing because no civil rights social movements have, or likely ever will, overturn white hegemony. Though White participants and participants of color had different reasons for shying away from an open discussion of systemic racism, they converged on the same political problem: many Americans prefer to discuss volitional explanations for racial disparities and inequities rather than sociological or structural explanations.[41]

If many Americans, including many Americans of color, resist talking about statistical evidence of systemic racism, how would they respond to different kinds of political messages intended to drum up public support for anti-racist, antipoverty social policies? Here, the empirical evidence is slightly more mixed but not terribly optimistic for racial justice messages. Several scholars have found that race-neutral arguments for social benefit policies or criminal justice reform generated more widespread public support than race-targeted justifications for those same policies, though these effects sometimes differed across the race and political partisanship of respondents.[42]

López and his colleagues in the Race-Class Narratives Project also tested how survey and focus group participants from across the country reacted to a variety of political advertisements and messages that presented different justifications for fighting inequality in American society. The general pattern of their findings was that White Americans tended to split relatively evenly when asked to judge whether they preferred conservative, "dog whistle" messages that played on racialized fear of immigrants and crime or colorblind, liberal, economic-populist messages that talked broadly about income inequality and wealthy elites "rigging the system." This split was especially pronounced among "persuadables," the majority of White Americans whom they found to lack strong attachments to either the Democratic or Republican parties. In contrast, they found that a majority of White participants consistently preferred "race-class" messages over dog whistle messages when the former was introduced into the discussion; race-class messages were also more attractive to respondents than purely economic messages that said nothing about race whatsoever. López and colleagues employed several different race-class messages, but they shared a common theme of Americans of all races and backgrounds coming together to build a better country.

They also conducted one test that was directly pertinent to this study:

> We asked people which came closer to their views: a right-wing probusiness story, or a progressive agenda promoting activist government. In doing so, we offered respondents two versions of the progressive message, with and without the italicized text: "To make life better for working people we need to invest in education, create better paying jobs, and make healthcare more affordable for *white, Black, and brown* people struggling to make ends meet." How did the two versions of the progressive message compare? The race-silent progressive message bested the probusiness message by a margin of 33 points. This result confirms that voters generally prefer progressive over probusiness economic policies. But what happened when the progressive policy position included the phrase "white, Black, and brown?" The winning margin over the conservative policies increased to 41 points, a significant improvement. Mentioning that all racial groups would benefit drove up support for investing in education, creating better-paying jobs, and making healthcare more

affordable. Support for progressive policies did not fall off a cliff when race was mentioned. It dramatically increased when combined with assurances that all racial groups will benefit.[43]

Reflecting on the total findings of their research, López and colleagues concluded, "1) People are worried about racial division. They want messages that touch on this, and they respond positively to messages that expressly communicate that all racial groups, whites included, will do better by coming together. 2) What tends to lose the persuadable middle is naming racism solely in terms of harms to communities of color in a manner that implicitly excludes and perhaps even faults whites. Assuring voters that whites will benefit from activist government proved to be an essential element in generating enthusiasm."[44]

Reconsidering Targeting within Universalism and the Politics of Recognition versus Redistribution in the Twenty-First Century

The political problem, then, is how to assemble majority support (or at least acquiescence) for public policies that would ameliorate the socioeconomic symptoms of systemic racism and concentrated disadvantage given the evidence of White Americans' consistent resistance to race-targeted programs. Decades ago, several scholars argued that the most viable political solution to this problem was "targeting within universalism."[45] In other words, craft social policies that could benefit a wide swath of Americans, such as Social Security or universal subsidized childcare, in such a manner that they would disproportionately benefit Americans of color not because of their race, but because systemic racism causes Americans of color to disproportionately suffer poverty and its associated ills. Sociologist William Julius Wilson called this a "hidden agenda," the purpose of which is to "improve the life chances of groups such as the ghetto underclass by emphasizing programs in which the more advantaged groups of all races can positively relate."[46] Similarly, political scientist Charles V. Hamilton wrote,

> I suggested that there were certain clear political advantages to be derived from emphasizing issues that lent themselves to what I called "de-racialized solutions." By this I meant that certain issues, such as full

employment, a meaningful national health insurance law, and a sound income-maintenance program, would (or at least ought to) appeal to broad segments of the electorate across racial lines. My position then and now is that there are millions of unemployed whites as well as Blacks who need decent paying jobs; that health-care costs threaten poor and marginal income whites as well as Blacks.[47]

Hamilton's position echoed that of Bayard Rustin and the Freedom Budget for All Americans that I discussed in the introductory chapter.[48]

Critics of these positions typically make two arguments. First, they note that universal social benefits policies excluded Black people for the first few decades of their existence.[49] Perhaps because White people received a "head start" on the intergenerational accumulation of wealth that was facilitated by universal benefits programs, such programs that continue to operate today have failed to close the racial wealth gap.[50] Most of America's government-subsidized financial benefit programs that are "submerged" in the tax code disproportionately benefit White and more affluent Americans.[51] In other words, universal programs have not undone the concentrated harms that systemic racism created in Black communities (and other communities of color). Second, critics take issue with "hiding" the anti-racist purpose of social policies.[52] They argue that minimizing or avoiding forthright, public discussion of systemic racism prioritizes White Americans' prejudices, fears, and cultural neuroses over Black Americans' righteous calls for justice, thereby reinforcing the white hegemonic status quo.[53] For such critics, it is critical that White Americans acknowledge the harms of systemic racism and support ameliorative politics and policymaking solely because they are anti-racist, not because they will help impoverished White people too.[54]

I emphasize that I am conducting a political analysis in this book, not advancing a moral or ethical argument. When White Americans refuse to face the sociological harms of systemic racism, they give systemic racism further power.[55] White Americans should support anti-racist policies simply because it is the moral thing to do. However, political victory in a democracy is achieved by growing one's coalition of supporters.[56] This requires finding allies among people who do not initially or entirely agree with you; preaching solely to one's own choir is a recipe for political gridlock and the maintenance of the status quo. Unfortunately, only a minority of White Americans are "racial liberals" who consistently score low on social scientists' various measures of racist stereotypes, prejudices, and resentment.[57] Though their total share of the voting population is slowly declining over time, Whites remain a large majority of voters.[58] Grappling with White backlash remains a political necessity in America if one hopes to see anti-racist policies become reality.[59] The question then becomes, how should we navigate the minefield of White racial resentment in the twenty-first century?

It is important to remember that my focus in this book is the politics of community-based crime prevention policy. Policymaking cannot be entirely separated from electoral politics, but I am not focused on the study of campaign messages to win elections, nor do I wish to speak solely to liberals and Democrats. I want to see conservatives and Republicans support community-based crime prevention too.[60] I am more interested in assessing sitting legislators' ability to enact new crime prevention policies without provoking public backlash and suffering at the ballot box. This shifts our focus somewhat away from politicians' responsibility to represent their constituents in a holistic sense and toward their ability to use public policy to ameliorate social problems. This should lower the "winner-takes-all" stakes of a focus on elections.

First, the good news for advocates of community investment. My national survey revealed that advocates begin from a position of greater strength than I think many people assumed. Direct community investment is supported by a majority of Black Americans but also a surprisingly large number of White Americans. To reiterate, my findings suggest that close to two-thirds of Black Americans prefer to invest in community institutions instead of criminal justice institutions to prevent crime, and about an additional fifth would support community investment as part of a balanced budget. Only about a third of White Americans prefer community investment, but if we add in the White people who support community investment alongside criminal justice investment in a balanced budget, the proportion of Whites who are open to community investment rises to half.

Republican respondents allocated less money toward community clinics, public schools, and job creation programs than Democrats or independents. However, when I examined respondents' overall budget preferences, a plurality of White, Republican, high school educated respondents who live outside metropolitan areas (which is the core of the Republican base) allocated all or most of their budgets toward the community institutions, and an additional quarter balanced their allocations between community institutions and criminal justice institutions. Support for community investment was even more widespread among White, Republican, college educated respondents who live in metropolitan areas. In other words, there does not appear to be consensus opposition to community investment among Republicans.

Politicians who favor community investment but fear that expressing that support would cost them votes should take even greater comfort from my findings in chapter 5. My analysis predicts that politicians who support community investment will receive the electoral support of a majority of Black Americans, a plurality of White Americans, a majority of Democrats, about a quarter of independents, and about a third of Republicans. Among the more skeptical groups of the population, the models predict that a politician's support for community investment would not affect the vote choices of a majority of independents and a plurality of Republicans one way or the other. Thus, at baseline, we are talking about a policy proposal that sparks enthusiasm among many Americans and indifference among many others. The data suggest that only a relatively slim minority of Americans would actively backlash against a politician who supports community investment. In other words, it appears that community investment does fall within Americans' "zone of acquiescence." As such, I dispute sociologist David Garland's assertation that "in the American polity, there is a settled political preference for penal rather than social measures. . . ."[61] Legislators who have a settled preference for punishment over community investment are, in fact, out of step with a great many American citizens.

The bad news is that racial division matters. Consistent with prior empirical evidence about racial priming and messaging, my data suggest that employing a racial justice centric message and advocating for an investment policy that would only benefit Black communities would cause politicians and advocates to lose support among White Americans. My findings are compatible with the advice to pursue a "hidden agenda." The White respondents to my survey did not backlash against proposals to invest in communities that suffer from high rates of crime, poverty, or welfare use. Nor did they consistently backlash against the proposal to invest in inner-city communities, surprisingly.[62] Remember that because of enduring segregation, when we talk about communities that experience those social problems, we are largely talking about majority-Black and majority-Latino communities—in urban areas, at least.[63] We're just talking about those communities in a manner that rhetorically emphasizes the social problems that justify focused investment, not the race of their residents. My findings suggest that contemporary advocates have a real shot at building a majority political coalition to support targeted investment into communities of concentrated disadvantage if they are willing to sacrifice the politics of recognition (of racial justice as the expressed justification for action) in order to achieve a politics of redistribution (that would ameliorate the socioeconomic deprivations of systemic racism).[64]

When discussing the findings from the Race-Class Narratives Project, Ian Haney López reports that he faced the greatest resistance from young activists on college campuses. He wrote, "When I urge racial justice advocates to link racism to economic issues in order to enlist more whites, these committed activists react in a range of ways. Some say straight up that they would rather demand that society face the crimes of white racism—even if it means not much really changes on the ground—than to reframe whites as victims of racism, too."[65] As such, I anticipate that the framing aspect of my findings will be distasteful to some readers. I can respect that perspective, but I agree with the scholars who argue that it is more important to employ political strategies that will achieve electoral and policy victories that will improve both the material conditions of neighborhoods of concentrated disadvantage and the lives of the residents therein.[66]

I also argue that we should recognize progress. The original "targeting within universalism" perspectives emphasized carving out space for racial justice efforts within very broad social policies that would benefit most Americans.[67] It is understandable that many critics felt this perspective acquiesced to White Americans' in-group selfishness and willingness to only support policies from which they personally would benefit. However, the justice reinvestment questions I asked the participants in my research project were much more targeted in nature. The participants in my focus groups clearly understood that money should only be invested in at-risk neighborhoods, and many of them pointedly said that wealthy communities should be excluded from investment initiatives. This means that my participants did not advance an "all communities matter" argument that negated the particular needs of impoverished communities. As such, I believe that my findings resonate with those of López and his colleagues in the Race-Class Narratives Project. They suggest that Americans do support targeted efforts to address poverty, unemployment, and inequality, but most people believe that such efforts should include the truly disadvantaged and working poor of all races.

I take seriously the maxim that "deracialization" should be employed strategically.[68] So let us consider the full political context of the present era. Deracialization was an electoral strategy that was primarily designed to help Democratic candidates appeal to the White, working-class voters who were the party's base in the first half of the twentieth century but began shifting to the Republican party following the civil rights movement. In the twenty-first century, there are far more Americans of color than there were in the 1970s and 1980s. Plus, given high levels of "partisan sorting," White swing voters are both far less numerous and far less important to electoral outcomes today. Instead, many activists and scholars argue that modern election outcomes typically hinge on turning out the base, not persuading swing voters. Since the contemporary Democratic base is comprised of Americans of color and Whites with relatively liberal attitudes about race, it may be ill-advised of liberals to prioritize the views of centrist or conservative Whites over the interests and concerns of Black Americans.[69] Fair enough—if I were studying elections. But I'm not; I'm studying policymaking. That is a critical difference. Let's consider the implications.

Political scientist Christopher Stout found evidence that Black Americans might be mobilized to vote if a White candidate who campaigns on a platform of policies related to racial justice is on the ballot (though he admits that the depressed turnout among Black and Latino voters in the 2016 presidential election despite Hillary Clinton's numerous racial justice overtures is a powerful counterfactual to his argument).[70] I, too, found that Black Americans are more supportive of community investment than White Americans. Since Black Americans are disproportionately concentrated in the nation's cities, and cities overwhelmingly vote for Democratic candidates, the evidence suggests that municipal politics could be a domain in which a racial justice focused community invest-ment campaign could be electorally advantageous. However, for such a strategy to be successful, it would need to be restricted to a municipal policy that is self-contained and self-funded within the city that created it.[71] It is likely that a race-targeted, racial justice justified community investment initiative would face greater resistance from the moderate and conservative White voters who grow more populous the farther one moves away from the nation's urban cores.

Many of the commentaries I have read that contribute to the racial justice versus race-neutral economic justice debate engage at a rather abstract level. Few rigorously consider the challenges of political geogra-phy. Liberal voters are disproportionately concentrated in cities. Ameri-ca's single-member, winner-takes-all district system puts the Democratic party at a distinct electoral disadvantage. Conservative politicians win a far greater number of suburban and rural districts than liberals with only 51% to 60% of the votes. Liberal candidates tend to win urban districts with larger vote shares, but any vote beyond 51% in a single-member district is wasted. This fact goes a long way toward explaining why the Republican party controls a majority of state legislatures in the United States and wields disproportionate power in the US Senate.[72]

This pattern has important implications for policymaking. Any politi-cal initiative or campaign that appeals only to liberal voters and voters of color will likely be most viable in cities but more politically polar-izing in suburban and rural areas. Two major challenges flow from this fact. First, beginning in the 1980s, Congress both reduced the overall grant aid that it supplied to states and cities, and Republican-controlled Congresses and Republican presidential administrations gave state leg-islatures greater control over allocation of federal money. These changes created numerous fiscal challenges for cities. Many cities might struggle to fund a robust community investment initiative using solely their own tax revenue.[73]

Second, state legislatures are increasingly passing laws that "preempt" (curtail or negate) municipal policies. Republican-controlled legislatures in states with a larger proportion of conservative citizens are more likely to pass preemption laws in order to negate progressive policymaking at the municipal level.[74] Related to the topic of crime prevention, there have been many examples of Republican-controlled state legislatures interfering with cities' attempts to pass local gun control ordinances, and several legislatures recently moved to preempt the power of local "progressive" prosecutors.[75] In 2021, Florida passed a law to criminalize participation in a riot that also contained a provision that will allow a prosecutor or local commissioner to appeal to the state any local government's efforts to reduce the municipal law enforcement budget. Similarly, bills were introduced into the Iowa legislature that would strip local governments of state funding if cities or counties defunded their own law enforcement budgets.[76] In other words, several Republican-controlled legislatures moved swiftly to preempt local efforts to "defund the police."[77] As much as they might wish it, liberal city dwellers cannot completely insulate themselves from the political influence of their more conservative suburban and rural fellow state citizens. An investment policy that would allocate some resources toward impoverished rural communities in addition to urban communities of concentrated disadvantage would hopefully face less opposition from conservative state legislators who represent rural and suburban districts and have the power to undermine city policies if provoked.

We should recognize where there is growth potential for mobilizing public support for community investment. My findings show that support is already quite high among a large proportion of Black Americans. Black respondents who were told that "African American communities" would receive reinvestment funds did not allocate significantly more money toward community institutions than Black respondents in the control group. In fact, Black respondents in this condition allocated significantly less money toward public schools than control group Black respondents.[78] Nor did exposure to the "African American communities" cue increase Black respondents' odds of saying that they would be more likely to support a politician who advanced community investment. These findings suggest that an explicit, racial justice political campaign would not be necessary to mobilize Black Americans behind this policy proposal. This echoes evidence that Black Americans expressed high support for President Obama's American Recovery and Reinvestment Act and the Affordable Care Act even though he campaigned for both of those policies in deracialized terms.[79]

In contrast, my evidence indicates that an explicit, racialized community investment campaign would alienate some White voters—and that might squander growth potential. Remember my finding in chapter 5 that Republican nonvoters' community investment preferences more closely resembled those of independents and Democrats, not their fellow Republicans who actively vote. Community investment advocates might be able to mobilize support among disengaged Republicans (who are disproportionately White), bringing them into the political process with a promise that government will work to invest in their economically struggling communities too.[80] Such an inclusive campaign might cut through the (inaccurate) belief held by many conservative-leaning White Americans that government only offers financial assistance to struggling people of color, not struggling White people.[81]

Finally, I want to be quite clear that I am not arguing against the use of racial justice centric messages and advocacy in a blanket manner. Rather than thinking in terms of a racial justice versus class justice binary, it is more accurate to recognize that race and class are correlated with each other along a spectrum in the United States. There are some injustices that are specifically caused by racial discrimination. Within the criminal justice realm, a major injustice is police officers racially profiling Americans of color.[82] Racial profiling does not affect White Americans. As such, it would make no sense to attempt to discuss the issue in a race-neutral or racially inclusive manner and doing so would simply reinforce colorblind racism's denial that people of color have a qualitatively different life experience in America than White people do.[83]

In contrast, poverty, deindustrialization, joblessness, and mass incarceration affect communities of all racial compositions across the country, even if they disproportionately affect communities of color.[84] Many rural communities solicited prison construction in a desperate attempt to create jobs in the wake of deindustrialization and local economic collapse.[85] This includes many rural communities in the South with large Black and Latino populations whose residents of color took jobs in the correctional facilities as correctional officers or other staff.[86] Consequently, a political economy analysis offers a more holistic lens to understand the synchronous rise to dominance of both mass incarceration and neoliberalism than a theory that focuses narrowly on racial oppression to the exclusion of labor and social class dynamics. It is a "both-and" social problem, not an "either-or" problem.

Furthermore, the twenty-first century has seen a notable change in criminal justice practice. Prison and jail admission rates are now higher in suburban and rural counties than they are in urban counties.[87] Analyzing prisons admissions data from 2009 to 2016 in Massachusetts, sociologist Jessica Simes found that the relationship between living in a community of concentrated disadvantage and experiencing a heightened likelihood of incarceration generalizes beyond large cities to smaller cities and suburban and rural areas.[88] Notably, she found that two small, satellite cities with over 80% non-Hispanic White populations were statistical outliers that disproportionately contributed to the state's prison admissions. Simes also demonstrated that incarcerated White people who lived in small cities came from communities of substantially higher levels of concentrated disadvantaged than Whites who lived in Boston prior to imprisonment. The opposite pattern was true for incarcerated Black residents, which suggests that the relationship between race, disadvantage, and incarceration now varies across regions even within states.[89] When scholars and advocates have an opportunity to show Americans of all races how social problems and predatory systems create widespread suffering, the data suggest they should attempt to build interracial solidarity and support for targeted investment policies through racially inclusive messaging.[90]

Which Kinds of Community Investment Policies?

In this book, I wanted to determine whether America's long-standing failure to implement robust, widespread community investment policies reflects public opinion, as many generations of politicians seem to have assumed. My focus group and survey data say nothing about which kinds of community investments would be most evidence based and produce the best social outcomes. That is a question I will leave to policy analysts to study in greater detail with comparative data across cities and states. Here, I will only offer brief recommendations based upon prior literature.

The federal and state governments have launched a variety of community investment initiatives over the past thirty years. However, they differ in some important theoretical and substantive ways from the types of investments that I believe many of the advocates and scholars

I have referenced in this book had in mind.[91] Economic development zones were the dominant model of government-initiated "place-based policies" enacted since the 1990s. Under these initiatives, the federal and state governments offer some combination of grants and tax deductions to incentivize private investors to finance development in the designated zones. Many of these economic development zones have, indeed, been implemented in the kinds of neighborhoods that advocates of the original vision of justice reinvestment argued should receive funds.

Empirical assessments of these zones have generated very mixed results. One study found that the federal Empowerment Zone program enacted under the Clinton administration "generated jobs in targeted communities and raised local earnings without generating large increases in population or housing rents."[92] However, the researchers found little evidence that the workers who economically benefitted from jobs in zone communities lived there; rather, they commuted from outside the zones, thereby diffusing some of the income tax revenue benefits to other, less needy neighborhoods. Another study concluded that the Empowerment Zone established in Boston during the G.W. Bush administration facilitated the creation of many new Black-owned businesses in the neighborhoods of Dorchester and Roxbury, but it did not cause significant declines in the overall levels of poverty or unemployment in the zone neighborhoods.[93]

Other scholars are more pessimistic and conclude that the bulk of the empirical literature fails to establish solid evidence that enterprise zones consistently create jobs or reduce poverty. Some research indicates that most of the investment that occurs in economic development zones flows into capital, especially real estate.[94] For-profit capital investments like real estate infrequently benefit the long-term residents of economic zone communities because those residents are typically too poor to afford the new properties. Developers who take advantage of the economic development zone tax incentives rely on attracting wealthier people to move into the neighborhood to make a return on their investment. While there can be some social and economic benefits to diversification of this nature, there is greater concern that an influx of new, wealthier residents simply sparks gentrification that displaces the historic residents of the neighborhood.[95] Even worse, evidence indicates that poorer residents who remain in place may become increasingly vulnerable to aggressive police surveillance and arrest at the behest of the more affluent residents who are concerned about the "order" of their new neighborhood.[96]

Several recent studies demonstrate that investment in nonprofit organizations and homeownership reduces crime. One example is Seattle's Neighborhood Matching Fund (NMF), which disburses grants to "organizations [that] must demonstrate that their projects *will provide a public benefit that is free to anyone* [and] that the project was planned and will be carried out by the neighbors who will actually benefit from the project. . . ."[97] Evidence indicates that the amount of NMF funding was significantly related to crime declines, and that this effect was strongest in the poorest neighborhoods. One study found a negative relationship between increases in the number of local nonprofit organizations and neighborhood crime rates, even though most of the nonprofits focused on broad quality of life issues, not crime prevention specifically.[98] Several studies found that increased mortgage lending also reduces neighborhood crime.[99] Likewise, evidence indicates that blight remediation efforts, such as the demolition of abandoned properties and the transformation of vacant lots into parks or community gardens, also reduces neighborhood crime.[100] The key difference in contrast to the economic development zones is that these investment programs directly fund both poorer prospective homeowners, which could help them resist displacement in the face of gentrification, and nonprofit organizations whose missions is to improve the "human resources and physical infrastructure" of disadvantaged neighborhoods. In other words, these programs invest in poor Black neighborhoods "as is," improving quality of life for established residents, not wealthy newcomers.[101] In sum, investments into public and nonprofit institutions advance the mission of justice reinvestment, whereas for-profit investments more often lead to gentrification and increased class tension.

Defunding the Police?

The public debate about "defunding the police" that followed the 2020 murder of George Floyd encompassed a range of perspectives.[102] We can think of these perspectives arrayed on a spectrum. On the most conservative side of the spectrum (in the sense of making incremental changes, not speaking in terms of political ideology) are advocates who call for reforms to police training, procedure, policy, and accountability. On the most radical side of the spectrum are advocates who call for the entire institution of policing in the United States to be disbanded or abolished and replaced with non-law-enforcement, community-based institutions tasked with ensuring public safety.[103] Somewhere in the middle are others who argue that the police should not be the first responders to deal with people who are experiencing homelessness, drug addiction, or mental health crisis. Instead, we should partially reduce police department budgets and reallocate that money into alternative first responders, such as social workers or crisis intervention specialists. Defunding advocates also commonly argued that some money that is taken away from police departments should be directly invested into disadvantaged communities in order to ameliorate the social causes of crime in the first place.

Because I based my research project on the justice reinvestment paradigm, I asked my participants to assume that the reinvestment money they were allocating came from reducing the budgets of prisons, not police departments. As such, I cannot speak directly to a key component of the "defund the police" debate, but my findings can shed some light around the margins. Recall from chapter 3 that about a third of Black respondents and one-fifth of White respondents to my national survey allocated their entire budgets into community institutions and gave police and probation no money at all. I infer that these are the Americans who may be most open to abolition arguments since they already chose to show no fiscal support for law enforcement. They are a minority of both racial groups, though. On the other hand, about 10% of Black respondents and close to 30% of White respondents allocated all or most of their budgets into police, probation, or a tax rebate, or some combination of the three. I infer that these Americans would either support incremental reforms to police departments or resist calls for reform altogether. They would also likely reject abolition arguments since they chose to express some fiscal support for law enforcement. Close to half of Black respondents and about a third of White respondents either balanced their budgets or allocated a small portion of their money toward criminal justice institutions alongside greater investment into community institutions. I infer that these are the Americans who might be open to the defunding arguments that the responsibilities of police should be scaled back, and greater investment should be made into communities and alternative forms of crime prevention.

Other polls indicate that only a minority of Americans supports reducing police budgets. A June 2020 Pew Research Center survey found that only 26% of Americans replied that spending on police in their area should be decreased, compared to 31% who favored increased spending and 42% who replied that funding should stay about the same. There were differences in responses across racial lines. Forty-two percent of Black Americans replied that spending on police should be decreased compared to only 21% of Whites and 24% of Hispanics. Support for reducing police spending was highest among Americans aged eighteen to twenty-nine (45%) but dropped dramatically among older people. Forty-one percent of Democrats supported reducing police spending contrasted to only 8% of Republicans.[104]

A variety of different national polls conducted in 2020 and 2021 found a general pattern that only a minority of Americans of all racial groups express support for defunding the police when the policy is not explained. This pattern of findings suggests that most Americans (again, of all racial groups) believe that there should be a role for police in society; ergo, the police dismantling or abolition perspective will likely face the most political opposition. In contrast, when pollsters talk about reallocating some money from police toward alternative first responders to handle crises other than violent crime, support jumps among Americans. The proposal to better fund alternative first responders and crime prevention initiatives does garner support from a majority of respondents in several polls.[105] This pattern holds even when examining many polls of Black Americans, specifically.[106] Notably, scholars who have specifically interviewed poorer Black Americans who live in heavily policed neighborhoods rather consistently find heterogenous opinions. Though distrust and criticism of the police is widespread among Black residents of these communities, that distrust does not always translate into a desire to expel police from their communities. Rather, a common sentiment expressed by many Black Americans who live in heavily policed communities is that they want to experience the same kind of respectful, noninvasive policing that more affluent White communities experience.[107] Even a team of researchers who interviewed protesters at the pro-police-reform 2020 March on Washington found widespread support for community investment among interviewees, but protesters were more divided in their opinions about reforming, defunding, or disbanding the police.[108]

Disbanding the institution of policing is not a consensus position among Americans at large or even among the communities of Black Americans who are most likely to suffer harassment and violence at the hands of police. However, if we separate the question of slashing police budgets from the question of better funding community-based crime prevention and first responders with public health training, then both my findings and those of other national surveys suggest that a large number of Americans endorse the investment side of abolition arguments. It is the divestment side of the argument that appears to be more politically divisive.[109]

Limitations and Directions for Future Research

I end by noting several limitations of this book, both to delineate the scope of my findings and to raise questions that are ripe for future research. First, as I explained in the introductory chapter, I chose to limit this research project to White and Black Americans so that my measures and hypotheses would cleanly fit within the theories I employed. Racial priming theory was originally focused on the Black-White divide in America, and most empirical tests of racial priming have also focused on those two racial groups. I felt it would be inappropriate to add participants from other racial or ethnic groups without first developing theoretical expectations for those groups' crime prevention preferences and their reactions to racialized cues.[110] A proper test that respects the unique histories and cultural backgrounds of different racial and ethnic groups would also need to expand the range of racial cues employed.[111] As such, the crime prevention investment preferences of Latino Americans, Asian Americans, Native Americans, and other Americans of color very much remains a question in need of empirical answers.

However, the omission of non-White or Black racial and ethnic groups would only significantly undermine my conclusions in this book under two conditions. The first condition would be if the average crime prevention investment preferences of non-Black Americans of color fell "outside" the range of preferences expressed by White and Black Americans—in other words, if any group supported criminal justice investment to a greater extent than White Americans or community investment to a greater extent than Black Americans. I can look to other surveys to make an evidence-based guess as to whether that might be the case.

In one study that was a source of inspiration for this project, a nationally representative sample of Americans constructed a hypothetical crime prevention budget in the year 2000. The researchers found that Black Americans allocated the most money toward "prevention programs to help keep youth out of trouble": 44.3% of their budgets, on average. In contrast, White Americans allocated 35.7% and Latinos, 32.3%, on average, which means that Latinos were slightly less supportive of a crime prevention program than Whites, although the difference between these two racial-ethnic groups was not statistically significant. Similarly, White and Latino respondents allocated nearly identical amounts toward "more prisons" (9.0% and 10.0%, respectively) both of which were significantly more than Black respondents' average allocation (4.4%). Respondents' average allocations toward "more police on the street" did not significantly differ across race (Whites = 21.6%, Blacks = 18.1%, Latinos = 19.5%).[112]

A 2010 nationally representative survey asked respondents, "Which of the following approaches to lowering the crime rate in the United States comes closer to your own view—do you think more money and effort should go to attacking the social and economic problems that lead to crime through better education and job training or more money and effort should go to deterring crime by improving law enforcement with more prisons, police, and judges?" The results of this survey indicated that 60% of White, 85% of Black, and 73% of "nonwhite" Americans (an admittedly blunt category) replied that more money should go toward attacking the causes of crime, whereas 35% of White, 23% of Black, and 12% of nonwhite respondents preferred improving criminal justice.[113] A nationally representative survey of likely voters conducted in 2017 by Lake Research Partners found that 78% of White, 83% of Black, and 72% of Latino respondents supported a proposal to move funding from incarceration to community-based public safety programs.[114] A national sample of registered voters conducted in 2020 by the Morning Consult + *Politico* National Tracking Poll found that 30% of White,

51% of Hispanic, and 61% of Black respondents somewhat or strongly supported "redirecting funding for the police department in your local community to support community development programs."[115]

In summary, the prior evidence is both sparse and somewhat mixed. It appears that when Latinos' justice policy preferences do not fall "in between" those of Whites and Blacks, they may be slightly more conservative than Whites, but not to a degree that is substantively or significantly different. It is impossible to draw direct comparisons since these were all different surveys that asked differently worded questions, but the inconsistency suggests that Latinos' opinions about community investment require additional clarification. This goes double for Asian Americans and Native Americans since they were not even identified in the prior surveys that contained the most relevant questions I could find. The evidence is much more consistent that Black Americans express the greatest support for community-based initiatives and the least support for criminal justice interventions of any other racial-ethnic group. It does seem that they represent the most liberal pole of the policy preference spectrum when it comes to crime prevention. Whether Latinos, Asian Americans, Native Americans or other Americans of color hold more conservative opinions on this topic than Whites—in general or only regarding particular questions—is less clear.

The second condition that would be a serious problem for my study would be if non-Black Americans of color reacted to racial primes in a substantively different manner than either White Americans or Black Americans. One racial priming study that analyzed survey data from Washington state found that both Whites and Latinos who more strongly blame racial disparities in punishment on Blacks' personal shortcomings backlashed when exposed to information about racial disparities in the death penalty. Members of these racial groups expressed stronger support for the death penalty after exposure to the racial injustice argument, which suggests that antiblack racial primes may affect Latinos in much the same way they affect Whites.[116] This gives us reason to suspect that, like Whites, Latinos may also resist allocating resources to "African American communities," specifically. On the flip side, another study found that Latinos perceive significantly higher levels of racial discrimination against Blacks in society than Whites perceive; perhaps this shared "sociological perspective" might make Latinos more open to targeted investment in Black communities.[117] This, too, is an important question for future research. I am aware of no prior studies that have tested how Asian Americans or Native Americans react to racialized cues.[118]

A second limitation of my study is that I asked participants to assume that they were allocating additional money that had been saved by reducing incarceration rates. I am fairly confident that my findings help us understand how White and Black Americans prioritize different crime prevention proposals in relation to each other.[119] They do not clarify how much money Americans would be personally willing to pay in taxes to fund community investment or other crime prevention initiatives should fiscal "reclamation" initiatives like justice reinvestment fail to generate adequate funds. This is an important distinction since resistance to raising taxes is a core component of "not in my backyard" attitudes that some scholars argue played an important role in middle-class Americans' punitive attitudes during the "tough on crime" era.[120] However, we should not assume *a priori* that Americans would be unwilling to pay any taxes whatsoever to fund community investment. A recent study demonstrated that Americans' crime prevention policy preferences are sensitive to projected tax increases, but most Americans were willing to pay at least a little bit more in taxes to support effective crime prevention. Furthermore, truly effective prevention policies should lower taxes in the long run by preventing the myriad costly social harms of crime on the back end, and Americans respond positively to arguments about a policy's projected likelihood of reducing taxes.[121]

Third, my framing experiment included only a single, brief racialized cue—the adjectives used to describe the communities that would receive reinvestment funds. I consider this study to be a test of the baseline likelihood of political backlash among White or Black Americans to alternative rhetorical messages about community investment. It does not test more sophisticated questions about longer messages delivered in the dynamic environment of an actual political campaign or social movement. Many scholars have demonstrated that the effects of frames on public opinion can be attenuated if people are exposed to multiple competing messages, or if they discuss competing frames with other people.[122] Furthermore, people react just as strongly to the identity of the person who delivers a framed message as they do to the content of the message itself.[123] I am aware of no studies that have tested these more complicated framing dynamics in regard to crime and justice issues; such research is ripe for innovation in the study of public opinion about criminal justice.

Finally, I found little evidence in my data that Americans who live in urban areas have significantly different crime prevention investment preferences than Americans who live in rural areas. Given the robust evidence of urban-rural polarization in many other aspects of contemporary American politics, this null finding surprised me.[124] The optimistic interpretation is that criminal justice continues to be one of the very few "de-balkanized" issues for which there is bipartisan appetite for reform in the early twenty-first century.[125] The pessimistic interpretation is that my national survey failed to adequately capture the voices of rural Americans. Only 240 respondents (11.5% of the sample) hailed from nonmetropolitan areas, and only 81 of these rural respondents were Black. Small samples increase the statistical margin of error, so it is possible that my survey data simply contained too few rural Americans to detect significant urban-rural differences in opinion.

To make matters worse, most nationally representative surveys that were conducted in the months leading up to both the 2016 and 2020 presidential elections underpredicted the magnitude of Donald Trump's electoral support, especially among rural Americans.[126] These polling errors may have been a function of Republicans' profound loss of trust in American institutions over the course of the twentieth century.[127] If the people who conduct surveys are perceived by Republican-leaning Americans to be "biased elites," those Americans will be less likely to participate in the survey. If political beliefs now drive survey nonresponse, even the most prestigious survey firms will be incapable of generating data that reflects the preferences of Republican Americans in an unbiased manner because they are simply not present in the data. For all these reasons, I am hesitant to confidently accept my finding of no urban-rural differences in community investment preferences. I urge criminologists and other scholars who study the politics of punishment to gather new data that robustly represents the perspectives of Americans who live in urban, suburban, and rural areas.[128] Only then can we know for sure whether support for criminal justice reform truly crosses the urban-rural divide as my results suggest.

Conclusion

This book reveals that a substantial number of Americans across racial divides support targeted investment into the public, not-for-profit institutions and programs that are the lifeblood of communities, such as public schools, healthcare clinics, and job creation programs. Politicians no longer have any excuse to ignore residents of communities of concentrated disadvantage who argue that proper crime prevention must begin with community investment and revitalization, not a single-minded focus on arrests and punishment. Theirs is not an isolated, minority perspective. Many of their fellow Americans who live in more affluent neighborhoods share their crime prevention policy preferences and appear willing to support targeted investment into communities that are besieged by high rates of crime, poverty, and unemployment. With the use of careful, inclusive rhetoric, my findings suggest that advocates have a very real shot at mobilizing a large coalition of citizens to stand up for policies that would build public safety by nourishing community wellbeing rather than constantly swelling the criminal justice system. Americans want safety beyond punishment. It is high time for politicians to listen to them.

ACKNOWLEDGMENTS

The research project that gave rise to this book began nearly a decade ago. Writing my first monograph has been a long, challenging, and rewarding experience. It could not have happened without the support of various people and institutions along the way.

I am grateful to the United States National Institute of Justice for funding this research project through its W. E. B. Du Bois Fellowship for Research in Race, Gender, Culture, and Crime (Award No. 2015-IJ-CX-0003). Without the money to field the focus groups and national survey, I would have had no data to analyze, and this book would have never come into existence. The opinions, findings, and conclusions or recommendations expressed in this book are mine alone and do not necessarily reflect those of the Department of Justice.

I thank the staff of the survey research center who recruited the focus group participants on my behalf and provided the venue for the qualitative data collection. I choose not to name them or the center itself as an added layer of protection for the privacy of my participants, but I can confidently say that the focus groups would not have happened without their diligence and labor. I also thank my research assistants who helped me observe the focus groups, code the data, and compile prior research for the literature review: Lena Campagna, Kate Phelps, and Jay Byron. Their assistance was invaluable. I thank various colleagues who read draft versions of components of this research over the course of many years, including Andrea Leverentz, Liz Brown, Frank Cullen, and many anonymous peer reviewers. Their feedback improved this work immensely. I also thank my editor at NYU Press, Ilene Kalish, for guiding me through the long process of writing and preparing the manuscript for publication.

I wish to extend a special acknowledgement to Representative Bobby Scott who hired me as an American Political Science Association Congressional Fellow and gave me invaluable, firsthand insight into the legislative policymaking process during the year in which I worked in his office. I also sincerely thank David Daily, Rashage Green, and Carrie Hughes, the members of "Team Scott" who supported me and taught me so much over the course of my fellowship. They were both excellent coworkers and dear friends.

I would not be the person or scholar I am today without the love and support of my family. My parents, Thomas and Madeleine, supported my education throughout my whole life and instilled in me the values to care about social justice. They also talked me "off the ledge" many days during graduate school when I doubted my ability to successfully complete the program. Finally, I offer my most heartfelt thanks to my husband, Aaron, for his unconditional love and support. He has stood by me as I withstood the rigors of doctoral education and experienced the challenges of life as an assistant professor entering academia. After listening to me prattle on about criminal justice for years, he surely deserves a criminology degree himself!

APPENDIX: RESEARCH METHODOLOGY

Focus Groups

The greatest strength of qualitative research methods, such as interviews or focus groups, is to understand the breadth, depth, and complexity of people's thoughts and behaviors. Rather than simply choosing prewritten responses to questions on a quantitative survey, a qualitative method allows participants to fully express themselves in their own words.[1] A unique aspect of focus groups that sets them apart from one-on-one interviews is their group context, which allows the researcher to observe how participants interact with each other and judge whether or not that interaction influences the things that they say, offering insight into group-based discussion and decision-making.[2] Prior "deliberative polls" found that people's punishment preferences become less punitive after engaging in dialogue about policy with other group participants.[3]

Prior research led me to expect that both race and social class would impact people's opinions about crime and criminal justice. Non-White Americans and poorer individuals of all races are significantly more likely to experience involuntary, coercive contact with the criminal justice system than wealthier White people.[4] According to procedural justice theory, people's satisfaction with the criminal justice system is shaped less by outcomes than by process; people who feel that criminal justice agents (police, judges, and so forth) treat them with fairness and due process are more likely to perceive the justice system to be legitimate than people who feel that they are treated unfairly.[5] Other research suggests that the relationship between race and perceptions of fairness is influenced by social class. One study demonstrated that both White and Black people of low socioeconomic status expressed similar levels of mistrust toward the justice system that were significantly greater than the distrust expressed by wealthier respondents, and the between-race difference in perceptions of injustice increased as a linear function of socioeconomic status.[6]

In order to maximize the likelihood of observing the influence of race and social class at work in people's thought processes, I chose to segment the focus groups. Segmentation is the process of choosing group composition according to characteristics of the participants that are germane to the topic of discussion.[7] Methodologists argue that within-group homogeneity on key background characteristics increases participants' level of comfort and willingness to speak. However, where appropriate, elements of heterogeneity may be introduced if the researcher wishes to study the impact of social differences on group discussion. I segmented the groups across race and level of education (a proxy for social class). Two focus groups contained only White participants, two focus groups contained only Black participants, and two focus groups were split between both Black and White participants. Within each pair of racial groups, one focus group contained respondents who were pursuing or attained an associate's, bachelor's, or postgraduate degree, and the other focus group contained participants who possessed, at maximum, a high school degree or GED.[8] Thus, all groups were segmented to be relatively homogeneous in regard to educational attainment, four of the groups were segmented to be homogeneous in regard to race, and two of the groups were segmented to be heterogeneous in regard to race. This segmentation allowed me to observe how race and social class influenced the discussions.

In May 2016, I worked with a university-based survey research center whose staff recruited participants via an advertisement posted on the website Craigslist. This ad invited volunteers to join focus groups to discuss "people's opinions about crime and criminal justice." To be eligible to participate, a person needed only to speak English, identify as Black or White, and be over eighteen years of age. Sixty-nine people who met these criteria responded to the advertisement; the forty-four participants were chosen from this group simply due to scheduling availability. Each focus group included six to eight participants who were evenly split between men and women. All participants were residents of the city of Boston or nearby towns. I refer to participants with pseudonyms throughout the book to protect their identities. I present shorthand information about participants in parentheses when I quote them. For example, "(Christopher, 68, B, CE, FG3)" indicates that Christopher was sixty-eight years old, Black, college educated, and a participant in Focus Group 3. "(Camille, 29, W, HSE, FG6)" indicates that Camille was twenty-nine years old, White, high school educated, and a participant in Focus Group 6.

Participants provided additional information about themselves on a short exit survey. In addition to basic demographic questions, the survey also asked the following:

1. What is the highest grade or level of school that you have completed?
   a. Response options: 8th grade or less; Some high school, but did not graduate; High school graduate or GED; Some college but no degree; Associate's degree; 4-year college degree; More than 4-year college degree
2. Are you employed in a criminal justice profession, like police officer or court clerk? If yes, what is your job? [No participant provided an affirmative response to this question.]
3. Is anyone in your family employed in a criminal justice profession, like police officer or court clerk? If yes, what is their job?
4. Have you ever served on a jury?
5. Have you ever been a witness at a trial?
6. Have you ever been questioned by a police officer because he/she thought you broke a law?
7. Have you ever been arrested?
8. Have you ever spent any time in jail or prison?
9. How much time did you spend in prison or jail?
   a. Response options: Less than 1 year; One to 5 years; More than 5 years
10. What was your total family income, from all sources, before taxes, in 2015?
    a. Response options presented as an ordinal scale of $30,000 increments.

Table A.1 presents the additional information that participants provided on the exit surveys. I note in quotation marks where participants wrote editorial comments on the survey sheet.

TABLE A1. Information about Focus Group Participants

	Gender	Race	Age	Education	Family CJS Job	Jury or Witness	Police Questioned	Arrested	Probation	Jail	Income (in thousands of dollars)
Focus Group 1—Mixed Race, College Educated											
Amber	Female	White	49	Associate's deg.	"State police"						70–99
Debbie	Female	White	64	Grad. deg.		Both	Yes				10–39
Brandon	Male	Black	49	Associate's deg		Witness	Yes	Yes	Yes	< 1	10–39
Lance	Male	Black	60	Grad. deg.			Yes				10–39
Lacey	Female	White	69	Grad. deg.			"Not Sure"	Yes			40–69
Jeffrey	Male	White	67	4-year deg.		Jury	Yes	Yes			< 10
Bettie	Female	Black	23	Associate's deg.							10–39
Patricia	Female	Black	49	Some college, no deg.							40–69
Focus Group 2—Mixed Race, High School Educated											
Baldwin	Male	Black	52	HS deg.		Witness	Yes	Yes	Yes	> 5	40–69
Chrissy	Female	Black	46	HS deg.		Witness	Yes	Yes	Yes	1 to 5	10–39
Ginger	Female	White	55	Some college, no deg.							40–69
Jacalyn	Female	Black	32	HS deg.		Witness	Yes	Yes	Yes	< 1	10–39
James	Male	White	46	HS deg.		Witness	Yes	Yes	Yes	< 1 ("Waiting for pretrial")	10–39
Roger	Male	White	63	Some HS, no deg.			Yes	Yes	Yes	< 1	10–39
Timothy	Male	Black	54	Some HS, no deg.	Yes (no details provided)	Witness	Yes ("Didn't like it")	Yes	Yes	< 1	< 10

Name	Gender	Race	Age	Education	Occupation					Number
Focus Group 3—Black, College Educated										
Paige	Female	Black	66	Grad. deg.		Both				100-129
Melissa	Female	Black	44	Grad. deg.		Jury	Yes			40-69
Christopher	Male	Black	68	Grad. deg.		Both				10-39
Sheldon	Male	Black	30	Grad. deg.			Yes			10-39
Rachelle	Female	Black	60+	Grad. deg.		Both	Yes			40-69
Candice	Female	Black	49	Some college, no deg.		Jury				40-69
William	Male	Black	67	4-year deg.			Yes	Yes	< 1	10-39
Adam	Male	Black	37	4-year deg.			Yes	Yes		10-39
Focus Group 4—Black, High School Educated										
Joseph	Male	Black	54	HS deg.		Jury		Yes		10-39
Matthew	Male	Black	55	HS deg.			Yes	Yes	> 5	40-69
Dorian	Male	Black	35	HS deg.	"Police officer"		Yes	Yes	> 5	40-69
Linda	Female	Black	56	Some HS, no deg.						< 10
Susan	Female	Black	53	Some HS, no deg.	"Paralegal"		Yes	Yes	1 to 5	< 10
Mary	Female	Black	33	HS deg.						10-39
Focus Group 5—White, College Educated										
Dylan	Male	White	25	4-year deg.			Yes			10-39
Inez	Female	White	72	4-year deg.						40-69
Marianne	Female	White	30	Grad. deg.						40-69
Alice	Female	White	54	Associate's deg.						70-99
Bruce	Male	White	58	4-year deg.						100-129
Wallace	Male	White	57	4-year deg.						10-39
Janet	Female	White	56	Grad. deg.						40-69
Nathan	Male	White	55	Some college, no deg.			Yes	Yes	< 1	10-39

(continued)

TABLE A1. (cont.)

	Gender	Race	Age	Education	Family CJS Job	Jury or Witness	Police Questioned	Arrested	Probation	Jail	Income (in thousands of dollars)
Focus Group 6—White, High School Educated											
Frederick	Male	White	20	Some college, no deg.							100–129
Pamela	Female	White	60	HS deg.			Yes	Yes	Yes		10–39
Albert	Male	White	43	HS deg.	"Police"	Jury	Yes	Yes	Yes	1 to 5	< 10
Jack	Male	White	71	HS deg.	"Prison guard"		Yes	Yes			10–39
Jason	Male	White	46	HS deg.			Yes	Yes	Yes	1 to 5 ("For a crime I did not commit")	10–39
Camille	Female	White	29	Some HS, no deg.			Yes	Yes	Yes	1 to 5	< 10
Judy	Female	White	70	HS deg.		Jury	Yes				< 10

Participants ranged between twenty and seventy-two years of age with a skew toward middle-age or elderly participants; only ten participants were younger than forty years old. Seven participants reported a total family income of less than $10,000 in the prior year, twenty reported between $10,000 and $39,000, twelve reported between $40,000 and $69,000, two reported between $70,000 and $99,000, and three reported between $100,000 and $129,000. The general patterns of disparate contact between poorer Americans and Black Americans and agents of the justice system were reflected in these focus group participants' experiences. Note how prevalent a history of arrest or punishment, or both, was among the high school educated participants of both races, contrasted to how uncommon it was among the college educated participants. On the other hand, several of the college educated participants disclosed in the group discussions that they worked or volunteered with organizations or professions that interacted with offenders, such as social work, prisoner reentry services, or other types of social service nonprofits.

The research team conducted all focus groups at a survey research center on an urban university campus. Participants sat around a table in a small conference room and could eat provided snacks and refreshments if they chose. A professional researcher at the survey center with experience running focus groups moderated all six groups. The moderator guided the participants through an iterative series of five pairs of writing prompts and discussion questions. She ensured that all five questions were discussed in each group (which sometimes necessitated curtailing a portion of the discussion if it was running too long), and she called upon quiet participants to ensure that everyone spoke. This means that these focus groups were more structured in nature as opposed to participant driven and free flowing.[9] However, the moderator did allow participants to talk about broader issues of social structure, community quality of life, and local governance, and she only redirected conversation back to the specific topics of crime and criminal justice if she perceived that the tangential discussions were straying too far from the purpose of the focus groups.

For each question, participants were first asked to brainstorm individually and write their ideas on a provided answer sheet. The moderator guided the participants in a discussion about the answers they wrote before repeating the process with the next writing prompt, followed by more group discussion. The focus groups proceeded as follows: first, respondents were asked to think of five things that cause crime, then they were asked to think of five things that can be done to prevent or reduce crime. Third, participants were asked to imagine that Massachusetts possessed extra money in its criminal justice budget that could be spent on crime prevention.[10] Participants were asked to decide how that money should be spent, and they were given a budget allocation worksheet to write down the percentage amount of money they would like to put into six different criminal justice or community-based institutions; they were also given the option to propose their own budget categories. Finally, the moderator described the basic justice reinvestment paradigm of using community-based sanctions instead of incarceration for offenders in order to save money and asked participants to state their reaction to the paradigm. The shortest focus group discussion lasted a little over an hour (Focus Group 6). The other five focus groups lasted between an hour and a half and two hours. Each participant was compensated forty dollars at the conclusion of the discussions.

Methodologists are engaged in a long-standing debate about the degree to which focus groups can measure people's individual opinions versus measure sentiments that are inseparable from the group discussion context.[11] To an extent, my design allowed me to measure both types of opinions. The written worksheets allowed me to compare participants' individual reactions to the discussion prompts with the statements they vocalized during the group discussion. I could thus identify sentiments that participants altered in the course of the discussion, new ideas they vocalized but did not initially write on their own, and ideas that they wrote but did not vocalize in the group.[12]

I personally observed the focus groups from behind a one-way mirror along with graduate research assistants and took field notes on participants' statements and interactions with each other. The focus group discussions were audio-recorded, and the recordings were later professionally transcribed. I took an inductive approach to data analysis, which proceeded as follows: first, I created a tentative coding scheme as I coded the first focus group transcript. Second, my research assistants independently coded the first focus group using my tentative coding scheme. Third, the three of us met and discussed the degree to which my preliminary coding scheme fit the data. Based upon this discussion, I reorganized the grouping of some top-level and sub-level codes, re-named some codes for greater clarity, and created new codes. All three of us then proceeded to code the second focus group transcript using the revised coding scheme. We once again met to discuss the "degree of fit" between the revised coding scheme and the second focus group, and all three of us agreed that the revisions were appropriate and made analysis easier. We repeated this process a third time for the third focus group and made one last round of revisions to the coding scheme; the final round of revisions entailed far fewer changes since the research assistants and I felt that most of the coding scheme fit the data well. Finally, I coded (or recoded) all six focus groups myself from scratch using the final iteration of the coding scheme.[13] We coded the data using Nvivo software.

Methodologists caution that social status can inhibit participants' willingness to speak in a focus group.[14] I minimized the likelihood that perceived differences in social class might have affected participants' comfort by making each group relatively homogeneous on levels of for-mal education. The two social categories that I think might have been most likely to affect participants' comfort were gender and race. The gender composition of all groups was split, and I intentionally designed Focus Groups 1 and 2 to be mixed race. By contrasting Groups 1 and 2 against the racially homogenous groups, I sought to empirically assess whether Black participants were less willing to share critical sentiments about the criminal justice system in the presence of White participants.

Somewhat to my surprise, I ultimately concluded that neither gender nor race systematically affected participants' willingness to speak during the discussions. Certainly, some highly vocal participants dominated the discussions, while other participants stayed largely silent unless directly queried by the moderator. However, I discerned no clear pattern that differentiated the dominant participants from the shy participants across groups. For example, Debbie, Jeffrey, and Lacey—three White people—were the most talkative, dominant participants in Focus Group 1, while Patricia and Lance, two Black participants, spoke very little. Viewed in isolation, this group would raise concerns that Black participants felt hesitant to speak about crime and justice around White people. In con-trast, Chrissy and Jacklyn, two Black women, dominated discussion in

Focus Group 2; James, a White man, and Baldwin, a Black man, were nearly as vocal as Chrissy and Jacklyn. Ginger, a White woman, and Timothy, a Black man, were the quietest participants in this group. Thus, Group 2 showed nearly the opposite race-gender participation dynamic as Group 1. Nor did the other groups show a clear pattern of women falling silent in the presence of men. Rachelle (FG3), Mary (FG4), Inez (FG5), and Judy (FG6) were all among the most talkative participants in this study. In addition, I saw no evidence that the moderator's identity (a White woman) significantly impeded discussion. As I noted in prior chapters, the Black participants of Focus Group 3 and 4 showed no hesitancy in talking openly about systemic racism and White oppression in front of the moderator.

Across all the focus groups, Ginger was the only participant whom I perceived to fall silent as the discussion progressed because of the way that the other group members responded to her. Ginger was the only participant in Focus Group 2 who had not experienced some form of coercive contact with the criminal justice system. She viewed the justice system in the most optimistic, trusting light out of all the people in this group, and the other participants frequently responded to Ginger's statements of hope for the system with stories of their own, negative experiences. This was not solely a function of race; other White participants in the group also disagreed with several of Ginger's statements. My research assistants and I noticed that Ginger was an active participant at the beginning of the discussion but had stopped speaking by the end. We perceived that she felt "shut down" as the discussion progressed.

Speech is typically less formal than written prose.[15] I chose to lightly edit the participants' statements when I directly quoted them in this book in order to "smooth out" interjections and repetition that did not contribute to the substantive meaning of their statements. I present a few examples of quotes from the original transcripts versus my edited versions in table A.2 to give my readers a better sense of the changes I made.

National Survey

The national survey respondents were selected from the Knowledge-Panel®, an online panel of over 40,000 US households. At the time I wrote this book in 2022, the KnowledgePanel was maintained by the

TABLE A2. Examples of Original Transcript Quotes versus Edited Quotes Presented in Text

Original Quote from Transcript	Edited Quote Presented in Text
So, better opportunities for everyone as a whole, because like in the inner, in the inner city, you know, the youth there that, that, resort to selling drugs . . .	Better opportunities for everyone as a whole, because like in the inner city, you know, the youth there that resort to selling drugs . . . (Chrissy, 46, B, HSE, FG2)
Um, I want to say, uh, when you talk about, um, causes of crime . . . Okay, you have to look at the individual first, and look at the pressures on the individual and you have pressures like, uh, serial unemployment or underemployment. You have, uh, serial homelessness. Uh, you have incompetent political and social leadership. You have a de-emphasis of, uh, art and music and, uh, you have, uh, lousy teaching or school, or, okay, those are all the pressures pointing at the individuals who say, "I'm gonna act out, I'm gonna commit the crime." Okay, but all the pressures are there if, um, if people decide, if—if leadership decided, "We're gonna do something about those causes so that the individual won't have those pressures," I think crime would go down.	I want to say, when you talk about causes of crime . . . Okay, you have to look at the individual first, and look at the pressures on the individual and you have pressures like serial unemployment or underemployment. You have serial homelessness. You have incompetent political and social leadership. You have a de-emphasis of art and music and you have lousy teaching or school, or, okay, those are all the pressures pointing at the individuals who say, "I'm gonna act out, I'm gonna commit the crime." Okay, but all the pressures are there if people decide, if leadership decided, "We're gonna do something about those causes so that the individual won't have those pressures," I think crime would go down. (Christopher, 68, B, CE, FG3)
I was going to say, that's like desperation. I . . . I have that one thing with something, the poverty, the unemployment, the need for cash. And then just desperation. But that's . . . that's an extreme.	I was going to say, that's like desperation. I have that one thing with something, the poverty, the unemployment, the need for cash. And then just desperation. But that's an extreme. (Wallace, 57, W, CE, FG5)
Well, I . . . I . . . I think of, um, places that society has abandoned, you know, in . . . in terms of that, I mean, in California and . . . and Detroit and, um, parts of Illinois, I mean, it's just there . . . there are no jobs. There's no hope. And these are . . . what do the smart people do? They get together, they join gangs. They . . . they rob, they steal, they figure out a way to survive. I don't blame them. So why . . . why . . . why are these places being abandoned? I mean, it doesn't seem like local government, their state governments, or the feds are really doing anything.	Well, I think of places that society has abandoned in terms of that . . . , I mean, in California and Detroit and parts of Illinois, it's just there are no jobs. There's no hope. And these are . . . what do the smart people do? They get together, they join gangs. They rob, they steal, they figure out a way to survive. I don't blame them. So why are these places being abandoned? I mean, it doesn't seem like local government, their state governments, or the feds are really doing anything. (Inez, 72, W, CE, FG5)
Well, that would be a start. And, and, and, and have better labels for videos, too. Movies and videos. Because I think . . . I mean, I was sitting in front watching a TV show the other day, I had no idea there was gonna be nudity in it, and this was, um, this was at 7:00 p.m., and I had somebody in the room that was very young.	Well, that would be a start. And have better labels for videos, too. Movies and videos. Because I think . . . I was sitting in front watching a TV show the other day, I had no idea there was gonna be nudity in it, and this was at 7:00 p.m., and I had somebody in the room that was very young. (Debbie, 64, W, CE, FG1)

survey firm Ipsos. At the time the survey was fielded in 2016, it was maintained by the survey firm GfK. Participants are recruited into the KnowledgePanel using an equal probability selection method based upon Address Based Sampling using the Delivery Sequence File of the United States Postal Service. A significant strength of the Knowledge-Panel is that the survey administrators provide a web-enabled device and free internet service to any randomly selected household that does not possess an internet connection, thereby overcoming the challenge of ensuring that households without home internet are properly represented in online survey research. Panel participants complete surveys online, and in general, participants are allowed to complete no more than one survey per week. Participants are eligible for small incentives, such as raffles for cash rewards or prizes.[16] Internet surveys based upon probability samples, like the KnowledgePanel, possess significantly higher external validity than nonrandom samples.[17] Some evidence specifically indicates that data gathered from KnowledgePanel participants can be generalized to the population of US residents age thirteen or older.[18] I additionally applied survey weights to many of the quantitative analyses I conducted in this book to increase representativeness. These survey weights were created using population benchmarks from the March 2016 Current Population Survey.

A total of 3,916 non-Hispanic White and Black residents of the United States were randomly selected from the KnowledgePanel to participate in this survey. The survey was fielded between September 27 and October 10, 2016. Among those sampled, 2,010 participants completed the survey, yielding a completion rate of 51%. Reporting response metrics for probability-based online panels is complicated because they involve multiple stages of selection and participation: first, the selection into the panel, second, maintaining active status on the panel, and third, the completion of each specific survey.[19] The cumulative response rate for this survey was: household recruitment rate (12.4%), multiplied by household entry profile completion rate (64.9%), multiplied by study completion rate (51.3%), which equals 4.1%. Though this cumulative response rate may strike some readers as dangerously low, survey methodologists have produced an impressive body of research which demonstrates that nonresponse bias (the degree to which a survey's sample statistics deviate from the corresponding "true" population parameters as a function of too few people completing the survey) is not a simple function of total response rate.[20]

On average, it took participants six minutes to complete the survey. To ensure data quality, I screened the participants who took two or fewer minutes to complete the survey, which placed them in the fastest 5% of the sample. Many of these fastest participants showed a great deal of "straight-lining" (giving the same answer to batteries of questions), which raises the concern that they sped through the survey without paying attention. Additional tests revealed that these participants gave significantly different responses to most questions than slower participants, and nearly 40% of these respondents answered the survey experiment manipulation check question incorrectly, which suggests that they were not properly treated, and the reliability of their responses is low.[21] As such, I chose to drop from the analysis participants who took two or fewer minutes to complete the survey, which resulted in a loss of 198 respondents (yielding an analysis sample of 1,812 respondents).[22]

Variable Construction

Racism

I employed the "racial resentment" scale composed of the following items: (1) "Irish, Italians, Jewish, and other minorities overcame prejudice and worked their way up; African Americans should do the same without special favors"; (2) "It's really a matter of some people just not trying hard enough; if African Americans would only try harder they could be just as well off as whites"; (3) "Generations of slavery have created conditions that make it difficult for African Americans to work their way out of the lower class"; (4) "Over the past few years, African Americans have gotten less than they deserve"; (5) "Most African Americans who receive money from welfare programs could get along without it if they tried"; (6) "Government officials usually pay less attention to a request or complaint from an African Americans person than from a white person."[23] All six items were followed by a Likert response scale of "agree strongly," "agree somewhat," "neither agree nor disagree," "disagree somewhat," and "disagree strongly." I reverse-coded items 3, 4, 5, and 6 so that higher scores on all items indicated greater levels of agreement with the beliefs that Black people do not adhere to the

"Protestant work ethic" and that racial discrimination is no longer a problem in society.[24]

Though these items are typically combined into a single scale, a principal factors analysis with oblique rotation revealed two factors with eigenvalues greater than one (2.52 and 2.51). The racial resentment items listed above loaded onto the two factors in the following manner (rotated factor loadings listed in parentheses): Factor 1—items 1 (0.71), 2 (0.76), and 5 (0.62); Factor 2—items 3 (0.66), 4 (0.73), and 6 (0.67). The nature of these loadings is consistent with the argument that the racial resentment items, when combined into a single scale, conflate people's negative dispositional judgments of Black people with their perceptions of racial discrimination in society.[25] I find that Factor 1 captures people's volitional endorsement of the laziness stereotype about Black people while Factor 2 captures people's denial of the continued existence of discrimination in society. The laziness scale has a Cronbach's alpha of 0.81 and the discrimination scale has a Cronbach's alpha of 0.82.

Criminal Justice System Fairness

I wrote five items to measure respondents' level of confidence that the justice system treats Black and White people equally. The items shared the same format: "How much confidence do you have that [ITEM] treat African Americans and Whites equally?" The five items were "the police," "prosecutors," "judges," "probation officers," and "prison guards." All items shared the same response options, which were "a lot of confidence," "some confidence," and "no confidence at all." A principal factors analysis with oblique rotation generated more ambiguous findings compared to the racial resentment items. Two factors generated eigenvalues greater than one, after rotation (3.56 and 3.34). However, several aspects of the factor loadings were problematic. Two items (judges and probation officers) cross-loaded onto both factors (their weaker factor loadings, on opposite factors, were 0.35 and 0.31, respectively). If I use the threshold of factor loadings greater than 0.35, Factor 1 would contain police, prosecutors, and judges while Factor 2 would contain only probation officers and prison guards. However, some scholars argue that factors containing fewer than three items are unstable and unreliable.[26] Given the empirical ambiguity of the factor analysis and the lack of extant theory that would explain why people's perceptions of criminal justice system fairness would differ across justice subsystems, I chose to proceed conservatively and combine all five items into a single scale as I first intended when I wrote the items. This scale has a Cronbach's alpha of 0.94.

2012 Voter

A single question identified people who voted in the previous presidential election: "In talking to people about elections, we often find that a lot of people were not able to vote because they weren't registered, they were sick, or they just didn't have time. Did you happen to vote in the 2012 elections for the U.S. President or Congress?" The response options were "Yes" (80.49% of the analysis sample) and "No" (19.51% of the analysis sample).

Political Ideology

Respondents' political ideology was measured with the question, "In general, do you think of yourself as 1) Extremely liberal, 2) Liberal, 3) Slightly liberal, 4) Moderate, middle of the road, 5) Slightly conservative, 6) Conservative, or 7) Extremely conservative." I combined the "extremely liberal" and "slightly liberal" respondents with the "liberal" respondents, and likewise for the conservative respondents, to create a three-category variable that identified Liberals, Moderates, and Conservatives. The analysis sample was 29.66% Liberal, 39.05% Moderate, and 31.28% Conservative.

Political Party Identification

Respondents' party identification was measured with a series of questions. Respondents first indicated if they called themselves a Republican, a Democrat, an independent, "another party," or had "no preference." Respondents who identified with either of the two parties were then asked if they were a "strong" or "not very strong" affiliate of that party. Respondents who gave one of the other three answers were then asked, "Do you think of yourself as closer to the 1) Republican Party or

Democratic Party?" Respondents who answered yes were coded as leaning toward one of the parties. I collapsed the "strong," "not very strong," and "lean" categories into single partisan categories, and I collapsed independents, "another party," and "no preference" respondents into a single Independent/Undecided category. The analysis sample was 30.96% Republican, 64.96% Democrat, and 4.08% independent. The overrepresentation of Democrats is likely because 50% of the sample was Black Americans who disproportionately affiliate with the Democratic Party.

Demographic Characteristics

KnowledgePanel participants complete a demographic profile when they enroll in the panel, and GfK and Ipsos provide basic demographic variables as part of all data sets. The codebook did not include the full, original wording of the questions used to measure demographic characteristics, but most of them are self-evident.

I created a three-category variable to identify respondents whose highest level of completed formal education was a high school degree (35.10% of the analysis sample), those who completed some college courses but did not receive a college degree (34.55%), and those who possessed a Bachelor's degree or some level of graduate education (30.35%).

The composition of the analysis sample was 46.96% male and 53.04% female. The mean age of the sample was fifty-two years, the median age was fifty-four years, and the standard deviation was 16.5 years. Seventy-five percent of the sample was age thirty-nine or older. I followed the Pew Research Center's definition of generational cohort membership.[27] I identified the "Silent Generation" as people who were age seventy-one or older in 2016 (13.63% of the sample), "Baby Boomers" as people who were between ages fifty-two and seventy (42.94%), and "Gen X" as those between ages thirty-six and fifty-one (22.35%). Since the minimum age to participate in the survey was eighteen, only a small number of Gen Z Americans were eligible as of 2016. As such, I combined "Gen Z" and the "Millennials" into a single category of all people who were age thirty-five or younger (21.08%).

The sample was heavily skewed toward urban residents; 88.30% of respondents reported living in a metropolitan statistical area (as defined by the US Census), while 11.70% reported living outside a metropolitan statistical area. Also following the definitions of the US Census, 16.94% of the analysis sample lived in states in the Northeast, 45.64% lived in the South, 21.80% lived in the Midwest, and 15.62% lived in the West.

Household income was measured as an ordinal, categorical variable that ranged from "less than $5,000" to "$250,000 or more." The modal category was "$100,000 to $124,000" (12.53% of the analysis sample), but 85% of respondents reported a lower level of total household income. Half of the sample reported $59,999 or less income, and one-quarter of the sample reported $29,999 or less income. Regarding home ownership, 65.51% reported being a homeowner and 34.49% being a renter or having some other type of unspecified living situation. The data included a seven-category employment status variable that I collapsed into four categories: employed either by self or as a paid employee (56.46% of the analysis sample), unemployed either temporarily or looking for work (11.59%), retired (25.94%), and disabled (6.02%). Finally, I created a dummy variable to identify respondents who had one or more minors under the age of eighteen in their household (25.61%) versus those who reported no minors in the household (74.39%); I treat this variable as a proxy for being the parent or guardian of a child, but I acknowledge the ambiguity in the original measure.

Table A.3 presents the descriptive statistics of all the variables I included in the quantitative analyses throughout the book.

The data that I analyzed in this book are publicly archived and available for use and replication at the National Archive of Criminal Justice Data.[28]

TABLE A3. Descriptive Statistics of Analysis Variables

Variable	Observations	Mean	Std. Deviation	Min.	Max.
Dependent Variables					
% Budget to Police	1812	14.37	26.19	0	100
% Budget to Probation	1812	14.98	24.00	0	100
% Budget to Clinics	1812	15.27	22.59	0	100
% Budget to Schools	1812	17.40	24.13	0	100
% Budget to Jobs	1812	20.73	28.05	0	100
% Budget to Tax Rebate	1812	16.42	29.52	0	100
Budget Preference Categories	1797	2.87	1.63	1	6
CJS Invest. Vote Preference	1797	2.12	0.74	1	3
Comm. Invest. Vote Preference	1789	2.39	0.74	1	3
Moderating and Control Variables					
Racism-Laziness Stereotype	1788	8.72	3.39	3	15
Racism-Discrimination	1792	8.56	3.45	3	15
Criminal Justice System Fairness	1783	8.33	3.12	5	15
2012 Voter	1804	0.80	0.40	0	1
Political Ideology	1790	2.02	0.78	1	3
Political Partisanship	1812	2.34	0.92	1	3
Education	1812	0.95	0.81	0	2
Age	1812	52.14	16.54	18	89
Generation	1812	1.67	1.04	0	3
Metro Resident	1812	0.88	0.32	0	1
Geographic Region of Residence	1812	2.60	0.94	1	4
Household Income	1812	11.71	4.85	1	21
Homeowner	1812	0.66	0.48	0	1
Employment Status	1812	1.82	1.02	1	4
Parent	1812	0.26	0.44	0	1

Full Regression Output

TABLE A4. Results of Multinomial Logit Regression Analysis of Budget Preference Categories on Demographic and Ideological Variables

| | Only Community vs. . . . | | | | |
	Mostly Community	Balanced	Mostly CJS or Tax	Only CJS or Tax	Only Tax
White	0.99	0.96	1.82	1.10	0.93
	(0.66–1.48)	(0.61–1.50)	(0.96–3.48)	(0.65–1.87)	(0.51–1.71)
Some College, No Degree	1.11	1.05	1.32	1.18	1.17
	(.75–1.64)	(0.70–1.59)	(0.77–2.25)	(0.75–1.87)	(0.66–2.07)
Bachelor's Degree or Higher	0.96	0.65	1.03	0.71	0.80
	(0.63–1.46)	(0.41–1.05)	(0.55–1.95)	(0.40–1.25)	(0.43–1.49)
Independent	1.71	0.64	0.12*	0.59	3.13
	(0.65–4.53)	(0.22–1.87)	(0.01–0.97)	(0.19–1.84)	(0.92–10.68)
Democrat	0.97	0.82	0.52*	0.56*	0.93
	(0.57–1.66)	(0.50–1.35)	(0.28–0.97)	(0.33–1.00)	(0.50–1.73)
Moderate	0.92	1.14	2.95**	1.38	1.32
	(0.65–1.31)	(0.74–1.73)	(1.41–6.19)	(0.83–2.31)	(0.70–2.48)
Conservative	1.01	1.33	3.43**	1.60	1.54
	(0.62–1.67)	(0.79–2.23)	(1.52–7.73)	(0.86–2.98)	(0.74–3.22)
Metro Area Resident	1.07	0.74	0.83	0.94	0.63
	(0.61–1.87)	(0.45–1.23)	(0.41–1.68)	(0.53–1.67)	(0.33–1.22)
Age	1.01	1.00	1.01	1.01	1.01
	(0.99–1.02)	(0.99–1.02)	(0.99–1.03)	(1.00–1.03)	(0.99–1.03)
Male	0.72*	0.75	1.05	1.12	1.99**
	(0.52–0.98)	(0.53–1.05)	(0.67–1.65)	(0.77–1.63)	(1.22–3.24)
Northeast	0.76	1.02	1.34	0.77	1.24
	(0.49–1.18)	(0.65–1.60)	(0.71–2.53)	(0.46–1.29)	(0.66–2.30)
Midwest	0.85	0.98	1.10	0.84	1.19
	(0.57–1.28)	(0.64–1.50)	(0.60–2.01)	(0.52–1.37)	(0.64–2.19)
West	0.85	0.93	1.60	1.03	1.00
	(0.54–1.35)	(0.56–1.52)	(0.86–2.98)	(0.58–1.80)	(0.50–2.00)
Income	1.04	1.05*	1.00	1.06*	1.09**
	(1.00–1.08)	(1.00–1.10)	(0.94–1.06)	(1.00–1.12)	(1.02–1.16)
Homeowner	0.95	1.49	1.10	1.11	1.20
	(0.66–1.37)	(0.99–2.24)	(0.63–1.92)	(0.70–1.76)	(0.67–2.17)
Parent	0.91	1.02	0.70	1.07	0.85
	(0.63–1.31)	(0.68–1.54)	(0.39–1.26)	(0.68–1.66)	(0.48–1.50)
Unemployed	1.26	0.60	0.76	1.58	1.39
	(0.75–2.11)	(0.32–1.11)	(0.37–1.55)	(0.87–2.86)	(0.64–2.99)
Retired	0.57*	0.83	0.68	0.87	0.63
	(0.36–0.91)	(0.50–1.37)	(0.33–1.37)	(0.50–1.49)	(0.32–1.26)
Disabled	1.36	1.49	0.96	1.40	1.08
	(0.70–2.62)	(0.70–3.17)	(0.28–3.21)	(0.60–3.26)	(0.34–3.41)
Racism-Discrimination	0.96	0.99	1.03	1.02	1.13*
	(0.89–1.03)	(0.96–1.07)	(0.94–1.12)	(0.94–1.10)	(1.03–1.24)
Racism-Laziness	0.95	1.05	1.04	1.13**	1.20***
	(0.89–1.01)	(0.99–1.12)	(0.95–1.14)	(1.04–1.22)	(1.11–1.30)
CJS Fairness	0.96	0.98	1.09	1.11*	0.94
	(0.89–1.04)	(0.91–1.06)	(0.99–1.20)	(1.02–1.20)	(0.85–1.05)

Notes: Effects presented are relative risk ratios with 95% confidence intervals in parentheses. "Only community" is the omitted, comparison category of the dependent variable.
* = p <0.05, ** = p <0.01, *** = p <0.001

Table A5.1. Results of Multinomial Logit Regression Analysis of Criminal Justice Investment Vote Preference on Experimental Condition, Budget Preference, and Demographic and Ideological Variables

| | No Change vs. . . . | |
	Less Likely	More Likely
Experiment Conditions		
· High Crime Treatment	1.274 [0.743,2.185]	1.245 [0.739,2.100]
· High Poverty Treatment	0.767 [0.440,1.335]	1.175 [0.699,1.976]
· Welfare Treatment	1.220 [0.737,2.018]	1.133 [0.697,1.841]
· Inner City Treatment	1.388 [0.805,2.393]	0.962 [0.573,1.613]
· Rural Treatment	1.266 [0.726,2.207]	0.933 [0.556,1.565]
· African American Treatment	0.916 [0.529,1.586]	0.979 [0.585,1.638]
Budget Preference Categories		
· Mostly Community	0.683* [0.476,0.979]	1.420 [0.930,2.170]
· Balanced	0.367*** [0.223,0.605]	3.375*** [2.228,5.111]
· Mostly CJS or Tax	0.145*** [0.0459,0.455]	5.115*** [3.002,8.715]
· Only CJS or Tax	0.387** [0.198,0.755]	6.554*** [4.112,10.45]
· Only Tax	1.080 [0.628,1.858]	0.746 [0.394,1.412]
2012 Voter	1.634* [1.080,2.473]	1.716** [1.181,2.493]
White	0.766 [0.518,1.131]	0.905 [0.623,1.313]
Some College, No Degree	1.080 [0.734,1.589]	1.199 [0.867,1.657]
Bachelor's Degree Or Higher	1.390 [0.898,2.151]	1.325 [0.912,1.926]
Democrat	0.203*** [0.0784,0.524]	0.0992*** [0.0296,0.332]
Independent	0.624 [0.381,1.024]	0.750 [0.511,1.100]
Moderate	0.718 [0.504,1.024]	0.530*** [0.372,0.754]

	No Change vs. . . .	
	Less Likely	More Likely
Conservative	0.702 [0.437,1.126]	0.551** [0.365,0.833]
Metro Area Resident	1.012 [0.614,1.668]	0.994 [0.670,1.474]
Silent Generation	0.956 [0.486,1.882]	0.898 [0.508,1.587]
Baby Boomers	0.958 [0.620,1.480]	0.881 [0.578,1.342]
Generation X	1.349 [0.879,2.070]	0.842 [0.553,1.283]
Male	1.195 [0.884,1.615]	1.068 [0.817,1.396]
Northeast	0.838 [0.556,1.263]	1.044 [0.721,1.512]
Midwest	0.990 [0.675,1.452]	1.118 [0.778,1.606]
West	0.961 [0.605,1.524]	1.027 [0.696,1.514]
Income	0.959* [0.921,0.999]	0.997 [0.964,1.031]
Homeowner	0.960 [0.669,1.377]	1.018 [0.731,1.417]
Parent	1.057 [0.749,1.492]	0.958 [0.681,1.349]
Unemployed	0.995 [0.615,1.612]	1.394 [0.889,2.185]
Retired	0.761 [0.470,1.232]	0.901 [0.604,1.346]
Disabled	0.742 [0.369,1.491]	0.997 [0.551,1.804]
Racism-Discrimination	0.971 [0.910,1.036]	1.034 [0.978,1.094]
Racism-Laziness	0.957 [0.902,1.016]	1.093** [1.035,1.153]
CJS Fairness	0.908** [0.845,0.976]	0.999 [0.942,1.060]
N	1729	

Notes: Effects presented are relative risk ratios with 95% confidence intervals in parentheses. The dependent variable response option, "It probably wouldn't change my vote one way or the other," was the omitted comparison category.
*= $p < 0.05$, **= $p < 0.01$, ***= $p < 0.001$

TABLE A5.2. Results of Multinomial Logit Regression Analysis of Community Investment Vote Preference on Experimental Condition, Budget Preference, and Demographic and Ideological Variables

	No Change vs. . . .	
	Less Likely	More Likely
Experiment Conditions		
· High Crime Treatment	0.809 [0.389,1.681]	1.267 [0.738,2.176]
· High Poverty Treatment	1.539 [0.776,3.054]	0.976 [0.583,1.634]
· Welfare Treatment	1.315 [0.691,2.502]	0.827 [0.504,1.358]
· Inner City Treatment	1.499 [0.779,2.886]	1.041 [0.625,1.734]
· Rural Treatment	0.833 [0.418,1.661]	0.794 [0.474,1.329]
· African American Treatment	1.926* [1.023,3.626]	1.326 [0.790,2.224]
Budget Preference Categories		
· Mostly Community	1.731 [0.907,3.302]	0.924 [0.627,1.361]
· Balanced	0.990 [0.521,1.881]	0.532** [0.357,0.794]
· Mostly CJS or Tax	2.054* [1.041,4.053]	0.429** [0.239,0.769]
· Only CJS or Tax	1.396 [0.766,2.542]	0.169*** [0.105,0.272]
· Only Tax	1.940* [1.010,3.727]	0.270*** [0.151,0.482]
2012 Voter	2.234** [1.325,3.768]	1.435 [0.982,2.097]
White	0.903 [0.522,1.563]	1.290 [0.876,1.899]
Some College, No Degree	0.827 [0.536,1.275]	0.926 [0.657,1.305]
Bachelor's Degree Or Higher	0.765 [0.461,1.269]	0.905 [0.613,1.337]
Democrat	0.467 [0.165,1.321]	0.266** [0.101,0.698]
Independent	0.670 [0.404,1.110]	1.106 [0.752,1.626]
Moderate	0.323*** [0.194,0.538]	0.662* [0.464,0.945]

	No Change vs. . . .	
	Less Likely	More Likely
Conservative	0.577 [0.327,1.019]	0.494** [0.325,0.752]
Metro Area Resident	1.065 [0.632,1.795]	0.886 [0.585,1.342]
Silent Generation	1.101 [0.498,2.436]	0.857 [0.470,1.561]
Baby Boomers	1.054 [0.619,1.797]	0.731 [0.472,1.132]
Generation X	0.772 [0.428,1.390]	1.052 [0.685,1.617]
Male	1.588* [1.106,2.280]	1.135 [0.858,1.500]
Northeast	1.011 [0.620,1.647]	0.940 [0.628,1.407]
Midwest	0.908 [0.581,1.419]	0.797 [0.558,1.139]
West	1.237 [0.746,2.050]	0.881 [0.587,1.321]
Income	0.977 [0.931,1.025]	0.997 [0.961,1.035]
Homeowner	1.514 [0.984,2.328]	1.171 [0.834,1.644]
Parent	1.520 [0.993,2.327]	1.126 [0.803,1.579]
Unemployed	1.534 [0.871,2.702]	0.855 [0.528,1.384]
Retired	0.594 [0.340,1.036]	0.936 [0.636,1.378]
Disabled	1.145 [0.542,2.420]	0.815 [0.439,1.512]
Racism-Discrimination	1.019 [0.934,1.113]	0.929** [0.881,0.981]
Racism-Laziness	1.055 [0.977,1.140]	1.004 [0.954,1.057]
CJS Fairness	1.028 [0.951,1.111]	0.912** [0.856,0.971]
N	1721	

Notes: Effects presented are relative risk ratios with 95% confidence intervals in parentheses. The dependent variable response option, "It probably wouldn't change my vote one way or the other," was the omitted comparison category.
$* = p < 0.05$, $** = p < 0.01$, $*** = p < 0.001$

NOTES

INTRODUCTION

1 Hill et al. 2020; New York Times 2021.

2 Buchanan et al. 2020.

3 Baldassare 2019; National Advisory Commission on Civil Disorders and Kerner 1968.

4 Cobbina 2019; Lowery 2016.

5 Guynn 2015; Lebron 2021; Ransby 2015; Taylor 2016.

6 Beckett and Herbert 2009; Clear and Frost 2015; Garland 2001; 2020; Gilmore 2007; Hinton 2016; Sharkey 2018; Simon 2007; Wacquant 2009.

7 King 2020.

8 Hatzipanagos 2020.

9 National Advisory Commission on Civil Disorders and Kerner 1968, 1.

10 Le Blanc 2013.

11 Rustin 1964, 25, 26.

12 A *"Freedom Budget" for All Americans* 1966, 12.

13 Glazer and Sharkey 2021.

14 Beltramini 2017; Johnson 2017.

15 The pattern of wealthier newcomers displacing longtime residents when neighborhood property values rise is called "gentrification." For evaluations of enterprise zone programs, see Drucker and Lipton 2019; Neumark 2020; Neumark and Simpson 2015; Tankersley 2020; Theodos et al. 2020; Trickey 2020.

16 Dunworth and Mills 1999.

17 Bridenball and Jesilow 2005; Kraska 2007; Miller 2001.

18 Cramer et al. 2014; La Vigne et al. 2016; Monteiro and Frost 2015; Sabol and Baumann 2020.

19 Tucker and Cadora 2003, 2.

20 Austin et al. 2013; Cleve and Mayes 2015; Sabol and Baumann 2020; Sakala et al. 2018; Welsh-Loveman and Harvell 2018.

21 David Garland (2020) refers to programs that assist only individuals who are already entangled in the justice system as "penal assistance."

22 Sharkey 2018; see also Hackworth 2019.

23 Branas et al. 2016; Kondo et al. 2018; Krivo, Lyons, and Vélez 2021; Kubrin and Weitzer 2003; Peterson and Krivo 2010; Raleigh and Galster 2015; Sampson, Raudenbush, and Earls 1997; Sampson, Morenoff, and Raudenbush 2005; Sampson and Wilson 1995; Savage, Ellis, and Wozniak 2019; Savage and Wozniak 2016.

24 Dagan and Teles 2016, 74.

25 Full details about the methodology used to create the punitive sentiment measure can be found in Enns (2016). Ramirez (2013) used the same basic methodology as Enns and demonstrated very similar patterns of changes in mass punitive sentiment over time.

26 Thielo et al. 2016.

27 Pickett and Baker 2014; Unnever et al. 2010.

28 See also Eckhouse 2019.

29 Page and Jacobs 2009.

30 Enns and Koch (2013) provide a counterpoint. At the macro level, they demonstrate that the overall public policy mood in the early 2000s was significantly more conservative than it was during the 1960s, indicating lower mass public support for government intervention and welfare policies. This mass public conservative shift was present in all states, even those with relatively more liberal populations. Resolving the discordance between individual-level surveys that show high public support for antipoverty spending with the aggregate-level evidence of conservative public mood is a challenge that I cannot resolve in this book.

31 This GSS survey question was identical to the spending on government assistance to the poor question, except instead of asking about "assistance to the poor," the question asked about "welfare."

32 Hochschild 1995; Hunt 1996, 2007; Manning et al. 2015; Silva 2013.

33 Page and Jacobs 2009, 96–97.

34 Katz 2013.

35 Petersen et al. 2012.

36 Allport 1979; Eberhardt 2019; Kahneman 2011.

37 For the pre-twentieth-century history of racial stereotyping as a means of enforcing white hegemony, see Du Bois 1935; Kendi 2016; Muhammad 2011; H. C. Richardson 2020. In the twentieth century, Franklin Delano Roosevelt compromised with conservative, prosegregation Southern members of Congress in order to pass his New Deal policies. These legislators inscribed into the New Deal policies a range of exceptions and loopholes that were designed to minimize Black Americans' access to benefits. For example, the Social Security Act of 1935 established federal programs that would disburse financial assistance to the elderly, the unemployed, and families with dependent children. However, Southern members of Congress amended the bill to make farmworkers and domestic workers (such as maids) ineligible for many of the benefits the law created. They did this knowing that Black Americans at the time were disproportionately employed in the agricultural and domestic labor forces; 65% of all Black Americans were initially ineligible for Social Security, and in some southern states, this percentage was as high as 80%. The Housing Act of 1937 allowed local banks and housing authorities to implement the infamous practice of "redlining"—denying federally subsidized mortgages to residents of neighborhoods that were

deemed undesirable, often because they were predominantly populated by Black Americans, the poor, or both. For the history of racially discriminatory public aid programs in the twentieth century, see Katznelson 2006; Quadagno 1996; Rothstein 2017.

38 Gilens 1999, 114; see also Katz 2013.

39 Quoted in López 2015, 58.

40 Hackworth 2019; Quadagno 1996.

41 McIlwain and Caliendo 2014; Sharkey 2018; Soss et al. 2011; Wacquant 2009.

42 Gilens 1999; Mettler 2018; Rosenthal 2021.

43 Cramer 2016; Hochschild 1995; Hunt 1996, 2007; Manning et al. 2015; Silva, 2013, 2019; Skocpol and Williamson 2016.

44 Mendelberg 2001. In the two decades since Mendelberg's book was published, political scientists have debated whether overtly racist beliefs of Black inferiority saw a widespread resurgence between the presidencies of Barack Obama and Donald Trump, meaning among more than the subset of people who espoused openly white supremacist beliefs. See Hopkins and Washington 2020; Jardina and Piston 2019; Tesler 2013; Yadon and Piston 2019.

45 López (2015) refers to implicitly racialized cues as "dog whistles"; they allow politicians to activate racist sentiments while retaining plausible deniability that their statements had anything to do with race. See also Hutchings and Jardina, 2009; Tesler 2017; Valenzuela and Reny 2021; Winter 2008.

46 Clear 2007; Krivo et al. 2020; Massey and Denton 1993; Peterson and Krivo 2010; Sampson 2017; Sampson and Loeffler 2010; Sampson and Wilson 1995; Tucker and Cadora 2003.

47 Gilens 1999; Hurwitz and Peffley, 2005; Wetts and Willer 2019; White 2007.

48 Hagan and Albonetti 1982; Travis et al. 2014; Western 2006; Western and Pettit 2010.

49 Sharkey 2018; Zimring 2008.

50 McCarthy 2020.

51 Enns 2016.

52 I emphasize that this book examines political and sociological forces in the United States alone. The early decades of the twenty-first century in the United States could only be considered low in crime and punitiveness compared to the nation's own history. The United States consistently experiences significantly higher rates of violent crime than other wealthy, democratic nations in Europe and the British Commonwealth. See Garland 2020; Miller 2016.

53 Garland 2001; Mead 1918.

54 Hershbein 2018.

55 U.S. Bureau of Labor Statistics 2016.

56 Cynamon and Fazzari 2016; Schaeffer 2020; Desilver 2018.

57 Chetty et al. 2017; Jennings 2016; Schuster and Ciurczak, 2018.

58 Case and Deaton 2020; Metzl 2020; Skolnick 2018.

59 Beckett 1997; Beckett and Francis 2020; K. Drakulich et al. 2017, 2020; Tilley 2020; Zoorob 2019.

1. WHAT DO PEOPLE BELIEVE CAUSES CRIME?

1 Baumgartner and Jones 2009; Kingdon 1984; Stone 1989.

2 Iyengar 1991; Jonson et al. 2013.

3 Quoted in Scheingold 2011, 75. Other writers echoed Scheingold's observations about the causes and consequences of policy makers' changing understanding of crime from the 1960s through the 1990s (Garland 2001; Gottschalk 2006; Hinton 2016; Murakawa 2014). Flanagan (1987) considered how changes in lay citizens' understanding of the causes of crime may have influenced policy makers.

4 Arnold 1992.

5 Agnew 1992; Merton 1938.

6 I identify all focus group participants with their pseudonym, their age, their race (Black or White), their educational status (high school educated, HSE, or college educated, CE), and the focus group they attended.

7 Jacklyn and Matthew's arguments here echo the argument made by the sociologist Elijah Anderson (1999) in his book, *Code of the Street*.

8 Unnever and Cullen 2009.

9 Cauffman et al. 2016. One participant all but used criminologists' jargon, "the age-crime curve": Mary (33, B, HSE, FG4) said, "Well, for one, when I was in my twenties, I know a lot of . . . The only difference between some murderers and some didn't get caught is just they didn't get caught. And then I do know when people . . . Like, I'm a spiritual person, and I feel like Jesus was like 33 when he started his journey. And there's something when you're about that age, you kind of know your purpose. So I do think a lot of people, when they're in their thirties, would not do some of the things they did in their twenties."

10 Akers 1998; Sutherland 1947.

11 Anderson 1999.

12 Ferguson et al. 2014; Ferguson and Markey 2019; Ferguson and Savage 2012; Savage 2004, 2008; Savage and Yancey, 2008; S. Smith et al. 2018.

13 Kubrin 2005.

14 Gottfredson and Hirschi 1990; Hirschi 2002; Hoeve et al. 2009; Pagani 2009; Savage and Wozniak 2016.

15 Wilson 2012.

16 The age "60+" is not a typo. Rachelle declined to specify her exact age. She wrote "60+" on her exit survey.

17 Anderson 1990; Bunyasi and Smith 2019; Cohen 1999.

18 Dawson 1995.

19 Sampson 2004; Sampson et al. 1999.

20 Elijah Anderson (1999) also observed that adult residents of the communities he studied expressed fear of a new generation of teenagers that they perceived to be dangerous and unpredictable.

21 Some theorists discussed personal morality in quite stark terms. In *Thinking about Crime*, the political scientist James Q. Wilson (1975, 235) famously wrote, "Wicked people exist. Nothing avails except to set them apart from innocent people."
22 Hirschi 2002; Wikström et al. 2012.
23 Gottfredson and Hirschi 1990.
24 Britt and Rocque 2016.
25 Bersani and Doherty 2013; Hirschi 2002; Sampson and Laub 1993.
26 Nagin 2013.
27 Maruna 2007.
28 Cohen and Felson 1979.
29 Becker 2018.
30 Lerman and Weaver 2014b; Maruna 2007; Middlemass 2017; Pager 2008.
31 Hinton 2016; Scheingold 1991, 2011; Tonry 2004.
32 Hagan 2010.
33 Cochran, Boots, and Heide 2003; Cullen et al. 1985; Falco and Turner 2014; Grasmick and McGill 1994; Green, Staerkle, and Sears 2006; Peffley, Hurwitz, and Mondak 2017; Pickett and Baker 2014; Ramirez 2015; Thompson and Bobo 2011; Unnever et al. 2010; Updegrove et al. 2021; Wozniak 2016; R. L. Young 1991.
34 Erskine 1974.
35 Flanagan 1987.
36 Gabbidon and Boisvert 2012; Hart 1998; Sims 2003.
37 Thompson and Bobo 2011.
38 Sasson 1995.
39 See also Jonson et al. 2013; Unnever et al. 2010.
40 Enns 2016; Ramirez 2013.

2. BRAINSTORMING RESPONSES TO CRIME

1 Kingdon 1984.
2 Bursik and Grasmick 1993; Carr 2003; Hunter 1985; Leverentz and Williams 2017.
3 Bell 2016; Brunson 2007; Carr et al. 2007; Desmond et al. 2016; Leverentz 2011; Leverentz and Williams 2017; Peffley and Hurwitz 2010; Prowse et al. 2020; Soss and Weaver 2017; Zaykowski et al. 2019.
4 Enns and Wlezien 2011.
5 Statements of a "mixed attributional nature" were not unique to Focus Group 2. Another illustrative example came from Amber (49, W, CE, FG1): "Well, people cause crimes. It depends, like I would say neighborhood crimes and guns and weapons, but it all ties back into people. And the economy is like, if you don't have the good economy, a lot of people aren't gonna be happy. So, then it comes to the government, too, because, you know, the economy, people aren't happy. So, it depends like what type of neighborhood you live in too. It depends; a lot of crimes happen in bad neighborhoods and it also happens in good neighborhoods too." For cogent sociological explanations of the reasons why many Americans of color endorse both volitional and structural attributions of responsibility see

Bobo 1991 and Hunt 1996. For additional evidence that large numbers of Black Americans recognize systemic racism but also endorse American values of hard work, personal responsibility, and individualism, see Hochschild 1995, Manning et al. 2015, and Smith 2014.

6 The school shooting that received the most extensive media coverage in the years preceding the focus groups was the 2012 mass shooting at Sandy Hook Elementary School in Newtown, CT, in which twenty young students were killed, as well as six members of staff.

7 Miller 2008, 108.

8 I draw the phrase "selective hearing" from Hinton et al. 2016.

9 Fagan et al. 2015.

10 Braga et al. 2019; Brunson 2007; Carr et al. 2007; Desmond et al. 2016; Peffley and Hurwitz 2010; Prowse et al. 2020; Soss and Weaver 2017.

11 In Massachusetts, Medicaid and the Children's Health Insurance Program (CHIP) are combined into one program called MassHealth.

12 Bell 2016; Zaykowski et al. 2019.

13 Walker 2014.

14 Peck 2015; Peffley and Hurwitz 2010.

15 Prowse et al. 2020; Soss and Weaver 2017.

16 Dawson 1995.

17 Cramer 2016; Hochschild 2018; Silva 2019.

18 Denver et al. 2018; Pager, 2008; Uggen et al. 2014; Vuolo et al. 2017.

19 Dawson 1995.

20 Muhammad 2011.

21 Anderson 1999; Carter et al. 2017; Parker and Maggard 2009; A. A. Young 2007.

22 Forman 2017; Fortner 2015; Gaubatz 1995; Peffley and Hurwitz 2010; Wilson and Dunham 2001.

23 Cambridge is a sister city to Boston that lies directly across the Charles River. It is home to Harvard University, the Massachusetts Institute of Technology, and many companies that specialize in digital technology or biotechnology. It has a reputation for being more affluent and more politically progressive than Boston, overall.

24 Eck and Maguire 2000; Weisburd and Eck 2004.

25 Dear 1992.

26 Newton and Belmont are affluent suburbs of Boston.

27 Jennings et al. 2015.

28 Atkinson 2012; Simes 2021.

29 Schueler 2019; Schueler et al. 2017.

30 Gilens 1999; Hochschild 2018; Rosenthal 2021.

31 Scheingold 1991, 2011.

32 Ramey and Shrider 2014; Sharkey et al. 2017; Bursik and Grasmick 1993; Morenoff et al. 2001; Sampson et al. 1997.

33 Krivo et al. 2020; Peterson et al. 2000; Peterson and Krivo 2010; Sampson et al. 2005.

34 Massey and Denton 1993; Rothstein 2017; Wilson 1987.
35 Glazer and Sharkey 2021; Tucker and Cadora 2003.
36 Anderson 1990; Bunyasi and Smith 2019; Cohen 1999.
37 See also Unnever 2008.
38 Braga et al. 2019; Carr et al. 2007; Desmond et al. 2016; Peffley and Hurwitz 2010; Prowse et al. 2020; Soss and Weaver 2017.
39 Forman 2017; Fortner 2015.
40 Bobo 1991; Hinton et al. 2016; Miller 2008.
41 Duxbury 2021a, 2021c.
42 Lacey and Soskice 2015.

3. PUBLIC PREFERENCES FOR A CRIME PREVENTION BUDGET

1 Mears et al. 2015.
2 Tucker and Cadora 2003, 2.
3 Durán 2009; Zatz and Krecker 2003.
4 Braga et al. 2019; Brunson 2007; Forman 2017; Fortner 2015; Prowse et al. 2020; Rios 2011.
5 Rios 2011.
6 "The T" is the name of Boston's public subway and commuter bus system.
7 Dorchester and Roxbury are neighborhoods within the city of Boston that contain a high concentration of residents who are poorer, working class, or people of color, or a combination of the three. Newton is an affluent, predominantly White suburb that borders Boston.
8 Muñoz et al. 2015.
9 Kelling and Wilson 1982.
10 Cohen and Felson 1979.
11 Gaubatz 1995.
12 Gaubatz 1995, 158.
13 Gaubatz 1995, 159
14 Enns 2016; Ramirez 2013.
15 MBTA stands for the "Massachusetts Bay Transportation Authority," which runs Boston's public transportation systems.
16 I lightly edited this exchange to eliminate instances of inaudible crosstalk in the transcript when participants were speaking over each other.
17 Corburn et al. 2022; Matthay et al. 2019; Wikoff et al. 2012; Wolf et al. 2015.
18 Forman 2017; Fortner 2015.
19 Gilens 1999; Hancock 2004; Soss et al. 2011; Wacquant 2009.
20 "Methadone Mile" is a pejorative term Bostonians use to refer to an area of the city where several hospitals, homeless shelters, and drug treatment facilities are located. Because of the concentration of services in this region, it tends to attract many people who are experiencing homelessness or drug addiction; see Marcelo 2017; Ramos and Allen 2016; Zalkind 2017.

21 Bunyasi and Smith 2019; Byrnes and Henricks 2014; Hyra 2006; Pattillo 2003.
22 Most surveys of public opinion about criminal justice simply ask people to state the degree to which they support or oppose a variety of punishments, like the death penalty or long prison sentences. Far fewer surveys asked respondents to choose between alternative policy options. A close read of such studies reveals that, when asked to choose between punishment versus rehabilitation or crime prevention, more Americans typically prefer the latter over the former (Atkin-Plunk 2020; Atkin-Plunk and Sloas 2019; T. Baker et al. 2015; 2016; M. A. Cohen, Rust, and Steen 2006; Dunbar 2020; Dunbar et al. 2022; Mancini et al. 2010; Mears, Pickett, and Mancini 2015; Metcalfe and Pickett 2018; Nagin et al. 2006; Peter D. Hart Research Associates 2002; Piquero and Steinberg 2010; Sloas and Atkin-Plunk 2019; Thielo et al. 2016; Thompson and Bobo 2011; Vuk et al. 2020; Welch, Butler, and Gertz 2019). The pattern of findings in these prior studies suggests that the spending preferences of the participants in my focus groups were not wildly different from the spending preferences of Americans from other parts of the country.
23 La Vigne et al. 2016; Tucker and Cadora 2003.
24 I was inspired by the work of Cohen et al. (2006) to include a tax rebate option in the survey budget question.
25 Lewis-Beck et al. 2009.
26 Cramer 2016; Gimpel et al. 2020; Johnson and Scala 2020; Rodden 2019.
27 To simply the multinomial logit analysis, I collapsed the 4% of "mostly tax, then community" respondents into the "mostly community" category, the 3% of "mostly tax, then CJS [criminal justice system]" respondents into the "mostly CJS or tax" category, and the roughly 1% of "mostly tax, split rest" respondents into the "balanced" category (percentages derived from the combined sample of White and Black respondents).
28 Long and Freese 2014.
29 When calculating the predicted probabilities for these "ideal types," I held constant at their mean values several other variables: age, gender, household income, homeownership, parenthood, employment status, racism (separate variables for denial of systemic discrimination and laziness stereotypes), and perceived fairness of the criminal justice system. To ensure that controlling for household income did not artificially suppress social class divisions across education levels, I replicated these models but dropped the income control. This change only altered the predicted probabilities by 1% to 4% across categories and ideal types—a minimal and substantively inconsequential difference.
30 Dagan and Teles 2016.

4. HOW FRAMING AFFECTS PUBLIC INVESTMENT PREFERENCES

1 Gilens 1999; Hancock 2004; Katznelson 2006; Quadagno 1996.
2 Clear 2007; Krivo et al. 2020; Peterson and Krivo 2010; Sampson and Loeffler 2010; Weisburd 2015.

3 Tucker and Cadora 2003.

4 Chong and Druckman 2007; Kahneman 2011; Zaller 1992.

5 López 2015; Mendelberg 2001.

6 Perlstein 2012. I chose to censor the "n-word" in the original quote.

7 Gilens 1999; Hurwitz and Peffley 2005; Rosenthal 2021.

8 See Schneider and Ingram (1993) and Sniderman et al. (1996) for discussions of particularized versus general policies. When I pretested the survey instrument, I asked a separate group of respondents to write the words or phrases that came to mind when they were shown each treatment phrase ("rural communities," "inner city communities," etc.). Not all respondents mentioned race, but several respondents did write the words "Black" or "minorities" in reaction to the prompts "inner city," "African American," "high poverty," and "residents on welfare." Respondents only wrote the response "White" in reaction to two prompts: "rural" and "residents on welfare." In the latter case, the respondent wrote, "White communities that are rural."

9 Cramer 2016; Gimpel et al. 2020; Johnson and Scala 2020; Rodden 2019; Skocpol and Williamson 2016.

10 Mendelberg 2001; but see Valentino et al. (2018) for evidence that explicit versus implicit racial cues may no longer cause Americans to react differently in the twenty-first century.

11 Hutchings and Jardina 2009.

12 Abdi 2007.

13 Chong and Druckman 2007.

14 Following prior racial priming studies, I tested whether the effects of cue exposure in my experiment were moderated by respondents' beliefs about race relations in the United States (such as racial resentment) or belief that the criminal justice system treats people of all races fairly (Hurwitz and Peffley 2005; Peffley, Hurwitz, and Mondak 2017; Peffley and Hurwitz 2010). Overall, I found very little evidence that these beliefs moderated cue exposure. I report these limited results elsewhere (Wozniak 2020b), so I do not repeat them here for the sake of parsimony.

15 With the wider variation afforded to me in the national survey sample, I chose to separate respondents who had a high school degree or less formal education, those who took some college classes but did not graduate, and those who had a bachelor's degree or greater education. I made this choice because of evidence that many people who take on debt to attend college but do not graduate actually end up in the most precarious financial situation of all (Perna, Kvaal, and Ruiz 2017).

16 I followed the Pew Research Center's (2015) cut points to define generational cohorts. I identified the "Silent Generation" as people who were age seventy-one or older in 2016, "Baby Boomers" as people who were between ages fifty-two and seventy, and "Gen X" as those between ages thirty-six and fifty-one. Since only adults of at least eighteen years of age were selected into the national survey sample, there were few members of Generation Z in the data. I combined Generation

Z and Millennial respondents into a single category of all people who were age thirty-five or younger for analysis.

17 In this section, I report differences between predicted probabilities in terms of differences from subtraction. I make this choice because I feel that talking about a "percentage change in percentages" gets very confusing. For example, I should say that exposure to the African American communities cue made White respondents 79.6% less likely to fall into the "mostly community" category than control group respondents because the difference between the predicted probabilities of 22.6% and 4.3% is 18%, and 18% is 79.6% of 22.6%. However, I feel that the subtraction-based differences are much easier to understand than the "difference in differences."

18 Neither beliefs in racial stereotypes of laziness, nor beliefs about racial discrimination in society, nor beliefs about the fairness of the justice system moderated the effects of cue exposure on respondents' overall budget preferences.

19 See also Lee et al. 2021.

20 Krivo et al. 2020; Peterson and Krivo 2010; Weisburd 2015.

21 Peterson and Krivo 2010; Sampson et al. 2005.

22 Baranauskas 2020; Braga et al. 2010.

23 Jennings 2019.

24 Simes 2021.

25 See also broader evidence that Americans' punitive opinions (Enns 2016) and perceptions of local crime (Holbrook and Weinschenk 2020) are significantly related to and responsive to objective crime conditions.

26 K. M. Drakulich 2012, 2013; Leverentz 2011; Leverentz et al. 2018; Quillian and Pager 2001; Sampson and Raudenbush 2004.

27 For a thorough overview of the historical social construction of crime as an urban phenomenon, see chapter 2 in Simes (2021).

28 Cicero et al. 2014.

29 Zaller 1992.

30 Sniderman et al. 1996.

31 Bonilla-Silva 2017.

32 Bonilla-Silva 2017.

5. THE POLITICAL BOUNDARIES OF PUBLIC SUPPORT FOR SAFETY BEYOND PUNISHMENT

1 Dagan and Teles 2016.

2 Enns 2016; Stimson 2018.

3 Brown 2011; Herbst 1998.

4 Enns and Wlezien 2011; Fenno 2002; Lacey and Soskice 2015; Lewis-Beck et al. 2009; Mayhew 1974.

5 Arnold 1992; Stimson 2018.

6 Jonson, Cullen, and Lux 2013; Wood 2009.

7 Beckett 1997; Beckett and Sasson, 2003; Enns 2016; Hinton 2016; Mancillas 2018; Murakawa 2014.

8 P. Baker 2018; Beckett 1997; Cohen 2019; Lerman and Weaver 2014a; Pfaff 2018; Schwartzapfel and Keller 2015.

9 Murakawa 2014.

10 Dagan and Teles 2016.

11 Lewis-Beck et al. 2009.

12 Schlozman et al. 2012.

13 Scheingold 1991, 2011; Sharkey 2018.

14 Duxbury 2021a, 2021c; Lacey and Soskice 2015; Miller 2008; Ramirez 2015.

15 Ellis and Stimson 2012.

16 Brown et al. 2019; Silver and Pickett 2015.

17 Ellis and Stimson 2012.

18 For the sake of parsimony, here I am referring only to between-group differences that were statistically significant at $p \leq 0.05$ after applying a Bonferroni adjustment for multiple comparisons.

19 Even though the multinomial logit model indicated that the framing experiment did not significantly affect respondents' expressed likelihood of voting for a politician who supported criminal justice investment, framing is important for both theory and politics, so I estimated the predicted probabilities for the control group and the two treatment groups that most consistently generated significant framing effects in chapter 4 ("rural communities" and "African American communities"). No matter how I "sliced" the sample, no subgroup of respondents who were exposed to either of the treatment cues were significantly more likely to say that a politician's support for criminal justice investment would increase their likelihood of voting for that candidate contrasted to respondents in the control group who were not exposed to a community description cue. This finding suggests that Americans will either like or dislike a politician's choice to invest in criminal justice institutions as a function of their personal characteristics or beliefs, and their feelings will not substantively change no matter how the candidate talks about crime prevention budget choices.

20 Bonilla-Silva 2017; K. Drakulich et al. 2020.

21 I also estimated the predicted probabilities for the framing experiment control and treatment groups that were significant in chapter 4. This analysis produced a few differences across categories that seemed substantively significant, even though none of them were statistically significant. White respondents were predicted to be about 13% less likely to say that they would be "more likely" to vote for a politician who funded community institutions in African American communities and about 14% more likely to say that they would be "less likely" to vote for such a politician compared to a politician who funded "community institutions" with no further descriptor. Republicans in the "African American communities" group were predicted to be about 16% more likely to say that they would be "less likely" to vote for a politician who funded community institutions compared to control group Republicans and about 10% less likely to say that they would be "more likely" to vote for such a politician. Republicans in the "African

American communities" group were the only category of respondents predicted to have a higher likelihood of expressing that a politician's support for community investment would make them "less likely" to vote for him or her (estimated 42%) than the likelihood of saying that such support would make their vote "more likely" (23%) or not affect their vote one way or the other (35%). Independents exposed to the "rural communities" cue were about 15% more likely to say that a politician's support for community investment would not affect their vote and about 19% less likely to say this kind of investment would make them "more likely to vote" for such a politician than independents in the control group. However, in all these cases, the confidence intervals around the predicted probabilities were so large that we cannot be confident that these differences are statistically significant. Thus, these results suggest that the way politicians talk about community invest-ment *may* affect constituents' vote preferences more than talking about criminal justice investment, but these data do not allow us to be sure that this is the case.

22 Ellis and Stimson 2012; but see Brown et al. 2019.
23 Dagan and Teles 2016.

CONCLUSION

1 A "Freedom Budget" for All Americans 1966; Harris and Curtis 2018; National Advisory Commission on Civil Disorders and Kerner 1968; Rustin 1964; Sharkey 2018; Tucker and Cadora 2003.
2 Dagan and Teles 2016.
3 Hunt 1996.
4 Leverentz and Williams 2017.
5 Eckhouse 2019; Hinton et al. 2016; Miller 2008.
6 Unnever et al. 2010.
7 Pickett and Baker 2014.
8 See Pickett and Baker 2014; and Unnever et al. 2010.
9 Pickett 2019; Stimson 2015.
10 Enns 2016; Nicholson-Crotty et al. 2009; Stimson 2015, 2018.
11 Page and Shapiro 2010.
12 Enns 2016; Ramirez 2013.
13 Forman 2017; Fortner 2015.
14 Miller 2008, 2016.
15 Miller 2008, 155–56.
16 Eckhouse 2019; Hinton et al. 2016.
17 Alexander 2012; Clear 2007; Prowse et al. 2020; Soss and Weaver 2017; Tonry 1995.
18 Simes 2021.
19 Clear 2007; Rose and Clear 1998; Travis et al. 2014; Wakefield and Uggen 2010.
20 Duxbury 2020, 2021a, 2021b; Eckhouse 2019.
21 T. Baker et al. 2016; Cullen et al. 2007.
22 Cullen et al. 2000.
23 Jonson, Cullen, and Lux 2013.

24 Unnever, Cullen, and Jones (2008) present a notable exception. They analyzed data
    from the 2000 American National Election study to assess Americans' preference
    for addressing the social, "root causes" of crime versus punishing offenders.

25 Mendelberg 2001; see also López 2015.

26 Huber and Lapinski 2008; Hurwitz and Peffley 2005; Peffley and Hurwitz 2009;
    Tesler 2017; Valentino 1999; White 2007; Winter 2008.

27 Hutchings and Jardina 2009; Tesler 2017; Wetts and Willer 2019.

28 Huber and Lapinski 2008; Jardina 2019; Reny et al. 2020; Tesler 2016; Valentino
    et al. 2018.

29 Stephens-Dougan 2020.

30 For detailed information about my tests of the moderating effect of racial resent-
    ment (or lack, thereof), see Wozniak 2020.

31 Hurwitz and Peffley 1997, 391.

32 I explore the distinctions the participants in my focus groups drew between
    violent and nonviolent offenders, as well as between offenders who committed
    violent acts of varying severity, in a separate publication. See Wozniak, 2020a.

33 Chiricos et al. 2004; Miller 2016; Muhammad 2011; Russell-Brown 2009.

34 Hurwitz and Peffley 1997.

35 Schneider and Ingram 1993.

36 Cramer 2016; Gest 2016; Hochschild 2018; Rosenthal 2021.

37 Fraser 1995; Hamilton 1977; Johnson 2017; Kelley 1997; Reed, A. 1999, 2016; Reed,
    T. 2015, 2020; Roediger 2019; Rustin 1964; Skocpol 1991; Sniderman et al. 1996;
    Wilson 1978, 1987; Coates 2016; Fukuyama 2018; Johnson 2017; Levitz 2021; Lilla
    2017; Maxwell 2021; Reed 2018; Reed 2020; Stout 2020.

38 Creighton and Wozniak 2019; Hetey and Eberhardt 2014; Peffley and Hurwitz 2010.

39 López 2019, 107.

40 López 2019, 108.

41 Pertinent to this point, Unnever (2008) found that Black Americans were
    substantially more likely to believe that racial bias in the criminal justice system
    contributes to the disproportionate incarceration of Black men than White
    Americans. White and Black Americans were comparably likely to believe that
    poverty contributes to racial disparities in incarceration. But even though they
    recognized the role of racial bias in the justice system, Black Americans were
    also more likely than White Americans to place dispositional responsibility upon
    Black people themselves by arguing that failure to teach children right from
    wrong plays a significant role in incarceration disparities. Unnever's findings echo
    those of Hunt (1996, 2007) who found that Black and Latino Americans endorsed
    both structural and volitional explanations for poverty and Black-White income
    inequality.

42 Gottlieb 2017; Sniderman et al. 1996; Stout 2020.

43 López 2019, 186–87.

44 López 2019, 187–88.

45 Skocpol 1991; Wilson 1987.

46 Wilson 2012, 155.

47 Hamilton 1977, 3.

48 Rustin 1964.

49 Katznelson 2006; Quadagno 1996.

50 Casey and Hardy 2018; Darity 2016; Joint Economic Committee 2020.

51 Mettler 2011, 2018.

52 Kraus et al. 2019.

53 Chow and Knowles 2016.

54 DiAngelo 2018.

55 Bonilla-Silva 2017; Kraus et al. 2019.

56 Schattschneider 1960.

57 Manning et al. 2015; Wetts and Willer 2019; Yadon and Piston 2019.

58 File 2017.

59 Levitz 2021.

60 Dagan and Teles 2016; Gingrich and Nolan 2011; Norquist 2017; Percival 2015.

61 Garland 2020, 337.

62 I am aware of no compelling evidence that the phrase "inner-city communities" has ceased to be racialized in Americans' minds. Indeed, when I pretested my survey instrument, some participants reported that they associated Black people with "inner cities." As another notable example, a White rioter who stormed the US Capitol building and assaulted a Capitol Police officer on January 6, 2021 complained to his lawyers that he was shocked to be jailed alongside "people who committed inner-city crimes" (Colarossi 2021).

63 Krivo et al. 2020; Massey and Denton 1993; Peterson and Krivo 2010; Sampson and Wilson 1995.

64 Fraser 1995.

65 López 2019, xvi.

66 Hamilton 1977; Johnson 2017; Reed, A. 2018; Reed, T. 2020; Wilson 1987.

67 Skocpol 1991; Wilson 1987.

68 Hamilton 1977.

69 Stout 2020.

70 Stout 2020.

71 Such municipal-level programs do exist, such as the Neighborhood Matching Fund that has operated in Seattle since 1980. See Ramey and Shrider 2014.

72 Cramer 2016; Gimpel et al. 2020; Johnson and Scala 2020; Rodden 2019.

73 Hackworth 2019; Quadagno 1996.

74 Flavin and Shufeldt 2020; Fowler and Witt 2019; Riverstone-Newell 2017.

75 Goldrosen 2021; Tartakovsky 2013.

76 Epstein and Mazzei 2021.

77 KVUE Staff 2022; Pfaff 2021.

78 This particular finding echoes Johnson's (2017) observation that several of the early leaders of the Black Lives Matter movement parted ways because of a policy disagreement over the merits of public schools versus charter schools.

As I explained in earlier chapters, several of the Black participants in my focus groups were similarly quite ambivalent about Boston public schools.

79 Lewis et al. 2013.

80 Allard 2017; Kneebone and Holmes 2016.

81 Gest 2016; Hochschild 2018; Rosenthal 2021.

82 Gaston 2019; Gaston and Brunson 2020; Roach et al. 2020; Vito et al. 2020.

83 Bonilla-Silva 2017.

84 Allard 2017; Baccini and Weymouth 2021; Eason 2017b; Eason et al. 2017; Gest 2016; Gilmore 2007; Gottschalk 2016; Kneebone and Holmes 2016; Muro et al. 2019; Silva 2013, 2019; Simes 2021.

85 Eason 2017b; Gilmore 2007; Thorpe 2014.

86 Eason 2017a.

87 Beckett and Beach 2021; Kang-Brown and Subramanian 2017.

88 Simes 2018.

89 Simes 2020.

90 López 2019.

91 Glazer and Sharkey 2021; Rustin 1964; Sharkey 2018; Tucker and Cadora 2003.

92 Busso et al. 2013, 898.

93 Jennings 2011.

94 Drucker and Lipton 2019; Neumark 2020; Neumark and Simpson 2015; Tankersley 2020; Theodos et al. 2020; Trickey 2020.

95 Jennings 2016; J. Richardson et al. 2020.

96 Beck 2020; Cahill et al. 2019; Pattillo 2008.

97 Ramey and Shrider 2014, 8 (emphasis added); see also Shrider and Ramey 2018.

98 Sharkey et al. 2017.

99 Shrider and Ramey 2018; Vélez et al. 2012; Vélez and Richardson 2012.

100 Kondo et al. 2018.

101 Pattillo 2008.

102 Cobbina-Dungy et al. 2022; Lowe 2020.

103 Kaba 2020.

104 Pew Research Center 2020.

105 North 2020; Rakich 2020; Saletan 2021; Vaughn et al. 2022.

106 Fortner 2020.

107 Carr et al. 2007; Miller 2008; Phelps et al. 2019; Pryce and Chenane 2021.

108 Cobbina-Dungy et al. 2022.

109 As I finished writing this book in 2022, the mainstream of the Democratic Party had largely concluded that defunding the police was not a winning political stance; see Manchester 2022. President Joseph Biden even argued in his 2022 State of the Union Address that the best answer to crime is "not to defund the police; it's to fund the police"; see Blake 2022.

110 Harris-Lacewell, 2003.

111 In *Ignored Racism: White Animus toward Latinos*, Ramirez and Peterson (2020) make an important contribution that begins to correct scholars' relative

underappreciation of the experiences of non-Black racial minorities in the study of racism and politics. See also the important, recent work by Reny, Valenzuela, and Collingwood (2020) on anti-immigrant and anti-Latino primes.

112 Cohen, Rust, and Steen 2006.

113 SCJS 2010.

114 Gotoff et al. 2017.

115 Morning Consult + Politico 2020.

116 Peffley et al. 2017.

117 Hurwitz et al. 2015.

118 Hutchings and Jardina 2009.

119 Kahneman et al. 1999.

120 Dear 1992; Lacey and Soskice 2015.

121 Pickett, Ivanov, and Wozniak 2020.

122 Chong and Druckman 2010, 2013; Druckman 2004; Druckman and Nelson, 2003.

123 Doherty and Stancliffe 2017; Druckman 2001; Druckman et al. 2013; Stephens-Dougan 2020; Turner 2007.

124 Cramer 2016; Gimpel et al. 2020; Johnson and Scala 2020; Rodden 2019.

125 As I finished writing this book in 2022, the political winds continued to shift. Gun violence surged in many cities between 2020 and 2021, and hopes for continued bipartisan criminal justice reform grew dimmer as Republican candidates once again campaigned on "tough on crime" platforms heading into the 2022 midterm elections (Levine 2022). However, many studies that have been conducted since at least the year 2000 consistently found that most Americans express support for making investments into crime-prevention initiatives outside of the criminal justice system. I cannot know whether public spending preferences have changed since I gathered my data in 2016, but I suspect that Republican politicians are once again out of touch with Americans' more egalitarian opinions about crime prevention.

126 Clinton et al. 2021; Kennedy et al. 2018; Shepard 2021; Skelley 2021.

127 Ekins 2021.

128 See, for example, Leverentz and Williams 2017.

APPENDIX: RESEARCH METHODOLOGY

1 Tewksbury 2009.

2 Doble 1987; Krueger and Casey 2014; Morgan 1998; Sasson 1995; Stewart and Shamdasani 2014.

3 Green 2006; Hough and Park 2002.

4 Gottschalk 2006; Krivo et al. 1998; Peterson and Krivo 2010; Travis et al. 2014; Weaver et al. 2019; Western 2006; Western and Pettit 2010.

5 Tyler 2006.

6 Hagan and Albonetti 1982.

7 Morgan 1998.

8 The segmentation was not flawless. Both Ginger in Focus Group 2 and Frederick in Focus Group 6 reported on their exit surveys that they had taken some college classes but never graduated. Participants with any exposure to college-level education were supposed to be placed into the college educated groups, and Focus Groups 2 and 6 were segmented on high school level education. Since my survey research center consultants constituted the focus groups, I do not know how this mistake occurred. However, neither Ginger nor Frederick stuck out to me as noticeably different from their fellow participants in any meaningful way, so I do not think that this mistake created a fatal flaw in the data.

9 Ryan et al. 2014.

10 The nature of this question reflects the structure of the justice reinvestment initiative (Cramer et al. 2014; La Vigne et al. 2016). States first "free up" money in the budget by reducing the state's incarceration rate. This "extra" money is then reinvested in alternatives to incarceration. Reinvestment does not occur until money is "recovered" from the corrections line item in the budget.

11 Hollander 2004; Ryan et al. 2014.

12 Vicsek 2007.

13 Campbell et al. 2013.

14 Hollander 2004.

15 Vicsek 2010.

16 Weinberg et al. 2014.

17 MacInnis et al. 2018; Yeager et al. 2011.

18 Chang and Krosnick 2009.

19 Callegaro and DiSogra 2008.

20 Groves 2006; Groves and Peytcheva 2008; Pickett et al. 2018.

21 At the end of the survey, participants were asked, "Earlier in this survey, we asked you to imagine that a politician in your state voted to spend money on funding healthcare, public schools, or job creation programs in communities. Do you remember which kind of communities would receive funding for these programs? Please choose which kind of communities you read about in an earlier question. Since we're asking you to remember what you read, there is only one correct answer to this question." Respondents were presented with three incorrect descriptors of communities ("wealthy," "with many children," or "manufacturing") as well as the accurate treatment text to which they were randomly assigned. This question allowed me to identify respondents who did not appear to be properly treated, though I acknowledge a margin of error inherent in human recollection. See Mutz (2011) for a discussion of manipulation checks in experimental survey research.

22 Osborne 2013.

23 Kinder and Sanders 1996.

24 Simmons and Bobo 2018; Sniderman and Piazza 1993; Tarman and Sears 2005; Tuch and Hughes 2011.

25 Peffley et al. (2017) also found a two-factor structure when they employed the racial resentment items.
26 Costello and Osborne 2005.
27 Pew Research Center 2015.
28 See Wozniak (2018) for information to access the archived data.

BIBLIOGRAPHY

"A 'Freedom Budget' for All Americans." 1966. New York: A. Philip Randolph Institute.

Abdi, Hervé. 2007. "The Bonferroni and Sidak Corrections for Multiple Comparisons." In *Encyclopedia of Measurement and Statistics*, edited by Neil Salkind, 103–6. Thousand Oaks, CA: SAGE.

Agnew, Robert. 1992. "Foundation for a General Strain Theory of Crime and Delinquency." *Criminology* 30 (1): 47–87.

Akers, Ronald L. 1998. *Social Learning and Social Structure: A General Theory of Crime and Deviance*. Boston: Northeastern University Press.

Alexander, Michelle. 2012. *The New Jim Crow: Mass Incarceration in the Age of Colorblindness*. New York: New Press.

Allard, Scott W. 2017. *Places in Need: The Changing Geography of Poverty*. New York: Russell Sage Foundation.

Allport, Gordon W. 1979. *The Nature of Prejudice*. 25th Anniversary Edition. Cambridge: Perseus Books.

Anderson, Elijah. 1990. *Streetwise: Race, Class, and Change in an Urban Community*. Chicago: University of Chicago Press.

———. 1999. *Code of the Street: Decency, Violence, and the Moral Life of the Inner City*. New York: W. W. Norton.

Arnold, R. Douglas. 1992. *The Logic of Congressional Action*. New Haven, CT: Yale University Press.

Atkin-Plunk, Cassandra A. 2020. "Should All Violent Offenders Be Treated Equally? Perceptions of Punishment and Rehabilitation for Violent Offenders with Varying Attributes." *Victims & Offenders* 15 (2): 218–42. https://doi.org/10.1080/15564886 .2019.1711277.

Atkin-Plunk, Cassandra A., and Lincoln B. Sloas. 2019. "Support for Balanced Justice and Rehabilitation for Justice-Involved Veterans." *Criminal Justice Review* 44 (2): 165–82. https://doi.org/10.1177/0734016818793698.

Atkinson, Jay. 2012. "Lawrence, MA: City of the Damned." *Boston Magazine*, February 28, 2012. https://www.bostonmagazine.com/news/2012/02/28/city-of-the-damned -lawrence-massachusetts/.

Austin, James, Eric Cadora, Todd Clear, Kara Dansky, Judith Greene, Vanita Gupta, Marc Mauer, Nicole Porter, Susan Tucker, and Malcolm C. Young. 2013. "Ending Mass Incarceration: Charting a New Justice Reinvestment." Washington, DC: Sentencing Project. https://www.ncjrs.gov/App/AbstractDB/AbstractDBDetails.aspx?id =264175.

Baccini, Leonardo, and Stephen Weymouth. 2021. "Gone for Good: Deindustrialization, White Voter Backlash, and US Presidential Voting." *American Political Science Review* 115 (2): 550–67. https://doi.org/10.1017/S0003055421000022.

Baker, Peter. 2018. "Bush Made Willie Horton an Issue in 1988, and the Racial Scars Are Still Fresh." *The New York Times*, December 4, 2018. https://www.nytimes.com/2018/12/03/us/politics/bush-willie-horton.html.

Baker, Thomas, Hayley M. D. Cleary, Justin T. Pickett, and Marc G. Gertz. 2016. "Crime Salience and Public Willingness to Pay for Child Saving and Juvenile Punishment." *Crime & Delinquency* 62 (5): 645–68. https://doi.org/10.1177/0011128713505487.

Baker, Thomas, Christi Falco Metcalfe, Tamar Berenblum, Gali Aviv, and Marc Gertz. 2015. "Examining Public Preferences for the Allocation of Resources to Rehabilitative Versus Punitive Crime Policies." *Criminal Justice Policy Review* 26 (5): 448–62. https://doi.org/10.1177/0887403414521462.

Baldassare, Mark, ed. 2019. *The Los Angeles Riots: Lessons for the Urban Future*. 2nd ed. New York: Routledge.

Baranauskas, Andrew J. 2020. "Exploring the Social Construction of Crime by Neighborhood: News Coverage of Crime in Boston." *Sociological Focus* 53 (2): 156–76. https://doi.org/10.1080/00380237.2020.1730280.

Baumgartner, Frank R., and Bryan D. Jones. 2009. *Agendas and Instability in American Politics*. 2nd ed. Chicago: University of Chicago Press.

Beck, Brenden. 2020. "Policing Gentrification: Stops and Low-Level Arrests during Demographic Change and Real Estate Reinvestment." *City & Community* 19 (1): 245–72. https://doi.org/10.1111/cico.12473.

Becker, Howard S. 2018. *Outsiders*. 3rd ed. New York: Free Press.

Beckett, Katherine. 1997. *Making Crime Pay: Law and Order in Contemporary American Politics*. New York: Oxford University Press.

Beckett, Katherine, and Lindsey Beach. 2021. "The Place of Punishment in Twenty-First-Century America: Understanding the Persistence of Mass Incarceration." *Law & Social Inquiry* 46 (1): 1–31. https://doi.org/10.1017/lsi.2020.4.

Beckett, Katherine, and Megan Ming Francis. 2020. "The Origins of Mass Incarceration: The Racial Politics of Crime and Punishment in the Post–Civil Rights Era." *Annual Review of Law and Social Science* 16 (1): 433–52. https://doi.org/10.1146/annurev-lawsocsci-110819-100304.

Beckett, Katherine, and Steve Herbert. 2009. *Banished: The New Social Control in Urban America*. New York: Oxford University Press.

Beckett, Katherine, and Theodore Sasson. 2003. *The Politics of Injustice: Crime and Punishment in America*. Thousand Oaks, CA: SAGE Publications.

Bell, Monica C. 2016. "Situational Trust: How Disadvantaged Mothers Reconceive Legal Cynicism." *Law & Society Review* 50 (2): 314–47. https://doi.org/10.1111/lasr.12200.

Beltramini, Enrico. 2017. "Freedom Budget for All Americans and Economic Equality." *Journal of Economic and Social Thought* 4 (1): 55–66. https://doi.org/10.1453/jest.v4i1.1213.

Bersani, Bianca E., and Elaine Eggleston Doherty. 2013. "When the Ties That Bind Unwind: Examining the Enduring and Situational Processes of Change behind the Marriage Effect." *Criminology* 51 (2): 399–433.

Blake, Aaron. 2022. "Biden Tries to Nix 'Defund the Police,' Once and for All." *Washington Post*, March 2, 2022. https://www.washingtonpost.com/politics/2022/03/02/biden-nix-defund-police/.

Bobo, Lawrence. 1991. "Social Responsibility, Individualism, and Redistributive Policies." *Sociological Forum* 6 (1): 71–92.

Bonilla-Silva, Eduardo. 2017. *Racism without Racists: Color-Blind Racism and the Persistence of Racial Inequality in America.* 5th ed. Lanham, MD: Rowman & Littlefield Publishers.

Braga, Anthony A., Rod K. Brunson, and Kevin M. Drakulich. 2019. "Race, Place, and Effective Policing." *Annual Review of Sociology* 45 (1): 535–55. https://doi.org/10.1146/annurev-soc-073018-022541.

Braga, Anthony A., Andrew V. Papachristos, and David M. Hureau. 2010. "The Concentration and Stability of Gun Violence at Micro Places in Boston, 1980–2008." *Journal of Quantitative Criminology* 26 (1): 33–53. https://doi.org/10.1007/s10940-009-9082-x.

Branas, Charles C., Michelle C. Kondo, Sean M. Murphy, Eugenia C. South, Daniel Polsky, and John M. MacDonald. 2016. "Urban Blight Remediation as a Cost-Beneficial Solution to Firearm Violence." *American Journal of Public Health* 106 (12): 2158–64. https://doi.org/10.2105/AJPH.2016.303434.

Bridenball, Blaine, and Paul Jesilow. 2005. "Weeding Criminals or Planting Fear: An Evaluation of a Weed and Seed Project." *Criminal Justice Review* 30 (1): 64–89. https://doi.org/10.1177/0734016805275682.

Britt, Chester L., and Michael Rocque. 2016. "Control as an Explanation of Crime and Delinquency." In *The Handbook of Criminological Theory*, edited by Alex R. Piquero, 205–31. Malden, MA: Wiley Blackwell.

Brown, Elizabeth K. 2011. "Constructing the Public Will: How Political Actors in New York State Construct, Assess, and Use Public Opinion in Penal Policy Making." *Punishment & Society* 13 (4): 424–50. https://doi.org/10.1177/1462474511414779.

Brown, Elizabeth K, Kelly M Socia, and Jasmine R Silver. 2019. "Conflicted Conservatives, Punitive Views, and Anti-Black Racial Bias 1974–2014." *Punishment & Society* 21 (1): 3–27. https://doi.org/10.1177/1462474517736295.

Brunson, Rod K. 2007. "'Police Don't Like Black People': African-American Young Men's Accumulated Police Experiences." *Criminology & Public Policy* 6 (1): 71–101. https://doi.org/10.1111/j.1745-9133.2007.00423.x.

Buchanan, Larry, Quoctrung Bui, and Jugal K. Patel. 2020. "Black Lives Matter May Be the Largest Movement in U.S. History." *The New York Times*, July 3, 2020. https://www.nytimes.com/interactive/2020/07/03/us/george-floyd-protests-crowd-size.html.

Bunyasi, Tehama Lopez, and Candis Watts Smith. 2019. "Do All Black Lives Matter Equally to Black People? Respectability Politics and the Limitations of Linked Fate."

Journal of Race, Ethnicity, and Politics 4 (1): 180–215. https://doi.org/10.1017/rep.2018
.33.

Bursik, Robert J., and Harold G. Grasmick. 1993. *Neighborhoods and Crime: The Dimensions of Effective Community Control.* New York: Lexington Books.

Busso, Matias, Jesse Gregory, and Patrick Kline. 2013. "Assessing the Incidence and Efficiency of a Prominent Place Based Policy." *American Economic Review* 103 (2): 897–947. https://doi.org/10.1257/aer.103.2.897.

Byrnes, Bill, and Kasey Henricks. 2014. "'That's When the Neighborhood Went South': How Middle Class Blacks and Whites Police Racial Boundaries of Stigmatized Blackness." *Sociological Spectrum* 34 (5): 381–402. https://doi.org/10.1080/02732173
.2014.937650.

Cahill, Caitlin, Brett G. Stoudt, María Elena Torre, Darian X, Amanda Matles, Kimberly Belmonte, Selma Djokovic, Jose Lopez, and Adilka Pimentel. 2019. "'They Were Looking at Us Like We Were Bad People': Growing Up Policed in the Gentrifying, Still Disinvested City." *ACME: An International Journal for Critical Geographies* 18 (5): 1128–49.

Callegaro, Mario, and Charles DiSogra. 2008. "Computing Response Metrics for Online Panels." *Public Opinion Quarterly* 72 (5): 1008–32. https://doi.org/10.1093/poq
/nfn065.

Campbell, John L., Charles Quincy, Jordan Osserman, and Ove K. Pedersen. 2013. "Coding In-Depth Semistructured Interviews: Problems of Unitization and Intercoder Reliability and Agreement." *Sociological Methods & Research* 42 (3): 294–320. https://doi.org/10.1177/0049124113500475.

Carr, Patrick J. 2003. "The New Parochialism: The Implications of the Beltway Case for Arguments Concerning Informal Social Control." *American Journal of Sociology* 108 (6): 1249–91.

Carr, Patrick J., Laura Napolitano, and Jessica Keating. 2007. "We Never Call the Cops and Here Is Why: A Qualitative Examination of Legal Cynicism in Three Philadelphia Neighborhoods." *Criminology* 45 (2): 445–80. https://doi.org/10.1111/j.1745-9125
.2007.00084.x.

Carter, TaLisa J., Karen F. Parker, and Heather Zaykowski. 2017. "Building Bridges: Linking Old Heads to Collective Efficacy in Disadvantaged Communities." Supplement, *Sociological Forum* 32 (S1): S1093–111. https://doi.org/10.1111/socf.12368.

Case, Anne, and Angus Deaton. 2020. *Deaths of Despair and the Future of Capitalism.* Princeton, NJ: Princeton University Press.

Casey, Marcus D., and Bradley L. Hardy. 2018. "The Evolution of Black Neighborhoods Since Kerner." *RSF: The Russell Sage Foundation Journal of the Social Sciences* 4 (6): 185–205. https://doi.org/10.7758/RSF.2018.4.6.09.

Cauffman, Elizabeth, Caitlin Cavanagh, Sachiko Donley, and April Gile Thomas. 2016. "A Developmental Perspective on Adolescent Risk-Taking and Criminal Behavior." In *The Handbook of Criminological Theory*, edited by Alex R. Piquero, 121–42. Malden, MA: Wiley Blackwell.

Chetty, Raj, David Grusky, Maximilian Hell, Nathaniel Hendren, Robert Manduca, and Jimmy Narang. 2017. "The Fading American Dream: Trends in Absolute Income Mobility since 1940." *Science* 356 (6336): 398–406. https://doi.org/10.1126/science.aal4617.

Chiricos, Ted, Kelly Welch, and Marc Gertz. 2004. "Racial Typification of Crime and Support for Punitive Measures." *Criminology* 42 (2): 358–90.

Chong, Dennis, and James N. Druckman. 2007. "Framing Theory." *Annual Review of Political Science* 10: 103–26.

———. 2010. "Dynamic Public Opinion: Communication Effects over Time." *American Political Science Review* 104 (4): 663–80.

———. 2013. "Counterframing Effects." *Journal of Politics* 75 (1): 1–16. https://doi.org/10.1017/S0022381612000837.

Chow, Rosalind M., and Eric D. Knowles. 2016. "Taking Race Off the Table: Agenda Setting and Support for Color-Blind Public Policy." *Personality and Social Psychology Bulletin* 42 (1): 25–39. https://doi.org/10.1177/0146167215611637.

Cicero, Theodore J., Matthew S. Ellis, Hilary L. Surratt, and Steven P. Kurtz. 2014. "The Changing Face of Heroin Use in the United States: A Retrospective Analysis of the Past 50 Years." *JAMA Psychiatry* 71 (7): 821–26. https://doi.org/10.1001/jamapsychiatry.2014.366.

Clear, Todd R. 2007. *Imprisoning Communities: How Mass Incarceration Makes Disadvantaged Neighborhoods Worse*. New York: Oxford University Press.

Clear, Todd R., and Natasha A. Frost. 2015. *The Punishment Imperative: The Rise and Failure of Mass Incarceration in America*. New York: NYU Press.

Clinton, Josh, Jennifer Agiesta, Megan Brenan, Camille Burge, Marjorie Connelly, Ariel Edwards-Levy, Bernard Fraga, Emily Guskin, D. Sunshine Hillygus, Chris Jackson, Jeff Jones, Scott Keeter, Kabir Khanna, John Lapinski, Lydia Saad, Daron Shaw, Andrew Smith, David Wilson, and Christopher Wlezien. 2021. "Task Force on 2020 Pre-election Polling: An Evaluation of the 2020 General Election Polls." Alexandria, VA: American Association for Public Opinion Research. https://www.aapor.org/Education-Resources/Reports/2020-Pre-Election-Polling-An-Evaluation-of-the-202.aspx.

Coates, Ta-Nehisi. 2016. "Why Is Bernie Sanders Against Reparations?" *Atlantic*, January 19, 2016. https://www.theatlantic.com/politics/archive/2016/01/bernie-sanders-reparations/424602/.

Cobbina, Jennifer E. 2019. *Hands Up, Don't Shoot: Why the Protests in Ferguson and Baltimore Matter, and How They Changed America*. New York: NYU Press.

Cobbina-Dungy, Jennifer, Soma Chaudhuri, Ashleigh LaCourse, and Christina De-Jong. 2022. "'Defund the Police:' Perceptions among Protesters in the 2020 March on Washington." *Criminology & Public Policy* 21 (1): 147–74. https://doi.org/10.1111/1745-9133.12571.

Cochran, John K., Denise Paquette Boots, and Kathleen M. Heide. 2003. "Attribution Styles and Attitudes toward Capital Punishment for Juveniles, the Mentally

Incompetent, and the Mentally Retarded." *Justice Quarterly* 20 (1): 65–93. https://doi
.org/10.1080/07418820300095461.

Cohen, Andrew. 2019. "Are Voters Ready to Move on From Willie Horton?" *Marshall
Project*, August 2, 2019. https://www.themarshallproject.org/2019/08/02/are-voters
-ready-to-move-on-from-willie-horton.

Cohen, Cathy J. 1999. *The Boundaries of Blackness: AIDS and the Breakdown of Black
Politics*. Chicago: University of Chicago Press.

Cohen, Lawrence E., and Marcus Felson. 1979. "Social Change and Crime Rate Trends:
A Routine Activity Approach." *American Sociological Review* 44 (4): 588–608. https:
//doi.org/10.2307/2094589.

Cohen, Mark A., Roland T. Rust, and Sara Steen. 2006. "Prevention, Crime Control,
or Cash? Public Preferences towards Criminal Justice Spending Priorities." *Justice
Quarterly* 23 (3): 317–335.

Colarossi, Natalie. 2021. "Eye-Gouging Capitol Rioter in 'Shock' over Detention with
'Inner-City Crimes' Inmates: Lawyer." *Newsweek*, April 10, 2021. https://www
.newsweek.com/eye-gouging-capitol-rioter-shock-over-detention-inner-city-crimes
-inmates-lawyer-1582644.

Corburn, Jason, Yael Nidam, and Amanda Fukutome-Lopez. 2022. "The Art and
Science of Urban Gun Violence Reduction: Evidence from the Advance Peace
Program in Sacramento, California." *Urban Science* 6 (1): 6. https://doi.org/10.3390
/urbansci6010006.

Cramer, Katherine J. 2016. *The Politics of Resentment: Rural Consciousness in Wisconsin
and the Rise of Scott Walker*. Chicago: University of Chicago Press.

Cramer, Lindsey, Samantha Harvell, Dave McClure, Ariel Sankar-Bergmann, and Erika
Parks. 2014. "The Justice Reinvestment Initiative: Experiences from the Local Sites."
Washington, DC: Urban Institute.

Creighton, Mathew J., and Kevin H. Wozniak. 2019. "Are Racial and Educational Inequities in Mass Incarceration Perceived to Be a Social Problem? Results from an Experiment." *Social Problems* 66 (4): 485–502. https://doi.org/10.1093/socpro/spy017.

Cullen, Francis T., Gregory A. Clark, John B. Cullen, and Richard A. Mathers. 1985.
"Attribution, Salience, and Attitudes toward Criminal Sanctioning." *Criminal Justice
and Behavior* 12 (3): 305–31.

Cullen, Francis T., Bonnie S. Fisher, and Brandon K. Applegate. 2000. "Public Opinion
about Punishment and Corrections." *Crime and Justice* 27: 1–79.

Cullen, Francis T., Brenda A. Vose, Cheryl N. Lero Jonson, and James D. Unnever.
2007. "Public Support for Early Intervention: Is Child Saving a 'Habit of
the Heart'?" *Victims & Offenders* 2 (2): 109–24. https://doi.org/10.1080
/15564880701263015.

Cynamon, Barry Z., and Steven M. Fazzari. 2016. "Inequality, the Great Recession and
Slow Recovery." *Cambridge Journal of Economics* 40 (2): 373–99. https://doi.org/10
.1093/cje/bev016.

Dagan, David, and Steven Teles. 2016. *Prison Break: Why Conservatives Turned Against
Mass Incarceration*. New York: Oxford University Press.

Darity, William A., Jr. 2016. "How Obama Failed Black Americans." *Atlantic*, December 22, 2016. https://www.theatlantic.com/politics/archive/2016/12/how-barack-obama -failed-black-americans/511358/.

Dawson, Michael C. 1995. *Behind the Mule: Race and Class in African-American Politics*. Princeton, NJ: Princeton University Press.

Dear, Michael. 1992. "Understanding and Overcoming the NIMBY Syndrome." *Journal of the American Planning Association* 58 (3): 288–300. https://doi.org/10.1080 /01944369208975808.

Denver, Megan, Justin T. Pickett, and Shawn D. Bushway. 2018. "Criminal Records and Employment: A Survey of Experiences and Attitudes in the United States." *Justice Quarterly* 35 (4): 584–613. https://doi.org/10.1080/07418825.2017.1340502.

Desilver, Drew. 2018. "For Most Americans, Real Wages Have Barely Budged for Decades." *Pew Research Center* (blog). August 7, 2018. https://www.pewresearch.org /fact-tank/2018/08/07/for-most-us-workers-real-wages-have-barely-budged-for -decades/.

Desmond, Matthew, Andrew V. Papachristos, and David S. Kirk. 2016. "Police Violence and Citizen Crime Reporting in the Black Community." *American Sociological Review* 81 (5): 857–76. https://doi.org/10.1177/0003122416663494.

DiAngelo, Robin J. 2018. *White Fragility: Why It's So Hard for White People to Talk about Racism*. Boston: Beacon Press.

Doble, John. 1987. *Crime and Punishment: The Public's View*. New York: Public Agenda Foundation for the Edna McConnell Clark Foundation.

Doherty, David, and James Stancliffe. 2017. "Interpreting and Tolerating Speech: The Effects of Message, Messenger, and Framing." *American Politics Research* 45 (2): 224–55. https://doi.org/10.1177/1532673X16667090.

Drakulich, Kevin M. 2012. "Strangers, Neighbors, and Race: A Contact Model of Stereotypes and Racial Anxieties About Crime." *Race and Justice* 2 (4): 322–55. https: //doi.org/10.1177/2153368712459769.

———. 2013. "Perceptions of the Local Danger Posed by Crime: Race, Disorder, Informal Control, and the Police." *Social Science Research* 42 (3): 611–32. https://doi.org /10.1016/j.ssresearch.2012.12.012.

Drakulich, Kevin, John Hagan, Devon Johnson, and Kevin H. Wozniak. 2017. "Race, Justice, Policing, and the 2016 American Presidential Election." *Du Bois Review: Social Science Research on Race* 14 (1): 7–33. https://doi.org/10.1017 /S1742058X1600031X.

Drakulich, Kevin, Kevin H. Wozniak, John Hagan, and Devon Johnson. 2020. "Race and Policing in the 2016 Presidential Election: Black Lives Matter, the Police, and Dog Whistle Politics." *Criminology* 58 (2): 370–402. https://doi.org/10.1111/1745-9125.12239.

Drucker, Jesse, and Eric Lipton. 2019. "How a Trump Tax Break to Help Poor Communities Became a Windfall for the Rich." *New York Times*, August 31, 2019. https: //www.nytimes.com/2019/08/31/business/tax-opportunity-zones.html.

Druckman, James N. 2001. "On the Limits of Framing Effects: Who Can Frame?" *Journal of Politics* 63 (4): 1041–66. https://doi.org/10.1111/0022-3816.00100.

———. 2004. "Political Preference Formation: Competition, Deliberation, and the (Ir)
Relevance of Framing Effects." *American Political Science Review* 98 (4): 671–86.

Druckman, James N., Erik Peterson, and Rune Slothuus. 2013. "How Elite Partisan
Polarization Affects Public Opinion Formation." *American Political Science Review*
107 (1): 57–79.

Druckman, James N., and Kjersten R. Nelson. 2003. "Framing and Deliberation: How
Citizens' Conversations Limit Elite Influence." *American Journal of Political Science*
47 (4): 729–45.

Du Bois, W. E. B. 1935. *Black Reconstruction in America.* In *The Oxford W.E.B. Du Bois,*
19 vols., edited by Henry Louis Gates, Jr. New York: Oxford University Press.

Dunbar, Adam. 2020. "Follow the Money: Racial Crime Stereotypes and Willingness
to Fund Crime Control Policies." *Psychology, Public Policy, and Law* 26 (4): 476–89.
https://doi/10.1037/law0000234.

Dunbar, Adam, Aaron Kupchik, Cresean Hughes, and Raven Lewis. 2022. "Fear of a
Black (and Poor) School: Race, Class, and School Safety Policy Preferences." *Race
and Justice* 12 (2): 344–67. https://doi.org/10.1177/2153368719881679.

Dunworth, Terence, and Gregory Mills. 1999. "National Evaluation of Weed and Seed."
US Department of Justice, Office of Justice Programs. Washington, DC: National
Institute of Justice. https://nij.ojp.gov/library/publications/national-evaluation
-weed-and-seed-research-brief.

Durán, Robert J. 2009. "Legitimated Oppression: Inner-City Mexican American Experiences with Police Gang Enforcement." *Journal of Contemporary Ethnography* 38
(2): 143–68. https://doi.org/10.1177/0891241607313057.

Duxbury, Scott W. 2020. "Fear or Loathing in the United States? Public Opinion and
the Rise of Racial Disparity in Mass Incarceration, 1978–2015." *Social Forces* 100, no.
2 (December): 427–53. https://doi.org/10.1093/sf/soaa112.

Duxbury, Scott W. 2021a. "Who Controls Criminal Law? Racial Threat and the Adoption of State Sentencing Law, 1975 to 2012." *American Sociological Review* 86 (1):
123–53. https://doi.org/10.1177/0003122420967647.

———. 2021b. "Whose Vote Counts for Crime Policy? Group Opinion and Public
Representation in Mass Incarceration, 1970–2015." *Public Opinion Quarterly* 85 (3):
780–807. https://doi.org/10.1093/poq/nfab037.

Eason, John M. 2017a. "Prisons as Panacea or Pariah? The Countervailing Consequences of the Prison Boom on the Political Economy of Rural Towns." *Social
Sciences* 6 (1): 7. https://doi.org/10.3390/socsci6010007.

———. 2017b. *Big House on the Prairie: Rise of the Rural Ghetto and Prison Proliferation.*
Chicago: University of Chicago Press.

Eason, John M., Danielle Zucker, and Christopher Wildeman. 2017. "Mass Imprisonment across the Rural-Urban Interface." *ANNALS of the American Academy of Political and Social Science* 672 (1): 202–16. https://doi.org/10.1177/0002716217705357.

Eberhardt, Jennifer L. 2019. *Biased: Uncovering the Hidden Prejudice That Shapes What
We See, Think, and Do.* New York: Viking.

Eck, John E., and Edward R. Maguire. 2000. "Have Changes in Policing Reduced Violent Crime? An Assessment of the Evidence." In *The Crime Drop in America*, edited by A. Blumstein and J. Wallman, 207–65. New York: Cambridge University Press.

Eckhouse, Laurel. 2019. "Race, Party, and Representation in Criminal Justice Politics." *Journal of Politics* 81 (3): 1143–52. https://doi.org/10.1086/703489.

Ekins, Emily. 2021. "Why Did Republicans Outperform the Polls Again? Two Theories." *FiveThirtyEight* (blog). March 2, 2021. https://fivethirtyeight.com/features/why-did -republicans-outperform-the-polls-again-two-theories/.

Ellis, Christopher, and James A. Stimson. 2012. *Ideology in America*. Cambridge: Cambridge University Press.

Enns, Peter K. 2016. *Incarceration Nation: How the United States Became the Most Punitive Democracy in the World*. New York: Cambridge University Press.

Enns, Peter K., and Julianna Koch. 2013. "Public Opinion in the U.S. States: 1956 to 2010." *State Politics & Policy Quarterly* 13 (3): 349–72. https://doi.org/10.1177 /1532440013496439.

Enns, Peter K., and Christopher Wlezien, eds. 2011. *Who Gets Represented?* New York: Russell Sage Foundation.

Epstein, Reid J., and Patricia Mazzei. 2021. "G.O.P. Bills Target Protesters (and Absolve Motorists Who Hit Them)." *New York Times*, April 21, 2021. https://www.nytimes .com/2021/04/21/us/politics/republican-anti-protest-laws.html.

Erskine, Hazel. 1974. "The Polls: Causes of Crime." *Public Opinion Quarterly* 38 (2): 288–98.

Fagan, Jeffrey, Anthony A. Braga, Rod K. Brunson, and April Pattavina. 2015. "An Analysis of Race and Ethnicity Patterns in Boston Police Department Field Interrogation, Observation, Frisk, and/or Search Reports." Boston: ACLU of Massachusetts. http://raceandpolicing.issuelab.org/resources/25203/25203.pdf.

Falco, Diana L., and Noelle C. Turner. 2014. "Examining Causal Attributions Towards Crime on Support for Offender Rehabilitation." *American Journal of Criminal Justice* 39 (3): 630–41. https://doi.org/10.1007/s12103-013-9231-5.

Fenno, Richard. 2002. *Homestyle: House Members in Their Districts*. Longman Classics Edition. New York: Pearson Longman.

Ferguson, Christopher J., and Patrick Markey. 2019. "PG-13 Rated Movie Violence and Societal Violence: Is There a Link?" *Psychiatric Quarterly* 90 (2): 395–403. https: //doi.org/10.1007/s11126-018-9615-2.

Ferguson, Christopher J., Cheryl K. Olson, Lawrence A. Kutner, and Dorothy E. Warner. 2014. "Violent Video Games, Catharsis Seeking, Bullying, and Delinquency: A Multivariate Analysis of Effects." *Crime & Delinquency* 60 (5): 764–84. https://doi .org/10.1177/0011128710362201.

Ferguson, Christopher J., and Joanne Savage. 2012. "Have Recent Studies Addressed Methodological Issues Raised by Five Decades of Television Violence Research? A Critical Review." *Aggression and Violent Behavior* 17 (2): 129–39. https://doi.org/10 .1016/j.avb.2011.11.001.

File, Thom. 2017. "Voting in America: A Look at the 2016 Presidential Election." *United States Census Bureau* (blog). May 10, 2017. https://www.census.gov/newsroom/blogs /random-samplings/2017/05/voting_in_america.html.

Flanagan, Timothy J. 1987. "Change and Influence in Popular Criminology: Public Attributions of Crime Causation." *Journal of Criminal Justice* 15 (3): 231–43. https://doi .org/10.1016/0047-2352(87)90046-8.

Flavin, Patrick, and Gregory Shufeldt. 2020. "Explaining State Preemption of Local Laws: Political, Institutional, and Demographic Factors." *Publius: The Journal of Federalism* 50 (2): 280–309. https://doi.org/10.1093/publius/pjz024.

Forman, James. 2017. *Locking Up Our Own: Crime and Punishment in Black America*. New York: Farrar, Straus and Giroux.

Fortner, Michael Javen. 2015. *Black Silent Majority: The Rockefeller Drug Laws and the Politics of Punishment*. Cambridge, MA: Harvard University Press.

———. 2020. "Reconstructing Justice: Race, Generational Divides, and the Fight Over 'Defund the Police.'" Washington, DC: Niskanen Center. https://www .niskanencenter.org/reconstructing-justice-race-generational-divides-and-the-fight -over-defund-the-police/.

Fowler, Luke, and Stephanie L Witt. 2019. "State Preemption of Local Authority: Explaining Patterns of State Adoption of Preemption Measures." *Publius: The Journal of Federalism* 49 (3): 540–59. https://doi.org/10.1093/publius/pjz011.

Fraser, Nancy. 1995. "From Redistribution to Recognition? Dilemmas of Justice in a 'Post-Socialist' Age." *New Left Review* (212): 68–149.

Fukuyama, Francis. 2018. "Against Identity Politics: The New Tribalism and the Crisis of Democracy Essays." *Foreign Affairs* 97 (5): 90–115.

Gabbidon, Shaun L., and Danielle Boisvert. 2012. "Public Opinion on Crime Causation: An Exploratory Study of Philadelphia Area Residents." *Journal of Criminal Justice* 40 (1): 50–59. https://doi.org/10.1016/j.jcrimjus.2011.11.008.

Garland, David. 2001. *The Culture of Control: Crime and Social Order in Contemporary Society*. Chicago: University of Chicago Press.

———. 2020. "Penal Controls and Social Controls: Toward a Theory of American Penal Exceptionalism." *Punishment & Society* 22 (3): 321–52. https://doi.org/10.1177 /1462474519881992.

Gaston, Shytierra. 2019. "Producing Race Disparities: A Study of Drug Arrests across Place and Race." *Criminology* 57 (3): 424–51. https://doi.org/10.1111/1745 -9125.12207.

Gaston, Shytierra, and Rod K. Brunson. 2020. "Reasonable Suspicion in the Eye of the Beholder: Routine Policing in Racially Different Disadvantaged Neighborhoods." *Urban Affairs Review* 56 (1): 188–227. https://doi.org/10.1177/1078087418774641.

Gaubatz, Kathlyn Taylor. 1995. *Crime in the Public Mind*. Ann Arbor: University of Michigan Press.

Gest, Justin. 2016. *The New Minority: White Working Class Politics in an Age of Immigration and Inequality*. New York: Oxford University Press.

Gilens, Martin. 1999. *Why Americans Hate Welfare: Race, Media, and the Politics of Antipoverty Policy*. Chicago: University of Chicago Press.

Gilmore, Ruth Wilson. 2007. *Golden Gulag: Prisons, Surplus, Crisis, and Opposition in Globalizing California*. Oakland: University of California Press.

Gimpel, James G., Nathan Lovin, Bryant Moy, and Andrew Reeves. 2020. "The Urban–Rural Gulf in American Political Behavior." *Political Behavior* 42 (4): 1343–68. https://doi.org/10.1007/s11109-020-09601-w.

Gingrich, Newt, and Pat Nolan. 2011. "Prison Reform: A Smart Way for States to Save Money and Lives." *Washington Post*, January 7, 2011. http://www.washingtonpost.com/wp-dyn/content/article/2011/01/06/AR2011010604386.html.

Glazer, Elizabeth, and Patrick Sharkey. 2021. "Social Fabric: A New Model for Public Safety and Vital Neighborhoods." New York: The Square One Project. https://squareonejustice.org/paper/social-fabric-a-new-model-for-public-safety-and-vital-neighborhoods-by-elizabeth-glazer-and-patrick-sharkey-march-2021/.

Glueck, Katie. 2022. "Staunch Critic of the N.Y.P.D. Grapples with Deaths of 2 Officers." *New York Times*, January 26, 2022. https://www.nytimes.com/2022/01/26/us/politics/kristin-richardson-jordan-nypd.html.

Goldrosen, Nicholas. 2021. "The New Preemption of Progressive Prosecutors." *Illinois Law Review Online* 150 (April): 150–57. https://www.illinoislawreview.org/online/the-new-preemption-of-progressive-prosecutors/.

Gotoff, Daniel, Celinda Lake, and Corey Teter. 2017. "Survey Findings on Community Investment." Washington, DC: Lake Research Partners. https://www.urban.org/sites/default/files/polling_memo.pdf.

Gottfredson, Michael R., and Travis Hirschi. 1990. *A General Theory of Crime*. Stanford: Stanford University Press.

Gottlieb, Aaron. 2017. "The Effect of Message Frames on Public Attitudes Toward Criminal Justice Reform for Nonviolent Offenses." *Crime & Delinquency* 63 (5): 636–56. https://doi.org/10.1177/0011128716687758.

Gottschalk, Marie. 2006. *The Prison and the Gallows: The Politics of Mass Incarceration in America*. New York: Cambridge University Press.

———. 2016. *Caught: The Prison State and the Lockdown of American Politics*. Princeton, NJ: Princeton University Press.

Grasmick, Harold G., and Anne L. McGill. 1994. "Religion, Attribution Style, and Punitiveness Toward Juvenile Offenders." *Criminology* 32 (1): 23–46. https://doi.org/10.1111/j.1745-9125.1994.tb01145.x.

Green, David A. 2006. "Public Opinion versus Public Judgment about Crime: Correcting the 'Comedy of Errors.'" *British Journal of Criminology* 46 (1): 131–54.

Green, Eva G. T., Christian Staerkle, and David O. Sears. 2006. "Symbolic Racism and Whites' Attitudes toward Punitive and Preventive Crime Policies." *Law and Human Behavior* 30 (4): 435–54.

Groves, Robert M. 2006. "Nonresponse Rates and Nonresponse Bias in Household Surveys." *Public Opinion Quarterly* 70 (5): 646–75.

Groves, Robert M., and Emilia Peytcheva. 2008. "The Impact of Nonresponse Rates on Nonresponse Bias: A Meta-Analysis." *Public Opinion Quarterly* 72 (2): 167–89.

Guynn, Jessica. 2015. "Meet the Woman Who Coined #BlackLivesMatter." *USA TODAY*, March 4, 2015. https://www.usatoday.com/story/tech/2015/03/04/alicia-garza -black-lives-matter/24341593/.

Hackworth, Jason. 2019. *Manufacturing Decline: How Racism and the Conservative Movement Crush the American Rust Belt.* New York: Columbia University Press.

Hagan, John. 2010. *Who Are the Criminals? The Politics of Crime Policy from the Age of Roosevelt to the Age of Reagan.* Princeton, NJ: Princeton University Press.

Hagan, John, and Celesta A. Albonetti. 1982. "Race, Class, and the Perception of Criminal Injustice in America." *American Journal of Sociology* 88 (2): 329–55.

Hamilton, Charles. 1977. "Deracialization: Examination of a Political Strategy." *First World,* 1977.

Hancock, Ange-Marie. 2004. *The Politics of Disgust: The Public Identity of the Welfare Queen.* New York: NYU Press.

Harris, Fred, and Alan Curtis, eds. 2018. *Healing Our Divided Society: Investing in America Fifty Years after the Kerner Report.* Philadelphia: Temple University Press. http://tupress.temple.edu/book/20000000009771.

Harris-Lacewell, Melissa V. 2003. "The Heart of the Politics of Race: Centering Black People in the Study of White Racial Attitudes." *Journal of Black Studies* 34 (2): 222–49. https://doi.org/10.1177/0021934703255596.

Hart, Timothy C. 1998. "Causes and Consequences of Juvenile Crime and Violence: Public Attitudes and Question-Order Effect." *American Journal of Criminal Justice* 23 (1): 129–43. https://doi.org/10.1007/BF02887287.

Hatzipanagos, Rachel. 2020. "What 'Defund the Police' Might Look Like." *Washington Post,* June 12, 2020. https://www.washingtonpost.com/nation/2020/06/12/black -lives-matter-defund-police-is-country-ready/.

Herbst, Susan. 1998. *Reading Public Opinion: How Political Actors View the Democratic Process.* Chocago: University of Chicago Press.

Hershbein, Brad. 2018. "How the Great Recession Hurt the Middle Class—Twice." *Brookings* (blog). December 4, 2018. https://www.brookings.edu/blog/up-front/2018 /12/04/how-the-great-recession-hurt-the-middle-class-twice/.

Hetey, Rebecca C., and Jennifer L. Eberhardt. 2014. "Racial Disparities in Incarceration Increase Acceptance of Punitive Policies." *Psychological Science* 25 (10): 1949–54. https://doi.org/10.1177/0956797614540307.

Hill, Evan, Ainara Tiefenthäler, Christiaan Triebert, Drew Jordan, Haley Willis, and Robin Stein. 2020. "How George Floyd Was Killed in Police Custody." *New York Times,* August 13, 2020. https://www.nytimes.com/2020/05/31/us/george-floyd -investigation.html.

Hinton, Elizabeth. 2016. *From the War on Poverty to the War on Crime: The Making of Mass Incarceration in America.* Boston: Harvard University Press.

Hinton, Elizabeth, Julilly Kohler-Hausmann, and Vesla M. Weaver. 2016. "Did Blacks Really Endorse the 1994 Crime Bill?" *New York Times,* April 13, 2016. https://www

.nytimes.com/2016/04/13/opinion/did-blacks-really-endorse-the-1994-crime-bill .html.

Hirschi, Travis. 2002. *Causes of Delinquency*. 2nd ed. Piscataway, NJ: Transaction Publishers.

Hochschild, Arlie Russell. 2018. *Strangers in Their Own Land: Anger and Mourning on the American Right*. New York: New Press.

Hochschild, Jennifer L. 1995. *Facing Up to the American Dream: Race, Class, and the Soul of the Nation*. Princeton, NJ: Princeton University Press.

Hoeve, Machteld, Judith Semon Dubas, Veroni I. Eichelsheim, Peter H. van der Laan, Wilma Smeenk, and Jan R. M. Gerris. 2009. "The Relationship Between Parenting and Delinquency: A Meta-Analysis." *Journal of Abnormal Child Psychology* 37 (6): 749–75. https://doi.org/10.1007/s10802-009-9310-8.

Holbrook, Thomas M., and Aaron C. Weinschenk. 2020. "Information, Political Bias, and Public Perceptions of Local Conditions in U.S. Cities." *Political Research Quarterly* 73 (1): 221–36. https://doi.org/10.1177/1065912919892627.

Hollander, Jocelyn A. 2004. "The Social Contexts of Focus Groups." *Journal of Contemporary Ethnography* 33 (5): 602–37. https://doi.org/10.1177/0891241604266988.

Hopkins, Daniel J, and Samantha Washington. 2020. "The Rise of Trump, the Fall of Prejudice? Tracking White Americans' Racial Attitudes via a Panel Survey, 2008–2018." *Public Opinion Quarterly* 84 (1): 119–40. https://doi.org/10.1093/poq/nfaa004.

Hough, Mike, and Alison Park. 2002. "How Malleable Are Attitudes to Crime and Punishment? Findings from a British Deliberative Poll." In *Changing Attitudes to Punishment: Public Opinion, Crime, and Justice*, edited by Julian V. Roberts and Mike Hough, 163–83. Portland, OR: Willan Publishing.

Huber, Gregory A., and John S. Lapinski. 2008. "Testing the Implicit-Explicit Model of Racialized Political Communication." *Perspectives on Politics* 6 (1): 125–34.

Hunt, Matthew O. 1996. "The Individual, Society, or Both? A Comparison of Black, Latino, and White Beliefs about the Causes of Poverty." *Social Forces* 75 (1): 293–322. https://doi.org/10.2307/2580766.

———. 2007. "African American, Hispanic, and White Beliefs about Black/White Inequality, 1977–2004." *American Sociological Review* 72 (3): 390–415.

Hunter, Albert. 1985. "Private, Parochial, and Public Social Orders: The Problem of Crime and Incivility in Urban Communities." In *The Challenge of Social Control: Citizenship and Institution Building in Modern Society*, edited by Gerald D. Suttles and Mayer N. Zald, 230–42. Norwood, NJ: Ablex.

Hurwitz, Jon, and Mark Peffley. 1997. "Public Perceptions of Race and Crime: The Role of Racial Stereotypes." *American Journal of Political Science* 41 (2): 375–401. https://doi.org/10.2307/2111769.

———. 2005. "Playing the Race Card in the Post–Willie Horton Era." *Public Opinion Quarterly* 69 (1): 2005.

Hurwitz, Jon, Mark Peffley, and Jeffery Mondak. 2015. "Linked Fate and Outgroup Perceptions: Blacks, Latinos, and the U.S. Criminal Justice System." *Political Research Quarterly* 68 (3): 505–20. https://doi.org/10.1177/1065912915589597.

Hutchings, Vincent L., and Ashley E. Jardina. 2009. "Experiments on Racial Priming in Political Campaigns." *Annual Review of Political Science* 12: 397–402. https://doi.org /10.1146/annurev.polisci.12.060107.154208.

Hyra, Derek S. 2006. "Racial Uplift? Intra-Racial Class Conflict and the Economic Revitalization of Harlem and Bronzeville." *City & Community* 5 (1): 71–92. https://doi .org/10.1111/j.1540-6040.2006.00156.x.

Iyengar, Shanto. 1991. *Is Anyone Responsible? How Television Frames Political Issues.* Chicago: University of Chicago Press.

Jardina, Ashley. 2019. *White Identity Politics.* Cambridge: Cambridge University Press.

Jardina, Ashley, and Spencer Piston. 2019. "Racial Prejudice, Racial Identity, and Attitudes in Political Decision Making." In *Oxford Research Encyclopedia of Politics.* https://doi.org/10.1093/acrefore/9780190228637.013.966.

Jennings, James. 2011. "The Empowerment Zone in Boston, Massachusetts 2000–2009: Lessons Learned for Neighborhood Revitalization." *Review of Black Political Economy* 38 (1): 63–81. https://doi.org/10.1007/s12114-010-9080-0.

———. 2016. "Gentrification as Anti-Local Economic Development: The Case of Boston, Massachusetts." *Trotter Review* 23 (1): 1–16.

———. 2019. "Select Overview of Poverty in Boston and Three Neighborhoods: Roxbury, Dorchester, and Mattapan." Presented at the Presentation to the Boston Health Care for the Homeless Program, Boston, MA, October 29, 2019. https://sites .tufts.edu/jamesjennings/files/2019/10/reportsPRoxburyDorchesterMattapanOct-29 -2019.pdf.

Jennings, James, Barbara Lewis, Richard O'Bryant, Rachel Bernard, Linda Sprague Martinez, and Russell Williams. 2015. "Blacks in Massachusetts: Comparative Demographic, Social, and Economic Experiences with Whites, Latinos, and Asians." Boston: William Monroe Trotter Institute. https://sites.tufts.edu/jamesjennings/files /2018/06/reportsBlackComparativeExperience2015.pdf.

Johnson, Cedric. 2017. "The Panthers Can't Save Us Now." *Catalyst* 1 (1): 56–85.

Johnson, Kenneth M., and Dante J. Scala. 2020. "The Rural-Urban Continuum of Polarization: Understanding the Geography of the 2018 Midterms." *Forum* 18 (4): 607–26. https://doi.org/10.1515/for-2020-2102.

Joint Economic Committee. 2020. "The Economic State of Black America 2020." Washington, DC: Joint Economic Committee. https://www.jec.senate.gov/public/index .cfm/democrats/2020/2/economic-state-of-black-america-2020.

Jonson, Cheryl Lero, Francis T. Cullen, and Jennifer L. Lux. 2013. "Creating Ideological Space: Why Public Support for Rehabilitation Matters." In *What Works in Offender Rehabilitation*, edited by Leam A. Craig, Louise Dixon, Theresa A. Gannon, 50–68. Chichester, UK: John Wiley & Son. https://doi.org/10.1002/9781118320655.ch3.

Kaba, Mariame. 2020. "Yes, We Mean Literally Abolish the Police." *New York Times*, June 12, 2020. https://www.nytimes.com/2020/06/12/opinion/sunday/floyd-abolish -defund-police.html.

Kahneman, Daniel. 2011. *Thinking, Fast and Slow.* New York: Farrar, Straus and Giroux.

Kahneman, Daniel, Ilana Ritov, and David Schkade. 1999. "Economic Preferences or Attitude Expressions? An Analysis of Dollar Responses to Public Issues." *Journal of Risk and Uncertainty* 19 (1–3): 203–35. https://doi.org/10.1007/978-94-017-1406-8_8.

Kang-Brown, Jacob, and Ram Subramanian. 2017. "Out of Sight: The Growth of Jails in Rural America." Vera Institute of Justice. https://www.vera.org/publications/out-of -sight-growth-of-jails-rural-america.

Katz, Michael B. 2013. *The Undeserving Poor: America's Enduring Confrontation with Poverty*. 2nd ed. Oxford: Oxford University Press.

Katznelson, Ira. 2006. *When Affirmative Action Was White: An Untold History of Racial Inequality in Twentieth-Century America*. New York: W. W. Norton.

Kelley, Robin D.G. 1997. "Identity Politics and Class Struggle." *New Politics* 6 (2): 84–96.

Kelling, George L., and James Q. Wilson. 1982. "Broken Windows." *Atlantic*, March 1982. https://www.theatlantic.com/magazine/archive/1982/03/broken-windows /304465/.

Kendi, Ibram X. 2016. *Stamped from the Beginning: The Definitive History of Racist Ideas in America*. New York: Nation Books.

Kennedy, Courtney, Mark Blumenthal, Scott Clement, Joshua D. Clinton, Claire Durand, Charles Franklin, Kyley McGeeney, Lee Miringoff, Kristen Olson, Douglas Rivers, Lydia Saad, G Evans Witt, Christopher Wlezien. 2018. "An Evaluation of the 2016 Election Polls in the United States." *Public Opinion Quarterly* 82 (1): 1–33. https://doi.org/10.1093/poq/nfx047.

Kinder, Donald R., and Lynn M. Sanders. 1996. *Divided by Color: Racial Politics and Democratic Ideals*. Chicago: University of Chicago Press.

King, Maya. 2020. "Black Lives Matter Goes Big on Policy Agenda." *POLITICO*, August 28, 2020. https://www.politico.com/news/2020/08/28/black-lives-matter-breathe -act-403905.

———. 2021. "First Covid Raised the Murder Rate. Now It's Changing the Politics of Crime." *POLITICO*, October 28, 2021. https://www.politico.com/news/2021/10/28 /covid-murder-crime-rate-517226.

Kingdon, John W. 1984. *Agendas, Alternatives, and Public Policies*. Boston: Little, Brown.

Kneebone, Elizabeth, and Natalie Holmes. 2016. "U.S. Concentrated Poverty in the Wake of the Great Recession." *Brookings* (blog). March 31, 2016. https://www .brookings.edu/research/u-s-concentrated-poverty-in-the-wake-of-the-great -recession/.

Kondo, Michelle C., Elena Andreyeva, Eugenia C. South, John M. MacDonald, and Charles C. Branas. 2018. "Neighborhood Interventions to Reduce Violence." *Annual Review of Public Health* 39: 253–71. https://doi.org/10.1146/annurev-publhealth -040617-014600.

Kraska, Peter B. 2007. "Militarization and Policing—Its Relevance to 21st Century Po-lice." *Policing: A Journal of Policy and Practice* 1 (4): 501–13. https://doi.org/10.1093 /police/pam065.

Kraus, Michael W., Ivuoma N. Onyeador, Natalie M. Daumeyer, Julian M. Rucker, and Jennifer A. Richeson. 2019. "The Misperception of Racial Economic Inequality." *Perspectives on Psychological Science* 14 (6): 899–921. https://doi.org/10.1177/1745691619863049.

Krivo, Lauren J., Christopher J. Lyons, and María B. Vélez. 2021. "The U.S. Racial Structure and Ethno-Racial Inequality in Urban Neighborhood Crime, 2010–2013." *Sociology of Race and Ethnicity* 7 (3): 350-68. https://doi.org/10.1177/2332649220948551.

Krivo, Lauren J., Ruth D. Peterson, Helen Rizzo, and John R. Reynolds. 1998. "Race, Segregation, and the Concentration of Disadvantage: 1980–1990." *Social Problems* 45 (1): 61–80.

Krueger, Richard A., and Mary Anne Casey. 2014. *Focus Groups: A Practical Guide for Applied Research*. 5th ed. Thousand Oaks, CA: SAGE.

Kubrin, Charis E. 2005. "Gangstas, Thugs, and Hustlas: Identity and the Code of the Street in Rap Music." *Social Problems* 52 (3): 360–78. https://doi.org/10.1525/sp.2005.52.3.360.

Kubrin, Charis E., and Ronald Weitzer. 2003. "Retaliatory Homicide: Concentrated Disadvantage and Neighborhood Culture." *Social Problems* 50 (2): 157–80.

KVUE Staff. 2022. "Gov. Abbott Adopts Rules Punishing Cities That 'Defund Police Departments.'" Kvue.Com. March 12, 2022. https://www.kvue.com/article/news/police/gov-abbott-rules-punish-cities-defund-police/269-97121a7c-19e9-4fd7-b266-de821772a52f.

Lacey, Nicola, and David Soskice. 2015. "Crime, Punishment and Segregation in the United States: The Paradox of Local Democracy." *Punishment & Society* 17 (4): 454–81. https://doi.org/10.1177/1462474515604042.

La Vigne, Nancy, Samantha Harvell, Jeremy Welsh-Loveman, Hanna Love, Julia Durnan, Josh Eisenstat, Laura Golian, Eddie Mohr, lizabeth Pelletier, Julie Samuels, Chelsea Thomson, and Margaret Ulle. 2016. "Reforming Sentencing and Corrections Policy: The Experience of Justice Reinvestment Initiative States." Washington, DC: Urban Institute.

Le Blanc, Paul. 2013. "Freedom Budget: The Promise of the Civil Rights Movement for Economic Justice." *WorkingUSA* 16 (1): 43–58. https://doi.org/10.1111/wusa.12022.

Lebron, Christopher J. 2021. *The Making of Black Lives Matter: A Brief History of an Idea*. Oxford University Press.

Lee, Heejin, Francis T. Cullen, Alexander L. Burton, and Velmer S. Burton. 2021. "Millennials as the Future of Corrections: A Generational Analysis of Public Policy Opinions." *Crime & Delinquency* Online first (July). https://doi.org/10.1177/00111287211022610.

Lerman, Amy E., and Vesla M. Weaver. 2014a. "Race and Crime in American Politics: From Law and Order to Willie Horton and Beyond." In *The Oxford Handbook of Ethnicity, Crime, and Immigration*, edited by Sandra Bucerius and Michael Tonry, 41–69. Oxford University Press. https://doi.org/10.1093/oxfordhb/9780199859016.013.003.

———. 2014b. *Arresting Citizenship: The Democratic Consequences of American Crime Control*. Chicago: University of Chicago Press.

Leverentz, Andrea. 2011. "Neighborhood Context of Attitudes toward Crime and Reentry." *Punishment and Society* 13 (1): 64–92.

Leverentz, Andrea, Adam Pittman, and Jennifer Skinnon. 2018. "Place and Perception: Constructions of Community and Safety across Neighborhoods and Residents." *City & Community* 17 (4): 972–95. https://doi.org/10.1111/cico.12350.

Leverentz, Andrea, and Monica Williams. 2017. "Contextualizing Community Crime Control: Race, Geography, and Configurations of Control in Four Communities." *Criminology* 55 (1): 112–36. https://doi.org/10.1111/1745-9125.12127.

Levine, Marianne. 2022. "Criminal Justice Reform Faces Political Buzzsaw as GOP Hones Its Midterm Message." *POLITICO*, April 14, 2022. https://www.politico.com/news/2022/04/14/criminal-justice-reform-midterms-00024991.

Levitz, Eric. 2021. "Avoiding White Backlash Is a Racial-Justice Issue." *New York Magazine*, May 2, 2021. https://nymag.com/intelligencer/2021/05/white-backlash-racial-justice-kalla-english-race-class-narrative.html.

Lewis, Angela K., Pearl K. Ford Dowe, and Sekou M. Franklin. 2013. "African Americans and Obama's Domestic Policy Agenda: A Closer Look at Deracialization, the Federal Stimulus Bill, and the Affordable Care Act." *Polity* 45 (1): 127–52. http://dx.doi.org.ezproxy.lib.umb.edu/10.1057/pol.2012.25.

Lewis-Beck, Michael S., William G. Jacoby, Helmut Norpoth, and Herbert F. Weisberg. 2009. *The American Voter Revisited*. Ann Arbor, MI: University of Michigan Press.

Lilla, Mark. 2017. *The Once and Future Liberal: After Identity Politics*. HarperCollins.

Long, J. Scott, and Jeremy Freese. 2014. *Regression Models for Categorical Dependent Variables Using Stata*. 3rd ed. College Station, TX: Stata Press.

López, Ian Haney. 2015. *Dog Whistle Politics: How Coded Racial Appeals Have Reinvented Racism and Wrecked the Middle Class*. Oxford University Press.

———. 2019. *Merge Left: Fusing Race and Class, Winning Elections, and Saving America.* The New York: New Press.

Lowe, Tracie. 2020. "Policing, Justice, and Black Communities: A Brief Guide for Understanding Police Defunding, Reform, Disbanding, and Abolition." Austin, TX: Institute for Urban Policy Research & Analysis. https://utexas.app.box.com/v/police-justice-series-2.

Lowery, Wesley. 2016. *They Can't Kill Us All: Ferguson, Baltimore, and a New Era in America's Racial Justice Movement*. Little, Brown.

MacInnis, Bo, Jon A. Krosnick, Annabell S. Ho, and Mu-Jung Cho. 2018. "The Accuracy of Measurements with Probability and Nonprobability Survey Samples: Replication and Extension." *Public Opinion Quarterly* 82 (4): 707–44. https://doi.org/10.1093/poq/nfy038.

Manchester, Julia. 2022. "Democrats Look to Shake off 'Defund the Police.'" Text. The Hill. February 6, 2022. https://thehill.com/homenews/campaign/592920-democrats-look-to-shake-off-defund-the-police-as-crime-rises/.

Mancillas, Linda K. 2018. *Presidents and Mass Incarceration: Choices at the Top, Repercussions at the Bottom*. ABC-CLIO.

Mancini, Christina, Kelle Barrick, Julia DiPonio, and Marc Gertz. 2010. "Taxation with Representation?: Examining Public Fiscal Support for Diverse Correctional Policies." *Criminal Justice Policy Review* 21 (1): 76–97. https://doi.org/10.1177 /0887403409336053.

Manning, Alex, Douglas Hartmann, and Joseph Gerteis. 2015. "Colorblindness in Black and White: An Analysis of Core Tenets, Configurations, and Complexities." *Sociology of Race and Ethnicity* 1 (4): 532–46. https://doi.org/10.1177/2332649215584828.

Marcelo, Philip. 2017. "In Boston, 'Methadone Mile', an Open-Air Drug Market." *Providence Journal*, October 5, 2017. https://www.providencejournal.com/news/20171005 /in-boston-methadone-mile-open-air-drug-market.

Maruna, Shadd. 2007. *Making Good: How Ex-Convicts Reform and Rebuild Their Lives.* American Psychological Association.

Massey, Douglas, and Nancy A. Denton. 1993. *American Apartheid: Segregation and the Making of the Underclass.* Harvard University Press.

Matthay, Ellicott C., Kriszta Farkas, Kara E. Rudolph, Scott Zimmerman, Melissa Barragan, Dana E. Goin, and Jennifer Ahern. 2019. "Firearm and Nonfirearm Violence After Operation Peacemaker Fellowship in Richmond, California, 1996–2016." *American Journal of Public Health* 109 (11): 1605–11. https://doi.org/10.2105/AJPH .2019.305288.

Maxwell, Zerlina. 2021. *The End of White Politics: How to Heal Our Liberal Divide.* Hachette Books.

Mayhew, David R. 1974. *Congress: The Electoral Connection.* 2nd ed. New Haven: Yale University Press.

McCarthy, Justin. 2020. "Perceptions of Increased U.S. Crime at Highest Since 1993." Gallup.Com. November 13, 2020. https://news.gallup.com/poll/323996/perceptions -increased-crime-highest-1993.aspx.

McIlwain, Charlton D., and Stephen M. Caliendo. 2014. "Mitt Romney's Racist Appeals: How Race Was Played in the 2012 Presidential Election." *American Behavioral Scientist* 58 (9): 1157–68. https://doi.org/10.1177/0002764213506212.

Mead, George H. 1918. "The Psychology of Punitive Justice." *American Journal of Sociology* 23 (5): 577–602.

Mears, Daniel P., Justin T. Pickett, and Christina Mancini. 2015. "Support for Balanced Juvenile Justice: Assessing Views About Youth, Rehabilitation, and Punishment." *Journal of Quantitative Criminology* 31 (3): 459–79. https://doi.org/10.1007/s10940 -014-9234-5.

Mendelberg, Tali. 2001. *The Race Card: Campaign Strategy, Implicit Messages, and the Norm of Equality.* Princeton, NJ: Princeton University Press.

Merton, Robert K. 1938. "Social Structure and Anomie." *American Sociological Review* 3 (5): 672–82.

Metcalfe, Christi, and Justin T. Pickett. 2018. "The Extent and Correlates of Public Support for Deterrence Reforms and Hot Spots Policing." *Law & Society Review* 52 (2): 471–502. https://doi.org/10.1111/lasr.12327.

Mettler, Suzanne. 2011. *The Submerged State: How Invisible Government Policies Undermine American Democracy*. University of Chicago Press.

———. 2018. *The Government-Citizen Disconnect*. Russell Sage Foundation.

Metzl, Jonathan M. 2020. *Dying of Whiteness: How the Politics of Racial Resentment Is Killing America's Heartland*. Basic Books.

Middlemass, Keesha. 2017. *Convicted and Condemned: The Politics and Policies of Prisoner Reentry*. NYU Press.

Miller, Lisa L. 2001. *The Politics of Community Crime Prevention: Implementing Operation Weed and Seed in Seattle*. Burlington, VT: Ashgate.

———. 2008. *The Perils of Federalism: Race, Poverty, and the Politics of Crime Control*. New York: Oxford University Press.

———. 2016. *The Myth of Mob Rule: Violent Crime and Democratic Politics*. New York: Oxford University Press.

Monteiro, Carlos E., and Natasha A. Frost. 2015. "Altering Trajectories through Community-Based Justice Reinvestment Pathways to Prison: Policy Essay." *Criminology & Public Policy* 14 (3): 455–64.

Morenoff, Jeffrey D., Robert J. Sampson, and Stephen W. Raudenbush. 2001. "Neighborhood Inequality, Collective Efficacy, and the Spatial Dynamics of Urban Violence." *Criminology* 39 (3): 517–60.

Morgan, David L. 1998. *The Focus Group Guidebook*. Thousand Oaks, CA: SAGE.

Morning Consult + Politico. "National Tracking Poll #200671." 2020. Morning Consult. https://assets.morningconsult.com/wp-uploads/2020/06/17071351/200671_crosstabs _POLITICO_RVs_v1_AUTO.pdf.

Muhammad, Khalil Gibran. 2011. *The Condemnation of Blackness*. Cambridge, MA: Harvard University Press.

Muñoz, Ana Patricia, Marlene Kim, Mariko Chang, Regine O. Jackson, Darrick Hamilton, and William A. Darity, Jr. 2015. "The Color of Wealth in Boston." Boston: Federal Reserve Bank of Boston. https://www.bostonfed.org/publications/one-time -pubs/color-of-wealth.aspx.

Murakawa, Naomi. 2014. *The First Civil Right: How Liberals Built Prison America*. New York: Oxford University Press.

Muro, Mark, Jacob Whiton, and Robert Maxim. 2019. "Automation Perpetuates the Red-Blue Divide." *Brookings* (blog). March 25, 2019. https://www.brookings.edu /blog/the-avenue/2019/03/25/automation-perpetuates-the-red-blue-divide/.

Mutz, Diana C. 2011. *Population-Based Survey Experiments*. Princeton, NJ: Princeton University Press.

Nagin, Daniel S. 2013. "Deterrence in the Twenty-First Century." *Crime and Justice* 42 (1): 199–263. https://doi-org/10.1086/670398.

Nagin, Daniel S., Alex R. Piquero, Elizabeth S. Scott, and Laurence Steinberg. 2006. "Public Preferences for Rehabilitation versus Incarceration of Juvenile Offenders: Evidence from a Contingent Valuation Survey." *Criminology & Public Policy* 5 (4): 627–51. https://doi.org/10.1111/j.1745-9133.2006.00406.x.

National Advisory Commission on Civil Disorders, and Otto Kerner. 1968. "Report of the National Advisory Commission on Civil Disorders." Washington, DC: US Government Printing Office.

Neumark, David. 2020. "Place-Based Policies: Can We Do Better Than Enterprise Zones?" *Journal of Policy Analysis and Management* 39 (3): 836–44. https://doi.org/10.1002/pam.22225.

Neumark, David, and Helen Simpson. 2015. "Place-Based Policies." In *Handbook of Regional and Urban Economics*, edited by Gilles Duranton, J. Vernon Henderson, and William C. Strange, 5:1197–287. Amsterdam: Elsevier. https://www-sciencedirect-com.ezproxy.lib.umb.edu/science/article/pii/B9780444595317000181?via%3Dihub.

New York Times. 2021. "How George Floyd Died, and What Happened Next." *New York Times*, May 25, 2021. https://www.nytimes.com/article/george-floyd.html.

Nicholson-Crotty, Sean, David A. M. Peterson, and Mark D. Ramirez. 2009. "Dynamic Representation(s): Federal Criminal Justice Policy and an Alternative Dimension of Public Mood." *Political Behavior* 31 (4): 629–55. https://doi.org/10.1007/s11109-009-9085-1.

Norquist, Grover. 2017. "Conservatives for Criminal Justice Reform." *Wall Street Journal*, September 26, 2017. https://www.wsj.com/articles/conservatives-for-criminal-justice-reform-1506463970.

North, Anna. 2020. "Do Americans Support Defunding Police? It Depends How You Ask the Question." *Vox*, June 23, 2020. https://www.vox.com/2020/6/23/21299118/defunding-the-police-minneapolis-budget-george-floyd.

Osborne, Jason W. 2013. *Best Practices in Data Cleaning: A Complete Guide to Everything You Need to Do Before and After Collecting Your Data*. Thousand Oaks, CA: SAGE.

Pagani, Linda S. 2009. "The Influence of Family Context on the Development and Persistence of Antisocial Behavior." In *The Development of Persistent Criminality*, edited by Joanne Savage, 37–53. New York: Oxford University Press.

Page, Benjamin I., and Lawrence R. Jacobs. 2009. *Class War? What Americans Really Think about Economic Inequality*. Chicago: University of Chicago Press.

Page, Benjamin I., and Robert Y. Shapiro. 2010. *The Rational Public: Fifty Years of Trends in Americans' Policy Preferences*. Chicago: University of Chicago Press.

Pager, Devah. 2008. *Marked: Race, Crime, and Finding Work in an Era of Mass Incarceration*. Chicago: University of Chicago Press.

Parker, Karen F., and Scott R. Maggard. 2009. "Making a Difference: The Impact of Traditional Male Role Models on Drug Sale Activity and Violence Involving Black Urban Youth." *Journal of Drug Issues* 39 (3): 715–39. https://doi.org/10.1177/002204260903900311.

Pattillo, Mary. 2003. "Negotiating Blackness, for Richer or for Poorer." *Ethnography* 4 (1): 61–93. https://doi.org/10.1177/1466138103004001004.

———. 2008. "Investing in Poor Black Neighborhoods 'as Is.'" In *Public Housing and the Legacy of Segregation*, edited by Margery Austin Turner, Susan J. Popkin, and Lynette A. Rawlings, 31–46. Washington, DC: Urban Institute Press.

Peck, Jennifer H. 2015. "Minority Perceptions of the Police: A State-of-the-Art Review." *Policing: An International Journal of Police Strategies & Management* 38 (1): 173–203. https://doi.org/10.1108/PIJPSM-01-2015-0001.

Peffley, Mark, and Jon Hurwitz. 2009. "Racial Stereotyping and Political Attitudes: The View from Political Science." In *The Political Psychology of Democratic Citizenship*, edited by Eugene Borgida, Christopher M. Federico, and John L. Sullivan, 247–74. New York: Oxford University Press.

———. 2010. *Justice in America: The Separate Realities of Blacks and Whites*. New York: Cambridge University Press.

Peffley, Mark, Jon Hurwitz, and Jeffery Mondak. 2017. "Racial Attributions in the Justice System and Support for Punitive Crime Policies." *American Politics Research* 45 (6): 1032–58. https://doi.org/10.1177/1532673X17692326.

Percival, Garrick L. 2015. *Smart on Crime: The Struggle to Build a Better American Penal System*. Boca Raton: CRC Press. https://doi.org/10.1201/b18693.

Perlstein, Rick. 2012. "Exclusive: Lee Atwater's Infamous 1981 Interview on the Southern Strategy." *Nation*, November 13, 2012. https://www.thenation.com /article/archive/exclusive-lee-atwaters-infamous-1981-interview-southern -strategy/.

Perna, Laura W., James Kvaal, and Roman Ruiz. 2017. "Understanding Student Debt: Implications for Federal Policy and Future Research." *ANNALS of the American Academy of Political and Social Science* 671 (1): 270–86. https://doi.org/10.1177 /0002716217704002.

Peter D. Hart Research Associates. 2002. "Changing Public Attitudes toward the Criminal Justice System: Summary of Findings." New York: Open Society Institute. https://www.opensocietyfoundations.org/reports/changing-public-attitudes-toward -criminal-justice-system.

Petersen, Michael Bang, Daniel Sznycer, Leda Cosmides, and John Tooby. 2012. "Who Deserves Help? Evolutionary Psychology, Social Emotions, and Public Opinion about Welfare." *Political Psychology* 33 (3): 395–418. https://doi.org/10.1111/j.1467 -9221.2012.00883.x.

Peterson, Ruth D., and Lauren J. Krivo. 2010. *Divergent Social Worlds: Neighborhood Crime and the Racial-Spatial Divide*. New York: Russell Sage Foundation.

Peterson, Ruth D., Lauren J. Krivo, and Mark A. Harris. 2000. "Disadvantage and Neighborhood Violent Crime: Do Local Institutions Matter?" *Journal of Research in Crime and Delinquency* 37 (1): 31–63.

Pew Research Center. 2015. "The Whys and Hows of Generations Research." Washington, DC: Pew Research Center. https://www.pewresearch.org/politics/2015/09/03 /the-whys-and-hows-of-generations-research/.

———. 2020. "Majority of Public Favors Giving Civilians the Power to Sue Police Officers for Misconduct." Washington, DC: Pew Research Center. https://www .pewresearch.org/politics/2020/07/09/majority-of-public-favors-giving-civilians -the-power-to-sue-police-officers-for-misconduct/.

Pfaff, John. 2018. "The Never-Ending 'Willie Horton Effect' Is Keeping Prisons Too Full for America's Good." *Los Angeles Times*, May 14, 2018. http://www.latimes .com/opinion/op-ed/la-oe-pfaff-why-prison-reform-isnt-working-20170514 -story.html.

———. 2021. "The Greatest Threat to Defunding the Police? State Pre-emption." *Appeal* (blog). April 29, 2021. https://theappeal.org/defund-the-police-pre-emption/.

Phelps, Michelle, Amber Joy Powell, and Christopher Robertson. 2019. "Legal Estrangement and Police Reform in Minneapolis." *Scatterplot* (blog). November 4, 2019. https://scatter.wordpress.com/2019/11/04/legal-estrangement-and-police -reform-in-minneapolis/.

Pickett, Justin T. 2019. "Public Opinion and Criminal Justice Policy: Theory and Research." *Annual Review of Criminology* 2: 405–28.

Pickett, Justin T., and Thomas Baker. 2014. "The Pragmatic American: Empirical Reality or Methodological Artifact?" *Criminology* 52 (2): 195–222. https://doi.org/10.1111 /1745-9125.12035.

Pickett, Justin T, Francis T. Cullen, Shawn D. Bushway, Ted Chiricos, and Geoffrey Alpert. 2018. "The Response Rate Test: Nonresponse Bias and the Future of Survey Research in Criminology and Criminal Justice." *Criminologist* 43 (1): 7–11.

Pickett, Justin T., Stefan Ivanov, and Kevin H. Wozniak. 2020. "Selling Effective Violence Prevention Policies to the Public: A Nationally Representative Framing Experiment." *Journal of Experimental Criminology* 18 (October): 387–409. https: //doi.org/10.1007/s11292-020-09447-6.

Piquero, Alex R., and Laurence Steinberg. 2010. "Public Preferences for Rehabilitation versus Incarceration of Juvenile Offenders." *Journal of Criminal Justice* 38 (1): 1–6. https://doi.org/10.1016/j.jcrimjus.2009.11.001.

Prowse, Gwen, Vesla M. Weaver, and Tracey L. Meares. 2020. "The State from Below: Distorted Responsiveness in Policed Communities." *Urban Affairs Review* 56 (5): 1423–71. https://doi.org/10.1177/1078087419844831.

Pryce, Daniel K., and Joselyne L. Chenane. 2021. "Trust and Confidence in Police Officers and the Institution of Policing: The Views of African Americans in the American South." *Crime & Delinquency* 67 (6–7): 808–38. https://doi.org/10.1177 /0011128721991823.

Quadagno, Jill. 1996. *The Color of Welfare: How Racism Undermined the War on Poverty*. Oxford University Press.

Quillian, Lincoln, and Devah Pager. 2001. "Black Neighbors, Higher Crime? The Role of Racial Stereotypes in Evaluations of Neighborhood Crime." *American Journal of Sociology* 107 (3): 717–67. https://doi.org/10.1086/338938.

Rakich, Nathaniel. 2020. "How Americans Feel About 'Defunding the Police.'" *FiveThirtyEight* (blog). June 19, 2020. https://fivethirtyeight.com/features/americans -like-the-ideas-behind-defunding-the-police-more-than-the-slogan-itself/.

Raleigh, Erica, and George Galster. 2015. "Neighborhood Disinvestment, Abandonment, and Crime Dynamics." *Journal of Urban Affairs* 37 (4): 367–96. https://doi.org /10.1111/juaf.12102.

Ramey, David M., and Emily A. Shrider. 2014. "New Parochialism, Sources of Community Investment, and the Control of Street Crime." *Criminology & Public Policy* 13 (2): 193–216. https://doi.org/10.1111/1745-9133.12074.

Ramirez, Mark D. 2013. "Punitive Sentiment." *Criminology* 51 (2): 329–64.

———. 2015. "Racial Discrimination, Fear of Crime, and Variability in Blacks' Preferences for Punitive and Preventative Anti-crime Policies." *Political Behavior* 37 (2): 419–39. https://doi.org/10.1007/s11109-014-9285-1.

Ramirez, Mark D., and David A. M. Peterson. 2020. *Ignored Racism: White Animus Toward Latinos*. Cambridge: Cambridge University Press.

Ramos, Nestor, and Evan Allen. 2016. "Life and Loss on Methadone Mile." *Boston Globe*, July 2016. https://apps.bostonglobe.com/graphics/2016/07/methadone-mile.

Ransby, Barbara. 2015. "The Class Politics of Black Lives Matter." *Dissent* 62 (4): 31–34. https://doi.org/10.1353/dss.2015.0071.

Reed, Adolph, ed. 1999. *Without Justice for All: The New Liberalism and Our Retreat from Racial Equality*. New York: Routledge.

Reed, Adolph. 2016. "The Post-1965 Trajectory of Race, Class, and Urban Politics in the United States Reconsidered." *Labor Studies Journal* 41 (3): 260–91. https://doi.org/10.1177/0160449X16655674.

———. 2018. "Antiracism: A Neoliberal Alternative to a Left." *Dialectical Anthropology* 42 (2): 105–15. https://doi.org/10.1007/s10624-017-9476-3.

Reed, Toure F. 2015. "Why Liberals Separate Race from Class." *Jacobin*, August 22, 2015. https://jacobinmag.com/2015/08/bernie-sanders-black-lives-matter-civil-rights-movement.

———. 2020. *Toward Freedom: The Case Against Race Reductionism*. London: Verso Books.

Reny, Tyler T., Ali A. Valenzuela, and Loren Collingwood. 2020. "'No, You're Playing the Race Card': Testing the Effects of Anti-Black, Anti-Latino, and Anti-immigrant Appeals in the Post-Obama Era." *Political Psychology* 41 (2): 283–302. https://doi.org/10.1111/pops.12614.

Richardson, Heather Cox. 2020. *How the South Won the Civil War: Oligarchy, Democracy, and the Continuing Fight for the Soul of America*. New York: Oxford University Press.

Richardson, Jason, Bruce Mitchell, and Jad Edlebi. 2020. "Gentrification and Disinvestment 2020." Washington, DC: National Community Reinvestment Coalition. https://ncrc.org/gentrification20/.

Rios, Victor M. 2011. *Punished: Policing the Lives of Black and Latino Boys*. New York: NYU Press.

Riverstone-Newell, Lori. 2017. "The Rise of State Preemption Laws in Response to Local Policy Innovation." *Publius: The Journal of Federalism* 47 (3): 403–25. https://doi.org/10.1093/publius/pjx037.

Roach, Kevin, Frank R. Baumgartner, Leah Christiani, Derek A. Epp, and Kelsey Shoub. 2020. "At the Intersection: Race, Gender, and Discretion in Police Traffic Stop Outcomes." *Journal of Race, Ethnicity, and Politics*, 1–23. https://doi.org/10.1017/rep.2020.35.

Rodden, Jonathan A. 2019. *Why Cities Lose: The Deep Roots of the Urban-Rural Political Divide*. New York: Basic Books.

Roediger, David R. 2019. *Class, Race, and Marxism*. London: Verso Books.

Rose, Dina, and Todd Clear. 1998. "Incarceration, Social Capital, and Crime: Implications for Social Disorganization Theory." *Criminology* 36 (3): 441–78.

Rosenthal, Aaron. 2021. "Submerged for Some? Government Visibility, Race, and American Political Trust." *Perspectives on Politics* 19 (4): 1098–1114. https://doi.org/10.1017/S1537592720002200.

Rothstein, Richard. 2017. *The Color of Law: A Forgotten History of How Our Government Segregated America*. New York: Liveright.

Russell-Brown, Katheryn. 2009. *The Color of Crime*. New York: NYU Press.

Rustin, Bayard. 1964. "From Protest to Politics: The Future of the Civil Rights Movement." *Commentary Magazine* 39 (2): 25–31.

Ryan, Katherine E., Tysza Gandha, Michael J. Culbertson, and Crystal Carlson. 2014. "Focus Group Evidence: Implications for Design and Analysis." *American Journal of Evaluation* 35 (3): 328–45. https://doi.org/10.1177/1098214013508300.

Sabol, William J., and Miranda L. Baumann. 2020. "Justice Reinvestment: Vision and Practice." *Annual Review of Criminology* 3 (1): 317–39. https://10.1146/annurev-criminol-011419-041407.

Sakala, Leah, Samantha Harvell, and Chelsea Thomson. 2018. "Public Investment in Community-Driven Safety Initiatives." Washington, DC: Urban Institute. https://www.urban.org/research/publication/public-investment-community-driven-safety-initiatives.

Saletan, William. 2021. "Americans Don't Want to Defund the Police. Here's What They Do Want." *Slate*, October 17, 2021. https://slate.com/news-and-politics/2021/10/police-reform-polls-white-black-crime.html.

Sampson, Robert J. 2004. "Neighborhoods and Community: Collective Efficacy and Community Safety." *Progressive Review*, 11 (2): 106–13.

———. 2017. "Urban Sustainability in an Age of Enduring Inequalities: Advancing Theory and Ecometrics for the 21st-Century City." *Proceedings of the National Academy of Sciences* 114 (34): 8957–62. https://doi.org/10.1073/pnas.1614433114.

Sampson, Robert J., and John H. Laub. 1993. *Crime in the Making: Pathways and Turning Points Through Life*. Cambridge, MA: Harvard University Press.

Sampson, Robert J., and Charles Loeffler. 2010. "Punishment's Place: The Local Concentration of Mass Incarceration." *Daedalus* 139 (3): 20–31. https://doi.org/10.1162/DAED_a_00020.

Sampson, Robert J., Jeffrey D. Morenoff, and Felton Earls. 1999. "Beyond Social Capital: Spatial Dynamics of Collective Efficacy for Children." *American Sociological Review* 64: 633–60.

Sampson, Robert J., Jeffrey D. Morenoff, and Stephen W. Raudenbush. 2005. "Social Anatomy of Racial and Ethnic Disparities in Violence." *American Journal of Public Health* 95 (2): 224–32.

Sampson, Robert J., and Stephen W. Raudenbush. 2004. "Seeing Disorder: Neighborhood Stigma and the Social Construction of 'Broken Windows.'" *Social Psychology Quarterly* 67 (4): 319–42. https://doi.org/10.1177/019027250406700401.

Sampson, Robert J., Stephen W. Raudenbush, and Felton Earls. 1997. "Neighborhoods and Violent Crime: A Multilevel Study of Collective Efficacy." *Science* 277 (5328): 918–24.

Sampson, Robert J., and William J. Wilson. 1995. "Toward a Theory of Race, Crime, and Urban Inequality." In *Crime and Inequality*, edited by John Hagan and Ruth D. Peterson, 37–54. Stanford: Stanford University Press.

Sasson, Theodore. 1995. *Crime Talk: How Citizens Construct a Social Problem*. New York: Aldine de Gruyter.

Savage, Joanne. 2004. "Does Viewing Violent Media Really Cause Criminal Violence? A Methodological Review." *Aggression and Violent Behavior* 10 (1): 99–128. https://doi.org/10.1016/j.avb.2003.10.001.

———. 2008. "The Role of Exposure to Media Violence in the Etiology of Violent Behavior: A Criminologist Weighs In." *American Behavioral Scientist* 51 (8): 1123–36. https://doi.org/10.1177/0002764207312016.

Savage, Joanne, Stephanie K. Ellis, and Kevin H. Wozniak. 2019. "The Role of Poverty and Income in the Differential Etiology of Violence: An Empirical Test." *Journal of Poverty* 23 (5): 384–403. https://doi.org/10.1080/10875549.2019.1577325.

Savage, Joanne, and Kevin H. Wozniak. 2016. *Thugs and Thieves: The Differential Etiology of Violence*. New York: Oxford University Press.

Savage, Joanne, and Christina Yancey. 2008. "The Effects of Media Violence Exposure on Criminal Aggression: A Meta-analysis." *Criminal Justice and Behavior* 35 (6): 772–91. https://doi.org/10.1177/0093854808316487.

Schaeffer, Katherine. 2020. "6 Facts about Economic Inequality in the U.S." *Pew Research Center* (blog). February 7, 2020. https://www.pewresearch.org/fact-tank/2020/02/07/6-facts-about-economic-inequality-in-the-u-s/.

Schattschneider, E. E. 1960. *The Semisovereign People: A Realist's View of Democracy in America*. New York: Prentice-Hall.

Scheingold, Stuart A. 1991. *The Politics of Street Crime: Criminal Process and Cultural Obsession*. Philadelphia: Temple University Press.

———. 2011. *The Politics of Law and Order: Street Crime and Public Policy*. 2nd ed. New Orleans: Quid Pro Books.

Schlozman, Kay Lehman, Sidney Verba, and Henry E. Brady. 2012. *The Unheavenly Chorus: Unequal Political Voice and the Broken Promise of American Democracy*. Princeton, NJ: Princeton University Press.

Schneider, Anne, and Helen Ingram. 1993. "Social Construction of Target Populations: Implications for Politics and Policy." *American Political Science Review* 87 (2): 334–47. https://doi.org/10.2307/2939044.

Schueler, Beth E. 2019. "A Third Way: The Politics of School District Takeover and Turnaround in Lawrence, Massachusetts." *Educational Administration Quarterly* 55 (1): 116–53. https://doi.org/10.1177/0013161X18785873.

Schueler, Beth E., Joshua S. Goodman, and David J. Deming. 2017. "Can States Take Over and Turn Around School Districts? Evidence From Lawrence, Massachusetts." *Educational Evaluation and Policy Analysis* 39 (2): 311–32. https://doi.org/10.3102/0162373716685824.

Schuster, Luc, and Peter Ciurczak. 2018. "Boston's Booming . . . But For Whom?" Boston: Boston Indicators. https://www.bostonindicators.org/reports/report-website-pages/shared-prosperity.

Schwartzapfel, Beth, and Bill Keller. 2015. "Willie Horton Revisited." *Marshall Project*, May 13, 2015. https://www.themarshallproject.org/2015/05/13/willie-horton-revisited.

SCJS. 2010. "Attitudes toward Approaches to Lowering the Crime Rate in the United States, by Demographic Characteristics, Unites States, 2010." Sourcebook of Criminal Justice Statistics. https://www.albany.edu/sourcebook/pdf/t200132010.pdf.

Sharkey, Patrick. 2018. *Uneasy Peace: The Great Crime Decline, the Renewal of City Life, and the Next War on Violence*. New York: W. W. Norton.

Sharkey, Patrick, Gerard Torrats-Espinosa, and Delaram Takyar. 2017. "Community and the Crime Decline: The Causal Effect of Local Nonprofits on Violent Crime." *American Sociological Review* 82 (6): 1214–40. https://doi.org/10.1177/0003122417736289.

Shepard, Steven. 2021. "Dem Pollsters Acknowledge 'Major Errors' in 2020 Polling." *POLITICO*, April 13, 2021. https://www.politico.com/news/2021/04/13/dems-polling-failure-481044.

Shrider, Emily A., and David M. Ramey. 2018. "Priming the Pump: Public Investment, Private Mortgage Investment, and Violent Crime." *City & Community* 17 (4): 996–1014. https://doi.org/10.1111/cico.12344.

Silva, Jennifer M. 2013. *Coming Up Short: Working-Class Adulthood in an Age of Uncertainty*. New York: Oxford University Press.

———. 2019. *We're Still Here: Pain and Politics in the Heart of America*. New York: Oxford University Press.

Silver, Jasmine R., and Justin T. Pickett. 2015. "Toward a Better Understanding of Politicized Policing Attitudes: Conflicted Conservatism and Support for Police Use of Force." *Criminology* 53 (4): 650–76. https://doi.org/10.1111/1745-9125.12092.

Simes, Jessica T. 2018. "Place and Punishment: The Spatial Context of Mass Incarceration." *Journal of Quantitative Criminology* 34 (2): 513–33. https://doi.org/10.1007/s10940-017-9344-y.

———. 2020. "The Ecology of Race and Punishment across Cities." *City & Community* 19 (1): 169–90. https://doi.org/10.1111/cico.12425.

———. 2021. *Punishing Places: The Geography of Mass Imprisonment*. University of California Press.

Simmons, Alicia D., and Lawrence D. Bobo. 2018. "Understanding 'No Special Favors': A Quantitative and Qualitative Mapping of the Meaning of Responses to the Racial Resentment Scale." *Du Bois Review: Social Science Research on Race* 15 (2): 323–52. https://doi.org/10.1017/S1742058X18000310.

Simon, Jonathan. 2007. *Governing through Crime: How the War on Crime Transformed American Democracy and Created a Culture of Fear*. New York: Oxford University Press.

Sims, Barbara. 2003. "The Impact of Causal Attribution on Correctional Ideology: A National Study." *Criminal Justice Review* 28 (1): 1–25. https://doi.org/10.1177/073401680302800102.

Skelley, Geoffrey. 2021. "Why Was the National Polling Environment So off in 2020?" *FiveThirtyEight* (blog). February 23, 2021. https://fivethirtyeight.com/features/why-was-the-national-polling-environment-so-off-in-2020/.

Skocpol, Theda. 1991. "Targeting within Universalism: Politically Viable Policies to Combat Poverty in the United States." In *The Urban Underclass*, edited by Christopher Jencks and Paul E. Peterson, 411–36. Washington, DC: Brookings Institution.

Skocpol, Theda, and Vanessa Williamson. 2016. *The Tea Party and the Remaking of Republican Conservatism*. New York: Oxford University Press.

Skolnick, Phil. 2018. "The Opioid Epidemic: Crisis and Solutions." *Annual Review of Pharmacology and Toxicology* 58: 143–59.

Sloas, Lincoln B., and Cassandra A. Atkin-Plunk. 2019. "Perceptions of Balanced Justice and Rehabilitation for Drug Offenders." *Criminal Justice Policy Review* 30 (7): 990–1009. https://doi.org/10.1177/0887403418762532.

Smith, Candis Watts. 2014. "Shifting from Structural to Individual Attributions of Black Disadvantage: Age, Period, and Cohort Effects on Black Explanations of Racial Disparities." *Journal of Black Studies* 45 (5): 432–52. https://doi.org/10.1177/0021934714534069.

Smith, Sven, Chris Ferguson, and Kevin Beaver. 2018. "A Longitudinal Analysis of Shooter Games and Their Relationship with Conduct Disorder and Self-Reported Delinquency." *International Journal of Law and Psychiatry* 58 (May): 48–53. https://doi.org/10.1016/j.ijlp.2018.02.008.

Sniderman, Paul M., Edward G. Carmines, Geoffrey C. Layman, and Michael Carter. 1996. "Beyond Race: Social Justice as a Race Neutral Ideal." *American Journal of Political Science* 40 (1): 33–55. https://doi.org/10.2307/2111693.

Sniderman, Paul M., and Thomas Leonard Piazza. 1993. *The Scar of Race*. Cambridge, MA: Harvard University Press.

Soss, Joe, Richard C. Fording, and Sanford F. Schram. 2011. *Disciplining the Poor: Neoliberal Paternalism and the Persistent Power of Race*. Chicago: University of Chicago Press.

Soss, Joe, and Vesla M. Weaver. 2017. "Police Are Our Government: Politics, Political Science, and the Policing of Race–Class Subjugated Communities." *Annual Review of Political Science* 20: 565–91. https://doi-org/10.1146/annurev-polisci-060415-093825.

Stephens-Dougan, LaFleur. 2020. *Race to the Bottom: How Racial Appeals Work in American Politics*. Chicago: University of Chicago Press.

Stewart, David W., and Prem N. Shamdasani. 2014. *Focus Groups: Theory and Practice*. 3rd ed. Thousand Oaks, CA: SAGE.

Stimson, James A. 2015. *Tides of Consent: How Public Opinion Shapes American Politics.* New York: Cambridge University Press.

———. 2018. *Public Opinion in America: Moods, Cycles, And Swings, Second Edition.* New York: Routledge.

Stone, Deborah A. 1989. "Causal Stories and the Formation of Policy Agendas." *Political Science Quarterly* 104 (2): 281–300. https://doi.org/10.2307/2151585.

Stout, Christopher T. 2020. *The Case for Identity Politics: Polarization, Demographic Change, and Racial Appeals.* Charlottesville: University of Virginia Press.

Sutherland, Edwin H. 1947. *Principles of Criminology.* 4th ed. Philadelphia: J. B. Lippincott.

Tankersley, Jim. 2020. "A Trump Tax Break Is Not Spurring Job Creation, Study Finds." *New York Times,* June 17, 2020. https://www.nytimes.com/2020/06/17/business/trump-opportunity-zone-jobs.html.

Tarman, Christopher, and David O. Sears. 2005. "The Conceptualization and Measurement of Symbolic Racism." *Journal of Politics* 67 (3): 731–61.

Tartakovsky, Joseph. 2013. "Firearm Preemption Laws and What They Mean for Cities." *Municipal Lawyer* 54 (5): 6–9.

Taylor, Keeanga-Yamahtta. 2016. *From #BlackLivesMatter to Black Liberation.* Chicago: Haymarket Books.

Tesler, Michael. 2013. "The Return of Old-Fashioned Racism to White Americans' Partisan Preferences in the Early Obama Era." *Journal of Politics* 75 (1): 110–23. https://doi.org/10.1017/S0022381612000904.

———. 2016. *Post-Racial or Most-Racial? Race and Politics in the Obama Era.* Chicago: University of Chicago Press.

———. 2017. "Racial Priming with Implicit and Explicit Messages." In *Oxford Research Encyclopedia of Politics.* https://doi.org/10.1093/acrefore/9780190228637.013.49.

Tewksbury, Richard. 2009. "Qualitative versus Quantitative Methods: Understanding Why Qualitative Methods Are Superior for Criminology and Criminal Justice." *Journal of Theoretical and Philosophical Criminology* 1 (1): 38–58.

Theodos, Brett, Eric Hangen, Jorge González-Hermoso, and Brady Meixell. 2020. "An Early Assessment of Opportunity Zones for Equitable Development Projects." Washington, DC: Urban Institute. https://www.urban.org/research/publication/early-assessment-opportunity-zones-equitable-development-projects.

Thielo, Angela J., Francis T. Cullen, Derek M. Cohen, and Cecilia Chouhy. 2016. "Rehabilitation in a Red State." *Criminology & Public Policy* 15 (1): 137–70. https://doi.org/10.1111/1745-9133.12182.

Thompson, Victor R., and Lawrence D. Bobo. 2011. "Thinking about Crime: Race and Lay Accounts of Lawbreaking Behavior." *ANNALS of the American Academy of Political and Social Science* 634 (1): 16–38. https://doi.org/10.1177/0002716210387057.

Thorpe, Rebecca. 2014. "Urban Divestment, Rural Decline and the Politics of Mass Incarceration." *Good Society* 23 (1): 17–29. https://doi.org/10.5325/goodsociety.23.1.0017.

Tilley, Brian P. 2020. "'I Am the Law and Order Candidate': A Content Analysis of Donald Trump's Race-Baiting Dog Whistles in the 2016 Presidential Campaign." *Psychology* 11 (12): 1941–74. https://doi.org/10.4236/psych.2020.1112123.

Tonry, Michael. 1995. *Malign Neglect: Race, Crime, and Punishment in America*. New York: Oxford University Press.

———. 2004. *Thinking about Crime: Sense and Sensibility in American Penal Culture*. New York: Oxford University Press.

Travis, Jeremy, Bruce Western, and F. Stevens Redburn. 2014. *The Growth of Incarceration in the United States: Exploring Causes and Consequences*. Washington, DC: National Academies Press. http://academicworks.cuny.edu/jj_pubs/27.

Trickey, Erick. 2020. "The Surprisingly Limited Success of Trump's Signature Antipoverty Program." *POLITICO*. September 29, 2020. https://www.politico.com/news/magazine/2020/09/29/cleveland-opportunity-zones-422728.

Tuch, Steven A., and Michael Hughes. 2011. "Whites' Racial Policy Attitudes in the Twenty-First Century: The Continuing Significance of Racial Resentment." *ANNALS of the American Academy of Political and Social Science* 634 (1): 134–52. https://doi.org/10.1177/0002716210390288.

Tucker, Susan B., and Eric Cadora. 2003. "Justice Reinvestment." *IDEAS for an Open Society*, 2003.

Turner, Joel. 2007. "The Messenger Overwhelming the Message: Ideological Cues and Perceptions of Bias in Television News." *Political Behavior* 29 (4): 441–64. https://doi.org/10.1007/s11109-007-9031-z.

Tyler, Tom R. 2006. *Why People Obey the Law*. Vol. 2. Princeton, NJ: Princeton University Press.

Uggen, Christopher, Mike Vuolo, Sarah Lageson, Ebony Ruhland, and Hilary K. Whitham. 2014. "The Edge of Stigma: An Experimental Audit of the Effects of Low-Level Criminal Records on Employment." *Criminology* 52 (4): 627–54. https://doi.org/10.1111/1745-9125.12051.

Unnever, James D. 2008. "Two Worlds Far Apart: Black-White Differences in Beliefs about Why African-American Men Are Disproportionately Imprisoned." *Criminology* 46 (2): 511–38.

Unnever, James D., John K. Cochran, Francis T. Cullen, and Brandon K. Applegate. 2010. "The Pragmatic American: Attributions of Crime and the Hydraulic Relation Hypothesis." *Justice Quarterly* 27 (3): 431–57. https://doi.org/10.1080/07418820902855362.

Unnever, James D., and Francis T. Cullen. 2009. "Empathetic Identification and Punitiveness: A Middle-Range Theory of Individual Differences." *Theoretical Criminology* 13 (3): 283–312.

Unnever, James D., Francis T. Cullen, and James D. Jones. 2008. "Public Support for Attacking the 'Root Causes' of Crime: The Impact of Egalitarian and Racial Beliefs." *Sociological Focus* 41 (1): 1–33. https://doi.org/10.1080/00380237.2008.10571321.

Updegrove, Alexander H., Danielle L. Boisvert, Maisha N. Cooper, and Shaun L. Gabbidon. 2021. "Criminological Explanations, Race, and Biological Attributions of Crime as Predictors of Philadelphia Area Residents' Support for Criminal Justice Policies." *Crime & Delinquency* 67 (3): 319–43. https://doi.org/10.1177/0011128720931437.

US Bureau of Labor Statistics. 2016. "Boston-Cambridge-Nashua Has Lowest Unemployment Rate among Large Metro Areas, October 2016." TED: The Economics Daily. December 8, 2016. https://www.bls.gov/opub/ted/2016/boston-cambridge-nashua-has-lowest-unemployment-rate-among-large-metro-areas-october-2016.htm.

Valentino, Nicholas A. 1999. "Crime News and the Priming of Racial Attitudes During Evaluations of the President." *Public Opinion Quarterly* 63 (3): 293–320.

Valentino, Nicholas A., Fabian G. Neuner, and L. Matthew Vandenbroek. 2018. "The Changing Norms of Racial Political Rhetoric and the End of Racial Priming." *Journal of Politics* 80 (3): 757–71. https://doi.org/10.1086/694845.

Valenzuela, Ali A., and Tyler Reny. 2021. "The Evolution of Experiments on Racial Priming." In *Advances in Experimental Political Science*, edited by Donald P. Green and James Druckman, 447–67. Cambridge: Cambridge University Press. https://doi.org/10.1017/9781108777919.031.

Van Cleve, Nicole Gonzalez Van, and Lauren Mayes. 2015. "Criminal Justice Through 'Colorblind' Lenses: A Call to Examine the Mutual Constitution of Race and Criminal Justice." *Law & Social Inquiry* 40 (2): 406–32. https://doi.org/10.1111/lsi.12113.

Vaughn, Paige E., Kyle Peyton, and Gregory A. Huber. 2022. "Mass Support for Proposals to Reshape Policing Depends on the Implications for Crime and Safety." *Criminology & Public Policy* 21 (1): 125–46. https://doi.org/10.1111/1745-9133.12572.

Vélez, María B., Christopher J. Lyons, and Blake Boursaw. 2012. "Neighborhood Housing Investments and Violent Crime in Seattle, 1981–2007." *Criminology* 50 (4): 1025–56. https://doi.org/10.1111/j.1745-9125.2012.00287.x.

Vélez, María B., and Kelly Richardson. 2012. "The Political Economy of Neighbourhood Homicide in Chicago: The Role of Bank Investment." *British Journal of Criminology* 52 (3): 490–513. https://doi.org/10.1093/bjc/azr092.

Vicsek, Lilla. 2007. "A Scheme for Analyzing the Results of Focus Groups." *International Journal of Qualitative Methods* 6 (4): 20–34. https://doi.org/10.1177/160940690700600402.

———. 2010. "Issues in the Analysis of Focus Groups: Generalisability, Quantifiability, Treatment of Context and Quotations." *Qualitative Report* 15 (1): 122–41.

Vito, Anthony G., Vanessa Woodward Griffin, Gennaro F. Vito, and George E. Higgins. 2020. "'Does Daylight Matter'? An Examination of Racial Bias in Traffic Stops by Police." *Policing: An International Journal* 43 (4): 675–88. https://doi.org/10.1108/PIJPSM-04-2020-0055.

Vuk, Mateja, Brandon K. Applegate, Heather M. Ouellette, Riane M. Bolin, and Eva Aizpurua. 2020. "The Pragmatic Public? The Impact of Practical Concerns on Support for Punitive and Rehabilitative Prison Policies." *American Journal of Criminal Justice* 45 (2): 273–92. https://doi.org/10.1007/s12103-019-09507-2.

Vuolo, Mike, Sarah Lageson, and Christopher Uggen. 2017. "Criminal Record Questions in the Era of 'Ban the Box.'" *Criminology & Public Policy* 16 (1): 139–65. https://doi.org/10.1111/1745-9133.12250.

Wacquant, Loïc. 2009. *Punishing the Poor: The Neoliberal Government of Social Insecurity*. Durham, NC: Duke University Press.

Wakefield, Sara, and Christopher Uggen. 2010. "Incarceration and Stratification." *Annual Review of Sociology* 36: 387–406.

Walker, Adrian. 2014. "Charles Stuart Case's Awful Legacy, in Black and White." *Boston Globe*, October 24, 2014. https://www.bostonglobe.com/metro/2014/10/23/recalling-city-least-cherished-anniversary-years-after-stuart-case/7AQjpmjT8a9uSbD5lEGZCP/story.html.

Weaver, Vesla M., Andrew Papachristos, and Michael Zanger-Tishler. 2019. "The Great Decoupling: The Disconnection Between Criminal Offending and Experience of Arrest Across Two Cohorts." *RSF: The Russell Sage Foundation Journal of the Social Sciences* 5 (1): 89–123. https://doi.org/10.7758/RSF.2019.5.1.05.

Weinberg, Jill, Jeremy Freese, and David McElhattan. 2014. "Comparing Data Characteristics and Results of an Online Factorial Survey between a Population-Based and a Crowdsource-Recruited Sample." *Sociological Science* 1 (August): 292–310. http://dx.doi.org.ezproxy.lib.umb.edu/10.15195/v1.a19.

Weisburd, David. 2015. "The Law of Crime Concentration and the Criminology of Place." *Criminology* 53 (2): 133–57. https://doi.org/10.1111/1745-9125.12070.

Weisburd, David, and John E. Eck. 2004. "What Can Police Do to Reduce Crime, Disorder, and Fear?" *ANNALS of the American Academy of Political and Social Science* 593 (1): 42–65.

Welch, Kelly, Leah Fikre Butler, and Marc Gertz. 2019. "Saving Children, Damning Adults? An Examination of Public Support for Juvenile Rehabilitation and Adult Punishment." *Criminal Justice Review* 44 (4): 470–91. https://doi.org/10.1177/0734016819833141.

Welsh-Loveman, Jeremy, and Samantha Harvell. 2018. "Justice Reinvestment Initiative Data Snapshot." Washington, DC: Urban Institute. https://www.urban.org/research/publication/justice-reinvestment-initiative-data-snapshot.

Western, Bruce. 2006. *Punishment and Inequality in America*. New York: Russell Sage Foundation.

Western, Bruce, and Becky Pettit. 2010. "Incarceration & Social Inequality." *Daedalus* 139 (3): 8–19. https://doi.org/10.1162/DAED_a_00019.

Wetts, Rachel, and Robb Willer. 2019. "Who Is Called by the Dog Whistle? Experimental Evidence That Racial Resentment and Political Ideology Condition Responses to Racially Encoded Messages." *Socius* 5 (January): 1–20. https://doi.org/10.1177/2378023119866268.

White, Ismail K. 2007. "When Race Matters and When It Doesn't: Racial Group Differences in Response to Racial Cues." *American Political Science Review* 101 (2): 339–54. https://doi.org/10.1017/S0003055407070177.

Wikoff, Nora, Donald M. Linhorst, and Nicole Morani. 2012. "Recidivism among Participants of a Reentry Program for Prisoners Released without Supervision." *Social Work Research* 36 (4): 289–99.

Wikström, Per-Olof H., Dietrich Oberwittler, Kyle Treiber, and Beth Hardie. 2012. *Breaking Rules: The Social and Situational Dynamics of Young People's Urban Crime.* Oxford: Oxford University Press.

Wilson, George, and Roger Dunham. 2001. "Race, Class, and Attitudes Toward Crime Control: The Views of the African American Middle Class." *Criminal Justice and Behavior* 28 (3): 259–78. https://doi.org/10.1177/0093854801028003001.

Wilson, James Q. 1975. *Thinking about Crime.* New York: Basic Books.

Wilson, William J. 1978. *The Declining Significance of Race: Blacks and Changing American Institutions.* Chicago: University of Chicago Press.

———. 1987. *The Truly Disadvantaged: The Inner City, the Underclass, and Public Policy.* Chicago: University of Chicago Press.

———. 2012. *The Truly Disadvantaged: The Inner City, the Underclass, and Public Policy.* 2nd ed. Chicago: University of Chicago Press.

Winter, Nicholas J. G. 2008. *Dangerous Frames: How Ideas about Race and Gender Shape Public Opinion.* Chicago: University of Chicago Press.

Wolf, A.M., A. Del Prado Lippman, C. Glesmann, and E. Castro. 2015. "Process Evaluation for the Office of Neighborhood Safety." Oakland, CA: National Council on Crime and Delinquency.

Wood, Jane L. 2009. "Why Public Opinion of the Criminal Justice System Is Important." In *Public Opinion and Criminal Justice: Context, Practice, and Values*, edited by Jane L. Wood and Theresa A. Gannon, 33–48. New York: Routledge.

Wozniak, Kevin H. 2016. "Perceptions of Prison and Punitive Attitudes: A Test of the Penal Escalation Hypothesis." *Criminal Justice Review* 41 (3): 352–71. https://doi.org/10.1177/0734016816654739.

———. 2018. Racialized Cues and Support for Justice Reinvestment: A Mixed-Method Study of Public Opinion, Boston, 2016. Ann Arbor, MI: Inter-university Consortium for Political and Social Research [distributor], 2018-05-16. https://doi.org/10.3886/ICPSR36778.v1

———. 2020a. "Public Discussion about Critical Issues in Criminal Justice Reform." *Journal of Qualitative Criminal Justice & Criminology* 8 (4): 401–29.

———. 2020b. "The Effect of Exposure to Racialized Cues on White and Black Public Support for Justice Reinvestment." *Justice Quarterly* 37 (6): 1067–95. https://doi.org/10.1080/07418825.2018.1486448.

Yadon, Nicole, and Spencer Piston. 2019. "Examining Whites' Anti-Black Attitudes after Obama's Presidency." *Politics, Groups, and Identities* 7 (4): 794–814. https://doi.org/10.1080/21565503.2018.1438953.

Yeager, David S., Jon A. Krosnick, LinChiat Chang, Harold S. Javitz, Matthew S. Levendusky, Alberto Simpser, and Rui Wang. 2011. "Comparing the Accuracy of RDD Telephone Surveys and Internet Surveys Conducted with Probability and Non-probability Samples." *Public Opinion Quarterly* 75 (4): 709–47. https://doi.org/10.1093/poq/nfr020.

Young, Alford A. 2007. "The Redeemed Old Head: Articulating a Sense of Public Self and Social Purpose." *Symbolic Interaction* 30 (3): 347–74. https://doi.org/10.1525/si.2007.30.3.347.

Young, Robert L. 1991. "Race, Conceptions of Crime and Justice, and Support for the Death Penalty." *Social Psychology Quarterly* 54 (1): 67–75. https://doi.org/10.2307/2786789.

Zalkind, Susan. 2017. "The Opioid Epidemic's Infrastructure Problem." *Pacific Standard*, September 25, 2017. https://psmag.com/social-justice/opioid-epidemic-infrastructure-problem.

Zaller, John. 1992. *The Nature and Origins of Mass Opinion.* New York: Cambridge University Press.

Zatz, Marjorie S., and Richard P. Krecker. 2003. "Anti-gang Initiatives as Racialized Policy." In *Crime Control and Social Justice: The Delicate Balance*, edited by Darnell F. Hawkins, Samuel L. Myers, and Randolph N. Stone, 173–96. Westport, CT: Greenwood Press.

Zaykowski, Heather, Erin Cournoyer Allain, and Lena M. Campagna. 2019. "Examining the Paradox of Crime Reporting: Are Disadvantaged Victims More Likely to Report to the Police?" *Law & Society Review* 53 (4): 1305–40. https://doi.org/10.1111/lasr.12440.

Zimring, Franklin E. 2008. *The Great American Crime Decline.* New York: Oxford University Press.

Zoorob, Michael. 2019. "Blue Endorsements Matter: How the Fraternal Order of Police Contributed to Donald Trump's Victory." *PS: Political Science & Politics* 52 (2): 243–50. https://doi.org/10.1017/S1049096518001841.

INDEX

Page numbers in *italics* indicate Figures or Tables.

ABOUT THE AUTHOR

KEVIN H. WOZNIAK is a member of the faculty of the School of Law and Criminology at the National University of Ireland Maynooth. He received his PhD in Justice, Law, and Society from American University and his BA in Psychology from Skidmore College. He is a former Congressional Fellow of the American Political Science Association, former W. E. B. Du Bois Fellow of the United States National Institute of Justice, and former member of the sociology faculty at the University of Massachusetts Boston. He studies the politics of crime and criminal justice.

www.ingramcontent.com/pod-product-compliance
Lightning Source LLC
Chambersburg PA
CBHW032101040426
42336CB00040B/627